ANTISEMITISM IN AMERICA TODAY

ANTISEMITISM IN AMERICA TODAY:
Outspoken Experts Explode the Myths

EDITED BY
JEROME A. CHANES

A BIRCH LANE PRESS BOOK
PUBLISHED BY CAROL PUBLISHING GROUP

A Birch Lane Press Book
Published by Carol Publishing Group

Birch Lane Press is a registered trademark of Carol Communications, Inc.
Editorial Offices: 600 Madison Avenue, New York, N.Y. 10022
Sales and Distribution Offices: 120 Enterprise Avenue, Secaucus, N.J. 07094
In Canada: Canadian Manda Group, One Atlantic Avenue, Suite 105,
  Toronto, Ontario M6K 3E7
Queries regarding rights and permissions should be addressed to Carol
Publishing Group, 600 Madison Avenue, New York, N.Y. 10022

Carol Publishing Group books are available at special discounts for bulk purchases, sales promotion, fund-raising, or educational purposes. Special editions
can be created to specifications. For details, contact: Special Sales Department,
Carol Publishing Group, 120 Enterprise Avenue, Secaucus, N.J. 07094

Manufactured in the United States of America
10 9 8 7 6 5 4 3 2 1

Library of Congress Cataloging-in-Publication Data
Antisemitism in America today : outspoken experts explode the myths /
  edited by Jerome A. Chanes.
      p.   cm.
  "A Birch Lane Press Book."
  ISBN 1-55972-290-8
    1. Antisemitism—United States.   2. United States—Ethnic
  relations.   I. Chanes, Jerome A.
  DS146.U6A59   1995
  305.892'4073—dc20   94-41154
                                                          CIP

To the memory of my mother

בײלה בת ר׳ משה הכהן ולאה

Berta Gottlieb Chanes

and my father

שמחה עמנואל בן ר׳ יעקב ורחל

Manuel S. Chanes

■ ■ ■

Contents

Contents

■■■

Acknowledgments

I have been fortunate to have enjoyed a relationship with a number of individuals who can justly be characterized as "mentors." Phil Jacobson of blessed memory, for many years a respected staff member of the National Jewish Community Relations Advisory Council (NJCRAC) and the American Jewish Committee, introduced me to the nuances of the public affairs debate, particularly in the areas of constitutional protections.

Albert D. Chernin, NJCRAC's executive vice chairman emeritus and one of the more thoughtful and creative "issues persons" in the Jewish community, brought me into the community-relations and public-affairs world and helped shape my perspectives on and understanding of the broadest conceivable range of issues. Al Chernin has been colleague, friend, frequent sparring partner, and above all good teacher. I am indebted to him.

Dr. Walter Lurie, also formerly of the NJCRAC staff and one of the respected elder statesmen of the Jewish community, has guided me toward an understanding of the community-relations dynamics of antisemitism.

Earl Raab, another of the elder statesmen, whose work is represented in this volume, has through his own estimable writings and many conversations and suggestions helped me find a voice with which to express my views.

My understanding of public policy and public affairs and of Jewish communal structure and function, and my work in the public affairs arena, has been enhanced by my association with a number of individuals who have been generous with their time, their effort, and their spirit. They include Dr. Donald Feldstein, a man of erudition and understanding; Rabbi Israel Miller, a genuine leader whose passionate devotion to human rights causes has been an inspiration to me—Rabbi Miller is a true role model; Arnold Aaronson and Samuel "Red" Spiegler, both formerly of the NJCRAC staff; Al Vorspan, who combines erudition, eminent practicality, and great one-liners—Al has taught many of us what passion about social justice is all about; Phil Baum of the American Jewish Congress; Dr. David Singer of the American Jewish Committee; Theodore Comet; Murray Friedman ("Why don't they listen to me?"); Martin J. Raffel, friend and colleague at NJCRAC; Chaim Dovid Zwiebel; and Rabbi David Saperstein, senior Jewish public affairs Washington representative—David, no matter how busy in his inside-the-Beltway *tummling*, has always found time to give me good guidance.

I owe a deep debt to Nathan Goldberg and Marshall Sklare. Professor Nathan Goldberg, of blessed memory, of Yeshiva University, first introduced me to the social scientific study of anti-semitism. I am sorry that Marshall Sklare did not live to see the seeds that he planted in my brain in his Brandeis University seminar come to fruition in this book and in other aspects of my work. Marshall articulated for me, as he did for just about everyone who has studied Jewish communal affairs, the vocabulary of American Jewish sociology.

Kenneth Jacobson has been my best and severest critic and my close friend for almost four decades. Ken, a genuine polymath, has over many years guided me in any number of crucial areas. I cite but two: the development of a jump shot, and clear thinking in critical-issues analysis.

Thanks to my friends and colleagues at the Graduate School and University Center of the City University of New York. Special thanks to Charles Kadushin for his unfailing good advice and good humor; and to Egon Mayer, the director of the Center for Jewish Studies at the CUNY Graduate Center, with which I am privileged to be associated as a research fellow.

Thanks also to Dean Sheldon R. Gelman of Yeshiva University's Wurzweiler School of Social Work, for his encouragement; to Professor Norman Linzer, for allowing me to bounce many of these ideas off of him and his classes; and, most of all, to my students past and present at the Wurzweiler School of Social Work. ". . . but from my students I have learned most of all."

To my friends and colleagues at the NJCRAC, a debt of gratitude is owed. I cite in particular Dr. Lawrence Rubin, NJCRAC's exec, who has long encouraged my research and writing; NJCRAC's director of public information, Kenneth Bandler, for his friendship and moral support; and Lynn Lyss, NJCRAC's chair.

Special mention needs be made of a number of individuals whose insights helped me sharpen my own perspectives, with whom I discussed theoretical and practical points, and who have helped in innumerable ways in this project. I am grateful to Helen Epstein who, when I first discussed the idea of this book with her, said, "Don't talk about it; *do* it"; Charney V. Bromberg for his friendship, and for bearing with me while I bounce ideas off him—I have never had a conversation with Charney in which I did not learn something; Dr. Michael Kotzin, ditto; Pearl K. Bell and Daniel Bell, each of whom suggested some points worthy of analysis; Dr. Barry Holtz, for his helpful suggestions when this book was but an idea in my mind; and to his wife, Dr. Bethamie Horowitz, for her infectious energy and her encouragement; Richard and Jeanne Siegel of their warm friendship and consistent encouragement; Menachem Z. Rosensaft, friend and gadfly, for the erudition he has generously shared with me and for his useful editorial comments; Ted Solotaroff, creator of an earlier, classic volume on antisemitism, Charles Herbert Stember's *Jews in the Mind of America*, who encouraged me to pursue this present project; Sandee Brawarsky, who, in her own quiet way, always has sensible suggestions; Nessa Rapoport; Barry Ungar, for discussions that have fertilized my thinking on a range of issues related to antisemitism; Michael A. Pelavin, for his friendship and challenging observations both; Dr. Leonard Cole; Arthur Hertzberg, teacher and gadfly, who has taught me how to say many things, and whose work graces this volume; Dr. Chaim Waxman; and Dr. Lawrence Grossman, for challenging everything I say.

A work such as this would not be possible without the cooperation of individuals who have the resource materials at their fingertips, and who have the insights to go with those resources. It is not possible to name all of these people, but let me take a crack at identifying some: the staff at the American Jewish Committee research department, particularly director David Singer and librarians Cyma Horowitz and Michele Anish; Tony Lerman, Howard Spier, and the research staff of London's Institute of Jewish Affairs (Antony Lerman's chapter on international anti-semitism is found in this volume). I regret that Frank Muller of the IJA library staff did not live to see this work; Alan M. Schwartz, Gail Gans, Gerald Baumgarten, Barbara Ehrlich, and especially Marc Caplan, all of the research department and library at Anti-Defamation League, have been unfailingly and consistently generous with their assistance, resources, and vast knowledge. "B'chochmo poseiach sheorim."

Finally, for a very different and very special reason, S. Douglas Stewart and Mike Rosenkrantz.

This book would not have been possible without the support of Mark and Sharon Bloome of the Heart of America Fund; Martha Kongsgaard and Peter Goldman; Jeremy Mack of the Mack Foundation; Sam and Lillie Fogelman; and Nancy and Fred Fagelman. Special thanks to Aviva Kempner of the Ciesla Foundation, for putting aside Hank Greenberg for a few minutes.

I was fortunate to receive a fellowship from the Memorial Foundation for Jewish Culture. Warmest thanks to Dr. Jerry Hochbaum for his consistent encouragement of my work.

I was most fortunate to have as an editor the estimable Hillel Black of Birch Lane Press. Hillel early on took this project under his wing and encouraged, cajoled, counseled, and befriended me and helped shape the contours of this book. I appreciate Hillel's wise and prudent counsel. Thanks as well to my publisher Steven Schragis for his support of this project, and to Susan Hayes for her valuable assistance.

I am deeply indebted to my agent, Ellen Geiger of Curtis Brown Ltd. Ellen, in fact, has been much more than agent. She is confidante, pal, and wise counselor. I thank as well Charlotte Sheedy, who helped initiate this project and who was most supportive in its initial stages.

This volume is dedicated to the memory of my mother and father, Berta Gottlieb and Manuel S. Chanes. Berta and Simcha offered the milestones to measure the distance of my understanding.

Last is first. More than to anyone, my gratitude goes to my beloved wife, Dr. Eva Fogelman, who has been a constant, unwavering source of encouragement and support. I thank Eva for her creative suggestions, keen insight, criticism, good humor, and most of all for her patience and love. Without her, this book would not have been done.

A Note on the Spelling and Usage of "Antisemitism"

Historian Yehuda Bauer writes as follows:

> The term "antisemitism" was coined in 1879 by a professed anti-semite, the German radical writer and politician Wilhelm Marr. The old term, "Jew-hatred," had become obsolete, for it described traditional, Christian antipathy toward Jews, and did not suit the modern, pseudo-scientific, nationalist, anti-Christian ideology which arose during the second half of the nineteenth century. The standard-bearers of the new—or revised—ideology sought a neutral, sanitized term that did not contain the word "Jew," and that would sound as though it had come from the world of the new social sciences. Marr's neologism came from the field of comparative philology, which had labeled certain languages, particularly Hebrew, Arabic, and Aramaic, as "Semitic."
>
> Sometimes in English the word is written with a hyphen. "Anti-Semitism," however, is altogether an absurd construction, since there is no such thing as "Semitism" to which it might be opposed. In German—and Hebrew—there is no hyphen; and the word has no precise meaning, although its connotations are well-understood. Despite the rather elliptical reference, Marr's readers, his colleagues, and his disciples did not have to struggle with the meaning of "antisemitism." They knew what he meant. [From "In Search of a Definition of Antisemitism," in *Approaches to Antisemitism: Context and Curriculum,* ed. by Michael Brown. New York and Jerusalem: The American Jewish Committee and the International Center for the University Teaching of Jewish Civilization, 1994.]

I would add that the use of the hyphen and upper case, as in "anti-Semitism," as Bauer points out, emphasizes a fictitious and imaginary "Semitism," characterizing a racially defined (rather than linguistic) "Semitic" group. Such a usage gives the antisemites a victory right off the mark.

Throughout this book, we will spell it "antisemitism."

PART ONE

INTRODUCTION

·1·

Antisemitism and Jewish Security in America Today: Interpreting the Data
Why Can't Jews Take "Yes" for an Answer?

JEROME A. CHANES

Antisemitism in the 1990s continues to confound and puzzle American Jews. Consider some recent appalling events and developments in the United States: the Crown Heights riots in which blacks attacked Jews in August 1991; the candidacies of David Duke; the outrages of Patrick J. Buchanan; the continuing swirl of activity surrounding Nation of Islam's virulent Minister Louis Farrakhan; George Bush's September 12, 1991, press conference in which he characterized legitimate Jewish grassroots advocacy as "powerful political forces"—was that antisemitism? asked many Jews; Professor Leonard Jeffries's contention that Jews were behind the slave trade. All these events have given American Jews heartburn and worse and raise serious questions, particularly with respect to evaluating data on antisemitism and interpreting those data in terms of threats to Jewish security. Clearly these and other developments indicate that certain taboos long thought to inhere in the society may be at risk.[1]

At the same time, American Jews ask how are we to parse data that assert that antisemitism is in fact on the decline?

All of these observations, other data from behavioral manifes-

Sections of this chapter were presented at the International Seminar for Researchers on Antisemitism, Institute of Jewish Affairs, London, December 6–8, 1993, and were subsequently published in *Patterns of Prejudice* vol. 28, nos. 3 & 4, 1994. Portions of this chapter also previously appeared in the author's "Antisemitism and Jewish Security in the United States, 1992: Why Are Jews Worried?" *Jerusalem Letter/Viewpoints* (Jerusalem Center for Public Affairs, May 1992).

tations, and statistics from polls and surveys, pose two fundamental questions: What do these manifestations and countervailing data mean with respect to the nature and extent of antisemitism in the United States? And how does our view of antisemitism affect the larger picture of Jewish security in America?

I am tempted to invoke Machiavelli, who is reputed to have said, "Others will tell you how things should be; let *me* tell you how they really are." The problem, when it comes to interpreting the data about antisemitism, is that everyone—and therefore no one—is an expert.

Interpretation of data on antisemitism in America is often a Rashomonlike exercise. Perception and interpretation have as much to do with psychological dynamics as with technical matters. While I do not want to enter into "shrink time"—one of the authors in this volume, psychoanalyst Martin Bergmann, does address the psychological dynamics of antisemitism (see chapter 5)—I will nonetheless return to some of the social-psychological dynamics involved in perceptions of antisemitism, notwithstanding what the data may show.

A number of specific questions should guide the analysis offered in this book. First, what do we know? What are the current available data on antisemitism in the United States? What is really happening out there and, just as important, what is *not* happening?

Second, how do we explain perceptions within the Jewish community of an antisemitism ascendant, even as data along a broad range of evaluative criteria tell us that antisemitism in America has declined and probably continues to decline—as Jewish perceptions of antisemitism? In 1983, in a survey conducted among American Jews by the American Jewish Committee, approximately one half of the respondents disagreed with the statement "Antisemitism is currently not a serious problem for American Jews." By 1988, the proportion had risen to 76 percent. And 1990 National Jewish Population Survey numbers show that 83 percent of American Jews either "strongly" or "somewhat" agree that antisemitism is a serious problem in the United States.[2] How can nine out of ten Jewish Americans say they "feel at home" in a country they think is rife with antisemitism?[3]

4

What accounts for the perception among most Jewish people that antisemitism is a serious problem in America, and that the status and security of Jews is at risk?

If things are so good out there, why do so many Jews think that things are so bad?

Third, when Jews say that antisemitism is a serious problem, what do they mean? What are they talking about?

Fourth, antisemitism emanating from the black community has clearly become a major source of Jewish concern. What do we know—and what do we *not* know—about antisemitism in the African-American community?

Fifth, what ought we be doing about antisemitism? What should we *not* be doing?

Sixth, what areas of study and research are indicated in areas of antisemitism about which we know very little?

Finally, what happens in a society such as ours, in which antisemitism in its various forms continues to wither away and the fear of a different threat to Jewish security—assimilation—is widespread?

The essays in *Antisemitism in America Today* address these and other questions and, in so doing, explore the level of security enjoyed by Jews in the United States. The picture that emerges from the tapestry woven by the chapters in this book challenges some conventional wisdom and raises a fundamental question: Why can't Jews take "yes" for an answer?

First, of course, there is the question of definition. What is antisemitism? There have been many efforts aimed at defining it, from the elaborate formulations reflected in attitudinal surveys to the classic one-liner: An antisemite is someone who dislikes Jews more than is absolutely necessary. And even this tired old saw tells us something about the nature, irrationality, and unpredictability of hatred of Jews. For the purpose of this discussion, however, we suggest a simple and stark definition of antisemitism: *all forms of hostility manifested toward the Jews throughout history.*

But it is difficult to define antisemitism with precision. Sometimes the best approach—paraphrasing former Supreme Court Justice Potter Stewart in his comment about obscenity—is "I can't define it, but I know it when I see it." However, this approach poses one problem: all too often incidents or expressions are characterized as antisemitism when they are really not; the gut feeling—the "kishke factor"—is important, but gut reactions must be carefully weighed with whatever hard data are available.

However one defines antisemitism, one distinction must be kept in mind: the distinction between antisemitism and many other forms of group conflict. Antisemitism presupposes that *the Jews are radically "other."* This simple central point is a universal, timeless characteristic of antisemitism.

To our set of questions:

First, on the question of the nature and extent of antisemitism in the United States, there are some fairly concrete data. To paraphrase the political commentator Ben Wattenberg, the good news is that the bad news isn't all bad.

There are two kinds of antisemitism—two kinds of anything, when it comes down to it. There is a crucial relationship between what people *think* and what people *do*, between *attitudinal* and *behavioral* antisemitism. Antisemitism of both kinds is assessed along a broad range of evaluative criteria.[4] The data on antisemitism, along these criteria, indicate that both behavioral and attitudinal antisemitism have declined in the United States over the past forty years, even as we must watch and concern ourselves with recurring danger signals. This finding, of course, is no great revelation, and is amply confirmed by evidence both anecdotal and research-generated, and fully explored by a number of essayists in this volume. Nonetheless, the finding calls for some analysis in terms of both behavioral and attitudinal manifestations.

Behavioral antisemitism is manifest, of course, in different ways—from swastika daubings to Jewish American Princess (JAP) jokes to political rhetoric. I submit that behavioral antisemitism "where it counts" is simply no longer a factor in American life. Such behavioral antisemitism includes large-scale discrimination against Jews; the cynical use of antisemitism in political rhetoric in order to achieve political gains, arguably the most virulent form of antisemitism; and, most important, the inability or reluctance of the Jewish community to express itself on issues of con-

cern because of anti-Jewish animus. This kind of antisemitism—
the kind that makes a difference in terms of the security and status of American Jews—has declined steadily and dramatically
over the past four decades and more.[5]

It follows that in any analysis of antisemitism in the United
States, a crucial distinction must be made. We need to distinguish
between antisemitism, which does exist and must be repudiated
and counteracted, and Jewish status, which is fundamentally
secure. Jewish security is strong largely because of a history and
tradition of constitutional protections that inform democratic
pluralism. While antisemitism and Jewish security are concentric
circles and therefore obviously related, the distinction between
them is important when discussing the issue in the context of
America in the 1990s.

What about attitudinal antisemitism? Here is where the issue of
data interpretation is best addressed and some exploration is
called for. Renae Cohen's chapter in this volume, "What We
Know, What We Don't Know About Antisemitism" (chapter 3),
provides a comprehensive survey and analysis of the data on attitudinal antisemitism.

It comes as a surprise to many that attitudinal antisemitism
in the United States has been a relatively little-studied phenomenon over the past three decades. In an age when social scrutiny
seems to extend into the most obscure corners of our experience,
we learn that antisemitism—an enduring social phenomenon and
one of special significance in our own time—has received scant
attention from America's social scientists until recently. Most
comprehensive, indeed landmark, studies were conducted during
the 1960s. Notable among these were the Anti-Defamation
League's *Patterns of American Prejudice*—the so-called Berkeley
studies—which developed a scale of antisemitic beliefs of non-
Jews and articulated the now-classic reverse correlation that the
higher the education level, the less likely are non-Jews to hold
antisemitic beliefs.[6]

The question is, What do Americans think about Jews? On
this fairly narrow question there are fairly conclusive findings.
The cumulative data of attitudinal surveys conducted by
Yankelovich, Roper, and their fellow researchers have consistent-

ly substantiated the view that the level of conventional antisemitic beliefs has continued in its forty-year decline. Simply put, there are fewer Americans who profess unfavorable images of Jews.

The usual explanation for this transformation is generational. As Earl Raab and others have shown, it is not that the antisemites are being converted, but that each succeeding age group tends to display fewer antisemitic attitudes than the preceding generation of that age group. Committed antisemites are swayed to virtue neither by events nor by prejudice-reduction programs. Raab puts it best: antisemites do not fade away; they simply die. See his chapter 4 in this volume, "Can Antisemitism Disappear?" Research findings clearly, strongly, and consistently suggest that a younger, better-educated, more affluent population is less antisemitic. This pattern, a negative correlation of education level and antisemitism, obtains across the board, including among blacks.[7]

While attitudinal surveys are always suspect—sometimes even for the right reasons—the lack of a truly comprehensive study since the American Jewish Committee's 1981 Yankelovich poll had greatly hindered the examination of present-day antisemitism in America.

Come now five studies in the past four years: the University of Chicago's National Opinion Research Center (NORC) 1990 General Social Survey, a comprehensive survey of ethnic groups commissioned by the American Jewish Committee (AJC) and conducted by NORC's Tom W. Smith[8]; a 1992 survey of American attitudes toward Jews conducted for the Anti-Defamation League (ADL) by Marttila and Kiley[9]; a 1992 intergroup relations study of New York City, done by the Roper Organization for the AJC[10]; a 1993 ADL/Marttila and Kiley survey on racial attitudes in America[11]; and, most recently, a 1994 comprehensive study (commissioned by the AJC) by NORC's Tom W. Smith confirming and synthesizing the findings of previous studies.[12]

It is instructive to analyze and compare the AJC/NORC and ADL/Marttila studies. (The American Jewish Committee Intergroup Relations Survey of New York, while containing valuable data, is a local study; the Marttila racial-attitudes survey addresses the question of prejudice in America generally, and calls for its own discrete treatment.)

The NORC 1990 General Social Survey data on fifty-eight ethnic groups—including one fictitious group, the "Wissians"; NORC found that significant numbers of Americans hold negative attitudes toward the "Wissians"—were "massaged" by NORC's Tom W. Smith for the AJC in order to elicit specific information about anti-Jewish attitudes.

NORC analyzed data related to six areas.[13] Among AJC/NORC's general findings were that first, and most generally, antisemitism and negative attitudes are at a low point. Specifically, only few members of certain minority groups harbor some negative attitudes toward Jews, and that conflict between Jews and non-Jews is less serious than are clashes between many other ethnic groups. NORC tells us also that latent sources of anti-semitism are not closely connected, and therefore are not likely to sustain one another. And the behavioral antisemitism that does exist in one area is almost always unconnected to that in another area. These are important findings. They suggest a pattern different from what existed in America fifty years ago.

Particularly intriguing are AJC/NORC's findings on Israel and antisemitism. It has long been known that anti-Israel and antisemitic attitudes are linked, that antisemitic attitudes are more common among those with negative attitudes toward Israel, and that anti-Israel attitudes are stronger among those with antisemitic beliefs. According to NORC this linkage is not especially strong. Attitudes toward Israel may be related to causes other than antisemitic attitudes—oil, Arabs, a particular world view, and so on.

Also instructive is the question of how Jews are perceived in terms of social standing, relative to other groups. Among religions, Jews come in tenth of twenty religious groups, below "Protestants" and Catholics, but above Mormons, Greek Orthodox, Christian Scientists, Unitarians (!), Spiritualists, and Jehovah's Witnesses.

A most significant area of the AJC/NORC study—as in any poll of attitudes toward Jews—is that of perceived power and influence. The "Jewish power" question is one to which significant import is given; it therefore merits some analysis. The way in which the question is asked makes a difference. If the question is open-ended—as in "Which groups have too much power?"—

Jews will consistently come out low. If the question is closed-ended and contextual—"Which groups from the following list have too much power?"—Jews still come out relatively low. If the question is completely closed-ended—"Do Jews have too much power in the United States?"—the numbers are higher.

The "Jewish power" question was asked by NORC not as "Do Jews have too much power in the United States?"—it should never be asked like this, because the data do not tell us much. It was asked, however—as it should be asked—as a contextual question: "Which of the following groups (twenty-three were listed: Arab oil nations, the media, labor unions, Orientals, blacks, the Catholic Church, banks and so on) have too much influence and power?" The Jews come out way down; about the only ones lower than the Jews were the Hispanics.

Seymour Martin Lipset, the political scientist, and others suggest that with regard to this issue, people are not antisemitic; they are anti-power.[14] That is, the issue is power, not Jews. People think that many groups have too much power in this society. But even this requires further nuance, and we will return to the question of interpreting the Jewish power question in our analysis of the Marttila poll.

Antisemitism in America is neither virulent nor growing, concludes the AJC/NORC study, consistent with the data from earlier polls. But NORC cautions that antisemitism in America is not a spent force, that Jews are yet recognized as an ethnic or religious out-group and are often accordingly judged and treated in a distinctive manner. Antisemitism has not disappeared; it has become dormant, and latent antisemitism does have the potential to become actualized. And antisemitic incidents do occur. Furthermore, antisemitic political groups may exist as isolated entities in the lunatic fringe. But lunatics can be dangerous.

A survey conducted by the polling firm Marttila and Kiley for the Anti-Defamation League in 1992 proves significant as well, but in a different way from the AJC/NORC study. For NORC, Tom W. Smith massaged general data in order to generate information about attitudes toward Jews. The ADL/Marttila study is the first comprehensive study specifically of attitudes toward Jews since the Yankelovich poll of 1981, and used once again the criteria for antisemitism (the "index") first developed by the Berkeley Studies and used by Yankelovich.

ADL/Marttila generally corroborated everything that we have known for many years, and most things that we have suspected, about attitudinal antisemitism. Marttila's central investigative device consists of an eleven-item scale—the "Index of Antisemitic Beliefs"—made up of questions designed to detect antisemitism.[15] Six or more yes answers make a person "most antisemitic"; two to five yeses result in a rating of "middle"; one or two yes answers, "not antisemitic."

General findings: twenty percent of Americans answered "yes" to six or more questions; they were therefore "most antisemitic." Forty-one percent were "middle," and 39 percent "not antisemitic."

Further, the survey results show a continuing pattern of decline—albeit a slow one—along a range of antisemitic beliefs. The negative correlation of "education up, antisemitism down" holds for all groups in the society, including blacks. Age is a factor: Americans over sixty-five are twice as likely as those under sixty-five to fall into the "most antisemitic" category. Important data in ADL/Marttila are those linking antisemitism and racism. Individuals who are "most racist" are likely to be "most antisemitic," and vice versa. One cautionary note in ADL/Marttila concerns the "Jewish power" question: the numbers are slightly up, between 24 and 31 percent, depending on the question asked.[16]

Perhaps the most surprising finding in the ADL/Marttila survey was the refutation of conventional wisdom that the more contact a person has with Jews, the less antisemitic that person will be. Not so, says Marttila. This finding requires further study.

One other fascinating finding of the study—taken, let us recall, during the last months of the Likud/Shamir government in Israel—is that criticism of Israel is no predictor for antisemitic attitudes. Indeed, many critics of Israel are well educated and embrace tolerant, pluralistic attitudes. (As a point of fact, there are some Jews who are "anti-Israel," and many Jews (perhaps a majority of American Jews, according to some polls) who opposed the policies of the Likud government under former prime minister Shamir.)[17]

The ADL/Marttila poll is valuable, even though it does not

tell us that much that is new. It is arguable that we should get off the antisemitism-polling fix and explore other areas. (Political scientist Seymour Martin Lipset, to cite one example, would prefer that social scientists study philosemitism; why do some people have an unusual affinity for—*like* or *love*—Jews?[18]) But with respect to data analysis and interpretation ADL/Marttila serves us well as a case study for data analysis. It is in this respect that I would suggest four questions about the ADL/Marttila poll, questions that illumine issues about the study of antisemitism in general.

The first question has less to do with the study and everything to do with the way in which the data were presented and interpreted. "Twenty percent of Americans are strongly antisemitic," asserts ADL/Marttila. Is this bad news or good news? Although 20 percent is hardly a trivial number—30 million antisemites out there is nothing to be laughed at—it seems to me that the news is not all that bad. The first questions any social scientist asks about any such assertion is, "Compared to *when,* and compared to *what?*" The 20 percent reported is down from the 29 percent of the 1964 ADL/Berkeley Studies. Further, with respect to the "compared to what?" question, ample data exist from any number of sources that indicate that 20 percent—or more—of any group hates any other group. So: good news or bad?

Second, some of the questions in the index may not have been perceived by respondents as reflecting negatively on Jews; they indeed may not measure antisemitism. A classic example of this flaw in questioning emerged in the 1986 poll of evangelical Christians in America conducted by the Anti-Defamation League. At the height of what was known as the "Christianization of America," the ADL asked the question, Are fundamentalists more antisemitic than the general population? Is it antisemitism that informs their agenda? And—no great surprise—the ADL found that fundamentalists factor out in levels of antisemitism about the same as everyone else, approximately 20 percent.

In the course of the survey, the ADL in effect asked the question: "Are Jews tight with their money?" A significant percentage of the respondents answered, "Yes, Jews are tight with their money." Antisemitism! But then, in a question that was brilliant in a post facto way, the follow-up question was asked: "Is this good?" Answer: "Yes, this is a good trait; Jews are thrifty," etc. Antisemitism? A number of questions in the "Index of Antisemitic Beliefs" may not be measuring antisemitism, but some other beliefs or feelings that may indeed represent some anti-Jewish animus, or may in fact be reflective of positive attitudes toward Jews.

Third, and more serious, attitudes are much more nuanced than the three groupings "most antisemitic," "middle," and "not antisemitic."[19] There is a basic ambiguity in most responses that needs to be noted. A respondent who answered "yes" to six or seven questions (some of which may in fact *not* measure antisemitism, as we just noted) has been just fine on four or five. (And even some of these questions may not measure antisemitism, as we have noted.) Even among the "most antisemitic," therefore, there exist identifiable pro-Jewish attitudes. (Among the "not antisemitic," the reverse is true: they may very well hold anti-Jewish attitudes.) A more sophisticated conceptual scheme is clearly needed, one that takes into account these ambiguities.

Fourth, and most troubling: ADL/Marttila—indeed, attitudinal surveys in general—are leading Jews toward a new definition of antisemitism: attitudes toward Jews that *Jews* find distasteful; attitudes that Jews wish "they," namely non-Jews, would not have; rather than the classic definition of antisemitism as expressed hostility toward Jews.

For example, the increase in numbers on the "Jewish power" question is indeed troubling. But consider: Jews in America *are* a power group; is it unreasonable for some people to ask whether Jews have too much power? The question is, how do individuals who hold such views *act* on those views? *The* fundamental question in antisemitism anywhere, at any time, is what is the relationship between *attitude* and *behavior?*

Mention ought be made of a sixth study, conducted by Louis Harris for the National Conference (formerly the National Conference of Christians and Jews), released in 1994, that evaluated the state of intergroup relations in the United States and provided a further context for the study of antisemitism.[20] With respect to prejudicial attitudes in general, the study found that members of minority groups are more likely than are whites to agree to negative stereotypes about other minority groups. In terms of antisemitism, the National Conference/Harris survey data revealed disturbingly high numbers in the responses to the "Jewish power" and "dual loyalty" questions, among both whites and minority group members. Forty-three percent of blacks and 22 percent of whites said that Jews "have too much control over business and the media." Forty-seven percent of blacks and 24 percent of whites responded that Jews "are more loyal to Israel than to America."

Of course, there are inherent problems with any survey data. Respondents may be disingenuous: "I may *think* it. I can't *say* it." Or questions may be flawed, or not sufficiently probing, or without good follow-up. Recall if you will the ADL questions of the fundamentalists.

In sum: Notwithstanding the problems with comparing the two large surveys owing to the many differences between them, some conclusions with respect to broad trends are called for. There is a steady, albeit slow lessening of expressed negativity toward Jews, with a possible exception of the stereotypes of Jewish power; a smaller percentage of the population scores as antisemitic; there is a more widespread acceptance of positive statements about Jews. The dual-loyalty numbers may have remained more or less constant over the years, but other statistics, exhibiting positive attitudes, have evidenced dramatic change: in 1958, 61 percent of Americans said they would vote for a Jew for president; in 1987, 89 percent of Americans said they would so vote.[21]

So much for attitudinal data. One further general observation about antisemitism in America, and some specific concrete issues that go to the core of data interpretation.

Cogent lessons should be learned about antisemitism from recent experiences. It is not what happened that often matters, but what did *not* happen. One way of measuring antisemitism is by looking at responses to "conflict" situations—situations that could tend to polarize society, with the expectation that antisemitism will increase. Consider the whole range of conflict situations over the past four decades—from the Rosenbergs' case in the 1950s to the oil crises of 1973–74 and 1979 (remember the

"Burn Jews, Not Oil" bumper stickers that nobody saw?), the Iran/Contra affair, with its Israeli connection; the conviction during the 1980s of Jewish public officials in New York and Maryland; the Boesky insider-trading case; the farm crisis in the mid-1980s; the Intifada; and, most dramatically, the Pollard spy case, invoking clearly the question of "dual loyalty"—all situations that everyone confidently expected would trigger expressions of antisemitism. In fact, none of these resulted in an increase of antisemitic expression or attitude in the United States—most instructive.[22]

While the response to conflict situations has been fairly standard over the years, as not resulting in increased antisemitic expression, mention ought be made of two events in recent years that suggest that inhibiting factors may be weakening somewhat. At his September 12, 1991, news conference, President George Bush referred to pro-Israel activists who had converged on Washington to press for loan guarantees, and characterized the Jewish grassroots advocacy as "powerful political forces." Those comments were a direct response to a conflict situation, and were very troubling to many American Jews. Was it antisemitism? In my view, the answer is no. Was it on the margin, signifying the breakdown of a taboo against political antisemitism? Certainly.

Serious concern was expressed as well over the August 26, 1990 (and subsequent) remarks of columnist Patrick J. Buchanan: "There are only two groups that are beating the drums of war in the Middle East—the Israeli Defense Ministry and its 'amen' corner in the United States." Buchanan's remarks—characterized by *New York Times* columnist A. M. Rosenthal as a "blood libel"[23]—were in direct response to a conflict situation, namely the then-developing Gulf Crisis, and were very troubling.

The context of Buchanan's remarks, of course, was Buchanan's questionable history with respect to Jews, very different from that of George Bush, whose remark might be considered sui generis. In both his syndicated columns and on television, Buchanan had over the years evidenced significant hostility to Israel and to many Jewish concerns. He has questioned the validity of continued American support of the Jewish state, proclaimed the innocence of suspected Nazi war criminal John Demjanjuk, and supported the presence of the Carmelite convent at the Auschwitz/Birkenau death camp.

The most difficult questions with respect to data interpretation in the United States have to do with antisemitism in the black community, arguably the main source of angst among Jews. The fact is that we know very little about the nature and extent of antisemitism among blacks.[24] There has never been a comprehensive study of black attitudes toward Jews, an issue complicated by black attitudes toward whites in general; the data that we have are limited and fragmentary—and mostly old. Until the 1960s the question of black views was sidestepped completely; since then— a bit of Charles Herbert Stember, a smidgen of Yankelovich, a statistical bite of Gary Marx, some Marttila, and a large amount of anecdotal evidence.[25]

Two observations. First: conventional wisdom about black antisemitism is largely unfounded. For example, the view that as education levels rise in the black community, so does antisemitism, and that the best-educated blacks are the most antisemitic, enjoys popular currency. (Remember the inverse relationship between educational level and antisemitism in the general community: as education levels go up, antisemitism goes down.)

But there are almost no data to justify the assertion that in the black community, as education goes up, so does antisemitism.[26] What can be said, based on the little that is known with certitude, is that the level of antisemitism drops steeply for both whites *and* blacks as education level rises, but less so for blacks—the reverse correlation exists, but is weaker. The Anti-Defamation League/Marttila and Kiley survey confirms this fact. Blacks do continue to be relatively more antisemitic than whites at any given education level. But this is very different from saying that they become more antisemitic as they become better educated.

But whatever the data do or fail to reveal, the reality exists that many blacks, for whatever reason, may not be constrained in their venting of antisemitic sentiment. Various polls taken over the years have substantiated the fact that the black population, who have always lagged well behind the general population in a range of economic and social indicators, is the only group in which the reservoir level of anti-Jewish feeling has not dropped— and may have in some areas increased—and in which the taboos against expression of antisemitism have eroded. Additionally,

16

they are less reluctant to repudiate antisemitism in their midst. For many American Jews this pattern is the tough reality of black antisemitism.

This form of black antisemitism requires analysis as well. The question is whether failure to repudiate antisemitic statements is *antisemitism*, or is it the reflection of other dynamics that are at work?

Indeed it was the failure of black leaders to repudiate antisemitism that was at the heart of any number of experiences during recent years. This was exemplified by the unhappy—and highly instructive—Cokeley affair in 1989. We recall that the obscene antisemitic (and anti-Christian) utterances of Steven Cokeley, black aide to then Chicago mayor Eugene Sawyer—including the appalling shocker that Jewish doctors were injecting black babies with AIDS—were awful enough. They were made even more so by the fact that Sawyer, instead of firing Cokeley within the hour that the story broke, temporized for five days. Equally disturbing was the fact that the black leadership of Chicago, including even Sawyer's black political rivals, did not immediately and vigorously denounce and repudiate Cokeley. The experience, once again, followed a pattern all too evident in recent years. More immediate and equally obvious examples: the failure of many black leaders to repudiate Nation of Islam Minister Louis Farrakhan. (See chapters 7 and 17, by Gary E. Rubin and Jonathan Rieder, respectively, in this volume.)

The pattern exemplified by the Cokeley affair and the Farrakhan experiences reflects the interpretation by each group of its priorities in light of its separate past. Blacks focus on *unity* and *solidarity*—which they indeed learned in part from the Jewish community—and argue that it was black disunity that simplified slavery and helped prevent black advancement in the century following emancipation. American Jews focus on—perhaps are even obsessed with—*denunciation* and *repudiation*. Jews would argue, and rightly so, that repudiation of antisemitism and of its practitioners by non-Jews—the willingness of those in leadership positions to speak out—is a key component in the counteraction of antisemitism. Jews argue that it was the failure to denounce Hitler's early evils that opened the way for the Holocaust.

It is important for Jews to understand that when "black antisemitism" is invoked, often what is being described may not be the attitude of the black population in general toward Jews—we do not know very much about that—but very different dynamics indeed, those of repudiation and solidarity. And this may be even more significant in terms of the tactics and strategies of our communal organizations. Denunciation and repudiation of antisemitism *are* key elements in the counteraction of antisemitism. Courageous black leaders have repudiated antisemitism, and need to continue to do so. But Jews ought not recklessly scapegoat the broader black population when hard data on that population are not in hand.

With respect to the riots in Crown Heights, there is no question that a serious antisemitic outburst occurred in August 1991; there is no question that an antisemitic murder was committed. But in analyzing those conditions in Crown Heights that led to the tragic events, a more nuanced approach is indicated. The key question here is whether Crown Heights is sui generis: can we—ought we—extrapolate Crown Heights to the black population in general or to other communities around the country?

The August 1991 events in Crown Heights had more to do with long-standing "tribal rivalries," to use the words of sociologist Jonathan Rieder, explored in detail in his chapter—rivalries of real estate, power, culture—than with a deep-seated antisemitism that indeed may not be present in a hardly monolithic black population in that neighborhood.

Further—and this goes to the heart of data interpretation—is the antisemitism of the black street kid yelling "Kill the Jew!" the same as the antisemitism of Professor Jeffries? The same as that of the white skinhead in Jersey City? We will not know very much about what goes on in neighborhoods like Crown Heights—where "Kill the Jew!" is directed at the most visible manifestation of white power—until we are ready to mount a serious ethnographic study on the street. Most important, it seems clear that the causes and events of Crown Heights would not be replicated elsewhere, and this is the key issue.[27]

Further: the Williamsburg section of Brooklyn has many of the same ingredients as did Crown Heights—"tribal" rivalries over land and power, a well-organized and politically savvy Hasidic group (in this case, the Satmar Hasidim), and a minority group that feels it has been given the short end of the stick. It is a tinderbox that could explode, the same situation as Crown Heights, only in Williamsburg there are no blacks—there are Hispanics. It was not "black antisemitism" that caused Crown Heights, it was tribal rivalry, primarily over land, exacerbated by individuals who exploited a tense situation.

As the United States increasingly becomes a multiethnic society, the pattern unfortunately reflects one of increasing ethnic strife. We are not in an era of antisemitism in this country; we are in an era of ethnic conflict. The problem is that in large measure ethnic groups sometimes are not affirming their unity by affirming the positive values of their heritages. For ethnic groups the only truly valid principle is this *positive* affirmation. Yet many groups are instead defining their unity in negative ways, either by the memory of their hurts (for the Jews the Holocaust and pogroms, to which blacks say, "You don't have a monopoly on the Holocaust; we had slavery"), or by focusing on the Enemy. What comes out of these projections is anger, which generates counteranger, which generates . . .

Neither group has anywhere to go in this kind of battle, and the traditional coalition that believes that bettering the conditions of society will lessen bias (including antisemitism)—a well-proven thesis—will split, as it has done. But if and as members of minority groups move into the system—as they become better educated and economically upwardly mobile—they become less antisemitic. The anger decreases. The attitudes of individuals may not have changed; the conditions have.[28]

Let us return to the questions with which I began, specifically to what explains the "perception gap" between the grass roots and the data.

First, it is necessary to understand what Jews are saying when they say that antisemitism is a serious problem. On this question there *are* some data. A study conducted by Brandeis University's Perlmutter Institute for Jewish Advocacy revealed that when asked about specific areas of "seriousness" of the antisemitism they were reporting, most respondents did not pinpoint economic, power, or political areas, but rather incidents of vandalism or

Israel-related activity. Or they are saying, "I heard from my neighbor that he heard on the radio . . ."[29]

So what explains the perception gap between the Jewish grass roots and the data? At bottom, it is clear that much of the anxiety felt by many American Jews is obviously related to our historical experience, particularly the Holocaust. History has made Jews unusually sensitive, and it is a sensitivity worth maintaining. This gut reaction—the "kishke" factor—is a response not to antisemitism but to a foreboding of latent antisemitism possibly turning into actual. We recall the classic one-liner: What's the definition of a Jewish telegram? "Start worrying. Letter follows." The 80 to 90 percent who are responding "yes" to the question "Is antisemitism a serious problem?" are responding not to antisemitism, but to the Jewish telegram.

Earl Raab, who has articulated much of the vocabulary of the Jewish community-relations field,[30] has written about this reaction at length. Raab suggests that the foreboding felt by most Jews is that of an antisemitism that is latent among many in the society, requiring some radical social dislocation to cause its actual expression. This foreboding is useful. It keeps Jews on their toes, and it should be held on to. But Raab suggests that it will not help us much if we just see anti-Israel activity as the latest version of atavistic Jew-hatred. At best, the foreboding does lead to an understanding that the best fight against latent antisemitism is the fight to strengthen positive American self-interest attitudes toward Jews.[31]

But there is more to the gap between the perception of antisemitism and the reality of Jewish security than just the foreboding of latent antisemitism. Social scientists should pay attention to their own numbers. Steven M. Cohen has found that more than half of all American Jews continue to hold traditional negative stereotypes of non-Jews.[32] Whatever the data on antisemitism's actual decline, these negative images resonate in the perception of an antisemitism reemergent. And this dynamic reinforces itself: the perception that non-Jews are hostile may very well lead Jews to avoid non-Jewish intimacies and associations. In turn, the absence of such contact sustains the negative image of the non-Jew and reinforces Jews' fear of non-Jews—in a word, of antisemitism.

Further, the perception of antisemitism found among many American Jews may be a vestige of a time when antisemitism in America was very real and when every Jew was insecure vis-à-vis non-Jews. If these outmoded social and cultural perceptions of the non-Jew persist, it may be too soon to measure the reactions of American Jews to questions about Jewish security against the *true* state of Jewish security.

Further, there is the intrusion of issues on the public-affairs agenda into the consciousness of many American Jews. The Christian "religious right" and the notion of America as a "Christian nation"* (see Mark Silk's analysis of the "new anti-secularism" in chapter 14 of this volume); the related attack on the separation of church and state, as a perceived quick fix for the dearth of values in the "public square" (witness the debate over prayer in the public schools)—threats all, in my view, to Jewish security—suggest to some Jews a renewed wafting of antisemitic odors. Questions with respect to the religious right went beyond, and were deeper than, the debate over public-policy issues. The controversy over the sometimes strange assertions found in the writings of the Reverend Pat Robertson, leader of the Christian Coalition, portraying a world-wide conspiracy of international bankers, communists, and freemasons—code words for classic antisemitica—further suggest that there remains a reservoir of antisemitism that may inform much of the activity of the religious right. At the very least, the apocalyptic vision that underlies much of the support of the religious right for the State of Israel is not especially friendly to Jews. Robertson has expressed his "sincere regrets" for his statements. But, as Mark Silk avers in his chapter in this volume, "Whatever one makes of this apologia, it is certainly true that Robertson chose to fish in some very dirty waters."

There are additional obvious influences on the perceptions of American Jews. Antisemitic activity in Europe has a psychologi-

---

*Revealing and instructive was the observation of Senator Howell Heflin of Alabama, who, in his opening remarks in Senate committee hearings in 1994 on language on religious harassment in the workplace for Equal Employment Opportunity Commission Guidelines, averred "We have [in this country] Americans, Jews, and others."

cal effect on Americans. American Jews also cannot discount the effects of traumas such as Crown Heights. Most important, in my view, is the effect of intergroup tensions in general in the United States. I suspect that the source of anxiety for most American Jews may not be antisemitism; it is the rise of intergroup conflict across the map. The relationship of intergroup tension to antisemitism in America is an area that requires significant study.

All of this suggests the question, not of who are the antisemites—who cares, really—but of who are those who are *not* antisemites. There would seem to be three types of people: philosemites, non-antisemites, and anti-antisemites.[33] The security of Jews does not depend on people being non-antisemites; for most people in the United States, Jews are simply not an issue.

And indeed, in the 1991 gubernatorial campaign in Louisiana 55 percent of the white vote went to former Klan leader David Duke not *because* of his racial views but *despite* those views; when self-interest is a factor, non-antisemites may ignore the antisemitism or racism of a candidate. According to exit polling, 27 percent of voters supported Duke because of his views on the state's economy, 39 percent because of government corruption, and only 12 percent because of Duke's views on racial issues.[34] This response to Duke strongly suggests that many in the non-antisemitic group will support an antisemite if some other area of self-interest is invoked. (See Mark Mellman's analysis of these data in chapter 9 of this volume.)

There is a substantial number of people who do not care about the Jews one way or another, but who are unconstrained enough to support an antisemite if such support appears to serve their needs. These are the *non*-antisemites. The dynamic at work in non-antisemitism lies at the interface of the social control and trigger mechanisms.

The real security of Jews lies in people being *anti*-antisemites, for whom antisemitism is totally illegitimate and must be repudiated. A relatively small number of people fall into this category, and not much is known about the taboo that informs anti-antisemitism. It is clearly an area for study.

Finally, What *don't* we know about antisemitism?

First, we need to know more about the taboos and controls

surrounding the *expression* of antisemitism that cause non-anti-semites to become anti-antisemites. With respect to triggers of antisemitism, it is not enough to mouth the simple formula "Bad times equals increased antisemitism." Bad economic times can be the background; they do not constitute the trigger. What is required is a combination and interaction of *background* and con-text; antisemitic *attitudes* of the population that are measured; and *trigger*.[35]

Second, there are forms of antisemitism that are difficult to observe and measure, namely hidden and latent antisemitism. Additionally, traditional, cruder forms of antisemitism may not have been eliminated, but may have been revamped and repack-aged for a new generation. This "new" antisemitism, articulated in a different, perhaps less blatant manner, more subtle and nuanced, calls for study. The difficulty is that while new forms of antisemitism may be open and observable (as compared with the hidden and latent kinds), they are often encrypted.[36]

A related question is that of threshold. The different points at which individuals *perceive* antisemitism need to be probed. What yardstick are people using when they measure situations that they themselves perceive or experience as antisemitism? Should survivors of the Holocaust, on the one hand, and college students who never experienced behavioral antisemitism until they reached the campus, on the other, be categorized in the same manner? (Both groups, from opposite ends of the spectrum, have very low thresholds for perceiving antisemitism.)[37] This is a dif-ficult and sensitive area.

Third: research and study are needed on the nature and extent of antisemitism in the black community. As I suggested earlier in this chapter, relatively little is known about antisemitism among blacks.

Fourth: we need a new look at the surveys. The existent sur-veys, which may be either antiquated or irrelevant, need to be retooled.

Fifth: a hierarchy of antisemitism needs to be developed. This is extremely important. Not all forms of antisemitism carry equal weight. It is ridiculous to equate political antisemitism—a most virulent form—with the telling of a JAP joke. No one would want to minimize any form of antisemitic expression—any person who is at the receiving end of such expression is an abused person—but until some serious weighting system is developed we will be at the mercy of those who would exploit antisemitism.

Sixth: we need to study the relationship of bigotry in general and antisemitism. The ADL/Marttila data are extremely valuable in this regard. Follow-up is called for.

Seventh, and most crucial: what is the relationship between attitude and behavior? This question has been around for decades, and has bedeviled research psychologists as much as sociologists.

And last: how do we assess, not antisemitism, but Jewish perceptions of antisemitism? My speculations and those of others in this area need more comprehensive analysis. What are the specific factors that influence or inform our perceptions? Why do American Jews respond more to the Jewish telegram than to realities?

Until fifty years ago, antisemitism was perfectly normal—indeed normative—in Jewish history.[38] In our own day, however, one might say that Adolf Hitler gave antisemitism a bad name, as did Father Coughlin and Gerald L. K. Smith in the United States. But once again, taboos against expressions of antisemitism, as against racism and bigotry in general, appear to be breaking down. Not many years ago, expression of antisemitism was not considered to be legitimate. But as the American Jewish Committee's David Singer has said, "Jesse Jackson was the first to show [in our day] that there is life after antisemitism."

Further, what is troubling about antisemitism in America today is not the reality of antisemitism; after all, antisemitism is always a reality. What appears to be different today is the fact that the efforts to introduce what was until now considered "fringe" or extremist manifestations of bigotry into the mainstream institutions of society as legitimate expression have increased. Items: Leonard Jeffries and higher education. Louis Farrakhan and the political arena. Holocaust denial and the academy and the press. A note on this last point: however few are the adherents to Holocaust "revisionism"—and by all accounts they are few indeed—Holocaust denial is a new vehicle for antisemitism that exploits the free discussion and the two-sides-to-the-question sense of fair play traditional to most Americans. Kenneth Stern explores this issue in detail in chapter 11.

Are there more negative dynamics at work today than there were ten years ago? Yes. Are there clouds in what five or ten years ago was a cloudless sky? Yes. Are they storm clouds? No, because the qualitative difference between a pluralistic America of 1994 and the Europe of 1934 remains, and this is a very significant difference.

And last: The American Jewish community has been hypnotized by antisemitism. We monitor it, we measure it, we chase after antisemites. But ultimately the important issue is not antisemitism; it is Jewish security. There are any number of things in America that have nothing to do with antisemitism that are terribly destructive to Jews; and there are many things in this country that could be fairly characterized as antisemitism that are superficial, that pose little or no danger to the Jewish polity or to individual Jews. Why can't American Jews take "yes" for an answer? And more basic, how, ultimately, can we measure Jewish security?

The historian Lucy Dawidowicz, writing in *Commentary* magazine in 1970, asked a simple question: "Can Anti-Semitism be measured?"[39] Dawidowicz suggested that survey analysis, which presents a picture frozen in a moment in time, is by its nature unequipped to investigate the historic images and themes that yet flourish, even in America; it is certainly unequipped to trace the passage of these themes from one culture to another. How much more difficult to locate a specific variety of antisemitism within a meaningful historical continuum, and translate this form of antisemitism in a responsible way for our communities. It is this last question that, ultimately, is our charge in interpreting antisemitism, and interpreting what we mean by Jewish security.

Antisemitism in America Today aims at synthesizing our knowledge and in some cases ignorance, our certitudes and speculations, about present-day antisemitism in the United States. Part One of the book—this introductory essay—has developed a thesis about antisemitism and Jewish security in America. Part two, on historical, sociological, and psychological perspectives, sets a context from these disciplines for part three, in which specific manifestations of antisemitism are discussed in detail, and are evaluated in terms of their impact on the American Jewish polity.

Six areas of significant concern—Israel, black-Jewish relations, extremist-group activity (including Holocaust denial, so-called Holocaust "revisionism"), Christian-Jewish relations, political antisemitism, and antisemitism on the campus—are explored. Reprinted as well in part three is part of Letty Cottin Pogrebin's classic essay, "Antisemitism in the Women's Movement."

Part four offers six unique perspectives on discrete issues in contemporary antisemitism. The book closes with an essay by Anne Roiphe, who asks, Is Antisemitism not our constant companion?

NOTES

1. Historian Robert Wistrich suggests a parallel development in Europe; it is of interest to compare the American with the European situation in terms of similarities and differences. See Robert S. Wistrich, *Anti-Semitism in Europe Since the Holocaust* (New York: American Jewish Committee, 1993), p. 19.

2. Barry Kosmin, *Highlights of the CJF 1990 National Jewish Population Survey* (New York: Council of Jewish Federations, 1990), p. 29.

3. See Earl Raab, "Taking the Measure of Anti-Semitism in the 21st Century," Address to the Plenary Session of the National Jewish Community Relations Advisory Council, February 16, 1992 (unpublished), p. 1. The author expresses his appreciation to Earl Raab for his guidance and counsel.

4. Among the criteria for assessing antisemitism developed by the National Jewish Community Relations Advisory Council are: prevailing attitudes toward Jews; acts of aggression, covert or overt, toward Jews; discrimination against Jews; expressions of antisemitism by public figures; expressions of antisemitism by religious figures; response to conflict situations; official reactions to antisemitism; antisemitic "mass" movements; personal experience with antisemitism; anti-Zionist manifestations in which the legitimacy of the State of Israel—and therefore the legitimacy of the peoplehood of the Jews—is questioned (this does not include criticism of the policies of the Israeli government). *NJCRAC 1985–86 Joint Program Plan* (New York: NJCRAC, 1986).

5. Other behavioral manifestations are certainly present in the United States, some disturbingly so. For example, the number of incidents of antisemitic vandalism, as monitored by the Anti-Defamation League's annual *Audit of Anti-Semitic Incidents*, increased each year from 1987 to 1991, declined in 1992, and increased again in 1993 and 1994. Analysts suggest that the ADL's audit must be evaluated in the context of the total number

of bias and prejudice-related incidents reported around the country, and assessed in terms of the nature of the incident and the identity of the perpetrator (for example, the skinhead, who expresses hate against many groups, including Jews; the teenaged swastika dauber; and so on).

6. *Patterns of American Prejudice* was published as a seven-volume series based on the University of California (Berkeley) *Five-Year Study of Anti-Semitism in the United States*, designed by the Survey Research Center at Berkeley and carried out by the University of Chicago's National Opinion Research Center under a grant from the Anti-Defamation League of B'nai B'rith. The eleven-item antisemitism scale developed by Gertrude Selznick and Stephen Steinberg for the Berkeley studies was the model for subsequent surveys, including the 1981 Yankelovich, Skelly, White poll commissioned by the American Jewish Committee and the 1992 Marttila and Kiley survey conducted for the Anti-Defamation League (see pp. 10–14). While there are numerous differences in the samples, study designs, and execution in the three surveys, the antisemitism scale used is substantially the same in all three. This has raised serious questions among researchers. See Tom W. Smith, "The Polls—a Review: Actual Trends or Measurement Artifacts? A Review of Three Studies of Anti-Semitism," *Public Opinion Quarterly* 57 (fall 1993): 380–93, for an exploration of these questions.

An earlier, landmark study, *The Authoritarian Personality*, by T. W. Adorno et al. (New York: Harper & Row, 1950), explored the personality of prejudice. In this American Jewish Committee study an earlier antisemitism scale was developed.

7. See, for example, the findings from the Anti-Defamation League/Marttila and Kiley survey.

8. *What Do Americans Think About Jews?* (New York: American Jewish Committee, 1991).

9. "Highlights from an Anti-Defamation League Survey on Anti-Semitism and Prejudice in America" (New York: Anti-Defamation League, November 16, 1993).

10. Carolyn E. Setlow and Renae Cohen, *1992 New York City Intergroup Relations Survey* (New York: American Jewish Committee, 1992).

11. "Highlights from an Anti-Defamation League Survey on Racial Attitudes in America" (New York: Anti-Defamation League, June 1993).

12. *Anti-Semitism in Contemporary America* (New York: American Jewish Committee, 1994). See Renae Cohen's chapter in this volume for an analysis of the 1994 AJC/NORC study.

13. The six areas examined by NORC/AJC were: (1) the perceived social standing of Jews compared to other ethnoreligious groups; (2) the images that people have of Jews compared to those of other ethnoreligious groups; (3) the perceived influence and power that Jews have compared to other groups; (4)

the warmth or closeness that people feel toward Jews compared to other groups; (5) social interactions between Jews and non-Jews in the areas of friendship and intermarriage; and (6) the perceived loyalty of Jews and the connection between anti-Israel and antisemitic attitudes.

14. Conversation with the author.

15. The eleven items in the index were: Jews stick together more than other Americans; Jews always like to be at the head of things; Jews are more loyal to Israel than to America; Jews have too much power in the United States today; Jews have too much control and influence on Wall Street; Jews have too much power in the business world; Jews have a lot of irritating faults; Jews are more willing than others to use shady practices to get what they want; Jewish businessmen are so shrewd that others don't have a fair chance in competition; Jews don't care what happens to anyone but their own kind; Jews are [not] just as honest as other businessmen.

16. The "Jewish power" question was asked both as an objective question and as a contextual question.

17. Compare the American Jewish Committee/NORC findings, above.

18. Remarks to Plenary Session of the National Jewish Community Relations Advisory Council, Washington, D.C., February 20, 1993 (unpublished).

19. See Gary E. Rubin, "A No-Nonsense Look at Anti-Semitism," *Tikkun*, May-June 1993, 46–48, 79–81; and chapter 7 in this volume.

20. *Taking America's Pulse: The National Conference Survey on Inter-Group Relations* (New York: The National Conference, 1994).

21. The apparent contradiction between a decline in attitudinal antisemitism and an increase over a period of years (until 1992) in the number of antisemitic incidents can be easily explained: among those relatively few who profess antisemitic attitudes, there has been in recent years a greater propensity to "act out" their beliefs in various forms of expression, consistent with the general erosion of traditional societal taboos that has been noted in the United States.

22. A comparison of the European and American experiences with respect to conflict situations is instructive. Do the same patterns obtain? Or is there more likely to be an antisemitic response to conflict situations in Europe?

23. September 14, 1990.

24. An essay on this issue that is dated, but nonetheless worth reading, is Leonard Dinnerstein's "Black Antisemitism" chapter in *Uneasy at Home: Antisemitism and the American Jewish Experience* (New York: Columbia University Press, 1987), pp. 218–254. Dinnerstein's essay offers a capsule review of such events as New York's Ocean Hill–Brownsville school-board turmoil and other events of the 1960s and early '70s, including early mani-

festations of "affirmative action." Caution, however: while Dinnerstein's essay is valuable, the polling data he cites are now woefully out of date.

25. For a valuable review of the data on black antisemitism, see Jennifer L. Golub, *What Do We Know About Black Anti-Semitism?* (New York: American Jewish Committee, 1990).

26. The only data that I could find are those from Ronald Tadao Tsukashima's study of Los Angeles, "The Social and Psychological Correlates of Anti-Semitism in the Black Community," Ph.D. dissertation, University of California, Los Angeles, 1973.

27. An NJCRAC survey of twenty-five communities of significant Jewish and black populations confirms this judgment (telephone interviews conducted by Jerome A. Chanes of the National Jewish Community Relations Advisory Council, September 1991, unpublished findings).

28. For a full exploration, see Arthur Hertzberg, "Is Anti-Semitism Dying Out?" *New York Review of Books*, June 24, 1993, pp. 51–57.

29. Unpublished findings, 1991.

30. See Earl Raab's "Can Antisemitism Disappear?" chapter 4 in this volume.

31. Raab, "Taking the Measure of Anti-Semitism in the 21st Century."

32. Steven M. Cohen and Charles S. Liebman, *Two Worlds of Judaism: The Israeli and American Experiences* (New Haven: Yale University Press, 1990).

33. The philosemitism phenomenon is a social-psychological phenomenon that calls for a discrete study.

34. *Exit Poll Cross Tabulations, Louisiana Runoff 1991* (New York: Voter Research and Surveys, 1991), photocopied. The raw data were interpreted by Mark Mellman of Mellman and Lazarus, Washington.

The question of whether there was receptivity to Duke's racist message even as his overt Klan connection was rejected or ignored is addressed by Mellman and others. Mellman points out that there are data to suggest that responses such as "reform the welfare system," conventionally considered to be code words for racism, are in fact nothing of the sort. Indeed, most Americans, when queried, respond that most people on "welfare" are white; and that welfare is an issue of being responsible for one's own actions, and not of race.

35. Raab, "Taking the Measure of Anti-Semitism," explores this area.

36. For a comprehensive discussion of hidden, latent, and "new" antisemitism, see Smith, *Anti-Semitism in Contemporary America*, pp. 19–22.

37. I thank Dr David Singer of the American Jewish Committee for suggesting this example.

38. This is not to say that Jewish history is the history of antisemitism; it is not. What historians Cecil Roth and Salo Baron characterized as "the

lachrymose theory of Jewish history" is a misrepresentation of the history of the Jews. Antisemitism is but one aspect, albeit a significant aspect, of Jewish history.

39. "Can Anti-Semitism Be Measured?" *Commentary*, July 1970, pp. 36–43.

PART TWO

PERSPECTIVES

·2·
Antisemitism in the United States: A Historical Perspective

JACK WERTHEIMER

Jack Wertheimer is the Joseph and Martha
Mendelson Professor of American Jewish History at
the Jewish Theological Seminary of America. He has
written and edited five books, most recently *A People
Divided: Judaism in Contemporary America.*

Jack Wertheimer develops a historical context for the discussion of antisemitism and Jewish security in the United States in the 1990s. In doing
so he addresses a basic question: Why indeed did antisemitism *not* take
firm root in this country, whatever its manifestations? Wertheimer's
approach to the historical analysis of antisemitism is to place antisemitism
in the context of other forms of intolerance, and therefore not to exaggerate the valence or power of this form of hatred, however dreadful its
manifestations may be.

J.A.C.

A historical examination of antisemitism in the United States
yields a striking paradox: every accusation of wrongdoing,
every stereotype and anti-Jewish ideology, every evil imputed to
Jews on the part of detractors in the United States has an identifiable counterpart in the repertoire of European Jew-haters; and in
turn, it seems unlikely that allegations made by antisemites
around the world in recent centuries have not surfaced in the
United States as well. By contrast, the manner in which Jew-
haters have mobilized public opinion in this country and the
organized forms of their attacks have differed significantly from
European versions of antisemitism. It is precisely the singular

expression of antisemitism in the United States that requires analysis if Jews and their allies are to respond effectively to contemporary Jew-hatred.

Many of the distinctive—and contradictory—characteristics of antisemitism in the United States were evident during the colonial period and the founding years of the American republic. Indeed, some patterns were already on display when the first group of Jews landed in North America. In 1654 a boatload of Sephardic Jews arrived in New Amsterdam (subsequently renamed New York), a colony of the Dutch West India Company. Fleeing from Recife, an island off the coast of Brazil that had been captured by the Portuguese, twenty-three impoverished Jews appealed to Peter Stuyvesant, the governor, for the right to settle in New Amsterdam. Stuyvesant, in turn, requested permission from his superiors in Amsterdam to expel the Jewish refugees. To justify his request, he invoked stock formulations of medieval antisemitism: the Jews, if admitted, would engage in "their customary usury and deceitful trading with Christians"; "they might become a charge in the coming winter"—that is, they are parasites; and they are "hateful enemies and blasphemers of the name of Christ."[1] Putting aside their fears that the colony would be "infected by people of the Jewish nation," Stuyvesant's superiors ordered him to admit the Jews in consideration of the losses they had sustained in defense of Recife, a Dutch colony, and the shares owned by Dutch Jews in Amsterdam who had petitioned the company to admit coreligionists to New Amsterdam.[2] Stuyvesant complied with these orders, but he restricted Jewish activities severely by denying Jews the right of public worship, land ownership, engaging in certain forms of trade, and bearing arms. Gradually, however, all of these barriers fell.

The initial encounter of Jews with a New World official thus included a range of conflicting circumstances. It was evident from Stuyvesant's initial response that European attitudes toward Jews had been imported to the New World. Stuyvesant evoked typically medieval Christian stereotypes and introduced discriminatory policies common in Europe—barring Jews from land ownership and bearing arms. He even went beyond prevailing practices in the Old World when he prohibited public worship.

But this traditional hostility was tempered by altered circumstances in the American colonies. Unlike the Old World, where limitations on Jewish participation were well defined and codified, the rights of Jews in the colonies were subject to rapid change. Jews benefited greatly from the fluidity of life in the colonies; since discriminatory policies were not well entrenched, individual Jews often found ways to circumvent or topple barriers. Within short order, they enjoyed opportunities denied to their contemporaries in Europe. It was symptomatic of the rapid change that Myer Myers assumed the presidency of New York's goldsmiths society in the mid–eighteenth century, a time when Jews were barred from even working as artisans throughout Europe, let alone holding high office in a guild.[3]

In addition to their new opportunities, Jews found themselves in the company of other minorities—many far more despised. Jews were not singled out as pariahs or uniquely victimized. Peter Stuyvesant, for example, was hostile to Jews, but he was even more brutal toward fellow Christians who failed to meet his standards. A staunch defender of the Dutch Reformed Church, Stuyvesant was ruthless toward Quakers, Lutherans, and Catholics.

From the outset of the American Jewish experience, then, an important pattern of group relations was set: Jews often encountered discrimination and certainly were subjected to verbal abuse, but they rarely suffered as grievously as other groups. The sheer heterogeneity of colonial America, the mixture of groups from many different nations and religious backgrounds, created an environment in which Jews were not the primary targets of bigots, and in fact never experienced the kind of abuse meted out to Christian outcasts, such as Catholics and Protestant dissenters. Ever since, the rich diversity of America has shielded Jews; they have been but one minority group in a vast nation consisting of immigrants from many lands and religious adherents of hundreds of denominations. Accordingly, even during the most serious surges in popular antisemitism, Jews did not encounter the hostility routinely inflicted upon racial minorities from Africa or Asia and religious minorities such as Catholics and Mormons. In a society as heterogeneous as America, antisemitism must compete with many other forms of bigotry, and therefore its intensity is diluted.

The small size of the Jewish population relative to the larger American society has provided additional protection. Simply put, Jews have been too insignificant a minority to provoke a strong antisemitic response. This was especially evident in the colonial era when Jews constituted no more than 1,500 souls out of a population of 2 million individuals. With no Jewish community numbering more than 200 to 300 people, there was little need to formulate unequivocal laws regarding the rights of Jews in a particular colony. Hence, there was considerable fluidity over time and from one colony to the next in the treatment of Jews.

The most important long-term consequence of this circumstance was the absence of any significant public debate over Jewish emancipation. A comparison with parallel developments in Europe is instructive. Since the end of the eighteenth century when the French National Assembly took up the question of Jewish rights, nations publicly debated the proper status of the Jews: Should they be treated as equal citizens? Could they be expected to demonstrate proper patriotism? Would they cease their distinctive patterns of behavior? Whenever such debates over Jewish rights or emancipation erupted, they were accompanied by highly public displays of political antisemitism which promoted discrimination against Jews. In the United States, by contrast, the framers of the Constitution chose not to discuss Jews as a separate group—and indeed, there is no reference at all to Jews in the Constitution. Jews were simply too insignificant a group to warrant sustained attention from the Founding Fathers. As a result, political antisemitism failed to emerge during the early years of the republic.

An exception to this generalization proves the rule: between 1818 and 1826, pro-Jewish legislators repeatedly introduced a bill to alter the Maryland state constitution in a manner that would provide Jews with the opportunity to vote and serve in office by taking an oath different from the one required of Christians. Once the question of Jewish rights was raised in the public square, a short-lived but bitter antisemitic controversy erupted over "the Jew Bill," as it was dubbed. Opponents of the bill united to form a "Christian ticket" and railed against the proposed changes:

"Preferring, as I do, Christianity to Judaism, Deism, Unitarianism, or any other sort of new fangled ism," wrote Benjamin

Galloway, a Federalist opponent of the bill's sponsor, "I deprecate any change in our State government, calculated to afford the least chance to the enemies of Christianity, of undermining it in the belief of the people of Maryland."[4] An explicit legislative initiative to remedy a form of discrimination against Jews *as a group* thus evoked a strong response by antisemites. In the case of the federal Constitution, by contrast, no questions about Jews as a collective entity were raised and accordingly, there was no "emancipation debate" or public expression of political antisemitism.

A third factor mitigating antisemitism in the United States was the uniquely American arrangement of church-state matters introduced during the earliest years of the republic. The Constitution and Bill of Rights created a political system dedicated to creedal freedom. No single religion was given special legal status. No religious hierarchy was officially privileged. To be sure, there has been a continuous effort on the part of some groups formally to Christianize America. But such campaigns have failed because of the strong tradition mandated by the Constitution to separate church and state, a tradition reinforced by the needs of a heterogenous nation consisting of numerous religious groupings. Many Christians belonging to denominations not regarded as mainline have been even more wary than Jews of efforts to breach the walls of separation.[5]

Constitutional protections, moreover, also provided Jews with the means to challenge discrimination and institutionalized bigotry. From the first years of the republic to the present day, defenders of the Jews have employed their guaranteed freedom of speech to challenge antisemites forthrightly. Commenting on this phenomenon, the historian Jonathan Sarna has observed: "As early as 1784, a 'Jew Broker'—probably Haym Solomon—responded publicly and forcefully to the anti-Semitic charges of a prominent Quaker lawyer, not hesitating to remind him that his 'own religious sectary' could also form 'very proper subjects of criticism and animadversion.' A few years later, Christian missionaries and their supporters faced Jewish polemics no less strident in tone." As Sarna points out, this pattern of response set during the early national period has persisted: "In defense of Jewish rights, [opponents of antisemitism] did battle even with the President of the United States."[6]

The sheer longevity of the American Jewish experience has also given courage to Jews engaged in battles against antisemitism. With a history dating back to 1654, the Jews can properly claim to have been present at the creation of the colonies that eventually joined to become the United States. They have pointed proudly—if in an exaggerated manner—to the contributions of Jews during the birth of the nation. Hence the obsession with the exploits of Haym Solomon. And they have gained heart from blessings conferred upon Jews by George Washington, the first president of the United States, who expressed his hope that "the children of the stock of Abraham who dwell in this land continue to merit and enjoy the good will of other inhabitants, while every one shall sit in safety under his own vine and fig-tree, and there shall be none to make him afraid."[7]

To be sure, such statements did not protect Jews from attacks, let alone sway antisemites. Rather, they served to encourage Jews engaged in self-defense to speak out forcefully, to feel that they were in the United States by right and not by sufferance. Emboldened by their pride in the role played by Jews in the American experiment and inspired by a line of predecessors dating back to the colonial era to feel at home in America, defenders of the Jews have castigated antisemitism as an "un-American," foreign import. Here, again, it is evident that patterns of relations established in the colonial and early national periods have shaped the relationship between Jews and the larger American society.

Historians have offered several different accounts of when American antisemitism actually began. All agree that instances easily can be adduced of cases dating to the colonial era and the first decades of the republic when individuals invoked negative stereotypes of Jews, engaged in missionary activities to convert them to Christianity, discriminated against Jews in hiring practices, and expressed their hostility in other ways. But one would be hard-pressed to find examples of blatantly public expressions of antisemitism. The "Jew bill" controversy in Maryland serves as a brief episode of such a public display, but it ended quickly and the bill, after all, passed. A recent study by Frederic Cople Jaher contends that "American anti-Semitism assumed its modern contours, if not its subsequent intensity and scope, from the later

1830s through the Civil War."[8] Arguing that "traditional prejudices were joined by newer forms of bigotry to create increasingly frequent anti-Jewish images and actions," Jaher identifies the immediate antebellum decades as the turning point.[9]

But the evidence Jaher cites demonstrates more continuity than change. Some of the abolitionists expressed criticism of the Jewish religion based upon typical Christian arguments; Dunn and Bradstreet agents portrayed Jewish-owned firms as unreliable, engaging as they did in "money making and money saving characteristics of their race;" and textbooks such as McGuffey's *Reader* "indoctrinated schoolchildren in Hebraic transgressions and devalued Judaism."[10]

However, these and other expressions of antisemitism rarely affected the lives of large numbers of Jews or intruded on the public sphere. On the contrary, Jaher and other historians of Jewish life prior to the Civil War are impressed with the remarkable strides taken by Jews toward equality. Their progress was even more dramatic coming as it did during a time when organized political parties officially sought to restrict Roman Catholics.

The expulsion of Jews from the territory of Tennessee in 1862 has prompted some historians to regard the Civil War as the critical turning point. In a sweeping indictment of all Jews, General Ulysses S. Grant charged that "the Jews as a class violat[ed] every regulation of trade established by the Treasury Department, and also department [of Tennessee] orders." Accordingly, he ordered them "expelled from the department within twenty-four hours from the receipt of this order."[11] This blanket stereotyping of all Jews as black-market profiteers by the official head of the territorial government held the potential for setting a terrible new precedent: "resembling a Czarist ukase more than an American governmental decree," writes historian Jaher, "Grant's order was the severest attempted official violation—civil or military, federal, state or local—of the rights to Jews in the history of this nation."[12] Far more important, however, was the immediate action taken by President Abraham Lincoln to countermand Grant's order. Thus, in the only instance in which an American government official instituted an official policy of anti-Jewish discrimination, the damaging act was quickly overturned and never again repeated.

Most historians trace the eruption of antisemitism in the public sphere to the closing decades of the century. The noted American historian Oscar Handlin identified populist resentment as the primary source of attacks upon Jews. In the post–Civil War period, an era of massive industrial transformation, rural inhabitants watched aghast as urban centers grew rapidly and dominated the nation's economy. According to Handlin, during the 1890s,

> the injured groups of American society, in agony, had issued the cries of an infant that has no words to express pain. Searching vainly for a means of relief, they could scarcely have guessed that the source of their trials was a change in the world in which they lived. And groping toward an understanding of that change, some perceived its instrument, the Jew. If all trade was treachery and Babylon the city, then the Jew—stereotyped, involved in finance, and mysterious—stood ready to be assigned the role of arch-conspirator. It was this suspicion that transformed the conception of the Jew after 1900, replaced the older images with that of the Elder of Zion.[13]

The dispossessed farmers of the American South and Midwest threw their support behind populist demagogues who blamed the economic distress on a cabal of financiers intent on manipulating markets for their own selfish gain. Interestingly, these demagogues inveighed against Jews living abroad who allegedly were exploiting hardworking Americans from the safety of Europe. Thus, an article in the *Illustrated America* of July 27, 1895, speculated:

> Might it not be that the money lenders of London, the magnificent, titled Shylocks of our modern world; who play with Czars, Emperors and Kings as a chess-player with castles, rooks and pawns, in the artificial production of a panic . . . may have purposely wrought the ruin of many American banks . . . because in America these gamblers of the banking world reap their riches harvest and wish to continue their tightest grip on the people?[14]

Although the primary culprits were identified as the agents of the House of Rothschild, populist writers also accused other Jewish financiers in Europe of unseemly financial machinations. Here, then, the nexus between European and American antisemitic motifs was clear: by tracing the source of the menace to European lands, populist antisemites were also drawing upon the vast anti-Jewish literature propagated in Europe during the late nineteenth century. There was little difference between these populist charges and the rantings of European antisemites intent on saving their countries from Jewish economic domination.

In time, the stereotype of the Jew as a Shylock figure was employed in the United States to further demonize Jewish financial dealings. The populist demagogue Ignatius Donnelly described in his antiutopian novel of 1890, *Caesar's Column*, how an oligarchy consisting mainly of Jews "wreak their cruel revenge on Christians for the ancient 'sufferings inflicted by their bigoted and ignorant ancestors upon a noble race.'"[15] Jewish malevolence, it was claimed by populist preachers, threatened not only the economic life of the country but its most cherished ideals. Writing in 1892, the well-known populist orator Tom Watson of Georgia asked: "Did [Thomas Jefferson] dream that in 100 years or less his party would be prostituted to the vilest purposes of monopoly, that red-eyed Jewish millionaires would be the chiefs of that party, and that the liberty and prosperity of the country would be sacrificed to Plutocratic greed in the name of Jeffersonian Democracy."[16]

The campaign launched by some populist demagogues in the waning years of the nineteenth century produced its most lethal consequences during and after World War I. First came the arrest and conviction of Leo Frank, a transplanted New Yorker who had come to Atlanta to supervise a family-owned factory. When a young employee named Mary Phagan was found murdered at the factory, Frank was arrested. In the minds of his accusers, he quickly came to embody all the imagined evils of Jews. A product of the hated Northern city, a Jew involved in business, Frank stood accused of dishonoring and murdering a child. Paranoid fears were further fueled by the arrival of big-city defense attorneys from New York.

All this was grist for the mill of populist demagogues. Writing during the trial, Tom Watson played upon deeply entrenched fears, describing Mary Phagan as "a daughter of the people, of the common clay, of the blouse and the overall, of those who eat bread in the sweat of the face, and who, in so many instances are the chattel slaves of a sordid Commercialism that has no milk of human kindness in its heart of stone;" He beatified Mary Phagan as "the little factory girl who held to her innocence."[17] Not long after the Governor of Georgia, John M. Slaton, commuted Leo Frank's death sentence in 1915, a mob seized him from prison and lynched him, a fate that befell no other American Jew, but that instilled fear in the hearts of Jews who lived in populist regions of the country.

A few years later, the specter of a Jewish conspiracy raised so frequently in populist rhetoric found full expression during the "Red Scare." In the wake of the Russian Revolution, American fears of Bolsheviks and anarchists heightened. Seeking to ferret out subversive elements, defenders of America tended to suspect recent immigrants to America, such as Italians and Russian Jews, of maintaining direct ties with European bomb-throwers. A link between Jews and Bolsheviks became a staple of antisemitic writings. When a subcommittee of the Senate Judiciary Committee met in 1919 to deal with the Communist menace, U.S. senators were particularly warned about Jewish troublemakers on New York's Lower East Side:

> A number of us were impressed with the strong Yiddish element in this thing right from the start, and it soon became evident that more than half of the agitators in the so-called Bolshevik movement were Yiddish. . . . I do not think the Bolshevik movement in Russia would have been a success if it had not been for the support it got from certain elements in New York, the so-called East Side. . . . After the revolution they swarmed in. . . . I do not want to be unfair, but I usually know a Jew when I see one.[18]

Among the most noteworthy accusers of Jews were other recent immigrants from Eastern Europe.

Equally pernicious were the attacks upon Jews mounted in publications sponsored by none other than Henry Ford. Convinced that Jews were up to no good, Ford opened a detective agency in New York to investigate Jewish influence. When the agency sent him a copy of the *Protocols of the Elders of Zion*, a fabrication of the tsarist secret police originally compiled at the end of the nineteenth century in French, Ford became obsessed with revealing the newfound truth of "the world-Jewish conspiracy." For almost two years, Ford's *Dearborn Independent* regularly featured accusations against "Jew finance," the malevolent role of Jews in sponsoring Communism, and the Jewish plot to exercise power—to the point of controlling U.S. presidents. Seeking to rally the forces of goodness against the Jewish conspiracy, Ford's publications sought to reveal all:

> "To the victor belong the spoils" is an old saying. And in a sense it is true that if all this power of control has been gained and held by a few men of a long-despised race, then either they are supermen whom it is powerless to resist, or they are ordinary men whom the rest of the world has permitted to obtain an undue and unsafe degree of power. Unless the Jews are supermen, the Gentiles will have themselves to blame for what has transpired, and they can look for rectification in a new scrutiny of the situation and a candid examination of the experiences of other countries.[19]

That the supporter of these conspiratorial fantasies was in fact one of the most powerful men in America, an industrialist who controlled the fate of thousands of workers, did not prevent the circulation of Ford's hysterical lies. Ironically, populist fears of Jewish financiers in time became the tool of America's preeminent industrialist. (Remarkably, Ford eventually apologized for his vicious attacks upon Jews, one of the few outspoken antisemites to take back his words. Even more important, more than one hundred prominent Americans, including Woodrow Wilson and William Howard Taft, denounced antisemitic campaigns in a statement issued early in 1921.)

As pressure built at the end of the nineteenth century for the dispossessed to blame Jews for their economic distress, an equal if not greater resistance to Jewish success grew among America's upper classes. Initially, this resistance took the form of discrimination practiced by American patricians to keep well-to-do Jews out of their elite social domains, particularly, summer resorts and social clubs.

The new trend became public knowledge when in 1877 Joseph Seligman, a prominent banker and friend of Lincoln and Grant, was barred from registering as a guest at the Grand Union Hotel in Saratoga Springs, New York, a posh summer resort. In light of Seligman's fame, the story was widely circulated in the press. "Newspaper editorials differed as to whether [the hotel] was right or not in barring Jews," writes historian Leonard Dinnerstein, "but the distasteful episode indicated that no matter how well-to-do or refined Jews might be they were socially undesirable and some later chroniclers erroneously marked this incident as the beginning of antisemitism in America."[20]

Two years later, another exclusionary incident dramatized the growing acceptance of social discrimination by America's elite. The president of the Manhattan Beach Corporation in Brooklyn, New York, announced a policy of barring Jews:

> Personally, I am opposed to Jews. They are a pretentious class who expect three times as much for their money as other people. They give us more trouble on our [rail]road and in our hotel than we can stand. Another thing is that they are driving away the class of people who are beginning to make Coney Island the most fashionable and magnificent watering place in the world.[21]

Thus it was precisely the most well-heeled of American Jews, mainly consisting of immigrants from Central Europe and their upwardly mobile children, who faced discrimination from upper-class Americans intent on protecting their exclusive domains. "If this is a free country," argued one such patrician, "why can't we be free of the Jews?"[22]

In time, less-established Jews also were targets of social discrimination. Indeed, John Higham, the historian most identified with an interpretation of American antisemitism that stresses the importance of social discrimination, has placed the problem within the context of immigrant mobility: "What finally set off . . . a pattern of social discrimination, in the 1870s, was not the arrival of immigrants; it was their rise. Though a remarkable number had prospered mightily, evidently few had yet acquired much education or polish. Discrimination began where Jews as a group pressed most heavily upon a limited field of opportunity."[23] As the waves of Jewish immigration from Russia, Austro-Hungary, and Rumania washed over American shores in the late nineteenth century and the first decades of the twentieth, the fear of upwardly mobile newcomers intensified, heightening xenophobia and anti-immigrant sentiment in the United States.

Before describing some symptoms of this aversion to the "new immigration," it is important to note the critical distinctions between an interpretation that stresses populist resentment as opposed to social discrimination as the source of American antisemitism. Whereas the former traces the roots of anti-Jewish animosities in the United States to those at the bottom rungs of America's socioeconomic ladder, the second stresses the role of more established classes in keeping upwardly mobile Jews in their place. In short, the critical question raised by these analyses is whether antisemitism originates at the top or the bottom of American society. These interpretations also differ in the credit they give to European antisemitic traditions for inspiring American bigots. Populist demagogues not only warned of the pernicious role played by European Jews, they clearly were inspired by European antisemites. By contrast, social discrimination is a response to local conditions that needs no support from imported ideas. Finally, this debate between historians is of more than academic interest: whereas the resentments of dispossessed Americans were fueled by traditional religious and cultural animosities toward Jews, social discrimination against Jews is part of a long history of conflict between more established Americans and recent immigrants. If American antisemitism stems primarily from such conflicts, rather than deeply entrenched folk beliefs and overarching ideologies of hatred, then there is reason to hope for a mitigation of antisemitism just as other forms of intergroup conflict have eased over time. The bitter enmity between Irish and German Americans, and between European and Asian Americans, has largely disappeared; so too one would expect antisemitism to ease considerably if its source is mainly conflict over an ethnic group's share of the American economic pie.

With the upsurge of Jewish immigration at the turn of the century, conflict between newly arrived Jews and their more established neighbors intensified. Accordingly, the drive to exclude Jews had grown to encompass not only the protection of elite social bastions, but the integrity of America's immigration policy. Claiming that Jewish and other immigrants from southern Europe threatened the very character of the country, a coalition of restrictionists, ranging from patrician Boston Brahmins, such as Senator Henry Cabot Lodge, to representatives of American labor, to medical officials, urged a tightening of immigration policy. *Frank Leslie's Weekly*, for example, warned in 1892 that East European Jews "are the most undesirable and least welcome of immigrants" because they "strain the country's power to assimilate." The popular journal went on to depict the immigrant enclave on Manhattan's Lower East Side:

> There exists on the east side of this town a great and coherent population of foreigners of a low order of intelligence, speaking their own languages, following their own customs, and absolutely blind or utterly indifferent to our ideals, moral, social, and political. . . . Go and see them swarm in the streets and the houses of the east side if you have doubts on the subject, and form your own conclusions as to the availability of the material for manufacture into the sort of citizen which the founders and fathers of the republic had in mind.[24]

Several intertwined motifs are evident in these remarks: Jews are portrayed as culturally and qualitatively different from other Americans; they are portrayed as less-than-human creatures who "swarm" in the houses and streets, and the quality of their racial stock is deemed inferior.

Indeed, racism became enmeshed with the restrictionist campaign. Learned scientists employed the recently invented intelligence test to demonstrate the mental deficiencies of Jewish immigrants. H. H. Goddard, director of the Vineland Institute for Feeble-Minded Girls and Boys in New Jersey, administered Binet tests to recent immigrants at Ellis Island and found that "83 percent of the Jews, 87 percent of the Russians, 80 percent of the Hungarians, and 79 percent of the Italians were feeble-minded—that is below mental age of twelve."[25] According to Goddard, "possibly the moron has his place" as a menial worker doing work "that no one else will do. . . . There is an immense amount of drudgery to be done."[26]

But other proponents of racial and eugenics science favored national quotas to restrict the inflow of racially "inferior" immigrants such as Jews from Eastern Europe.[27] As the restrictionist movement reached fever pitch, Madison Grant exhorted Americans to free themselves of the "widespread and famous belief in the power of environment, as well as education and opportunity, to alter heredity." Instead, he warned of the danger posed by "the Polish Jew, whose dwarf stature, peculiar mentality, and ruthless concentration on self-interest are being engrafted upon the stock of the nation."[28]

This racist campaign bore fruit immediately after World War I when the U.S. Congress passed legislation that favored immigrants from desired places of origin and sharply curtailed the opportunities of less-desired newcomers. Jewish immigration from Eastern Europe to the United States virtually ceased. Still, even this extreme form of American xenophobia did not take the form of an exclusive attack upon Jews: unlike restrictionists in England and Germany, for example, Americans who favored bars on immigration passed a law that included no specific quota on Jews, but rather limited immigration from countries of origin.

Although historians hold disparate views about when public antisemitism actually began in the United States, there is little doubt that the period between the two world wars represented the heyday of publicly expressed animosity toward Jews. One important sphere riddled with antisemitic discrimination was the academy. Virtually every private institution of higher learning, and many public ones as well, introduced selective admissions policies aimed at curbing the number of Jewish students, policies that lasted well into the 1950s at certain elite schools. Some institutions, such as Harvard, employed the subterfuge of seeking "geographic diversity" as a means to curtail the number of Jews who applied for admission from New York City. Others instituted quotas on Jewish students and openly asked applicants about their "religious affiliation," as well as questions about whether the applicant's parents had ever been known by another name—in other words, had they anglicized their name to cover up their Jewishness?

Selective admissions policies were justified by colleges and professional schools as a means to protect an institution of higher learning from decline. As A. Lawrence Lowell, president of Harvard University, put it: too many Jews at Harvard would result in the institution's losing "its character as a democratic, national university, drawing from all classes of the community and promoting a sympathetic understanding among them."[29]

Initially instituted to maintain the prestige of elite institutions by keeping out individuals deemed socially inferior, quotas had dire consequences for the job prospects and upward mobility of Jews. It was one thing when a talented Jew could not get into the most prestigious university and had to settle for an undergraduate education at an inferior school. It was quite another matter when the same Jew could not enter a graduate program in his or her chosen field and had to forgo a professional career entirely.

Social discrimination at universities quickly spread into the workplace as entire industries locked out Jews. Help-wanted advertisements during the interwar era routinely stated that Christians or Protestants only need apply. According to the historian Leonard Dinnerstein, "Utilities, banks, insurance companies, publishing houses, engineering and industrial companies, civic bodies for art and music, hospitals, universities, and law firms were among the major culprits" which discriminated with impunity against Jews.[30] Many made a virtue of their bigotry, as when Paul Cravath of a major New York law firm informed students at Harvard Law School of his firm's hiring preferences:

> Brilliant intellectual powers are not essential. Too much imagination, too much wit, too great cleverness, too facile fluency, if not leavened by a sound sense of proportion, are quite as likely to impede success as to promote it. The best clients are apt to be afraid of those qualities. They want as their counsel a man who is primarily honest, safe, sound and steady.[31]

It is impossible to calculate how many gifted Jews were unable to pursue their chosen field of work because of this blatant bigotry.

The entrenched and institutionalized discrimination practiced during the first half of the twentieth century constitutes the most pernicious expression of American antisemitism to date. Prejudice against Jews had moved beyond the sphere of private bigotry and the semiprivate realm of social discrimination to the marketplace; it had gone from subjective expressions of distaste and xenophobia to the objective expression of overt discrimination. It affected the career prospects of Jews, lessened their earning potential, and limited their mobility. Not accidentally, overt discrimination spread in this era to housing: apartment buildings in large cities prominently displayed signs stating that "Jews and Negroes" need not apply for rentals; and residential communities required new home buyers to sign "covenants" barring sales to unwanted groups, such as Jews. In response to these pressures, it became common for Jews to anglicize their names and downplay their distinctiveness.

The onset of the Great Depression and America's entry into the Second World War intensified antisemitic prejudices because Jews were blamed for these twin evils. When Charles A. Lindbergh, the great aviation hero, accused Jews of pushing the United States toward war with Nazi Germany, he struck a responsive chord. Some isolationists even characterized Franklin and Eleanor Roosevelt as dupes of the Jews if not Jews themselves.[32] Demagogues such as Father Charles Coughlin and William Pelley employed the media of the day, newspapers and the radio, to spread the message of antisemitism; and groups sponsored by Hitler's Germany sought to import Nazi antisemitism to the United States. "The barest scratching of an economic or political reactionary," wrote the reporter Stanley High in 1942, "almost unfailingly produces an anti-Semite."[33]

Public opinion polls confirmed what most Jews experienced. When Americans were asked whom they would least appreciate as neighbors, Jews were routinely cited right after "Negroes." When Americans were asked whom they suspected of having too much power, they pointed first at Jews. And when the question was posed, "Have you heard any criticism or talk against Jews in the last six months?" rising numbers answered affirmatively, so that by 1946 nearly two-thirds of respondents answered positively.[34] The wave of antisemitism that had engulfed Europe in the 1930s and 1940s swept the United States as well.

And then in the postwar era, the tide of antisemitism ebbed. Almost overnight, it became socially unfashionable to express anti-Jewish views in public. The same polls that found rising rates of response between 1940 and 1946 to the question "Have you heard any criticism or talk against Jews in the last six months?" traced a sharp decline thereafter: whereas 64 percent answered affirmatively in 1946, only 24 percent did so in 1950, and this figure was halved by the end of the decade.[35] Jews also made enormous strides in the 1950s and 1960s in all walks of life: industries that had previously barred Jews now promoted them to top executive positions; Jews assumed positions of influence at all levels of government—and were particularly overrepresented in the executive branch in Washington; remarkably, the very academic settings that had excluded Jews now vied to hire them in disproportionate numbers as professors. By the mid-1980s, Charles Silberman, himself an embodiment of the Jewish success odyssey, devoted a book to the stunning changes he had witnessed.[36]

Moreover, Judaism acquired a new respectability in American society, achieving parity with Protestantism and Catholicism in the "triple melting pot" of midcentury American religion. A 1951 cover story in *Time* magazine lauding the interfaith activities of Louis Finkelstein, chancellor of the Jewish Theological Seminary of America, was symptomatic of the new appreciation of Jews and Judaism by the elite white Anglo-Saxon Protestant patricians who had long governed the country.[37]

Antisemitism did not, of course, disappear from the American scene, but it assumed a lower profile and by the 1960s preoccupied Jews far less than previously. Periodically, antisemitism erupted in the public arena, as when synagogues were bombed in the South during the height of the civil rights movement; when Nazis sought to march in Skokie, Illinois, a largely Jewish suburb of Chicago; when some prominent Christian cleric or racist demagogue issued unflattering remarks about Jews; and when U.S. corporations bowed to the Arab boycott against Israel and discriminated against Jews. For the most part, however, antisemitism in the postwar era was confined to the private arena, as it had been for much of American history.

The relative calm was reflected in the changing priorities of Jewish organizations. Even community-relations groups that were dedicated to the defense of American Jews expended much energy in the post-1967 period to alleviating the plight of embattled and impoverished Jews abroad rather than fighting antisemitism at home. The key domestic concerns of defense agencies revolved around building interfaith and interethnic coalitions; strengthening legislation against hate crimes; formulating positions for the Jewish community on a range of social issues, ranging from affirmative action and civil rights questions to abortion policy and nuclear proliferation; and educating the American population about the nature of Jewish life.

In the closing decade of the century, a number of disturbing developments suggest the reemergence of more public forms of antisemitism.

Item: As the culture wars between American conservatives and liberals intensify, groups on the right of the political spectrum are calling for the reintroduction of religion into the public sphere. The reflex of Jewish groups is to fear such intrusions as a means of "Christianizing" America. Most Jewish groups have redoubled their efforts to shore up the walls of separation so that religion plays no public role, a stance other Jews regard as the antithesis of what separationism long implied, namely that religion would be protected, not guaranteed.

Item: There has been a troubling rise of anti-Jewish attitudes within the African-American community. Attitudinal surveys trace a far greater propensity on the part of educated black Americans to hold negative views of Jews, particularly as compared to educated whites. In recent years, several prominent black leaders have openly expressed hostility toward Jews, most notably in the vicious ranting of Louis Farrakhan and his minions, and in the ignorant teachings of Afrocentrists.

Item: Since 1967 it has been fashionable on the American left to couch anti-Jewish hostility in the language of anti-Zionism. Within the feminist movement,[38] fashionable academic circles, and other avant-garde groupings, there has long been a flirtation with the Palestinian liberation movement and a tendency to castigate Israel as a colonial power. This anti-Zionism, notes historian Henry Feingold, "demonstrates an unerring instinct for [attacking] what lies at the center of Jewish sensibility."[39]

Item: A number of conservative ideologues have displayed gross insensitivity toward Jews that has verged on outright antisemitic attacks. The inflammatory language of Patrick Buchanan during the Gulf War crisis was particularly offensive to Jews: Claiming that "there are only two groups that are beating the drums for war in the Middle East—the Israeli Defense Ministry and its 'amen' corner in the United States," Buchanan described the U.S. Congress as "Israeli-occupied territory"; he then singled out four prominent Jews who had advocated American intervention in Kuwait and noted that the actual fighting would be done by "kids with names like McAllister, Murphy, Gonzales, and Leroy Brown," thereby invoking an old canard about Jews shirking their military duties.[40]

Item: As interethnic rivalries reignite all over the world, some Jews fear that they will become targets of hate groups. Some worry about marginalization as new coalitions of the dispossessed are forming on college campuses and in the political arena, particularly since these groups show little sympathy for Jews and regard them as part of the victimizing establishment. Others fear the growth of the Aryan Nations and other violence-prone groups that define Jews and the "Zionist Occupation Government" in Washington as the enemy. Still others worry about the importation to the United States of anti-Jewish bigotry that now sweeps some sectors of formerly Communist countries.

As Jews confront these challenges, they would do well to consider the history of antisemitism in America. It is a history in which antagonism toward Jews never was entirely absent. And it is a history which encompasses virtually every variation of Jew-hatred known in other societies. Some antisemites in the United States have employed the traditional language of Christian Jew-hatred, whereas others have invoked more modern stereotypes, portraying Jews as racial inferiors, ideological conspirators, and political subversives; some antisemites in the United States have depicted Jews as arch capitalists and others as Communist fellow travelers. Despite these charges, Jews in the United States have been spared the types of onslaughts inflicted upon their coreligionists abroad: there have been no sustained pogroms, no cases of state-sponsored discrimination, and no concentration camps for Jews in the United States.

A critical distinguishing feature of the Jewish experience in the United States has been the failure of antisemites to institutionalize anti-Jewish discrimination. No American government has enacted a policy, let alone a legislative program, singling out Jews for special ill treatment. The one noteworthy exception proves the rule: Grant's general order expelling all Jews from the Territory of Tennessee was quickly rescinded and never repeated. As noted earlier in this essay, a range of historical circumstances, many dating back to the early years of the republic if not to the colonial era, account for the anomalous conditions of Jewish life in the United States. For the most part, antisemitism has been confined to the private realm of individual prejudice and social discrimination; rarely has it intruded into the sphere of public policy. As the historian Edward S. Shapiro has recently observed,

> Anti-Semitism is fundamentally at odds with the public culture of America as enunciated in the Declaration of Independence, the Bill of Rights, and the Gettysburg Address. One can search in vain for any major American anti-Semitic political figure or political movement or any important anti-Semitic theorist. Cut off from any significant constitutional or governmental basis, anti-Semitism in the United States has lacked a confident voice and has been relegated to the fringes.[41]

Since it is impossible to eradicate privately held antisemitic biases and stereotypes, those concerned with defending Jews would do best to concentrate their resources on battling efforts to inject antisemitism into the public sphere, and to react with special zeal to institutionalized discrimination against Jews. Using such a test, "defense" agencies in the recent past would have invested greater energy battling efforts by Arab countries to pressure American corporations to discriminate against Jewish employees than against the more overt but ultimately less significant expressions of antisemitism by bigots who painted swastikas on synagogues. In our own day, efforts to marginalize Jews in the academy and in public life warrant greater vigilance than hate-filled rhetoric.

As the sorry experience of discrimination at institutions of higher education and in the workplace during the interwar era attests, antisemitism can be institutionalized and highly damaging to Jewish prospects even if it is not sanctioned by governments. Jews need to remain particularly vigilant about the spread of antisemitic discrimination to this middle ground between governmental discrimination and social bias. If Jews are successfully barred from sectors of the economy, they may still find ways to prosper but their status in the United States will have deteriorated.

The most difficult—and divisive—issue in the present-day defense of Jewish interests revolves around questions of church-state separation. As conservative groups seek to give voice to religious teachings in the American public square, Jews reflexively recoil, fearing that such a program will automatically lead to the Christianization of the country and a steep rise in antisemitism. The historian David A. Gerber has cautioned against such an assumption by placing the separationist battles in a broader context:

> Throughout American history, pious Christians have sought legal guarantees for the sanctity of Sunday, the Christian Sabbath, or for hymn singing in the public schools and at Christmastime. One may accuse them of forgetting about the doctrine of separation of church and state and of insensitivity to Jewish feelings, but one need not assume intentional hostility toward Jews. . . . Many Christians seeking public supports for Christianity have simply forgotten that Jews were in their midst.[42]

As the struggles between liberals and conservatives intensify in the coming years, Jews will need to assess whether the reintroduction of some religious expression in American public life necessarily will unleash antisemitism or whether a more religious America will also be more civilized—and thereby offer Jews and other Americans greater safety.

NOTES

1. Morris U. Schappes, *A Documentary History of the Jews in the United States, 1654–1875* (New York: Schocken Books, 1971), pp. 1–2.

2. Ibid, pp. 4–5.

3. Jacob Rader Marcus, ed., *American Jewry. Documents of the Eighteenth Century* (Cincinnati: Hebrew Union College, 1959), p. 380; Henry L.

Feingold, *Zion in America: The Jewish Experience from Colonial Times to the Present* (New York: Twayne Publishers, 1974), p. 37.

4. Joseph. L. Blau and Salo W. Baron, *The Jews of the United States 1790–1840: A Documentary History*, vol. 1 (New York: Columbia University Press, 1963), p. 49. See pp. 33–55 for more documents relating to the Maryland "Jew Bill."

5. On efforts of Christianize the country and breach the walls of separation, see Robert T. Handy, *A Christian America: Protestant Hopes and Historical Realities* (New York: Oxford University Press, 1971); for a historical account of Jewish strategies to maintain a strong separation of church and state, see Naomi W. Cohen, *Jews in Christian America: The Pursuit of Religious Equality* (New York: Oxford University Press, 1992).

6. Jonathan D. Sarna, "Anti-Semitism and American History," *Commentary*, March 1981, p. 46.

7. George Washington, "A Reply to the Hebrew Congregation of Newport," in Paul R. Mendes-Flohr and Jehuda Reinharz, *The Jew in the Modern World: A Documentary History* (New York and Oxford: Oxford University Press, 1980), p. 363.

8. Frederic Cople Jaher, *A Scapegoat in the New Wilderness: The Origins and Rise of Anti-Semitism in America* (Cambridge, Mass.: Harvard University Press, 1994), p. 241.

9. Ibid.

10. Jaher, *Scapegoat*, ch. 5.

11. Bertram W. Korn, *American Jewry and the Civil War* (Philadelphia: Jewish Publication Society of America, 1951), pp. 122–23. Korn identifies the Civil War period as the turning point in the history of U.S. antisemitism: Grant's "order was only one example of a series of anti-Jewish libels which were propagated during the War in both the Union and the Confederacy. Anti-Jewish prejudice was actually a characteristic expression of the age, part and parcel of the economic and social upheaval effectuated by the war" (p. 156).

12. Jaher, *Scapegoat*, p. 199.

13. Oscar Handlin, "American Views of the Jew at the Opening of the Twentieth Century," in Leonard Dinnerstein, ed., *Anti-Semitism in the United States* (New York: Holt, Rinehart & Winston, 1971), p. 57.

14. Quoted in Michael N. Dobkowski, *The Tarnished Dream: The Basis of American Anti-Semitism* (Westport, Conn.: Greenwood Press, 1979), p. 170.

15. Ibid. p. 179.

16. Ibid. p. 177.

17. Leonard Dinnerstein, *The Leo Frank Case* (New York: Columbia University Press, 1968), p. 98.

18. Dr. George S. Simons, superintendent of the Methodist Episcopal Church in Russia and Finland, quoted in Dobkowski, *Tarnished Dream*, pp. 223–24.

19. "The International Jew," in Marc Lee Raphael, *Jews and Judaism in the United States: A Documentary History* (New York: Behrman House, 1983), p. 292.

20. Leonard Dinnerstein, *Antisemitism in America* (New York: Oxford University Press, 1994), pp. 39–40.

21. Quoted in Dinnerstein, ed., *Antisemitism in the United States*, p. 40.

22. Ibid.

23. John Higham, "American Antisemitism Historically Reconsidered," in Dinnerstein, ed., *Antisemitism in the United States*, p. 70.

24. Quoted in Dobkowski, *Tarnished Dream*, p. 147.

25. Stephen Jay Gould, "Science and Jewish Immigration," *Natural History*, December 1980, pp. 14–16.

26. Ibid, p. 16.

27. For a fine analysis of antisemitic racism in America prior to the passage of immigration restrictions, see Robert Singerman, "The Jew as Racial Alien: The Genetic Component of American Anti-Semitism," in David Gerber, ed., *Anti-Semitism in American History* (Urbana: University of Illinois Press, 1987), pp. 103–28.

28. Excerpt from *The Passing of the Great Race*, in Michael Selzer, ed., *Kike* (New York: Meridian Books, 1972), p. 77.

29. Quoted in Dinnerstein, *Antisemitism in America*, p. 86.

30. Ibid. p. 89.

31. Ibid. p. 89.

32. The failure of Roosevelt to mount a sustained effort to rescue European Jews and admit more Jewish refugees has prompted historians to debate whether antisemitism shaped American policy during the war years. Restrictionists in the State Department have been criticized severely for failing to act decisively, and some have been labeled as antisemites. The historian Henry Feingold has accused the State Department of blatant antisemitism, and especially singled out Breckinridge Long, an assistant secretary of state, of engineering plans to prevent Jewish immigration during World War II. See Feingold's *The Politics of Rescue: The Roosevelt Administration and the Holocaust, 1938–1945* (New Brunswick, N.J.: Rutgers University Press, 1970), pp. 131–37. This approach has been challenged by Alan M. Kraut and Richard D. Breitman in their essay "Antisemitism in the State Department, 1933–44: Four Case Studies," in David A. Gerber ed., *Anti-Semitism in American History* (Urbana: University of Illinois Press, 1987), pp. 167–97. Kraut and Breitman contend that "some State Department officials often perceived Jews in stereotypical patterns; however, their policies and behav-

ior often lacked a double standard. One might say that their attitude toward refugees was influenced by their anti-Semitism, but other motives, often ones even more powerful than ethnic prejudice, were primarily responsible for State Department policies that hampered the immigration of Jews imperiled by Nazi Germany" (p. 169). "Restrictionism," they conclude, "was not a euphemism for anti-Semitism" (p. 190).

33. Quoted in Dinnerstein, *Antisemitism in America*, p. 135.

34. Ibid. p. 132.

35. Ibid. p. 151.

36. Charles Silberman, *A Certain People: American Jews and Their Lives Today* (New York: Summit Books, 1985).

37. *Time*, October 15, 1951, pp. 52–57.

38. Letty Cottin Pogrebin, "Anti-Semitism in the Women's Movement," *Ms.*, June 1982.

39. Quoted in Dinnerstein, *Antisemitism in America*, p. 232.

40. William F. Buckley, Jr., *In Search of Anti-Semitism* (New York: Continuum Books, 1992), pp. 26–28.

41. Edward S. Shapiro, "American Anti-Semitism and the Historians," *Congress Monthly*, June/July 1994, p. 15.

42. David A. Gerber, "Anti-Semitism and Jewish-Gentile Relations in American Historiography and the American Past," in Gerber, ed., *Anti-Semitism in American History*, p. 6.

SELECTED BIBLIOGRAPHY ON THE HISTORY OF ANTISEMITISM IN THE UNITED STATES

Baltzell, E. Digby. *The Protestant Establishment*. New York: Random House, 1964. An account of social discrimination practiced by the American white Protestant elite to keep upwardly mobile Jews at arm's length in the first half of the twentieth century.

Cohen, Naomi W. *Jews in Christian America: The Pursuit of Religious Equality*. New York and Oxford: Oxford University Press, 1992. A probing analysis of Jewish fears concerning church-state relations over the course of American history.

Dinnerstein, Leonard. *Antisemitism in America*. New York and Oxford: Oxford University Press, 1994. The most valuable and up-to-date one-volume survey of American antisemitism historically considered. A first-rate introduction to the subject.

———. *The Leo Frank Case*. New York: Columbia University Press, 1968. A detailed examination of the trial and lynching of Leo Frank, the "American Dreyfus," in Atlanta on the eve of World War I.

Dobkowski, Michael N. *The Tarnished Dream: The Basis of American Anti-Semitism.* Westport, Conn.: Greenwood Press, 1979. This examination of major motifs appearing in antisemitic writings does not come to grips with the singularity of antisemitism in the United States.

Gerber, David A., ed. *Anti-Semitism in American History.* Urbana and Chicago: University of Illinois Press, 1987. An excellent collection of major essays on episodes and eras in the history of American antisemitism.

Higham, John. *Strangers in the Land.* New Brunswick, N.J.: Rutgers University Press, 1955. This pioneering study of American nativism and hostility to aliens was perhaps the first work to integrate antisemitism into the larger patterns of American history.

Jaher, Fredric Cople. *A Scapegoat in the New Wilderness: The Origins and Rise of Anti-Semitism in America.* Cambridge, Mass.: Harvard University Press, 1994. This work is strongest when it focuses sharply on developments prior to the Civil War, a period largely downplayed by most writers on American antisemitism. It is weaker when the author strays into sweeping assertions about the long history of antisemitism in Europe or in contemporary America.

Smith, Tom. W. *Anti-Semitism in Contemporary America.* New York: American Jewish Committee, 1994. A comprehensive analysis of the most recent sociological research on contemporary trends in American antisemitism.

Stember, Charles Herbert, et al. *Jews in the Mind of America* New York: Basic Books, 1966. An important collection of essays which analyze American opinion about Jews, particularly in the middle of the twentieth century.

Synott, Marcia Graham. *The Half-Opened Door: Discrimination and Admissions at Harvard, Yale, and Princeton, 1900–1970.* Westport, Conn.: Greenwood Press, 1979. A close examination of how three major universities implemented selective admissions policies to limit the enrollment of Jewish students.

Wechsler, Harold S. *The Qualified Student.* New York: John Wiley & Sons, 1977. A comprehensive account of means taken to select "qualified students" from the early decades of the century to more recent times.

Wyman, David, S. *The Abandonment of the Jews.* New York: Pantheon Books, 1984. The definitive, albeit highly judgmental, account of U.S. government policy regarding European Jewry during the Holocaust.

·3·

What We Know, What We Don't Know About Antisemitism: A Research Perspective

RENAE COHEN

Dr. Renae Cohen is senior research analyst in the
Department of Research and Publications at the
American Jewish Committee.

Among the "perspectives" that need to be addressed in any discussion of antisemitism is, almost tautologically, the measurement and assessment of the phenomenon. Renae Cohen's approach to the study of antisemitism is evident in the starting point—and ending point—of her essay: antisemitism is measured by any number of evaluative criteria, of which attitudinal measurement is but one.

With respect to the study of attitudinal antisemitism—"What do Americans think about Jews?"—Cohen conveys a coherent sense of what the studies and surveys have been all about (including the crucial questions "Compared to what?" and "Compared to when?") and synthesizes the findings that demonstrate a gradual and steady decline in antisemitic attitudes and stereotypes held by Americans.

J.A.C.

In a volume devoted to the thorough examination of contemporary antisemitism in the United States, the breadth of the subject becomes immediately apparent. Indeed, recognizing the multifaceted nature of antisemitism is essential to its assessment. In this vein, the National Jewish Community Relations Advisory Council (NJCRAC), the national coordinating body for the field of Jewish community relations, specifies ten criteria for assessing antisemitism.[1] Included on this list are expressions of antisemitism by political figures and by religious figures, anti-Zionist or anti-Israel manifestations, antisemitic "mass movements," covert or overt acts of aggression against Jews, and official reactions to antisemitism. NJCRAC points out that "no single factor, unrelated to other factors, can provide a definitive assessment of the state of antisemitism at any time."

One key criterion included on the NJCRAC list is the prevailing attitudes toward Jews. These are most commonly measured by survey research and polls, and this essay provides an overview of the survey research in the area of contemporary American antisemitism. Previous research and analysis in the area of contemporary antisemitism has pointed to the lessening of measurable anti-Jewish sentiment over the last decades.[2]

Before proceeding with the present review, it is important to note several key points. First, one should underscore that these surveys of attitudes, while a central component in any assessment of the state of antisemitism, do not measure antisemitism per se, but rather antisemitic or negative attitudes. Moreover, a note of caution is in order when considering the body of data resulting from surveys, in that the figures presented reflect expressed attitudinal antisemitism; there may also be considerable unexpressed antisemitism or negativity that is not reflected in the survey figures (see Smith, 1994, for a discussion of this phenomenon). Finally, while the survey research on contemporary antisemitism measures attitudes, beliefs, and feelings about Jews which may be negative or antisemitic in nature, it is important to note that there may exist attitudes that are positive as well.

For purposes of presentation, the survey research on antisemitic or negative attitudes and beliefs will be broken into two somewhat different, although not necessarily independent, categories. In the first approach, individual beliefs and attitudes are assessed (for example, that Jews have too much power), sometimes as part of a larger-scale survey instrument tapping other issues that may be related or unrelated to Jews. Attitudes toward Jews may be compared with attitudes toward other groups on particular items, when surveys provide for such comparisons (for example, where do Jews fall in a spectrum of groups who are rated as having "too much" power or influence?).

By examining this type of research, trends in the acceptance and rejection of individual antisemitic or negative beliefs may be assessed. However, when looking at similar items that appear in different surveys, problems in comparability may exist because of a number of factors, including subtle—and not-so-subtle—differences in the wording of particular items, the context in which similar or identical questions have appeared, different survey-research houses, and different surrounding items.

In the second approach, an antisemitism index is constructed from among the wide array of individual survey items which are presented as part of a large-scale survey of antisemitic attitudes, beliefs, and feelings, and a respondent is scored as "antisemitic" based on the number of negative responses on the scale. Such large-scale surveys also yield items that are not included in the index, but that may also be compared over time. Ideally, large-scale surveys intended to replicate one another should be designed with as few methodological differences as possible so that the studies can be accurately compared.

In light of these somewhat distinct approaches, this overview will first highlight some major findings for a number of key attitudes and beliefs, as well as some of the resulting trend data over time. We will then turn to the larger-scale assessments of antisemitic attitudes.

TRENDS IN ATTITUDES TOWARD JEWS

This section will focus on a number of attitudes and beliefs about Jews that have been measured over the years. In selecting the items for inclusion in this section, attention was paid to the salience and relevance of the items, along with the frequency of their appearance. Some of these key trend items have appeared in various large-scale surveys of antisemitic attitudes, but they will be cited in this section, not just in the second, because they often provide continuity in the trend line for specific attitudes.

An Early Exploration of Antisemitic Stereotypes, and a More Recent Application of the Technique

Attitudes and feelings toward Jews in the United States were assessed in the 1920s and '30s, often in the context of measuring stereotypes and feelings about a variety of groups.[3] In a frequently cited early study using the "adjective checklist" technique, one set of researchers probed the beliefs of undergraduate students about a number of groups, one of which was Jews (Katz and Braly, 1933). Subjects were presented with a list of positive and negative adjectives ("industrious, courteous, aggressive, deceitful, persistent" and the like) and asked to select those that they thought to be typical of certain groups.[4] This early study revealed that Jews were most often characterized as "shrewd" (79 percent rated Jews in this way), "mercenary" (49 percent), and "industrious" (48 percent); far fewer rated Jews as "intelligent" (29 percent), "ambitious" (21 percent), and "loyal to family ties" (15 percent).[5]

The research, conducted among Princeton University students, was repeated in the same location in 1950 (see Gilbert, 1951) and 1967 (see Karlins, Coffman, and Walters, 1969), and found a declining acceptance of a number of the negative stereotypes of Jews (for example, "shrewd": 1950, 47 percent; 1967, 30 percent; "mercenary": 1950, 28 percent; 1967, 15 percent). At the same time, the percentage rating Jews as "intelligent" and "ambitious" rose over the years ("intelligent": 1950, 37 percent; 1967, 37 percent; "ambitious": 1950, 28 percent, 1967, 48 percent). These characteristics may be associated with the image of Jews as successful, an image that may have strengthened over time.

While the basic paradigm of this early research has been questioned over the years (see Brigham, 1971; Ashmore and Del Boca, 1981), the method of asking respondents about the traits of various groups (sometimes using bipolar rating scales) has been used by many researchers, including major survey-research houses. For example, a more recent assessment using a varied technique was included in the 1990 General Social Survey (GSS) of the National Opinion Research Center (NORC), University of Chicago. In an item designed to assess the beliefs or images that Americans have about a number of ethnic groups (Asian Americans, blacks, Hispanic Americans, Jews, and Southern whites), respondents were asked to rate each group on a series of bipolar characteristics (rich/poor; hardworking/lazy; violence-prone/not violence-prone; unintelligent/intelligent; self-supporting/live off welfare; unpatriotic/patriotic).

Overall, Jews were the group rated most positively, and they were ranked first with regard to wealth, industry, nonviolence, intelligence, and self-support.[6] Indeed, the only characteristic on which Jews were not rated the most positively was patriotism (which may have tied into the perception of Jewish loyalty to Israel).[7]

Smith (1991), in evaluating these results, highlights this finding as one possible indicator of antisemitic sentiment. Moreover, he suggests that the positive ratings of Jews on the characteristics of wealth, industriousness, self-support, and intelligence may relate to the perception of Jews as disproportionately successful (Smith, 1991; 1994).

Both Jewish loyalty and Jewish power are variables on which a considerable amount of survey literature is available, and they will be explored in the next subsections.

Jewish Loyalty

One classic belief that has been measured is the notion of dual loyalty—that is, loyalty to the United States and to Israel—on the part of American Jews. In survey research assessing this view, the results have remained remarkably consistent since the mid-1960s (Rosenfield, 1982; Raab, 1989). For example, in a formulation employed in three large-scale investigations of antisemitism, respondents were asked to note whether the statement "Jews are more loyal to Israel than to America" was probably true or probably false. Approximately one-third of respondents believed that this was "probably true" in each of the surveys; what is remarkable here is that these studies were separated in time by twenty-eight years. Thus, in the 1964 fielding by the National Opinion Research Center and the 1981 fielding by Yankelovich, Skelly and White, 30 percent said that "Jews are more loyal to Israel than to America." The comparable figure in the 1992 fielding by Marttila and Kiley was 35 percent.

More recently, an August 1993 survey on intergroup relations conducted for The National Conference (formerly The National Conference of Christians and Jews) by LH Research found that 29 percent of respondents agreed that Jews "are more loyal to Israel than they are to America." When a similar item was fielded for the American Jewish Committee (AJC) by The Roper Organization in each year from 1984 to 1990, somewhat fewer respondents, from a high of 28 percent (May 1990) to a low of 21 percent (April 1989) agreed with the statement "Most American Jews are more loyal to Israel than to the United States." A plurality disagreed, from a high of 50 percent (January 1984) to a low of 43 percent (April 1989), with another quarter to just over one-third saying "don't know."

This item was also fielded for the AJC by Gallup six times between 1979 and early 1983 (August 1979, March/April 1980, October 1980, November 1981, March 1982, and January 1983). Roughly similar percentages agreed with the statement as in the three large-scale studies, from a high of 37 percent (January 1983) to a low of 29 percent (August 1979 and October 1980). Once again, a plurality disagreed, from a high of 50 percent (August 1979) to a low of 42 percent (January 1983).

Indeed, even when the question wording is somewhat more varied, and respondents are asked whether they believe that most American Jews "feel closer" to the United States or to Israel, the percentage of Americans saying that Jews feel closer to Israel is remarkably consistent with the other surveys. For example, in six surveys conducted for the AJC by Yankelovich, Skelly and White (April, June–July, and October, 1974; January 1975; January 1976; January-March 1981), the percentage of Americans saying that Jews feel closer to Israel ranged from a high of 34 percent (April 1974) to a low of 26 percent (January 1975).

In sum, various fieldings of the dual-loyalty item find that from about one-fifth to one-third of Americans believe that Jews are "more loyal" or "feel closer" to Israel than to the United States, with the results fairly consistent over time. Moreover, substantial minorities often do not reject this belief, instead expressing no opinion.

Jewish Power

Another negative theme that has emerged over the years is the perception of Jews as having too much power or influence.[8] This review will focus on the survey research tapping this belief in the general sense, rather than more particular beliefs such as that Jews have too much power in business (although such views have also been assessed by researchers).

The perception of Jewish power has been measured in a number of ways, with the nature of the survey item a key factor in any analysis of the results. In some cases, the question reads, "Do Jews have too much power?" In other cases, respondents are asked, "Which of the following groups has too much power?" Finally, respondents may be asked to rate each of a number of groups as having either too much, too little, or the right amount of power or influence. The effect of these differences in wording and context is often large. An earlier analysis of this item by Lipset (1987) indicated that when Jews appear as one of a number of groups which may be selected as having too much power, the number of respondents citing Jews as too powerful is much lower than when respondents are asked to rate only Jews. Moreover, when Jews are individually rated along with other groups, their relative position may be low.

The question "Do you think the Jews have too much power in the United States?" has been incorporated into various surveys since the late 1930s. Stember, in his 1966 analysis of the existing survey literature on this item, reported that a substantial minority endorsed the idea in the late 1930s (for example, 35 percent, November 1938; 41 percent, March 1938 and February 1939), with percentages increasing to a majority during and just after World War II (58 percent, June 1945; 55 percent, February 1946). High percentages also perceived "too much power and influence" in 1942 (44 percent) and 1945 (67 percent).

However, by June 1962, the percentage reporting that Jews had too much power decreased to 17 percent. Stember pointed out that figures were much lower when respondents were asked to select groups from a list, an early note on the difference between the findings on closed- and open-ended items about Jewish power.

Except for surveys using this multiple-choice format, national figures for "too much power" have ranged from 11 to 31 percent since 1962, while generally remaining within the range of 17 to 21 percent. Eleven percent of respondents in the 1964 ADL/SRC/NORC survey indicated that "the Jews have too much power in the United States," a further drop from the 17 percent figure obtained in 1962 on the same item. However, the figure increased to 20 percent when a similar item was fielded in the 1981 Yankelovich, Skelly and White/AJC survey.[9]

In a March 1986 ABC News/Washington Post survey which asked respondents to rate the level of influence for each of a number of groups, 20 percent of respondents indicated that Jews had too much influence. And in an April 1987 CBS News/New York Times item which asked whether Jews had too much power in the United States or not, 21 percent of respondents indicated that Jews had too much power.

In yet another formulation, in the 1990 General Social Survey (GSS) conducted by the National Opinion Research Center (NORC), respondents were asked to indicate whether each of a number of groups had too much, too little, or about the right amount of influence in "American life and politics." This survey yielded a similar figure to that in the 1981, 1986, and 1987 fieldings, with just over a fifth of Americans (21 percent) saying that Jews had "too much influence in American life and politics." Jews were more likely to be rated as having "too much" power and influence than blacks (14 percent), Southern whites (10 percent), Asian Americans (6 percent), and Hispanic Americans (5 percent), while somewhat less likely to be seen that way than whites in general (25 percent).

Finally, in the 1992 ADL/Marttila and Kiley survey of antisemitic attitudes, 31 percent of respondents stated that Jews had too much power—a significant increase in this belief. Subsequent fieldings of this item are necessary to determine whether the figure is an anomaly or whether it represents a true shift in belief.

A recent fielding of a comparable item in New York City for the American Jewish Committee by The Roper Organization revealed that nearly half of New Yorkers (47 percent) believe that Jews have "too much influence in New York City life and politics," as against Asians (9 percent), blacks (15 percent), Hispanics (8 percent), the Irish (10 percent), and Italians (20 percent). This strikingly high figure for Jews in New York City—a metropolitan area with a large Jewish population—is consistent with the finding that the greater the proportion of Jews who live in an area, the likelier respondents are to rate Jews as too powerful and influential (Smith, 1991).

In contrast to the aforementioned approaches, in surveys fielded for the AJC by The Roper Organization once a year from 1984 to 1990, respondents were asked, "Which, if any, of the following groups listed on this card do you believe have too much power in the United States?" Unlike the other surveys in this section, these polls asked respondents to select groups from a list without requesting an opinion about each group. In each survey, only 7 to 8 percent of Americans selected Jews. In contrast, many more selected "business corporations" (42 to 51 percent), "labor unions" (30 to 50 percent), "news media" (38 to 50 percent), and "Arab interests" (20 to 30 percent). Certain other groups were seen as too powerful somewhat more frequently than Jews ("Orientals," 11 to 23 percent; "blacks," 11 to 14 percent; "the Catholic Church," 8 to 13 percent), while Hispanics were seen in that way somewhat less frequently (4 to 6 percent).

Indeed, with the same format, relatively low percentages cited Jews in four surveys fielded by Gallup for the AJC. In November 1981 and March 1982 (half sample), Gallup asked whether any of a number of listed groups had too much "political influence"; in March 1982 (half sample) and January 1983, respondents were asked to select groups with too much "power." Eleven percent (November 1981) and 9 percent (March 1982) cited Jews as having too much "political influence"; 9 percent (March 1982) and 10 percent (January 1983) said Jews had "too much power."

Two general findings emerge from this review of some of the literature on Jewish power and influence. First, with the exclusion of the checklist format, the surveys have shown a decrease through the early 1960s in the view that Jews have too much power, followed by an increase to the approximately 20 to 30 percent figure that is found today (depending on the source).

The second finding concerns the effect of item wording and context. When respondents are asked to select groups from a list, Jews are less likely to be cited as having too much influence or power than when respondents are asked for an opinion about Jews (in either a single question about Jews, or in an item in which each of a number of groups is individually rated). Thus, recent results show that under 10 percent of respondents rate Jews as having too much power or influence in the first format, while usually at least 20 percent do so in the latter two formats.

Moreover, when Jews are one of a number of groups that are included in a list or are rated, their relative ratings vary depending on a number of factors, including the type of item, the other groups listed, and the ratings of the other groups (which themselves may vary considerably).

Some Other Relevant Survey Items

Before moving to the overview of the major surveys of antisemitic attitudes, we will briefly review three additional survey items on which attitudes toward Jews—as well as toward other groups—have often been assessed. The first item, addressing the willingness to vote for a Jewish presidential candidate, has revealed an increased acceptance of Jews over the years. For example, a July 1987 survey by Gallup indicated that 89 percent of respondents would be willing to vote for a Jew for president.[10] This figure is nearly double the 46 percent figure obtained by Gallup in 1937, and up significantly from the 62 and 63 percent figures obtained when this item was fielded by Gallup twice in 1958.

The next item involves the willingness to have neighbors who are Jews; in this area as well, acceptance of Jews is at a high level. For example, when the 1964 ADL/SRC/NORC study asked respondents how they would feel about having Jewish neighbors, only 7 percent said that they would "prefer not." The vast majority said that it "wouldn't make any difference" to them (86 percent) or that they "would like to have" some Jewish neighbors (6 percent), and 1 percent answered "don't know." The figures obtained in the 1981 Yankelovich, Skelly and White/AJC survey are nearly identical ("prefer not," 6 percent; "wouldn't make any difference," 87 percent; "like to have," 5 percent; not sure, 2 percent).[11]

Indeed, when Gallup asked respondents whether they "would or would not like to have [each of a number of different groups] as neighbors," 91 percent of respondents said they would like to have Jews as neighbors (January 1989). In a different formulation, Gallup presented respondents with a list of groups and asked them to sort out those they would not like to have as neighbors. Only 2 percent cited Jews in a December 1981 fielding; the figure in January 1987 was 3 percent.[12]

Finally, surveys have attempted to measure whether respondents' feelings toward Jews are generally positive and favorable or negative and unfavorable. Different approaches have been used to measure these feelings. The Gallup organization has asked respondents to indicate, on a ten-point scale ("scalometer"), whether their feelings toward a number of groups are favorable or unfavorable. The Survey Research Center (SRC) and NORC's General Social Survey (GSS) measure feelings toward different groups using a 101-point "feeling thermometer" that measures the warmth and favorability or coldness and unfavorability that respondents feel toward a number of groups.

Results on both of these items reveal generally favorable feelings toward Jews. For example, fieldings during the 1980s of the "feeling thermometer" item by SRC and NORC's GSS found the mean temperature for Jews to be between 61 (1988 and 1989 NORC/GSS) and 63 (1986 NORC/GSS and 1988 SRC).

And while the score for Jews tends to be somewhat lower than those for Catholics and Protestants, secondary analyses indicate these differences to be due solely to the size of each group, with the groups' self-ratings influencing the overall score (Smith, 1991). In his analysis of the data on this item, Smith reported "little change in either the relative or absolute rating of Jews over the last twenty years" (p. 13).

Summary of Individual Items

Positive findings that emerge from the survey literature include the diminished acceptance of many negative stereotypes about Jews over the years, along with a high acceptance of Jews as neighbors and potential presidential candidates, and generally positive feelings about Jews. These positive aspects stand alongside the perception of a significant minority that Jews are more loyal to Israel than to the United States. Moreover, while the belief that Jews have too much power and influence is now less popular than during the period between 1930 and 1960, it is nevertheless at least somewhat stronger than in the early 1960s (when comparing similarly worded items), and the figure is often higher than for other minority groups. When respondents are asked to select groups from a list, the figure for Jews is considerably lower than when other techniques are used.

These mixed findings about Jews are similar to those found in an analysis published in the early 1980s, which focused on some polling data about a number of ethnic groups (Smith and Dempsey, 1983). At that time, the researchers concluded that "there appears to be a small segment of the population concerned about Jewish achievements and, to a lesser extent, alleged Jewish subversion" (p. 586). This finding is supported by more current data as well. Attention is now turned to the large-scale survey instruments that have measured antisemitic beliefs and attitudes.

LARGE-SCALE SURVEYS OF ANTISEMITIC ATTITUDES

Over the years there have been numerous attempts to quantify attitudinal antisemitism in a broad fashion.[13] This section focuses on some of the key results of the three large-scale national surveys that have attempted to measure such attitudes. These studies, conducted in 1964, 1981, and 1992, examined a range of attitudes toward Jews, both positive and negative.

The latter studies were meant to replicate the earlier ones, but some complications arise from differences among the three; nevertheless, these surveys are widely regarded as benchmarks in the study of contemporary antisemitism, and the information that they provide has been useful in many ways.

First, they provide a comprehensive picture of the state of expressed attitudinal antisemitism at three time points over a nearly thirty-year period. Thus, rather than looking at one or two antisemitic beliefs, they encompass a range of attitudes on which a general conclusion may be based.

Second, to the degree that comparability is possible, they provide a series of questions whose results can be compared over the years. (Indeed, the results of some of these items have been reviewed in the first section of this overview.)

Finally, each of the surveys attempted to measure antisemitism using a scale consisting of a number of negative statements about Jews. These indices revealed the proportion of each sample that was thought to be extremely negative toward Jews, and these figures may be compared over time.

The first study was conducted in October 1964 by the Survey Research Center (SRC) of the University of California, Berkeley under a grant from the Anti-Defamation League of B'nai B'rith (ADL) as part of the ADL's *Five-Year Study of Anti-Semitism.* This survey, with fieldwork carried out by the National Opinion Research Center (NORC) at the University of Chicago, was fielded to a national sample, and resulted in a usable sample of nearly two thousand non-Jewish adults. The bulk of the survey, more than fifty items, related to Jews; these items were distributed among others concerning attitudes about a variety of other issues and groups.[14]

The second survey, designed as a follow-up to the 1964 study, was conducted during January–March 1981. Funded by the American Jewish Committee (AJC) and carried out by Yankelovich, Skelly and White, it was fielded among a sample of more than one thousand adults age eighteen and over. Again, much of the survey measured attitudes about Jews, although often in a comparative framework.[15]

The most recent study was funded by the Anti-Defamation League (ADL) and carried out in April–May 1992 by Marttila and Kiley. The survey instrument, fielded to over one thousand Americans, included more than fifty questions related to Jews, and was intended to serve as a third trend point.[16]

Before proceeding with an overview of these surveys, a key point should be noted. The second two surveys—the 1981 AJC/Yankelovich, Skelly and White survey and the 1992 ADL/Marttila and Kiley survey—were meant to provide benchmarks for comparison with the earlier surveys and, as such, were meant to include many of the same questions. It is unfortunate, then, that many of the replicated items—including the key item on Jewish power—varied in ways that could hamper comparability. Furthermore, the eleven-item index of antisemitic attitudes employed in each survey varied in both the exact wording of the items and the method of scoring respondents as antisemitic.

A recent review article specifies in detail the various inconsistencies—as well as consistencies—among the three surveys (Smith, 1993). It highlights differences among the surveys in design, content, repetition of items, and wording of items. The analysis indicates that such differences create problems both in comparing specific items over time and in comparing trends in the eleven-item index of antisemitic attitudes. Because of the many variations in the three surveys, this overview will proceed cautiously in examining trends over time, reviewing each survey individually rather than focusing exclusively on the time line.

The 1964 ADL/SRC/NORC Survey

The first broad, national survey to examine in detail a wide range of attitudes and beliefs about Jews was the 1964 survey sponsored by the ADL, designed by the Survey Research Center (SRC), and carried out by the National Opinion Research Center (NORC).

In analyzing the data from the 1964 survey, Selznick and Steinberg (1969) noted that while a relatively low percentage of respondents felt that Jews had too much power in the United States (11 percent), substantial numbers of respondents accepted some of the "traditional tenets of anti-Semitic ideology," as well as other negative beliefs. For example, large numbers believed that "Jews are more willing than others to use shady practices to get what they want" (42 percent), "Jews don't care what happens to anyone but their own kind" (26 percent), "Jews are [not] just as honest as other businessmen" (28 percent), "Jews always like to be at the head of things" (54 percent), "Jews stick together too much" (52 percent), "Jewish employers go out of their way to hire other Jews" (49 percent), "The movie and television industries are pretty much controlled by Jews" (47 percent), and "Jews have a lot of irritating faults" (40 percent).

The authors discussed the results of these and other negative beliefs in terms of six "traditional images about Jews," namely, as monied, clannish, prideful, unethical, power-hungry, and pushy and aggressive, citing the importance not only of the acceptance of individual beliefs, but also of the relationship between the acceptance of a number of beliefs.

In order to obtain an idea of the number of prejudiced and unprejudiced respondents, Selznick and Steinberg developed an "Index of Anti-Semitic Belief" based on eleven survey items.[17]

Respondents were then scored according to the number of negative beliefs that they accepted. On this basis, Selznick and Steinberg described 37 percent of the sample as prejudiced (those who accepted five or more beliefs), 32 percent as the middle antisemitic group (those who accepted two to four beliefs), and 31 percent as the least antisemitic group (those who accepted zero or one belief). The authors noted that the unprejudiced group expressed little negativity toward Jews, that the middle group held some of the less offensive beliefs, and that the antisemitic group held many more of the beliefs—and some of the more offensive ones—included in the index.

Despite the fact that over one-third of the sample was described as antisemitic, support for discrimination against Jews was found to be relatively low—often even among the most antisemitic group. Among the total sample, a majority supported the idea of hiring Jews, of having Jewish neighbors, and of voting for Jews. Moreover, a slight majority did not object to the idea of their child's marrying a Jew. However, only 58 percent of the sample said they would vote against an antisemitic candidate, a finding that, coupled with the high level of acceptance of antisemitic beliefs, the researchers felt could portend problems in the future.

Selznick and Steinberg also examined the sample for subgroup differences in negativity toward Jews; we will review a number of the more salient groups. Education was most strongly linked to antisemitic prejudice as measured by the eleven-item index, with more negativity expressed by the less-educated respondents. Age was also strongly related to antisemitism, with higher levels of antisemitism associated with greater age. Comparison between black and white respondents yielded somewhat more complex findings: blacks were more negative toward Jews on the five economic items on the index, while blacks and whites were more similar to one another in the expression of noneconomic antisemitism.

The 1981 AJC/Yankelovich, Skelly and White Survey

The second large-scale survey of antisemitic attitudes and beliefs was sponsored by the AJC and carried out by Yankelovich, Skelly and White in 1981. A central purpose of this survey was to "provide the first comprehensive trend study of anti-Semitism in the United States," the baseline being the 1964 NORC/ADL survey.

Analysis of the 1981 survey by Martire and Clark (1982) revealed that while positive beliefs about Jews were more widespread than negative ones, unfavorable beliefs nonetheless existed. Thus, while large numbers believed that Jews are hardworking (81 percent), have strong faith in God (71 percent), are warm and friendly people (64 percent), are just as honest as other businessmen (60 percent), and have contributed much to the cultural life of America (53 percent), substantial numbers believed that Jews stick together too much (40 percent), always like to be at the head of things (38 percent), go out of their way to hire Jews (37 percent), and have too much power in the business world (32 percent).

In comparing the trends from the 1964 baseline to the 1981 survey, one finds that respondents became somewhat more likely to see Jews as too powerful, although it should be noted that the item was worded differently. The item on dual loyalty remained constant among the total samples, with 30 percent attributing this to American Jews. However, Martire and Clark pointed out that respondents who expressed an opinion were more likely to perceive dual loyalty in 1981 than in 1964.

Nevertheless, Martire and Clark concluded, "Anti-Semitism has declined significantly in the United States since the mid-1960s" (p. 29). For example, respondents in the 1981 survey were less likely to see Jews as unethical (Jews are more willing to use shady practices: 1964 and 1981, 42 percent and 23 percent, respectively; Jewish businessmen are shrewd and tricky: 1964 and 1981, 35 percent and 20 percent, respectively) and as having other offensive personal qualities (Jews have irritating faults: 1964 and 1981, 40 percent and 19 percent, respectively; Jews care only about their own kind: 1964 and 1981, 26 percent and 16 percent, respectively).[18] Further, using an eleven-item "Index of Anti-Semitism" similar to that employed by Selznick and Steinberg and tapping the same beliefs, Martire and Clark described 23 percent of their sample as prejudiced (in accepting five or more beliefs), 32 percent as neutral, and 45 percent as unprejudiced—a seeming drop in negativity from the 1964 figure.[19] The authors described this decline in antisemitism as a result of generational change in the samples, with the older and more negative respondents replaced by younger and less negative ones.

In examining the various subgroup differences in the 1981 survey, the researchers found that education was, once again, the variable with the strongest relationship to antisemitic beliefs, with better-educated respondents less likely to express negativity. Age was again a key variable, with older respondents more likely than younger ones to express negativity. Finally, when considering only those respondents who expressed an opinion, blacks were found to be more negative than whites toward Jews. However, unlike the 1964 survey, this greater negativity was not restricted to the economic sphere but included items from the noneconomic sphere as well. The researchers further reported a strong relationship between xenophobia and antisemitism, but little relationship between economic and political concerns and antisemitism.

The 1992 ADL/Marttila and Kiley Survey

The final large-scale survey was sponsored by the Anti-Defamation League of B'nai B'rith and conducted in 1992 by Marttila and Kiley. A written document focusing on the highlights of the survey, prepared by the ADL in late 1992, noted that this was the third major survey of antisemitic attitudes and beliefs in the United States.

The report noted that respondents in 1992 were less likely than those in 1964 to accept (as well as more likely to reject) a variety of negative stereotypes about Jewish business practices and other negative statements about Jews. For example, the belief that Jews use shady practices dropped from 42 percent (1964) to 23 percent (1981) and 21 percent (1992); the corresponding figures for those rejecting this belief were 46 percent (1964), 46 percent (1981), and 73 percent (1992). Similarly, the belief that Jews are not as honest as other businessmen dropped from 28 percent (1964) to 17 percent (1981) and 16 percent (1992), while rejection increased, from 64 percent and 60 percent in 1964 and 1981, respectively, to 80 percent in 1992. Likewise, the belief that Jews have irritating faults declined over the years, from 40 percent in 1964 to 19 percent and 22 percent in 1981 and 1992, respectively; the corresponding figures for rejection of this stereotype rose, from 43 percent and 48 percent in 1964 and 1981, respectively, to 71 percent in 1992. Or again, the belief that Jews care only about their own kind dropped from 26 percent in 1964 to 16 percent in both 1981 and 1992; rejection of this stereotype increased from 62 percent and 59 percent in 1964 and 1981, respectively, to 81 percent in 1992.[20]

Acceptance of the notion of Jewish power seemed to have increased, with 31 percent believing that Jews have too much power in the United States. (This comparison may be hampered by the fact that the question on Jewish power was asked somewhat differently in the surveys, as discussed earlier.) The 1992 survey assessed the perceived power of other groups, as well, and the relatively high 31-percent figure may be compared with them. Thus, whites were cited as having too much power by nearly half of the sample (47 percent), followed by blacks (20 percent), Asians (17 percent), Italians (13 percent), and Hispanics (8 percent).

Thirty-five percent of the sample believed that Jews are more loyal to Israel than to the United States, up from 30 percent in both the 1964 and 1981 fieldings. Fifty-eight percent of respondents rejected this stereotype, up from 47 percent in 1964 and 32 percent in 1981. Moreover, on another item that assessed the level of patriotism on the part of each of six groups, 16 percent rated Jews as "less patriotic" than other Americans, lower than the comparable ratings for Asians (25 percent), Hispanics (25 percent), and blacks (22 percent), although at least somewhat higher than those for Italians (12 percent) and whites in general (4 percent).

The report also indicates that, while substantial numbers of Americans still accepted some stereotypes of Jewish clannishness (such as that Jews stick together too much and that Jewish employers hire other Jews), focus-group research suggested that these may not necessarily have been negative beliefs, and may have been of less significance than other beliefs. Finally, as with the 1981 survey, the results indicated that respondents were more likely to endorse positive statements about Jews than negative ones. Thus, for example, significant majorities believed that Jews "are a warm and friendly people" (84 percent), "have a strong faith in God" (85 percent), "are just as honest as other businessmen" (80 percent), and "have contributed much to the cultural life of America" (67 percent).

An index of antisemitic belief was once again constructed, using the eleven items that had been employed in each of the previous surveys, but with some variations on a number of the items. (In particular, the focus on international banking was changed to "too much control and influence on Wall Street.") The definition of those in the most, middle, and least antisemitic categories also differed from that used in each of the earlier surveys.[21] With those caveats in mind, the proportion of those scoring as the most antisemitic seems to have decreased since 1964, with 20 percent of the respondents in the 1992 survey, in accepting six or more of the statements on the eleven-item index, scoring as antisemitic.

The researchers attributed the generally decreased level of antisemitism over the years both to generational change, with the replacement of older and more antisemitic respondents with younger, less antisemitic ones, and to the slow change in the attitudes of older Americans over their lifetimes.

Consistent with the findings of the earlier surveys, education, age, and race were all linked to the expression of antisemitic beliefs. Thus, less-educated, older, and black respondents were more likely than better-educated, younger, and white respondents to express negativity toward Jews.

The researchers further noted that racism, xenophobia, and intolerance were all positively related to the expression of antisemitic beliefs. Consistent with previous findings, political and economic concerns were not strongly linked to the acceptance of antisemitic beliefs.

Brief Overview of the Three Surveys

We have pointed to the problems in comparing the surveys due to the many differences between them. Nevertheless, some tentative conclusions about broad trends are possible. In general, the results of the three surveys point to a lessening of expressed neg-

77

ativity toward Jews over the twenty-eight years between the first and last studies, with the notable exception of the stereotypes of Jewish power and, to a lesser extent, dual loyalty. This general lessening in the acceptance of antisemitic beliefs is coupled with a greater rejection of these beliefs over the years. Moreover, while the items have varied and the indices have been scored differently, the results seem to indicate that a smaller percentage of the population scores as antisemitic, with larger percentages accepting fewer negative statements. Finally, results show a more widespread acceptance of positive statements about Jews.

The review of both individual items and large-scale surveys has revealed a number of interesting and consistent findings. On the whole, expressed attitudinal antisemitism has declined over the years, with respondents less likely to endorse and often more likely to reject a variety of negative images about Jews. This decline in negativity is coupled with the widespread endorsement of positive statements about Jews, widespread acceptance of Jews in various social and political arenas, and generally warm feelings toward Jews.

Notwithstanding these positive developments, there are some causes for concern. The belief that Jews are too powerful may be on the increase, and seems higher now than it was in the early 1960s. Moreover, concern about dual loyalty on the part of American Jews is expressed by approximately one-third of all Americans. While previous analysis found little association between concerns about Jewish influence and Jewish patriotism (see Smith, 1991), other questions remain. Are there ramifications of these beliefs? Are they independent and do they simply stand alongside the positive feelings about Jews? Are they associated with other negative beliefs that are not measured by the surveys?

Of particular interest is the nature of the existing surveys and research items that are used to assess antisemitic sentiment, which have been in use for many years. It may be the case that some or many of them are of diminished relevance, and that the sphere of negativity toward Jews (as well as toward other groups) has taken a different form. Indeed, the current acceptance of particular stereotypes may not now have the same negative meaning for the respondents that it once did. For example, recall that while some stereotypes about Jewish clannishness were still accepted by substantial numbers of Americans in the most recent large-scale survey, focus-group research revealed that these may not have been negative beliefs.

Furthermore, other issues that are not currently probed to assess attitudinal antisemitism may now have more salience. Thus, while the relationship between anti-Israel and antisemitic attitudes is weak (Raab, 1986; Smith, 1991, 1994), it is positive and may represent one area in which a more current and complete examination is in order.

Moreover, as noted earlier, the concept of measured attitudinal antisemitism must also be carefully considered in that surveys, perfect or imperfect as they may be, will only measure what is expressed. Thus, in various ways and for a variety of reasons, the survey figures may not represent the full range of negativity toward Jews and other groups.

Finally, we return to the notion of antisemitism as being a multifaceted phenomenon that cannot be measured solely by surveys and other attitudinal assessments. In order to obtain a complete picture of the state of contemporary antisemitism at any particular time, assessments of attitudinal antisemitism must be evaluated together with a host of other criteria for assessing antisemitism. In the absence of these additional components, what is left is an incomplete and often imperfect measurement of the phenomenon.

NOTES

1. The NJCRAC engages and advises its membership organizations in the assessment of antisemitism in individual communities. In so doing, and in the process of assessing contemporary antisemitism on the national scene, these criteria were developed to assist in the assessment and discussion, as well as to aid in uniformity and consistency of evaluations. Thus, when using identical criteria, there is the possibility for more accurate comparisons across communities and over time.

2. For example, Stember, 1966; Qunley and Glock, 1979; Martire and Clark, 1982; Wuthnow, 1982; Raab, 1989; Smith, 1991; Anti-Defamation League, 1992; Smith, 1994 (see References).

3. See Katz and Braly (1935) for an overview of some early work in the area, and Stember (1966) for some early, relevant survey research.

4. The groups included Americans, Chinese, English, Germans, Irish, Italians, Japanese, Jews, "Negroes," and Turks.

5. Over the years other salient stereotypes have been measured; they will be examined in the next sections of this chapter.

6. Similar findings emerged when a number of unipolar characteristics were rated in a 1992 survey of New York City residents conducted for the American Jewish Committee by the Roper Organization (see Setlow and Cohen, 1993). Employing both positive and negative unipolar characteristics ("rich, lazy, intelligent, prone to violence, tolerant of other racial and ethnic groups, prefer to live off welfare"), respondents were asked to rate a number of groups (Italians, Hispanics, Jews, Asians, blacks, Irish) on each trait. Jews were likelier than any other group to be rated as rich and intelligent, and least or among the least likely to be rated as lazy, prone to violence, and preferring to live off welfare.

7. Nevertheless, Jews are not the only group described as unpatriotic, and are rated more favorably in this regard than blacks, Asians, and Hispanics.

8. While the belief that Jews have too much power is traditionally viewed as antisemitic, a number of researchers have questioned whether the attitude is indeed clearly negative (see Smith, 1994, for a full discussion of this issue).

9. An item tapping the belief that Jews have too much power was included in each of the three large-scale surveys of antisemitic attitudes. Unfortunately, in each of the surveys the item was asked in a somewhat different manner, so that the variance across years may be attributable to factors other than, or in addition to, a change in attitude. Thus, the item "Do you think the Jews have too much power in the United States?" was posed to respondents in the 1964 NORC/ADL survey. In the 1981 survey, respondents were asked to indicate if each of four groups (blacks, Italians, Jews, Japanese) had "too much power in the United States." In the 1992 survey, respondents were asked to rate if each of six groups (blacks, Italians, Jews, Asians, whites in general, Hispanics) "has too much power in the United States today or not."

10. This is higher than the figures obtained for a black candidate (79 percent) or an atheist (44 percent) in 1987.

11. The ratings for each of the other groups in the 1981 survey were as follows: Italian Americans ("wouldn't make any difference," 85 percent; "like to have," 6 percent; "prefer not," 6 percent; not sure, 3 percent) and Japanese Americans ("wouldn't make any difference," 82 percent; "like to have," 4 percent; "prefer not," 10 percent; not sure, 4 percent). All of these groups were rated more favorably than blacks ("wouldn't make any difference," 61 percent; "like to have," 5 percent; "prefer not," 31 percent; not sure, 3 percent).

12. The other responses in the December 1981 fielding were as follows: "members of minority religious sects or cults," 30 percent; "Cuban refugees," 25 percent; "Hispanics (Mexican, Puerto Rican, Cuban)," 18 percent; "Vietnamese refugees," 17 percent; "unmarried single people living together," 14 percent; "religious fundamentalists," 11 percent; "Protestants," 1 percent; "Catholics," 1 percent). The other responses in the January 1987 fielding were as follows: "members of minority religious sects or cults," 44 percent; "religious fundamentalists," 13 percent; "blacks," 13 percent; "unmarried single people living together," 12 percent; "Hispanics," 9 percent; "Protestants," 2 percent; "Catholics," 1 percent).

13. An early, ambitious, and well-known foray into the study of antisemitism in the 1940s resulted in the groundbreaking study commonly referred to as "The Authoritarian Personality." This AJC-sponsored research proposed a psychodynamic theory of prejudice, and examined the personality characteristics associated with authoritarianism, including antisemitism, ethnocentrism, and fascism. The findings and complete analysis are reported in detail in T. W. Adorno et al., 1950.

14. See Selznick and Steinberg, 1969, for the full text of the survey, as well as the complete analysis of the survey results.

15. See Martire and Clark, 1982.

16. See Anti-Defamation League, 1992.

17. The eleven items in the index measured the belief that Jews have too much power in the United States, care only about their own kind, are not as honest as other businessmen, have too much power in the business world, are more loyal to Israel than to America, control international banking, are shrewd and tricky in business, have a lot of irritating faults, use shady practices to get ahead, stick together too much, and always like to be at the head of things. See Selznick and Steinberg (1969) for a more complete description of the process of selecting the eleven items, their relationships with one another, their internal consistency, and the validity of the index as a whole.

18. Because of methodological differences, the 1981 survey resulted in an increased number of "don't know" responses. The result of this was probably to decrease the percentages of respondents both accepting and rejecting the beliefs about Jews. Excluding the "don't know" responses from these items results in differences of the same direction, but slightly different magnitude.

19. Again, different classification procedures, as well as variations in the wordings of a number of the items, complicate this comparison.

20. Again, the methodology used in the 1981 survey resulted in an increase in the number of "don't know" responses, probably resulting in a decrease of both positive and negative responses in 1981. Thus, the magnitude of any increase from 1981 to 1992 might be somewhat inflated. When the "don't know" responses for these items were excluded, a more linear

decrease in acceptance and increase in rejection of the negative stereotypes was evident. Indeed, Smith (1993) reported that exclusion of the "don't know" responses from each of the three surveys resulted in a generally linear decrease in antisemitism.

21. The 1964 and 1981 surveys categorized in the most antisemitic group those respondents who answered five or more statements on the eleven-item index in a negative manner. In the 1992 survey, respondents who answered six or more statements in a negative manner were so categorized. This change in cutoff point was based on the results of focus-group research and discussions with experts and scholars, which indicated that one or two of the items on the eleven-point scale might be ambiguous.

REFERENCES

Adorno, T. W et al. *The Authoritarian Personality.* New York: Harper and Brothers, 1950.

Anti-Defamation League of B'nai B'rith. *Highlights from an Anti-Defamation League Survey on Anti-Semitism and Prejudice in America.* New York: Anti-Defamation League, 1992.

Ashmore, Richard D., and Frances K. Del Boca. "Conceptual Approaches to Stereotypes and Stereotyping." In David L. Hamilton, ed., *Cognitive Processes in Stereotyping and Intergroup Behavior.* Hillsdale, N.J.: Erlbaum, 1981.

Brigham, John C. "Ethnic Stereotypes." *Psychological Bulletin* 76 (1971) 15–38.

Gilbert, G. M. "Stereotype Persistence and Change Among College Students." *Journal of Abnormal and Social Psychology* 46 (1951) 245–54.

Karlins, Marvin, Thomas L. Coffman, and Gary Walters. "On the Fading of Social Stereotypes: Studies in Three Generations of College Students." *Journal of Personality and Social Psychology* 13 (1969) 1–16.

Katz, Daniel, and Kenneth Braly. "Racial Prejudice and Racial Stereotypes." *Journal of Abnormal and Social Psychology* 30 (1935) 175–93.

———. "Racial Stereotypes of One Hundred College Students." *Journal of Abnormal and Social Psychology* 28 (1933) 280–90.

Lipset, Seymour M. "Blacks and Jews: How Much Bias?" *Public Opinion* 10 (July/August 1987) 4–5, 57–58.

Martire, Gregory, and Ruth Clark. *Anti-Semitism in the United States: A Study of Prejudice in the 1980s.* New York: Praeger, 1982.

The National Conference. *Taking America's Pulse: The Conference Survey on Inter-group Relations.* New York: The National Conference, 1994.

Quinley, Harold E., and Charles Y. Glock. *Anti-Semitism in America.* New York: The Free Press, 1979.

Raab, Earl. "Attitudes Toward Israel and Attitudes Toward Jews: The Relationship." In Michael Curtis, ed., *Antisemitism in the Contemporary World.* Boulder: Westview Press, 1986.

_____ . *What Do We Really Know About Anti-Semitism—And What Do We Want To Know?* New York: American Jewish Committee, 1989.

Rosenfield, Geraldine. "The Polls: Attitudes Toward American Jews." *Public Opinion Quarterly* 46 (1982) 431–43.

Selznick, Gertrude J., and Stephen Steinberg. *The Tenacity of Prejudice: Anti-Semitism in Contemporary America.* New York: Harper & Row, 1969.

Setlow, Carolyn E., and Renae Cohen. *1992 New York City Intergroup Relations Survey.* New York: American Jewish Committee, 1993.

Smith, Tom W. *Anti-Semitism in Contemporary America.* New York: American Jewish Committee, 1994.

_____ . "Studying Trends or Measurement Artifacts? A Review of Three Studies of Anti-Semitism." *Public Opinion Quarterly* 57 (fall 1993) 380–93.

_____ . *What Do Americans Think About Jews?* New York: American Jewish Committee, 1991.

_____ and Glenn R. Dempsey. "The Polls: Ethnic Social Distance and Prejudice." *Public Opinion Quarterly* 47 (1983) 584–600.

Stember, Charles H. *Jews in the Mind of America.* New York: Basic Books, 1966.

Wuthnow, Robert. "Anti-Semitism and Stereotyping." In Arthur G. Miller, ed., *In the Eye of the Beholder: Contemporary Issues in Stereotyping.* New York: Praeger, 1982.

·4·

Can Antisemitism Disappear?

EARL RAAB

Earl Raab is executive director emeritus of the San Francisco Jewish Community Relations Council and director emeritus of the Perlmutter Institute for Jewish Advocacy at Brandeis University. He is the coauthor (with Seymour Martin Lipset) of *Jews and the New American Scene.*

A key "perspective," in the discussion of any phenomenon, is the question of the possibility of the ending or elimination of that phenomenon. Earl Raab's essay flows naturally from Jack Wertheimer's chapter 2, which sets a historical perspective for American antisemitism. Raab, for many years a leading community-relations professional, analyzes antisemitism not in terms of its manifestations but of its terminability. His central thesis: antisemitism is not a genetic characteristic of this (or any) society. The nature of American society suggests possibilities that antisemitism can be eliminated. The implications of Raab's argument in terms of the future agendas of community-relations organizations are profound.

J.A.C.

"The Jews are the chosen people of the world's hatred. Judeophobia is hereditary and incurable," wrote Leo Pinsker, the nineteenth-century Zionist.

Most Jews would admit that hatred of Jews is not carried in some specific gene. But the majority do behave as though that hatred is incurable. Too much should not be made of the apparent inconsistency; it is largely a matter of confusing the possible with the probable.

It would be liberating in itself for us to understand that antisemitism *can* end, even if it doesn't. In addition, that understanding would make it easier to accept the probability that antisemitism *will* virtually end someday—earlier in some places than in others. And demystifying the phenomenon would allow us to better understand what remedies will most effectively hasten the realization of that probability.

A PRODUCT OF VARIABLE CIRCUMSTANCES

Antisemitism is, after all, a cultural artifact, created by social circumstances. There is some ironic truth in the usually malevolent statement that Jews are themselves responsible for the hatred directed against them. Jew-hatred was seeded in those particular religions which spring from Judaism, although such hatred has long fed on much more than primitive religious anger.

Early on, the hostile Christian societies of the Western world forced Jews into positions which made them economic as well as religious pariahs, and then, as nationalism developed, ethnic pariahs as well. Out of all these circumstances developed the culture of antisemitism, a cumulative reservoir of negative images and feelings transmitted from one generation to another, in certain areas of the world.

But it is possible to accept that antisemitism is a cultural rather than a genetic phenomenon, and still hold that this cultural reservoir is so powerful that it cannot be emptied, much less reduced. One conventional belief is that, whatever its cultural origins, it now lies there irreversibly, latent at best, like a reservoir not of water but of gasoline waiting to burst into flame whenever a match is lit.

In America alone, there is plenty of historical evidence to support the "lit-match" theory. In most of nineteenth-century America, anti-Catholicism was the bigotry of choice. Churches were burned, conspiracy theorists generally worried about "papists," and some local officials called for their people to collect arms in their cellars in order to repel the pope's invasion. Meanwhile, the relatively small number of Jews were largely ignored as they went about enjoying more political and economic freedom than could have been imagined in Europe.

But during the Civil War, "the match was lit" more than once. The citizens of Thomasville, Georgia, gave all the Jews in its environs twenty-four hours to get out of town and stay out. The town, like many others in the South, was in severe economic distress because of the Northern embargo. Prices were high, goods were scarce, the Jews there were mostly merchants or traders, and the Yankee navy was out of retaliatory reach. General Ulysses S. Grant, angered by illegal cotton traders, some of whom were Jewish, drew on the same reservoir of prejudice when he ordered *all* Jews as a class out of the area which he controlled.

When a number of Yankees became rich for the first time in America's boom toward the end of the century, they began to draw on ancient prejudice in order to exclude Jews from their resort hotels and social clubs. Their actions made it clear that a sense of status deprivation as well as economic distress provide motives for going to the poisoned well.

And as the century turned and large masses of immigrants entered the country, both motives came into play. The second Ku Klux Klan, a substantial force, was built on workingmen's economic distress and Protestant concern with status displacement. The old stereotypes of the Jew fit the bill, and antisemitism surged to the top of the bigotry hit list, staying there during the Depression.

INHIBITING FACTORS

A static—and superficial—view of such history might seem to support the "lit-match" theory: a "reservoir" of anti-Jewish prejudice which adverse circumstances can automatically activate into serious antisemitic behavior. But this is a too simple recipe for disaster.

In the first place, the "circumstances" or factors controlling such a conflagration are of two different kinds. There are *stimulating* factors, such as economic distress or pervasive concern about status deprivation. But there are also *inhibiting* circumstances or factors which can keep a lid on the behavioral activation of prejudiced attitudes, even if there are some significant stimulating factors. Inhibiting factors are those which make it more advantageous for a given set of people to repress their prejudice than to act it out.

Economic self-interest has at times worked as such an inhibitor. At one point, early in the civil rights era, it was found that the more affluent citizens of Atlanta were just about as prejudiced in attitude against blacks as were poorer Atlantans, but much more likely to submit to desegregation. Aside from being in a better position to avoid its consequences, they were concerned about the damage which would ensue to the image and economy of their community if there were massive, disruptive—and futile—opposition to the federal law. The same inhibiting factor played a role in David Duke's more recent run for the U.S. Senate seat from Louisiana. Among the more affluent, there was reported concern about the damage to the state's image and economy if Duke were to be elected.

Of course, economic self-interest can work both ways, as a stimulating factor for those whose times are bad, and an inhibiting factor for those whose times are good. There are other factors which are more singularly inhibiting in their effect, some of them peculiar to American society. A unique heterogeneity is one example which has had many applications. Early on, the unparalleled multiplicity of denominations, once referred to as a "swarm of sectaries" by a disgruntled Episcopalian official, made religious tolerance a political necessity. Upset by the failure of the Maryland legislature in 1819 to remove the time-honored requirement that public officials take a Christian oath, the *Philadelphia Aurora* editorialized: "If the legislature of Maryland have the right to disfranchise any portion of the freemen of that state because they believe in the God of Abraham, Isaac and Jacob, they may next decide which of the various sects are *true* Christians and disfranchise all the rest."

And, on a national level, both political parties are necessarily coalitional in nature, and have been inhibited from openly embracing a KKK type of bigotry, under pain of losing one or another constituency which they need for victory. Laws can also serve as inhibitors. It was once an axiom of civil rights opponents that "you can't legislate morality." They were, of course, wrong. The very existence of a legal prohibition, in a stable society, usually helps to establish a normative culture standard. And insofar as the law effectively changes behavior, the new behavior changes the cultural climate in which people learn.

The very integration of the Jews in America has been another inhibiting factor. When the Jews were expelled from Thomasville they were welcomed in Savannah, where a public protest against the expulsion was held in which the mainstream population participated. Jews had established themselves in Savannah from its inception, had served in official positions, and were active in the support of the Confederacy.

THE INCONSTANCY OF PREJUDICED ATTITUDES

It is not just a matter of bad times whipping bad attitudes into bad behavior; countervailing factors can block that behavior. And there is another false image inherent in a simple stimulus-and-response formula for antisemitic disaster: the assumption that the cultural reservoir of hostility is a fairly constant body of attitudes. The prevalence and salience of attitudinal prejudice, like the extent to which it is acted out, can and do diminish or expand.

It is startling to note the extent to which attitudes of prejudice against Jews have declined in America in the last half century. In the late 1930s, almost half of the American people said that Jewish businessmen were less honest than others; by 1964, that figure had dropped to about a quarter; and in 1991, to about a sixth. In the 1930s, more than half of the American population said they would vote against a Jewish presidential candidate; today, fewer than one out of ten say the same. Similar diminutions of hostility have been found in matters of hiring Jews or living next to them as neighbors. A corresponding reversal has been found in the expression of favorable feelings toward Jews; today, about as many indicate "warm and friendly" feelings toward Jews as they do toward Protestants and Catholics.

It is very possible that many people have become more sophisticated about the kind of answer they thought was expected to such questions. But that in itself is a powerful index of how the culture of antisemitism has changed.

It is not, by and large, that people with antisemitic attitudes have changed their minds. Rather, it is a generational change; younger generations of Americans have demonstrated lower levels of antisemitic attitude and behavior. Formal education has sometimes been credited for that change. And survey analysis consistently shows that there is a sharp inverse correlation between levels of education and of antisemitic belief. In 1991, 33 percent of those who had only a high school education or less scored "highest" on a scale of antisemitic attitudes, compared with 17 percent of college graduates. In 1940, about a quarter of the population above age twenty-five had graduated from high school and about one in ten from college. In the course of the postwar years, those figures have generally tripled.

It may be true that increases in cognitive knowledge can affect levels of prejudice. But even more certain is the fact that these newer generations—in school and out—have been subject to a changing general culture with respect to antisemitism.

THE EFFECT OF CHANGED BEHAVIOR ON ATTITUDES

That changing culture has not just been a matter of rhetoric; it includes prevailing behavior patterns. In the case of prohibitive laws, as previously suggested, people learn many of their attitudes from changed behavior patterns, including those within which they themselves behave. In the old South, a white child had witnessed enough black children drinking from separate, broken-down water fountains, and black adults working in menial and servile positions, to form a prejudiced set of attitudes about blacks before they were ever formally instructed in the matter.

The mountain of research done on black-white relationships during the early civil rights period established the fact that behavior often precedes attitude, rather than vice versa. In one typical study, white department store employees who had worked with at least one black colleague on an equal plane were half again more likely to be favorable toward employment integration than white employees who did not have that experience.[2]

The chicken-and-egg cycle in which cultural behavior changes cultural attitudes, which in turn further affect behavior, is notably applicable to the status of the American Jew. The radical improvement in the objective position of American Jews, in the way in which they have been integrated into society, reflects and further buttresses the radical improvement of surveyed opinion toward them.

A Jew recently was made president of Yale University. Only a few decades ago, there was a low quota on the admission of Jewish students at Ivy League colleges, almost no Jewish faculty, and a Jewish president would have been unthinkable. Now, the percentage of Jewish students at these elite universities is, in some cases, about ten times the proportion of Jews in the population. The size of the Jewish faculty has followed suit. And in recent years Princeton, Harvard, Dartmouth, the University of Pennsylvania, and Columbia, as well as Yale, have appointed Jewish presidents at one time or another.

This radically changed situation in the elite universities naturally coincides with just as drastic changes in the economic and social status of American Jews. The lists of the country's wealthiest businessmen in *Forbes* magazine in recent years include a highly disproportionate number of Jews. *Who's Who* records a similar disproportion of Jews. As a total group, Jews are at least as wealthy as Episcopalians and Presbyterians, who are much wealthier than other Protestants and Catholics. And, perhaps most significantly, a disproportionate number of Jews have been elected to Congress, and to other public positions, by constituencies which are 90 percent or more non-Jewish. That level of acceptance would not have been conceivable a few decades ago.

The radical difference in *behavior* toward Jews might indeed result from the fact that few of the conventional "stimulating" circumstances have been present since the end of World War II; there have been few "lit matches" set to the reservoir. Despite a couple of recessions and some abject pockets of poverty, the American population at large has experienced a swell of economic well-being unknown before the 1950s.

But, in addition, a number of directly "inhibiting" factors have been operative. Stringent civil rights laws have been passed, penalizing discriminatory behavior. The mainstream religious and civic institutions of the country have followed the temper of that legislation. An increasing ethnic heterogeneity, as a result of immigration, has made it even more difficult for a political party or mass movement of bigotry to develop. To add to the African-Americans, not to mention Jews, the swiftly growing edge of the population consists of other traditional targets of prejudice: Hispanics and Asians.

The integration of the Jews in the past few decades has also been swift and unprecedentedly thorough, affecting their vulnerability to hostility-stimulating factors, and exercising a directly hostility-inhibiting influence. Aside from being involved in more equal-status associations with other Americans, they are out there in stereotype-breaking positions. On the one hand, they are accepted as public policy makers. On the other, they are increasingly absent from those economic roles which helped to support the Shylock image. They are no longer the prototypical merchants and middlemen, or even the visible financiers. As businessmen and professionals, they are more and more often lost in the anonymous corporate structures. When Ivan Boesky was dramatically exposed as an arch-criminal of Wall Street, only about 2 percent of the population identified him as a Jew; he was primarily seen as part of the class of evil (and multidenominational) financiers.

In sum, the objective condition of the American Jew has improved to a degree never before seen in modern history, because of the lack of stimulating and the presence of inhibiting circumstances. The interacting level of attitudes in the mythical reservoir of prejudice has also drastically dropped—which should be no surprise since such attitudes are a product of the prevailing culture.

THE REVERSIBILITY OF PROGRESS

But that leaves a couple of crucial questions. To begin with, if today's circumstances can reduce behavioral and attitudinal levels of antisemitism, why can't tomorrow's circumstances reverse that process?

The reversibility of the good news is not to be taken lightly— nor do American Jews do so. About seven out of ten American Jews consistently say that antisemitism "is a serious problem in the United States today," and about the same proportion say that antisemitism is on the increase in this country. Yet most of them do not literally believe that. Certainly they do not believe that the important aspects of their personal lives are threatened by anti-Jewish hostility. Only about two out of ten say that anti-semitism is increasing on the economic front, or on the political front. And most of those do not say so out of personal experience, nor would the objective economic and political status of the Jews support such a conclusion.

The large proportion of American Jews who say they worry about antisemitism in this country are really expressing a con-cern not so much about its currency as about its *potential.* They have, of course, good historical reason to hold such a foreboding. Seemingly good conditions have been reversed before by bad cir-cumstances, in the group's American as well as world experi-ence.

But whether they all realize it or not, there is something more than a historical basis for their foreboding, as revealed in a fur-ther exploration of the dynamics of antisemitism. It has been noted that the "reservoir" of antisemitic attitudes can wax or wane, mutually interactive with the state of antisemitic behavior. That generalized construct describes one aspect of the flexibility of Judeophobia, but does not yet touch on the people who are involved in those dynamics.

With all due acknowledgment to the fact that typologies always mask a broad spectrum of human characteristics, a spec-trum which is usually in flux, evidence nevertheless suggests that, on the subject, there are three "kinds" of people at any given time. There are the "hard core," who have strongly hostile atti-tudes toward Jews and are ready to act them out. There are the "countercommitted," who, regardless of their level of attitudinal prejudice, and regardless of adverse circumstance, are committed for one reason or another against behaving in a discriminatory manner. And there are the "indifferent," who, regardless of their level of attitudinal prejudice, could too easily be influenced to engage in discriminatory behavior.

A couple of surveys illustrate these differences. In 1946, and then in 1964, respondents were asked whether they would be influenced to vote for an antisemitic congressional candidate because he was antisemitic, whether they would vote against him on that account, or whether his antisemitism wouldn't make any difference to their vote. In 1946, 23 percent said they would be influenced to vote *for* him because of his antisemitism; in 1964, only 5 percent gave that response. In 1946, 31 percent said they would vote *against* him on that account; in 1964, 58 percent gave that response. In both cases, about a third of the population said "it wouldn't make any difference." When a 1991 survey asked a differently worded question, involving a presidential candidate, a somewhat smaller percentage said they would vote for the candidate because of his antisemitism, and a somewhat larger percentage said they would be indifferent.

While the numbers derived from these single questions cannot be taken literally or used for precise analysis, they do roughly illustrate the kinds of grouping proposed above. They also corroborate the kind of progress which has been made in recent decades away from hard-core activism. And they nevertheless suggest the existence of a substantial body of "indifferents." That is the crucial body of people with respect to any potentially serious movement of antisemitism. They are admitting that certain circumstances could easily lead them to support an antisemitic politician, even if they do not currently register a high level of prejudice. Typical responses from some of those "indifferents" who were low on the scale of antisemitic attitudes were: "I don't think [his antisemitism] would influence me to vote one way or another," and, "If I liked the man, I'd vote for him anyway."

During the course of possibly the most dangerous antsemitic movement in America's history, that of Father Charles Coughlin in the 1930s, it was once determined that the attitudes of his followers were not significantly more antisemitic than those of the population which spurned him. Among other things, he promised an end to poverty in the midst of the Depression, and therefore many "indifferents" were willing to accept his antisemitism.

Without benefit of such survey illustrations, or the concept of "indifferents," many Jews intuit from their historical experience that there is a body of Americans who could rather easily be swayed by circumstances toward a more dangerous direction, even if they do not seem hostile today. That is the basis of the foreboding about the future displayed by so many Jews who are happy enough with the present.

And that is why so many Jews carefully scrutinize the scene for signs that those adverse circumstances are around the corner. It is this "around-the-corner" context in which they ask: If things are so good, why are they so bad? What about the skinheads, the general violence, the reported negative feelings of black Americans, a continued if diminished reservoir of stereotypes, hostility toward Israel? Are these not symptoms of a possible reversal?

THE PROBABILITY OF CONTINUED PROGRESS

The specific symptom around which there is probably the most misplaced concern is that of stepped-up vandalism, harassment, and violence against Jews and Jewish institutions. In 1992, for example, the Anti-Defamation League reported more than 1,700 antisemitic incidents. About half of them were acts of harassment, mostly personal, and about half were acts of physical vandalism, including twenty-eight incidents described as "particularly serious": arson, cemetery desecrations, and one bombing. There are also the occasional reports of the arrest of small, organized, and well-armed groups which have committed or intended to commit acts of violence against Jews as well as blacks, gays, and other traditional targets of bigotry. These manifestations have fluctuated from year to year, but have been apparently increasingly reported in recent years. They are not insignificant, but the nature of their significance is often mistaken.

First of all, there are—and probably will be for the indefinite future—the hard-core antisemites, those who are ready and willing to act on their highly prejudiced beliefs. It is obviously not a population which can be quantified with any accuracy. If one were to estimate the number engaged in the various acts reported by the Anti-Defamation League, then count all the members of ideologically bigoted organizations in America—such as the

KKK, the worst of the skinhead gangs, Aryan Nations, and the various neo-Nazi groups—and if one were to add the subscribers of all the ideologically bigoted periodicals, such as the Liberty Lobby's *Spotlight*, the total would be in the thousands, a fraction of 1 percent of the population. Or one might count, as in some state of readiness, those who are willing to anonymously admit on surveys that they would vote for antisemites and against candidates supported by Jewish organizations, and that they are indeed anti-Jewish and have reason to dislike Jews. That figure consistently comes to about 5 percent.

However, the fractional nature of that population is not as significant as the extent to which they are countercultural. They are clearly dangerous to the health and safety of their specific targets, and require society's avid attention on that account. But notably powerless in other terms, they do not have persuasive access to the mainstream. All law-enforcement agencies hunt them down when they commit overt acts; all public officials excoriate them, as do the mainstream media and authority figures in the civic and religious realms. If a mass movement of bigotry were to develop, it would undoubtedly include these people, but it would not stem from them or be led by them.

The perpetrators of the random and covert acts of vandalism and terrorism reported by the Anti-Defamation League are mostly young people. Many of them are not technically "hard-core" because their behavior is not always ideologically based, as it more often is in the organized groups. They are often young "indifferents," amoral, who act out their social pathology opportunistically against churches, synagogues, and other such institutions exactly because such behavior is so dramatically countercultural, and will predictably arouse social outrage.

It is not contradictory that the level of prejudice is gradually diminishing, at the same time that acts of violence against Jews and other ethnic targets are increasing. It is not that the proportion of antisemites is increasing, but that those who are antisemitic—and many of those who are indifferent but alienated—are more willing to express themselves in violent ways. But that phenomenon carries a certain significance of its own, more portentous than the immediate effect of the acts themselves.

The apparently increasing pattern of violence and uninhibited license in the society is not primarily or substantially directed against Jews. Other ethnic groups, homosexuals, and the general public are much more often targeted. Most of that behavior does not fall within the pathology of bigotry at all, much less hard-core antisemitism. Even when interethnic hostility breaks out as a result of conventional economic competition, Jews are less and less often the target of choice. When a Hispanic member of the city council of San Jose created a commotion in 1993 by blaming other ethnic groups for the disadvantaged position of Hispanics, she focused exclusively—and nastily—on Asians, African-Americans, and homosexuals. The culture of antisemitism apparently no longer applied, as once it would have.

Nevertheless, any serious breakdown of civility, of law and order, of restraint against violence, understandably raises the level of Jewish foreboding. The Jews' historical experience tells them that when the factor of inhibition unravels for society in general, it can unravel, somehow, for them as well.

"Black antisemitism" is a specific symptom of reversibility for many Jews. Black Americans were once prevalently seen as friendly allies of Jews in the struggle against bigotry. But there have been signs of an increasing hostility among blacks toward Jews. That hostility begins among a section of radical, elite, and intellectual blacks who, in classic style, have adopted various versions of Jewish conspiracy as the source of their discontent. Jews are blamed for much of the slave trade. Jewish doctors are accused of deliberately spreading AIDS among blacks. Israel is depicted as the imperialist oppressor of the Third World Palestinians.

Rank-and-file African-Americans have been only marginally affected by this kind of ideology, and their anger is no longer exacerbated by the existence of Jewish merchants and landlords. In the black ghetto riots and disturbances of recent years, Koreans and other Asians have been typical targets, not Jews. Nevertheless, the fulminations of the black antisemitic ideologues are disturbing, especially when they are broadcast by professors at leading universities. Surveys of black attitudes toward Jews indicate that while antisemitism decreases for black college graduates, it does not decrease as rapidly as it does for white college graduates.

The Jewish concern with this phenomenon is understandable

but sometimes exaggerated. After all, blacks are still the most embattled and powerless group in the society. They are not in a position to become part of a mass antisemitic movement, which would inevitably be an anti-black movement as well.

Some university settings and black Muslims aside, a new mainstream black leadership has developed which does not participate in the anti-Jewish demagoguery. The substantial black congressional caucus has been signally friendly to Israel and to the American Jewish communities with which they are politically related. The Jewish concern with evidence of black antisemitism is partly the bruising of a lover scorned. But there is undoubtedly a more cogent reaction, related to the riots, crime, and violence emanating from the desperate urban ghettos. They are symptoms of the kind of generally unrestrained society which generally frightens Jews.

Israel is the focus of another concern about the potential reversal of American Jewish security. As reported, the majority of American Jews do not believe that antisemitism in the current American economic or political scene is a serious problem, but they do express concern about vandalism, as a symptom of possible reversibility, and about Israel-connected hostility. In the first place, there is the probability that the Middle East will be the most potent site of antisemitism in the world. Even if a successful "peace process" develops between Israel and some of its Arab neighbors, the interethnic and interreligious hostility which has been generated in the course of the political struggles in the Middle East will not soon dissipate, especially as fanned by certain fundamentalist forces in the area. It is not likely that *this* reservoir of antisemitism—or that which still remains in Eastern or Western Europe—will be transmitted to the United States in the way that antisemitism was transmitted from Germany during the Nazi period. But its existence will be of fraternal concern for American Jews and will maintain an edge to their foreboding.

However, the main Israel-connected concern, as it touches on American Jewish security, is related to American-Israeli relations. American Jewry has been highly visible—and successful, despite occasional frictions—in its efforts to maintain the crucial American support of Israel. In many surveys since 1967, a quarter to a third of the American public has expressed the belief that American Jews are more loyal to Israel than to the United States. As long as Israel has remained the darling of the American public, as compared with the Arabs, that American belief has clearly not spurred hostility to the Jews because of their activity on behalf of Israel.

But many Jews have had some foreboding about the possible reversal of American feelings about Israel. A majority of Jews have tended to agree with the proposition that Americans could not be counted on for support of Israel "in a crunch." Indeed, if there were a rupture of American-Israeli relations, there could conceivably be a backlash against American Jews and their activities on behalf of Israel as well.

However, such a rupture is not likely. Even though the end of the Cold War has presumably reduced American concern about Soviet adventurism in the Middle East, it is still an area of significance for American national interest, and Israel is the only stable ally this country has in the area. More than that, Israel is the only "Western" society in the area. The majority of Americans affirm that Israelis are "more like us" than are the Arabs generally. That feeling has been strengthened by increased American animosity toward the anti-American expressions of some fundamentalist forces among the Arabs, and by some terrorist acts in America which have emanated from those forces. A serious rupture between Israel and the United States is not likely.

THE TERMINABILITY OF ANTISEMITISM

In sum, it is not difficult to envision turns of history which could both reignite the dormant pool of prejudice and erode the factors that inhibit an activated state of antisemitic behavior. Certain Israel-related events could have such an evil potential. So could a massive breakdown of moral and legal restraints in America. The possibility that such developments could take place sustains some sense of foreboding. The probability, however, is that no such adverse circumstances are likely to occur in the foreseeable future.

And in that foreseeable future, there will probably be no decrease in the factors which inhibit antisemitic behavior, such as stringent laws, the heterogeneity of the population, and the integration of the Jews—which may create other problems for the Jewish community, but only mitigates the problem of security. The probability is, in short, that the interactive cycle of diminishing antisemitic behavior and a diminishing reservoir of antisemitic attitudes will continue to gradually wind down.

But what of that slightly ominous phrase "in the foreseeable future?" How nervous do we have to be about the status of our Jewish grandchildren, about the occurrence of some event which is not "foreseeable"? No one can be too sanguine about the blind corners of history. But neither should we ignore the effect of *longevity* on cultural matters such as antisemitism.

If the cycle of antisemitic behavior and attitude continues to wind down, if the cultural reservoir of Judeophobia is unused long enough, there is no rational basis for believing that it will not virtually disappear. That would be the point of no return, of irreversibility.

This is not a call for complacency. We are not yet at that point. Even though it is probable that we will arrive there someday, we may never do so, because of unanticipated circumstances. A healthy sense of foreboding is still in order, and the effort must continue to strengthen inhibiting factors of restraint in the society. But whatever its probability, the possibility of antisemitism coming to an end is highly credible, and the process by which it would do so deserves more attention. The significance of positing the terminability of antisemitism is not just a matter of making prophecy—always a dubious enterprise, given the vagaries of history. It is more cogently a matter of clarifying the contemporary nature of antisemitism, and the nature of its most likely antidotes.

·5·
Antisemitism and the Psychology
of Prejudice

MARTIN S. BERGMANN

Martin Bergmann is clinical professor of psychology at
the New York University post-doctoral program in
psychoanalysis and psychotherapy, and training and
supervisory analyst at the New York Freudian Society.
He has published four books, most recently *In the
Shadow of Moloch: The Effect of the Sacrifice of
Children on Western Religion.*

Psychoanalyst Martin S. Bergmann offers a psychological perspective of
antisemitism. We cannot understand antisemitism without understanding
the psychology of the antisemite, says Bergmann. Antisemitism is not just
a social phenomenon; it has deep roots in the antisemite's psyche.
Bergmann blends his analysis of the psychology of the individual with that
of the different forms of antisemitism that have emerged throughout history—culminating with the experience of the past two centuries—in terms
of the social psychological profiles of these forms of anti-Jewish behavior.

With respect to the individual, Bergmann identifies two characteristics
that are determinative and universal in those who express racial prejudice
(including antisemitism): excessive hostility, exacerbated by feelings of inadequacy and perhaps paranoia; and the need to project aggression on others. Summing up psychoanalytically, Bergmann observes, "[The antisemite's] ego boundary is relatively weak and requires the protection of
prejudice in order to maintain it. What is projected are unacceptable and
repudiated parts of the self." And on the role of the state: "The expression of prejudice, and particularly the degree of violence, is dependent on
the authority of the state. [As an example,] with Hitler's rise to power a
paranoid personal antisemitism, nurtured by a tradition of Christian racial-

ism, was transformed into a political weapon with frightening results. . . . The counterproposition, as in the case of the United States, suggests a different reality."

Bergmann's essay moves the thinking about the psychology of antisemitism from an analysis of antisemitism in terms of social forces rather than personality structures and dysfunctions—the "state of the art" in the 1960s and '70s, which was by then moving from an "authoritarian personality" analysis*—back to an analysis of psychodynamics and psychological mechanisms of intolerance.

J.A.C.

THE CULTURAL HISTORY OF ANTISEMITISM

The first antisemite on record is Haman, who appears in the Book of Esther. In Esther 3:8, Haman gives his reasons for wishing to exterminate the Jews:

> Haman said to King Ahasuerus, "There is a certain people scattered abroad and dispersed among the people in all provinces of your kingdom; and their laws are diverse from all people; neither keep they the King's laws. Therefore it is not for the King's profit to suffer them."

In other words, the Jews were "other." Haman adds value to the petition by promising to pay ten thousand talents to the king's treasury if he is given a free hand to exterminate the Jews. We note two arguments employed by Haman: first, that the Jews are different from the other nations, and second, that they are scattered and lack a homeland. Both arguments will repeat themselves in the subsequent history of antisemitism.

Beyond the confines of the Bible, the first appearance of anti-Jewish sentiments took place in Alexandria, the Greek metropolis of Egypt. It was usually taken for granted that citizens of a town should honor the deity of that town. The monotheistic

*See in this regard Theodore Solotaroff and Marshall Sklare, Introduction to *Jews in the Mind of America* by Charles Herbert Stember et al. (New York: Basic Books, 1966).

Jews, and later the Christians, could not participate in such a communal fellowship. Their inability to participate in the ceremonies that united the community made them the target for hostility. Here we encounter for the first time the accusation that Jews kidnap men, fatten them, and offer them for sacrifice. This accusation is of particular interest, as I have shown in *In the Shadow of Moloch*, because Jews were the first to repudiate human sacrifice at a time when children were still sacrificed to various deities.

By an interesting psychological process, those who instituted the abolition of human sacrifices were accused throughout the ages of still practicing such sacrifice. What was projected on the Jews were cannibalistic impulses that found expression in human sacrifices. Tacitus, the Roman historian who described the victory of the Roman emperor Titus over the Jews and the destruction of the Temple in Jerusalem, portrays the Jews in ways that we today would characterize as antisemitic:

> The Jews are perverse and disgusting. They sit apart, eat apart, and sleep apart, and though singularly lusty, they abstain from intercourse with foreign women, but among themselves, nothing is unlawful. They have adopted circumcision as a mark of difference from other nations. They are honest among themselves, and compassionate, but show hatred for the rest of mankind. . . . Things sacred to us have no sanctity for them and they allow what is forbidden.[1]

Interestingly enough, Tacitus also adds that it was a crime among the Jews to kill any newborn infant. When we read Tacitus in the light of current psychological understanding, we note that his antisemitism is ambivalent, balancing praise with condemnation. In ancient Rome, the Jewish religion was a *religio licita*, a religion that had official sanction.

CHRISTIAN ANTISEMITISM

Christian antisemitism goes back to the Christian Scriptures, the so-called New Testament. On a religious level, the crucifixion of

Jesus was a necessary act of atonement and, strictly speaking, no one was to blame for it. It demands an internalized sense of guilt equivalent to a depression on the personal level. On a lower level it was not a cosmic necessity but was caused entirely by the wickedness of the Jews, who killed Christ. On an individual level this corresponds to a paranoid projection.

Yosef Haim Yerushalmi has drawn attention to the fact that for some time a theological debate took place within Christianity as to whether to retain the Hebrew Bible—the so-called Old Testament—or discard it and only use the Christian Scriptures ("New Testament").[2] Ultimately, the idea of retaining the "Old Testament" prevailed, probably because it provided Christianity with a prestigious antiquity. When this happened, and the Hebrew Scriptures were reinterpreted as prefiguring the coming of Christ, a sibling rivalry between the Church and the Synagogue developed as to who were God's elect, the Jewish people or the new ecclesia. In the Christian version, the Jews who were once chosen were now rejected because they refused to accept the happy tiding that the Messiah had come. The suffering of the Jews was punishment for their rejection of Christ.

From the twelfth century on, another accusation against the Jews was added, that of ritual murder.[3] It was believed that Jews needed the blood of Christian children for the baking of their unleavened bread during Passover. This accusation represents the projection outward of cannibalistic urges. It is the sacrament of the Eucharist that is mostly responsible for the simulation of such cannibalistic wishes. In John 6:51–55 we read:

I am the living bread which came down from heaven; if any man eat of this bread, he shall live forever; and the bread that I will give is my flesh; which I will give for the life of the world.

The Jews therefore strove among themselves, saying, How can this man give us flesh to eat?

Then Jesus said unto them, Verily, verily, I say unto you except you eat the flesh of the son of man and drink His blood, you have no life in you.

Who so eats my flesh, and drinks my blood, has eternal life; and I will raise him up at the last day.

For my flesh is meat indeed, and my blood is drink indeed.

It is interesting to note that Saint John retained the sense of horror that the Jews felt at the idea that they were to eat flesh and drink blood. The Eucharist is the central mystery of Christianity. It was inevitable that in the unconscious the Eucharist would evoke both cannibalistic wishes and the horror at such wishes. This explains why the cannibalistic wishes were projected on the Jews. Psychoanalysts know that cannibalistic wishes are part of early childhood expressions, both actively in the wish to devour and passively in the wish to be eaten. In further development these wishes undergo repression. At times they survive in the abhorrence of eating meat, or meat in which the blood has not been removed.

The accusation that the Jews killed the Savior resulted in a widespread antisemitism that was part of Christian culture. By contrast, the blood-libel accusation caused violent eruptions in which whole communities were wiped out. Thus, projection of cannibalistic impulses is conducive to the discharge of violent aggression, while the accusation of deicide, which relieves guilt, was seldom the direct cause of pogroms.

RACIAL ANTISEMITISM

Racial antisemitism emerged as a reaction to Jewish emancipation and its corollary development, Jewish assimilation. Closely connected with European Romanticism, this manifestation of antisemitism was opposed to the ethos of the Enlightenment and its idea of liberty and dignity for all. Racial antisemitism was always political in its striving, from the Dreyfus Affair in 1894 to the Nazi rule of Germany beginning in 1933. It was paranoid in nature in the sense that the Jews were described as organizing a world conspiracy ready to take over the world, and otherwise conspiring to undermine the state. It is a testimony to the complexity of social psychology that a person who is not himself clinically paranoid can nevertheless accept an ideology that is clearly paranoid in structure.

This is another example of group behavior, functioning to a significant degree independently of the personal realm. There were of course many adherents of racial antisemitism who were also personally paranoid, but for others the projection of the paranoia on the group may well have served to hold personal paranoia at bay.

With the rise of capitalism and the miseries brought about by industrialization, Jews were accused by economists such as Werner Sombart—who wrote about the role of the Jews in the rise of capitalism—of being responsible for introducing and fostering capitalism for profit. But Jews were also accused of undermining capitalism and promoting communism. Antisemitism became the expression of rage for many of the dislocated and disadvantaged. Clever politicians made good use of this antisemitism, often combining Christian and racial antisemitism into one.

THE PSYCHOLOGY OF ANTISEMITISM

Psychologically speaking, any racial prejudice, including antisemitism, is not of one piece. At least three different types of antisemitism can be differentiated: social, romantic, and persecutory. It is clear that the whole process of socialization that takes place during childhood requires the right to exclude. A kindergarten teacher once introduced the subject of overcoming prejudice, only to have one of the children exclaim, "But then what is the fun of playing?" Almost any gang in any neighborhood, on any street, is formed by excluding certain children. These exclusions may or may not be based on race or religion. They may be attributed to physical powers, size, or good looks.

I noticed the same process at work in the army during basic training. It seemed as if every platoon in the army became a group only by excluding certain members. Those who were excluded had certain characteristics, such as timidity, or exhibited compulsive or "feminine" behavior. As we have noted from numerous examples of previous decades, and of today, social prejudice can take the form of exclusion from clubs, fraternities, and neighborhoods.

It seems as if every group needs a scapegoat. The line of

demarcation between this ubiquitous need to exclude and racial prejudices is not always easy to draw, but it is nonetheless real. The bigot needs his prey, and cannot live without it; at the same time he aims toward the destruction of the object upon whom his aggression was projected, whereas the ordinary type of prejudice is gratified by the mere act of exclusion.

When intermarriage takes place between groups separated by social prejudice, it is usually regarded as a catastrophe to the families involved, and social contact with the offending family may be broken off. In addition to xenophobia—fear of the stranger— there is also the *attraction* to the stranger; traveling in foreign lands is a pleasure, and even the simple act of eating in restaurants of other national and ethnic groups leaves one with the feeling of having been freed from the oppression of one's own group.

The second type of antisemitism, which I call romantic antisemitism, is not common in the United States and therefore requires some explanation. The romantic antisemite feels that the evils of capitalism and the alienation that came with it can be redeemed by a sense of belonging to a community (*Gemeinschaft*). The Jews are seen as incapable of being assimilated into such a community. Jews need not be persecuted, but they should not have access to the cultural life of the nation.

I cite two examples of such antisemites. First, Richard Wagner. Some excerpts from his writings are illustrative:

> Although the peculiarities of the Jewish mode of speaking and singing come out the most glaringly in the commoner class of Jew, who has remained faithful to his father's stock, and although the cultured son of Jewry takes untold pains to strip them off, nevertheless they show an impertinent obstinacy in cleaving to him.

> The Jew has never had an art of his own. . . . He merely listens to the barest surface of our art but not to its life-bestowing inner organism; and through this apathetic listening alone can he trace external similarities—the most external accidents in our musical domain—and art must pass for its very essence.[4]

It so happened that in Wagner's lifetime there were Jewish composers, such as Meyerbeer and Mendelssohn, and the leading poet of the era was Heinrich Heine, a baptized Jew. But facts carry little weight where prejudice prevails. In the case of Heine, Wagner ignored Heine's masterpiece poem "The Lorelei," which every German child learned by heart, and felt that Heine became prominent only because of the relative sterility of poetry in his time.

A second example is Carl Jung, Sigmund Freud's heretical former disciple. In 1914, one year after his break with Freud, Jung developed a psychological theory that made the Jew fundamentally different from the German. In highly pictorial language, Jung describes the blond beast that is incarcerated in every Aryan and that threatens to break out now that Christianity has lost its hold. The Jew, on the other hand, who already had the culture of the ancient world, and who has also taken on the culture of the nations among whom he dwells, is devoid of roots and lacks the chthonic (underworld) quality that endangers the Aryan.

What is beguiling in Jung's statement is that the Jews are described, in flattering terms, as not being endangered by what Freud called the "id" and Nietzsche the "blond beast"; indeed, Jung defended himself against the charge of antisemitism by stating that German psychology finds Jewish psychology no more alien than Indian or Chinese. Just as he is not anti-Indian or anti-Chinese, argues Jung, he is not anti-Jewish. Jung ignored the fact that Freud, his previous mentor, lived and worked within the same orbit of culture. Furthermore, the fact that Indian and Chinese psychology differ from the European does not mean that there is a specific Indian or Chinese psychology. Those who accused Jung of antisemitism were justified, because after Hitler came to power Jung embraced Hitler with enthusiasm.

When Adolf Hitler was twelve years old, he saw his first opera, *Lohengrin.* He was swept away by the cry of the armed men in the final act. "A German sword for the German land! Thus will the power of the Reich be established!" Hitler maintained that "whoever wants to understand National Socialist Germany must know Wagner." We should note that romantic antisemitism can easily pass over into persecutory antisemitism.

Persecutory antisemitism cannot be discussed within the limits of individual psychology. That does not mean that it does not fulfill individual needs for all its participants, but that it can be understood only as a social and political phenomenon. The German character did not change substantially in 1933 when Hitler came to power. Nor did the character of the average Austrian change in 1938, the year of the Anschluss when he annexed Austria. Such changes cannot be explained in terms of individual psychology.

In his play *The Bacchae* the Greek dramatist Euripides had already, about 500 B.C.E., shown that individuals forming a crowd can become intoxicated, and in a frenzy do things that they would never allow themselves to do as individuals. In the nineteenth century the French sociologist Gustave Le Bon systematically studied the behavior of mobs that gathered during the French Revolution.[5] Le Bon noted that, as a member of a mob, a person has the possibility of losing his individual sense of discernment and will cast aside the internalized structure of prohibition that he carries with him. Freud added the idea that only relatively few people have an internalized moral structure, or "superego," which remains entrenched regardless of changes in conditions. Such people are remarkably independent of outer authority. Martin Luther's statement "Here I stand and I can do no other" represents such an independence of the moral point of view. The vast majority of people, however, are capable of projecting the moral authority outward on a leader, and when this leader frees them from the usual moral restraints, they follow him.

There are limits to the powers that even leaders can exercise. The pogrom sanctioned by the German government on the night of November 9, 1938—Kristallnacht—was visible to the entire world. This was a highly organized pogrom in which 267 synagogues were burned or razed, 7,500 Jewish businesses were destroyed, and 30,000 Jewish persons were deported to concentration camps.[6] The German government felt confident that this degree of antisemitism would be tolerated with only token opposition.

However, when it came to the so-called Final Solution, when Hitler decided on the systematic elimination of all Jews under his domination through mass killing in death camps, that decision was not shared with the German population and was kept secret. It is evident that Hitler did not feel that this degree of antisemitism would be embraced by Germany, even after years of National Socialist propaganda.

The reader will note that up to this point I have stressed a discharge theory of aggression; that is, the individual unburdens himself or herself to the extent to which he or she can project aggression outward. For example, after a lynching a mob feels exhilarated. A similar sense of exhilaration has been reported following the mass murders that have taken place in the former Yugoslavia.

However, the image of the concentration camp *Kommandant* who tortures and kills his victims during the daytime and returns home to a loving wife and children and listens to a Wagner opera is a fictional image. In our work with the children of Nazis, my colleagues and I have discovered that devoted Nazis were often very harsh and aggressive toward their own children, causing their children to identify themselves with the Jews.[7]

When Adolf Eichmann was brought to trial the world was horrified by what Hannah Arendt termed "the banality of evil."[8] The total absence of overt sadism in Eichmann was in a way more frightening than an outspoken sadist displaying emotions; Eichmann seemed to have none. The cruel and calculating way in which Eichmann sent millions to their deaths, as though he were shipping cattle across state borders, was chilling. It evoked the image of a universe in which all emotions of love and hate have been eliminated, and replaced by implementing the instruction of the evil ideal that Hitler represented. It will be recalled that, in his defense, Eichmann reiterated that he was merely obeying orders. Any sign of independent thinking had been eliminated.

In his book on the Nazi doctors, Robert Lifton illustrated another aspect of these issues.[9] Nazi doctors were trained within the medical ethos of healing and caring; they had taken the Oath of Hippocrates, to use their medical skills on behalf of their patients. But during the Nazi era, doctors used their medical knowledge to decide who should live and who should die, and for performing experiments of no medical value on death-camp inmates.

Lifton has stressed another psychological mechanism that made this activity possible: the capacity to split oneself into two parts. When a division occurs, two parts within a person do not communicate with each other. The two parts are so divided that they can coexist simultaneously. This state can be better maintained when the unacceptable or repudiated portion is projected. Henry Dicks, a noted English scholar in the field of family relationships, has demonstrated that such splitting and repudiation often take place in states of marital discord. Once feelings of remorse or guilt arise, this division mechanism loses its power to operate.[10]

Both projection and splitting are psychological mechanisms that, to be effective, must remain unconscious. Whatever reasons that are given for the persecution have the status of rationalization.

Rationalization takes place when the person has no way of knowing the unconscious reasons for what he or she is doing but must find ways of justifying such actions to himself or herself. It is on this level that we find the myth of prejudice. Strictly speaking, it is a misnomer to refer to racial prejudice when there are real reasons of danger or competition between two groups which may be contending, for example, for the same land. Psychologically speaking, this is the realm of group conflict. Wars, while they last, create their own mythology in defense of aggression. We must distinguish between aggression that arises from unconscious motives, and call that racial prejudice; and differentiate this prejudice from conscious competition between social groups.

The term "prejudice" derives from the Latin *prae judicium*. It refers to a judge who has already reached the verdict, indeed before the trial has begun. We all recall the cry in *Alice in Wonderland*, "Verdict first, trial later." If I am right in my suggestion that prejudice is always based on unconscious needs, it follows that it is futile to attempt to refute prejudice in individuals. Such refutations may soothe the wounds of the injured and affect the as-yet uncommitted observer, but they are powerless against a person for whom these prejudices have become a necessary mode of psychological functioning.*

Experienced psychotherapists know better than to try by argument to convince a person who suffers from delusion that he or

---

*Indeed, a number of authors have cited data supportive of Bergmann's assertion that "attitudes don't change." (Editor's note)

she is wrong. Freud suggested that at this point it is far more effective to search for the personal and biographical kernel of truth that is responsible for the emergence of the prejudices than to try to refute these prejudices by logical means. Such a search usually leads to the conclusion that the hostility was originally directed either against the self when, traumatically, one's belief in one's own omnipotence or power suffered a defeat, or that the aggression was originally aimed at the parent or other family members. When there is hostility toward a person upon whom one is dependent or whom one loves, it is psychologically important to deflect the hostility outside the family.

To give examples, during the Kristallnacht pogrom, an eye-witness reported:

> In Baden-Baden the Jewish men were marched through the city, then made to walk over prayer shawls, singing the "Horst Wessel Lied" twice.

In present-day Germany one often hears that those who have immigrated to that country leave their excreta in parks or upon lawns, thus befouling the German landscape. Dr. Arthur Flehinger reports that he was forced to read Hitler's *Mein Kampf* aloud while being struck on the back of his neck:

> During the lull we all had to troop out into the courtyard to relieve ourselves. We were not permitted to use the WCs; we had to face the synagogue while being kicked from behind.[11]

The Jews were universally described as smelly or dirty. Indeed, once incarcerated, the victims were denied access to baths and toilets so that the accusation became a reality, further facilitating the discharge of aggression. The person who holds the prejudice usually prides himself as being clean, and the object of prejudice as dirty. It is not immediately self-evident why this differentiation should be so crucial, and yet it seems to be a factor in every kind of prejudice. Prejudice against the homeless by many in present-day America constitutes a dramatic example, and is analogous to, this "clean-dirty" prejudice.

Psychologists have discovered that many mothers are unduly strict during the period of toilet training. The infant does not as yet have a disdainful attitude toward his feces and feels injured when they are flushed, believing that a precious part of himself has been lost and, often, that he himself could suffer a similar fate. This phase in the infant's development is often the first time the baby feels that the mother asks him to do something with which he does not wish to comply. Toilet training breaks the harmony that once prevailed between mother and baby. After the toilet battle is over, the clean child develops a reaction formation against the time when he was still dirty. The toilet-trained child despises and hates the younger sibling who has not yet gone through this process. It is this hatred that is projected in racial prejudice. In an adult, this whole process undergoes repression and is no longer available to conscious memory.

The other—almost as ubiquitous—accusation found in racial prejudice is of unbridled sexual passion. The object of prejudice is described as insatiable in his sexual appetites, ready to rape or seduce by whatever available means any woman he can find. He should never be trusted to be alone with a woman. Developmentally speaking, this accusation comes later than the one based on toilet training, but it nevertheless belongs to an early phase of development. It takes time for all of us to mature and to realize that our sexual needs are best met within a mutually loving relationship. In an earlier stage, we view sexual wishes as being entirely at the service of our gratification, without any regard for other persons. These wishes undergo repression. Here too, either what has been repressed or what could not be repressed but was unacceptable to the higher layers of the mind and caused discomfort, is projected onto the object of the prejudice.

The fact that prejudice everywhere has a general characteristic can tempt us to believe that it fulfills the same function for every individual; indeed, tasks of social psychologists would be much easier if we could point to such a general characteristic. But such generalizations prove useless when we get to know the person on a personal or deeper level. It is not possible without painstaking analysis to find who the real object of the prejudice stands for in the unconscious. The object of the hatred can be a sibling with whom the rivalry was intense, a father who was hated, or even a mother. It can come from different stages in personal development. From the perspective of the individual, every prejudice has its own biographical history.

Just how complex prejudice can be becomes clear in an example taken from Eva Fogelman's work on Christian rescuers of Jews during the Holocaust. A Polish priest, Father Falkowski, was a devout Catholic, one who believed that the Jews killed Christ. He also believed that the Jews were rightly punished by the Germans for their sins. But in spite of these prejudices, Falkowski became a rescuer of a Jew who escaped deportation to the Treblinka death camp.[12] How does one reconcile holding a prejudice, and treating someone from the hated group, who happens to be in need, humanely, indeed risking one's life for such a person?

To what extent is the minority group itself responsible for the prejudice against it? Strictly speaking, if the minority is really responsible for its destiny, we cannot speak of prejudice. But this is rarely the case. Prejudice implies that we do not see the person as an individual but only as a member of a group, We attribute to that person the characteristics that we assume are possessed by the group. Where the minority group is insecure, and the leaders of the group live on the margin between the minority and the majority, a special psychology of marginality develops. Persons living on the margin have no sure way of knowing when the hostility is directed toward them as members of a minority.

For example, it is well known that the German Jews succumbed to the illusion that the specific Jewish characteristics of the recent immigrants from Eastern Europe caused antisemitism, and that it would disappear once Jews resembled in appearance, speech, and culture their German neighbors. It therefore came as a shock to those Jews to realize that the assimilated Jew was no less abhorrent to the antisemite than the one who retained the speech and the appearance of the Jew still living in a ghetto.

In summary, I have argued that only two characteristics seem ubiquitous in anyone who is given to strong racial prejudices: excessive hostility, and a need as well as a capacity to project this aggression on other groups. In addition, such persons suffer from feelings of inadequacy and from the feeling that their own personal borders, psychologically speaking, are easily invaded by others. In psychoanalytic language, their ego boundary is relatively weak and requires the protection of prejudice in order to maintain it. What is projected are unacceptable and repudiated parts of the self. The expression of the prejudice, and particularly the degree of violence, is dependent on the authority of the state. When government sanctions antisemitism, antisemitism rises sharply. The counterproposition, as in the case of the United States, suggests a different reality.

For nearly two thousand years the dominant Christian society attempted to channel the nearly universal search for a scapegoat into a hatred for the Jews. On its highest level the Church recognized that the death of Christ was a theological necessity for which no one is to blame; but on a popular level the Jews, once chosen by God and now rejected, were blamed for deicide. Jews were segregated and even murdered.

But there was ambivalence as well. Thus the Jews were to be preserved until their final conversion to the "true faith." The French and American revolutions liberated the Jews and gave them equal rights. In part as a reaction against these developments, a new and virulent secular antisemitism emerged. And with Hitler's rise to power a paranoid personal antisemitism, nurtured by a tradition of Christian antisemitism and European racism, was transformed into a political weapon, with frightful results. Our society has not as yet found ways of diminishing the need for prejudice, nor have we found effective ways of preventing paranoid leaders from gaining political power.

NOTES

1. Tacitus, *Histories: Fifth Book* (Encyclopaedia Britannica, 1952).

2. Y. H. Yerushalmi, *Freud's Moses: Judaism Terminable and Interminable* (New Haven: Yale University Press, 1991).

3. See R. Po-chia Hsia, *The Myth of Ritual Murder: Jews and Magic in Reformation Germany* (New Haven: Yale University Press, 1988).

4. A. Goldman and E. Sprinchern, eds. *Jews in Music* (1964), pp. 51–54.

5. Freud described Le Bon's ideas in chapter 2 of his *Group Psychology and the Analysis of the Ego* (Standard Edition, vol. 18, 1921).

6. See "The Kristallnacht as a Public Degradation Ritual," *The Leo Baeck Institute Yearbook*, no. 32 (1987).

7. Martin S. Bergmann and Milton Jucovy, eds., *Generations of the Holocaust* (New York: Columbia University Press, 1990).

8. Hannah Arendt, *Eichmann in Jerusalem: A Report on the Banality of Evil* (New York: The Viking Press, 1963).

9. Robert J. Lifton, *The Nazi Doctors: Medical Killing and the Psychology of Genocide* (New York: Basic Books, 1986).

10. Henry V. Dicks, *Marital Tensions: Clinical Studies Toward a Psychological Theory of Interaction* (New York: Basic Books, 1967).

11. Quoted in Peter Lowenberg, "The Kristallnacht as a Public Degradation Ritual," *The Leo Baeck Institute Yearbook*, no. 32 (1987).

12. Eva Fogelman, *Conscience and Courage: Rescuers of Jews During the Holocaust* (New York: Doubleday, 1994), pp. 175–176.

PART THREE

MANIFESTATIONS OF ANTISEMITISM: ASSESSMENTS AND EVALUATIONS

·6·
American Jews, Israel, and the
Psychological Role of Antisemitism

BARRY RUBIN

Barry Rubin is a professor at the Hebrew University,
Jerusalem, and a senior fellow at its Harry S. Truman
Institute and at the University of Haifa's Jewish-Arab
Center. He is the author of twelve books on politics
and international affairs, including a history of Jewish
assimilation, *Assimilation and Its Discontents,* and
Israel-Arab Reader.

Political scientist Barry Rubin goes well beyond a mere analysis of the complicated relationship between American Jewry and the State of Israel.
Rubin's thesis is straightforward: in the 1990s, antisemitism is more
important in terms of how it affects and indeed shapes the *psychology* of
Jews, and hence Jews' responses to issues, than in its effect on Jews
themselves. Rubin uses the Arab-Israeli conflict as a foil for his views, and
his essay richly details many aspects of the conflict and of the Israeli-Ameri-
can relationship in terms of the ways in which these issues implicate how
American Jews view antisemitism.

But Rubin's discussion of Israel points to a more basic set of judgments. He suggests that, as Jews become either "normalized" in a Jewish state, or fully assimilated elsewhere (as in America), they are "pulled
in the opposite directions of greater self-affirmation or disintegration." In
this atmosphere, antisemitism is often used as a vehicle for Jewish solidarity. Not good, asserts Rubin. "Antisemitism was not a key to Jewishness but merely an obstacle to living it. The end of effective antisemitism
and acquisition of equality [evidenced, according to Rubin, in late-twentieth-
century America] raises far more starkly the old choice of using this freedom to enhance a Jewish civilization, or to escape from it."

Implicit in Barry Rubin's analysis—as in those of a number of authors in this volume—is the question of the counteraction of antisemitism as "a cornerstone of Jewish identity and activity," particularly with respect to Jewish communal agencies. Rubin's view is clearly a skeptical one.*

J.A.C.

The starting point for any honest discussion of antisemitism today is the phenomenon's unimportance. Never before, at least since the time Christianity seized power over the Roman Empire, has antisemitism been less significant than at present. One can count the number of skinheads, anti-Jewish groups in post-Soviet Eastern Europe, synagogue desecrations, or articles denying the Holocaust, but however distressing the continued existence of this scourge may be, its quantity is still minor and the significance on Western society and the lives of Jews even less.

Antisemitism has also been an insignificant factor in shaping American attitudes or U.S. policy on Israel or toward American Jews. When there was hostility expressed toward the Jewish state, it came about as the result of other issues: perceptions of the Middle East, definitions of U.S. interest, sympathy for the Arabs, or bilateral political friction. Some additional relevant factors, discussed below, concern the debate among Jews about their own identity, and the reaction to an era of pro-Jewish sentiment that enhanced Israel's image in American public opinion and thus aided Israel in the public-policy arena.

Antisemitism is an eternal phenomenon. But a number of forces make this issue far less relevant in the lives of Jews or in the world's politics and thought. These forces include Israel's creation, antisemitism's manifest horrible costs in the Shoah (the Holocaust), successful Jewish assimilation, huge population movements, the triumph of pluralism and democracy in the West, and the discrediting of anti-Jewish doctrines. A strong anti-antisemitism factor exists in contemporary American ideology and political life that never existed in pre-1945 Europe. In short,

---

*Compare in this regard the case that Abraham Foxman makes for a strong Jewish organizational response to antisemitism in chapter 15, "Antisemitism in America: A View from the 'Defense' Agencies."

despite antisemitism's huge historic significance, its contemporary role is far smaller. Most important, the expectation of antisemitism has more effect on the behavior and psychological insecurity of American Jews than it has practical effect on their lives or physical security.

Within the context of the American political debate, U.S. Middle East policy, or U.S.-Israel relations, not only is antisemitism marginal but its very expression makes one marginal. There are at least four more significant factors relating to antagonism toward Israel which are not explained by antisemitism:

- A debate among Jews on their own self-definition and attitudes on Israel, including powerful ideas developed during the assimilation process precisely to deny that Jews were a nation.
- Uncertainty by non-Jews on Israel's legitimacy, including its role in Jewish history, religion, or identity.
- What may be called anti-philosemitism, the view that pro-Israel factors had become too dominant in U.S. policymaking and public discourse.
- The notion that U.S. support for Israel endangered its strategic and economic interests in the Arab world.

CHANGES IN THE INERADICABLE:
THE MUTATIONS OF ANTISEMITISM

In 1898 Theodor Herzl, the founder of modern-day Zionism, wrote American Jews warning them of antisemitism's endurance and variability: "On iron rails men and goods speed across continents, great steamships hasten over the oceans of the world, in a single hour we receive news reports of events in places [once considered] inconceivably great distances. But one thing only is still as it was when the Turks conquered Byzantium, when Columbus set sail . . . when men rumbled over the highway in stagecoaches": the plight of our people. Antisemitism continued under new slogans "not only in the backward countries . . . but also in those that are called civilized. A dream, an illusion it was for us to believe that antisemitism would disappear."[1]

The "rational" basis to antisemitism, according to Zionist theory, was that the Jews were, in fact, different. Herzl wrote, "The nations in whose midst Jews live are all, either covertly or openly, antisemitic." The more Jews living in any country, the more intensive would be the majority's antagonism due to fear, mistrust, competition, and jealousy. In political terms, Jews were attacked by the most diverse, warring camps: capitalists saw them as revolutionaries; socialists portrayed them as plutocrats. The best way to deal with this problem was to acknowledge differences and explain them as equivalent to the contrasts among all nations rather than through wild notions of Jewish religious heresy, conspiracy, or racial inferiority.

Long before Israel's reestablishment, regardless of whether Jews were portrayed as people, religion, or race, their failure to accept totally dominant social norms opened them to the accusation of a dual loyalty. Count Clermont-Tonnerre told the French Revolution's assembly, "It is intolerable that the Jews should become a separate political formation or class in the country. . . . The existence of a nation within a nation is unacceptable to our country."[2]

This attitude would be eradicated neither by signs of Jewish virtue and willingness to assimilate nor by education or revolutionary change. But it could be altered by a change in the Jewish situation—the creation of the State of Israel, by a change in the status of Jews and of their self-image—fostering this hatred and making possible that plight. Establishing a national state for those who wished to live there would give the Jews equal standing with other peoples. Both the state and national movement would rebuild the character and fortunes of the Jewish people, gaining new respect for them as independent, hard working, and productive.

Assimilationist theory, in contrast, preferred to downplay or reduce any such distinctions. It argued that Jews were not a nation and eliminated references of a return to Zionism (Reform Judaism), or said that this was a purely Messianic task (Orthodox Judaism), or urged that Jews join with other downtrodden people to change the world through revolution (Marxists and other radicals) or through reform (liberalism). A large portion of the Jewish people put their energy into such individual solutions as conversion, intermarriage, a quiet drifting away from the community, or becoming patriots of the country and culture where they lived. The constant claim that Zionism and Israel's revival contradicted their identity and beliefs, that Jews are a religion and not a people, is a legacy continuing to shape the thinking of Jews and non-Jews alike.[3]

In practice, these dichotomies could be resolved by supporting Israel without the theoretical underpinning supplied by a Zionist view of the Jewish question. This strategy was remarkably effective, but also had some deficiencies, in that the urge toward continuity and development of the community might have been weakened. The nineteenth-century Jewish essayist Ahad Ha-Am was prophetic on how this would happen: "The very existence of the Jewish state will raise the prestige of those who remain in exile." It would give them self-esteem, something to work for, and the need for separate organizations.[4]

Yet by being advocates for other Jews' achievements, trying to battle or persuade other non-Jews, "those who remain in exile" became even more defensive and preoccupied with the outside world. They would continue to reap the material rewards of the fleshpots, but would participate only voyeuristically in the construction of a new Jewish psychology and civilization.

Meanwhile, antisemitism kept up with changes in Western society. The old hatred of Jews on religious grounds was put onto a racial basis, the ideology furnishing a foundation for the Nazis. These two stages corresponded to extremely different situations in relations between Jews and the larger society. When Jews retained their traditional practices and stood apart from a majority defining itself as Christian, they too were seen as a religion. As Jews began to assimilate while still retaining—subjectively, stylistically, or at least in the majority's eyes—distinctiveness, they were identified as a nonreligious, nonnational group, that is, as a "race," in that era's terminology.

Paradoxically, Israel's creation removed much of antisemitism's ability to hurt Jews while also giving it new material on a theoretical level in its new, postracial stage. If Jews were intent on complete assimilation or were only a religion—not a people—they did not need a state any more than such nonnational groups as "Christians" or "whites." Consequently, rather than Jews being depicted as an inferior race, Zionism could be portrayed by some antisemites as a form of racism rather than a type of nationalism.

Yet this rhetoric was far less important than the fact that the normalization wrought by Israel's creation meant that Jews could be treated in practice like other people, bringing Jews more safety, respect, and self-respect even when it did not win them popularity. "All we want is to be allowed to be ourselves on an equal basis with other peoples," explained Herzl. In this context, any antagonisic attitude toward Jews had three new features:

First, it partook far less of antisemitism, just as any criticism of Nigeria or China—or their inhabitants—was not necessarily a form of racism. Antisemitism had always been used to attack Jews in a situation where they were not engaging in any conflict. Jews never sought to undermine the Catholic Church or the "Aryan race." Now, however, Jews once again functioned as a nation and were involved in real battles. The Canaanites, Philistines, Babylonians, Assyrians, Greeks, and Romans all fought the ancient Jews and no doubt hated them. But this did not make "antisemitism" a meaningful issue in those ancient days.

Second, the new situation—the creation of the Jewish state—permitted non-Jews—or even Jews living in the Diaspora—to distinguish between "Jews" and "Israelis." As a largely successful effort to revitalize the Jewish people and by offering an identity inhibiting total assimilation, Israel posed a positive danger to powerful forces in the psyche of Diaspora Jews. Many had always sought protection by proving their detachment from any particular link or loyalty to other Jews. The French Jewish intellectual Bernard Lazare, disgusted by the cowardice of his community toward defending Captain Dreyfus, said of compatriots: "They are not content with being more jingoist than the native Frenchmen; like all emancipated Jews everywhere, they have also of their own volition broken all ties of solidarity" with their fellows abroad or who were recent immigrants.[5]

Third, it became possible to distinguish between antisemitism, a hatred of Jews and a desire to do them harm, and anti-Zionism, opposition to Israel's existence and a desire to hurt or destroy it. One could hate some Jews—Israelis and even their foreign Jewish supporters—without having to dispute Judaism or

Jews as such. Since the vast majority of Jews supported Israel's existence and security, however, this objectively puts such people in conflict with the wishes of the overwhelming majority. Anti-Zionism struck directly against one-third of all Jews and indirectly at almost all the rest. Thus, there was a real overlap between the two categories.

At the same time, though, these two spheres of antagonism can also be separated. A large element of the problem is that Jews and the world did not completely catch up to the new situation. Judaism and the Jews existed for 1,900 years without Israel, albeit with a strong emphasis on the importance of its eventual reestablishment. Many Jews have—for political, personal, philosophical, and even theological reasons—been anti-Zionist. Reform Jewish and ultra-Orthodox interpretations of Judaism, for example, have seen Israel as unnecessary or even positively detrimental, though both have steadily moved toward acceptance. Marxist and assimilationist Jews took similar positions, albeit from a standpoint of leaving Jewish ranks. Thus, while antisemitism and anti-Zionism overlap, they do not coincide completely.[6]

THE AFTERLIFE OF A DEFEATED ANTISEMITISM

Not only was a preoccupation with antisemitism a product of history (at a time when many still remembered the Shoah—the Holocaust—not to mention those who experienced it firsthand) but it was also the basis for the Jewish self-image of many—especially the most assimilated—as a "victim" people, as memory of oppression remained after a sense of community, customs, or ideas had vanished.

Being a victim, however, is not a status in which one revels but a view of self that can be rejected as quickly as possible, especially since being a Jew is one of the few victim states—in contrast to race and gender—which can be shed voluntarily. The history of assimilation begins with Jews first defining the situation of being a Jew as unattractive, then leaving the Jewish fold in huge numbers. And one of the most enduring forms of victimization is the obsession with defining one's present or past form as being victimized.

When Jay Leno was chosen to succeed the legendary Johnny Carson as host of *The Tonight Show*, he remarked that people in television told him that the job would probably never go "to a Jewish guy. The show is too mainstream for that."[7] But most of the people expressing this view were not antisemites but Jews who turned their erroneous belief that the masses would refuse to accept a Jew as late-night television's king into a self-fulfilling prophecy.

They should have considered the case of popular comedian Roseanne Barr, who became the closest thing to a national pariah after mangling "The Star-Spangled Banner" at a 1990 baseball game, then responding to boos by grabbing her crotch and spitting at fans. President Bush said, "It's disgraceful." ABC-TV, which aired her *Roseanne* program, issued a statement that Barr "meant no disrespect for the national anthem." Barr herself refused to apologize. But the fact that she was Jewish was never mentioned by those who accused her of unpatriotic behavior.[8]

At the opposite end of the spectrum, in June 1991 the Simon Weisenthal Center held a $50,000-a-table dinner to give an award to movie star Arnold Schwarzenegger, who reportedly contributed $5 million to build its Museum of Tolerance. Participants included Jewish executives heading virtually every movie studio, including Disney, whose late founder refused even to hire Jews. The Austrian-born actor's father may have been a Nazi party member and he himself a friend of Kurt Waldheim, Austria's ex-Nazi president. But "Arnold's very big right now, and everybody wants to work with him," a guest said. "Besides, this is Hollywood, and these guys would hire Hitler if it meant making money."[9] By the same token, though, European antisemites wanting to work in the film industry would have to accept Jewish authority there. Still, when Neal Gabler wrote his book on the old moguls—subtitled *How the Jews Invented Hollywood*—people in that same town were insecure enough to warn that the book would encourage antisemitism.

Even the worst-case nightmare scenarios, the conviction of Jonathan Pollard of spying for Israel and of Jewish brokers for manipulating Wall Street deals in the 1980s, had similarly little effect. In short, American Jews had gained tremendous cultural and intellectual power while evincing toward their own identity a mixture of self-assertion and fear of persecution and discrimination. Antisemitism's virtual absence changed the situation more than it did their thinking. In contrast to Europe, they were far better off, but a Hollywood-style happy ending merely made complete assimilation more likely. Indeed, by far the entertainment industry's most common theme about Jews—the romance of intermarriage—showed the intersection between disappearing antisemitism and disappearing Jews.

Of course, the fact that Jews felt comfortable with American life and their fair treatment by it were relatively recent phenomena. In 1922, Professor Harry Wolfson told his Harvard Jewish students—whose admission had been subject to quotas—that being Jewish was like being born blind, deaf, or lame, to be "deprived of many social goods and advantages." He urged them to "submit to fate" rather than "foolishly struggle against it" because "there are certain problems of life for which no solution is possible." As late as 1939, the American Jewish literary critic Ludwig Lewisohn could write, "For our numbers we have contributed singularly little to American literature."[10]

The great outpouring of creativity and success after 1945 came from a native-born generation torn between sentimental memory and fierce rejection of its background and the petit bourgeois banality its elders had embraced as quintessentially American. Of particular importance in undermining antisemitism and discrimination was the major role played by Jews in the cultural-political revolution that overthrew White Anglo-Saxon Protestant (WASP) ascendancy during the New Deal, motivated and informed less by communal interest than by liberalism and as vanguard for European immigrants from a dozen countries. With Jews seen as immigrants roughly equivalent to the others who descended the gangplanks at Ellis Island, it guaranteed their eventual acceptance into the society when a native-born generation grew up completely familiar with American ways. It also meant that, for most of them, Jewishness and Americanization would be inversely proportional.

There was no backlash against Jews, despite the omnipresence of this second and third generation in writing, filmmaking, book publishing, journalism, television, universities, and many other institutions. American society was different from Europe in three critical ways: first, racial antagonism generally took the place of antisemitism. Second, in Europe, Jews had been virtually the sole minority; in America they were one of many groups comprising a majority of the population. Ethnic identity increasingly meant charming variations in cuisine, not repugnant aliens subverting the nation's cultural integrity.

Third, in America, Jews were not dealing with an old, highly structured culture to which they had to clone themselves but a civilization still in the process of formation. American culture was recast by a Jewish/immigrant/racial minority alliance often led by Jews. American society came to embody an antisemite's worst nightmare: a country much influenced by the Jewish standpoint and experience, partly because many non-Jews saw their own problem of assimilation and adjusting to modern society in similar terms.

Given historic experience, declining religious adherence or old-country ethnicity, and the collapse of any Jewish culture, much of the shreds of any remaining identity revolved around antisemitism, a specter following them into assimilation but a phenomenon so rare that it must be searched out or provoked to justify this sensibility. As Jewish historian Gershom Scholem put it, "They [the Jews] may have been aware of their past, but they no longer wanted to have anything to do with the future of the Jews."[11]

Antisemitism was part of that past, rather than the creative enterprise which would have been demanded by a Jewish future. The threat came from assimilation, not oppression, but unable to face the former, Jewish intellectuals felt impelled to challenge the society to show its true, exclusionary, hypocritical face. They felt ambivalent about their success. Outraged by past abuse and servility, they were quick to overstate the implications of any new injustice or controversy. The need to find antisemites derived from their obsession about relations with Gentiles, rather than Jews, and a self-definition dependent on rejection. Self-assertion was a way to prove to themselves they were neither cowardly nor collaborating.

American culture from the 1960s and beyond was full of such restless figures who acted out a discomfort with American society justified as a struggle to make it better. "I can't stand rejection," said the provocative comedian Lenny Bruce. But he deliberately provoked anger, posing as a prophet inviting his own crucifixion, a scapegoat offering himself up for society's sins. "He seemed," said a biographer, "to get a kick out of rubbing salt in the wounds he made in many people's sensibilities."[12]

But he was far from the last of a breed that included such diverse types as Howard Stern, the nasty, profane radio host; Roseanne Barr, the sometimes abusive television actress; Roy Cohn, right-wing sleazy lawyer; Abbie Hoffman, left-wing anarchist clown; and Howard Cosell, straight-talking sports commentator ("Pro football has become a stagnant bore." "I am tired of the hypocrisy and sleaziness of the boxing scene."). They cheerfully advanced by turning themselves into public hate figures, smashing idols or running roughshod over public civility.[13]

This attitude paralleled what some Jewish intellectuals had managed to do in Berlin or Vienna. But acts which once risked provoking a pogrom during insecure centuries past now became a no-risk flaunting of freedom. Of course, this generation had far less to fear on either count, being far enough removed in space and time from real persecution to joke, as Woody Allen did, that a rabbi was so Reform that he was a Nazi.[14]

In "The Conversion of the Jews," Philip Roth runs through Jewish children's reactions to such painful questions as their viewing Christianity as a bizarre religion and questioning how Jews could be the Chosen People if everyone was created equal. The story ends with a boy forcing a rabbi to profess belief in Jesus to stop him from jumping off a roof.

Mel Brooks's film *History of the World* includes a fun romp through the Spanish Inquisition while another of his films, *The Producers*, shows how the more two Jewish impresarios set out to offend people—including a song entitled "Springtime for Hitler"—the more successful they become.

Yet what does all this chutzpah serve? An identity which exists only when jostled, which drowses when not being insulted, is satirized by Woody Allen's character at the start of *Annie Hall* who aurally transmutes the polite question, "Did you eat?" into the insult, "Did Jew eat?" Hypersensitivity to oppression where none exists was partly a sense of guilt over their degree of privilege. For them, it was easier to be Jews, but they had less desire to do so. Having the option to reveal or conceal a Jewish identity gave them more freedom but was also a demeaning, guilt-generating choice.

The same can be said of the contrast between their own situation and that of Jews suffering and dying in the Shoah or sacrificing to build Israel. In a Mordechai Richler novel, a Jewish refugee asks the author's stand-in character, "What's the worst thing that ever happened to you? Wait. I'll guess. Your dog was run over by a car. No, you were naughty and your mummy made you go to bed without your supper. Have you ever eaten the flesh of sewer rats?"[15]

The novelist Norman Mailer has more luck in achieving the paranoid apotheosis of finding an American Nazi and venting his angst with a great deal of satisfaction. Yet the silliness and safety of the confrontation only underscores its artificiality:

"You Jew bastard," he shouted. "Dirty Jew with kinky hair."
"You filthy Kraut."
"Dirty Jew."
"Kraut pig."[16]

This consummation came in complete safety. His interlocutor was not, of course, a "Kraut," a powerful German Nazi, but a member of a tiny, despised band. The confrontation shows Mailer's neurosis, not heroism. The post-1950s Jewish intellectuals knew, however, what their parents' generation did not yet understand: that a bad image would no longer bring anti-Jewish persecution. They rebelled against being paragons who, in Philip Roth's words, "would never do anything or be anything that couldn't be written up in the *Jewish News* under your graduation picture."[17]

The question "Who are the Jews?" was easiest to answer as: those who have been the object of antisemitism. But this response—indicating a vacuum of positive religious values, knowledge, or national identity—also required an exaggeration of the importance of antisemitism and the likelihood of Israel's demise, beliefs which, in turn, made assimilation seem more attractive and aliyah (emigration to Israel) less so.

FACTORS AFFECTING U.S. POLICY AND PUBLIC
OPINION TOWARD ISRAEL

As outlined above, when it comes to American attitudes toward Israel, antisemitism played an infinitesimal role in a special relationship that amounted to a close alliance. Israel was judged largely by realpolitik considerations. Where it was not, the additional factors usually redounded in its favor. And the exceptions often involved American Jews working out their own personal assimilation complexes.

There were, of course, small groups of even smaller importance located largely on the extreme political left and right trying to foment hatred. But the far left—including disproportionately large numbers of Jews—declined steadily since the early 1970s, and the far right lost ground even during the long, and relatively pro-Jewish, Reagan administration. Indeed, because of U.S.-Israel cooperation against the USSR and the pro-Israel sentiments of many Christian fundamentalists, the historic connection between conservative forces and antisemitism was weaker than ever before. Elements of the far left and far right were anti-Israel in no small part because they were themselves anti-American, showing how much the bilateral relationship was taken for granted.

The "normal" aspect of U.S.-Israel relations rested on the kind of state-to-state considerations that apply to other such bilateral links. The fact that the two countries had the same enemies—radical Arab regimes backed by the Soviet Union which sought to upset the regional status quo—proved a strategic factor encouraging cooperation. Against this fact was the largely fallacious argument that U.S. support for Israel endangered American interests in the Arab world, including encouraging moderate Arab states to align with the USSR.[18]

The anti-Americanism (including terrorism and hostage-taking) and extremism of Israel's enemies, plus the fact that the United States did generally maintain its position in the Arab world while still backing Israel, made the pro-Israel strategy triumph. But the balance was decisively tilted by several additional factors, including Western guilt over the Shoah; a common democratic system; strong popular support for Israel among Americans (a fact shown by every poll over many decades); sympathy (at least into the 1980s) with Israel as the underdog; the efforts of an active Jewish community; and—in contrast to historic anti-semitism—a largely common cultural heritage (when compared to Arabs and Muslims on the other side).

Periods of tension in the bilateral relationship were also unrelated to antisemitism. Of the two key periods of friction, differences over Lebanon in 1982–83 and the divisive period of 1989–92 (interrupted by the 1990–91 Kuwait crisis and Gulf War) grew out of disgreements over how best to advance the Arab-Israeli peace process. In both cases there was a divergence of views between the policies of the U.S. and Israeli governments.[19] Whether the U.S. position was right or wrong, it did not arise from any deliberate effort to injure Israel and, to some extent, coincided with the views of many Israelis. The most significant "extraneous" factor to a purely national security conception was not antisemitism but American Jews' insistence that countervailing special factors should overcome the appeal of Arab oil money, demographic weight, and apparent strategic value.

The most assiduously anti-Israel forces were disparate and disorganized: oil companies, academic Middle East specialists, and State Department bureaucrats argued that U.S. interests required a far less pro-Israel policy, out of sympathy for Arabs, mercenary motives, or a perception that Palestinians were being unfairly treated. Their frustration at losing battles repeatedly on the merits of the argument led them to view Israel's supporters as too powerful, a symptom of antisemitism but also a not altogether imaginary conclusion.

The State Department's evolution shows the fragility of any institutionalized anti-Israel posture. Historically, Middle East experts there saw their main task as maintaining good U.S.-Arab relations and all their experience was in the Arab world. By the 1970s, however, as the United States became more involved in Arab-Israeli peacemaking, Arab-Israeli mediation became the main priority. Consequently, such specialists' jobs and promotions required a more neutral stance and greater contact with Israel. During the Bush and Clinton administrations, Jews—once excluded from such jobs completely—held the main posts on the Middle

East diplomatic teams. And they were people who neither hid their affiliation nor bent over backward to prove their neutrality.

In an era when Jews had reentered history, there were real battles and issues at stake that fostered opposition and criticism whose causes transcended an arbitrary dislike of Jews. In part, there was some reaction against the pro-Jewish, pro-Israel sentiment so powerful during the post-1945 historical era by people who felt that Arabs had been treated unfairly or that Israel had been given too much leeway. Since Israel had become a country like other countries, such people could claim they merely wanted a more evenhanded perspective. Often the perpetrators were themselves Jews for whom a "man bites dog" story of Jews or Israelis being immoral or oppressive was a tempting one whose presentation could be portrayed as an act of intellectual independence, courage, and iconoclasm.

A number of other factors also made for distortions, including structural factors shaping the media, arising from its own requirements and the American way of viewing the world. The media would focus on the sensational, or would display an ignorance of context, a simplistic transliteration of American experience, an unfamiliarity in dealing with dictatorships and extremist ideologies. When America was not directly involved it was easier to romanticize rebels. An attacker of the World Trade Center was a terrorist; someone who machine-gunned an Israeli bus was called a guerrilla. But the same factor applied, for example, to the American media's coverage of the Irish Republican Army's attacks on British projects.

Israel also faced a complex situation which few Americans— including members of the elite—fully understood. A microscopic focus and inordinate attention given to events involving the Jewish state was bound to produce more critical coverage. Holding Israel to more moral judgments and higher standards than other countries arose from a difficulty in accepting that country as a normal state. After all, Israel had been founded in the Holy Land and under distinctive circumstances by a people preoccupied with ethical and religious issues, as a test case of whether suffering taught wisdom. Distorting as that situation might be, antisemitism was extremely rare. If anything, the problem was a reporters' fear—especially if Jewish—of being seen as biased toward Israel.

THE JEWISH FACTOR

Assimilating American Jews, however, were equally prone to puzzlement. Their uncertain self-image as Jews, hazy definition of that identity, career aspirations, yearning for assimilation, and attraction to other ideologies put some of them among those people most critical of or antagonistic toward Israel. They cared far more about the issue than others, did not fear being thought antisemitic, felt a proprietary right to criticize Israel or take sides in its debates, exploited their Jewish background by defying it to prove their American or humanist credentials. Their personal situations might confuse their perceptions of events without giving them any particular insight into the issues involved. A leading Arab-American scholar told one surprised audience, "If not for the American Jews, no one would care about the Palestinians."

Among this disparate group were columnists Anthony Lewis and Robert Novak, radical conspiracy theorists Noam Chomsky and Mark Lane, television reporter Mike Wallace, and author Seymour Hersh. Key anti-Israel books were even penned by ex-Israelis Ari Ben-Menashe and Victor Ostrovsky. *New York Times* reporter Thomas Friedman wrote the most successful of all volumes on the area, *From Beirut to Jerusalem,* carefully distancing himself from sympathy toward Israel and highlighting—far beyond a reporter's usual constraints—his disapproval of its behavior to boast of his own objectivity.

"I really dislike Judaism," said the American science and science fiction writer Isaac Asimov, son of Jewish immigrants, in a typical statement of the antagonistic assimilationist stance. "It's a form of particularly pernicious nationalism. I don't want humanity divided into these little groups that are firmly convinced, each one, that it is better than the others. . . . Every once in a while when I'm not careful, I think that the reason Jews have been persecuted as much as they has been to punish them for having invented this pernicious doctrine."[20]

Of course, the very fact that Asimov had such thoughts was

a fairly typical assimilationist response, since most non-Jews continued to accept the value of their own "little"—or, more likely, big—groups. Asimov adds that he coupled this view with "making sure that everyone knows I'm a Jew, so while I'm deprived of the benefits of being part of the group, I am sure that I don't lose any of the disadvantages, because no one should think I am denying my Judaism in order to gain certain advantages."[21] In fact, those taking this stance were living in times and places where a Jewish background brought a certain prestige. Moreover, by saying, in effect, that he once was part of the group but now is critical of it, an anti-Jewish Jew was parading proof of successful assimilation. Already in Ahad Ha-'Am's day, many decades earlier, there were many "who do not know their people, and hurl their utterances down from the lofty heights of Olympus," citing their Jewish background only to "rise above it."[22]

David Mamet's film *Homicide* shows how deeply this complex reached. A highly assimilated policeman, upset by an antisemitic remark, becomes involved with a ridiculously unlikely Israeli-directed underground group combatting neo-Nazis. In the end, it exploits him, makes him violate the law he swore to uphold, causing the death of his Irish partner—his real friend—and almost his own demise. Jewish identity thus appears a disastrous error, a betrayal of American pluralism, at the same time that antisemitism is overstated. Ironically, Mamet's declared purpose in writing the film was to assert his Jewish identity.[23]

The centrality of this Jewish factor is revealed by its presence at the heart of two critical moments in U.S.-Israel relations. Whatever anti-Jewish feelings President Richard Nixon might have had, the delay in resupplying Israel with military equipment during the 1973 war rested on a debate between Secretary of Defense James Schlesinger, a convert to Christianity, and Henry Kissinger. If there was a nonpolicy component it was between the psychologies of two Jews, not from the psyche of an antisemite.

The same can be said of the life sentence of Jonathan Pollard, who had spied for Israel. The main proponent of harsher punishment was Secretary of Defense Caspar Weinberger, apparently spurred by the need to separate himself from his own Jewish antecedents. A prominent lawyer who knew him claimed, "If Weinberger did not feel burdened by his name and his grandfather's religion" he would not have reacted so harshly, having long "leaned over backwards to show that there is absolutely nothing" Jewish about him.[24]

The obsession of American Jews with Israel's image in America reinforces this picture. First, as indicated above, the most critical material often came from Jewish reporters or editors trying to prove their objectivity in terms of self-image and career interests. Second, the elevation of image over reality sprang from the abstractness of their situation as Jews, a mental exercise rather than a daily experience or political framework. Third, they tended to view Israel in terms of its effect on their own standing and image in neighbors' eyes.

Their fears for Israel were a mixture of its problems and the insecurities of American Jews themselves. They worried that the United States would abandon Israel out of a historical experience, the nature of relations among states, and the weight of realpolitik arguments on the anti-Israel side. It was also somewhat difficult for those who had not experienced Jewish sovereignty to believe Israel could exist, paralleling those non-Jews who judged it as artificial or who consigned it to the realm of morality and choice, rather than necessity and the art of the possible. After all, the new nation was a young state created by a people who had known so many painful blows in history that Israel still reeled from the effects. A Jewish state seemed almost as much of an oxymoron as when Herzl first spoke of it a century earlier.

Thus, there was a constant fear that some new phenomenon was going to bring it crashing down. Diaspora Jews, very insecure as Jews no matter how strong they felt as Americans, projected this status onto Israel—which did, of course, have a serious basis for security concern—without fully comprehending the basis of Israel's power or the changes in character which a revision of situation had wrought on the Israeli descendants of ghetto Jews. No matter how powerful they felt as Americans or how proud they were of Israel's achievements, it was impossible to shake their image associating Jewishness with vulnerability.

This fear was enhanced by a continued intellectual dissonance in thinking of Jews as a people, promoted during many decades of the assimilation process, which made a Jewish state seem something of an oxymoron even to those supporting it.

Israel's survival rested first and foremost on its own strength whereas the Diaspora's survival rested on pleasing those around them—hence the latter's emphasis on public relations. Thus, the apprehension of Jews outside Israel gave them, by association, an exaggerated expectation of Israel's annihilation. The same defensiveness made them obsessed with Israel's treatment in the media, since they felt their status depended on neighbors' opinions. Opposition to Israel or its policies was seen as the most visible display of antisemitism, while they themselves fervently hoped Israel would do nothing to anger their governments or endanger their status.

The era beginning with the electoral victory of Menachem Begin and the Likud party in 1977 exacerbated some of these factors. The government that ruled Israel for most of the ensuing fifteen years was more at odds with U.S. policy and the liberal reflexes of many American Jews. *Time* magazine's incredible, objectively antisemitic gaffe in introducing the new prime minister—"Begin, rhymes with Fagan"—signaled a lack of sympathy made all the more revealing by the large Jewish presence in its editorial ranks.

U.S.-Israel disputes over the Lebanon crisis, the intifada, and the peace process overshadowed the earlier success at Camp David, thus setting a negative image for Israel's leaders. There were elements, perhaps, in the feistiness, nationalism, appearance, and style of prime ministers Begin and Yitzhak Shamir guaranteed to trigger antisemitic stereotypes in some sectors of America. It should be noted, however, that their successor Benjamin (Bibi) Netanyahu was lionized as he skillfully played the same political themes with a more familiar, palatable accent and charisma. At any rate, on a state-to-state level such factors were secondary to political issues or conflicts.

Where they were more significant was in alienating some of the most powerful, vocal sectors of American Jews who were intellectuals, decision makers, and media personalities outside the community. Liberals hoped that Israel would not do anything to embarrass them; conservatives—ironically those who most praised American society—often argued that the goyim were out to harm an imperiled Israel through unfair criticism. Through Israel, both sides felt some of the sense of peril so often associated with being a Jew: falling SCUDS, threatening enemies, an indifferent or hostile world, displaced refugees, slandered victims.

"Numerous Jews with no history of prior identification with Israel or other Jewish causes suddenly decided to speak out against Israel *as Jews*," charged Alan Dershowitz, though they would have been furious if asked to undertake any other protest on that basis. He believed their motive was to give "their 'hosts'—the 'real' Americans—to understand that *they* were the good Jews, not like the ones in Israel who were doing those embarrassing things. They were identifying themselves as Jews specifically in order to *disassociate* themselves from other Jews."[25]

There is clearly some truth in this assessment, though on a conscious level the great majority of such activists were motivated by a belief that they were simply applying consistent standards and even acting in Israel's self-interest. The point is, though, that the basis for this pattern of behavior included a considerable assimilationist complex, paralleling the Diaspora complex of Jews on the other side who refrained from criticism because it might be exploited by antisemites or other enemies of the Jews and Israel.

The underlying, controlling factor was the situation in which American Jews lived. Israelis constantly criticize their government and dissect its problems in far harsher terms than heard in the United States. But this activity takes place in a framework of supporting the state and society, demanding it be better. American Jews do not share these experiences and also worry about antagonistic critics who paint Israel as worse than it is, judge it by the worst possible case, seek to delegitimize it.

In short, American Jews feel themselves—not without justification—as fighting a propaganda war, one which affects their own image as well. This battle was the rationale for many American Jewish organizations, programs, and even for committed individuals as a reason not to "make aliyah"—to emigrate to Israel. In fact these matters had little or no effect on Israel, the Middle East, or U.S. policy and public opinion. But it had an enormous impact on the American Jewish psyche. Experience had given even the most assiduously assimilating Jews a different set of reflexes and perceptions than those of their neighbors. Assimilation itself involved a constant looking outward for models of imitation and obstacles to belonging. Israel depended on its social cohesion and its army; Diaspora Jews relied ultimately on the kindness of communal strangers, on a good reputation based on the historical lesson that there was only a short distance from slander to pogrom, from *Mein Kampf* to the concentration camp.

"Despite our apparent success, deep down we see ourselves as second-class citizens—as guests in another people's land," claimed Dershowitz. "We worry about charges of dual loyalty, of being too rich, too smart, and too powerful. Our cautious leaders obsess about what the `real' Americans will think of us."[26] He was right in detecting this pervasive insecurity, though he exaggerated the extent that it paralyzed action in more modern times. Further, such concerns were felt far less by Jewish leaders or activists—who freely chose such a public identification with that cause—than among those who tried to minimize any such connection.

But the underlying premise of Jewish attitudes can also be questioned. Why should non-Jews love Jews, share Jewish concerns, or be expected to know about Jewish sufferings? They have their own priorities and passions. Indifference and tolerance are the most one can expect in large-scale relations between groups. Philip Roth correctly noted:

> If some Jews are dreaming of a time when they will be accepted by Christians as Christians accept one another . . . it may be that they are dreaming of a time that cannot be, and of a condition that does not exist this side of one's dreams. Perhaps even the Christians don't accept one another as they are imagined to in that world from which Jews may believe themselves excluded solely because they are Jews. Nor are the Christians going to feel toward Jews what one Jew may feel toward another.[27]

Furthermore, real contradictions do exist. Roth asked, "Why shouldn't the Gentiles have suspicions?" A serious Jew believes "that on the most serious questions pertaining to man's survival—understanding the past, imagining the future, discovering the relation between God and humanity—that he is right and the Christians are wrong."[28] Obviously, deliberate and unnecessary provocation should always be avoided. But if Jews forget that differences exist, perhaps they might as well become Christians themselves. Examining or rejecting every Jewish act and belief on the basis of how others react to it—a common feature in assimilation—makes Jews the servants of non-Jewish opinion and interests. It often appears that, subconsciously, the love of others is demanded in order to persuade one that he is worthy of loving himself.

In terms of assimilation, Zionism was intended as a double solution. Those who so desired could live in a Jewish state. The rest—probably the majority—would remain outside and, if they wanted, find it easier to assimilate completely; those wishing to remain Jewish would gain a new lease on their identity through living evidence that theirs was not a fragmented, declining, inferior people. Wrote the nineteenth-century philosopher Moses Hess, "Jews have always, despite their dispersion, expressed their solidarity with this center. . . . Today with the disappearance of distances . . . it does not really matter for the Jewish state how many members of the Jewish people will live at home or abroad."[29]

This was the kind of sentiment expressed by the British industrialist/politician Alfred Mond in the 1930s: "The dignity and importance of our whole race will be enhanced by the existence of a national home where those of our people who have been compelled to live under less favorable conditions than we enjoy will be able to establish themselves on the soil of their ancestors."[30]

Israel's creation in 1948 and victory in the 1967 war inspired an upsurge of Jewish activism and identity in the United States. Such a hitherto hostile Marxist as Henry Roth exclaimed, "Sympathy flared up in the face of doctrine. . . . A miracle! The pall lifted that had so long encompassed him. What the hell was he waiting for? Here was a people reborn—*his* people—regenerated by their own will. Was he mad not to share in that regeneration?"[31]

Zionism re-created most of the basis of Jewish identity before the age of assimilation—residential concentration, majority status, and an autonomous administrative and legal system—adding to this state sovereignty for the first time in over two thousand years. It was also intensely practical. "My generation are men of thought, while they are men of deeds," wrote the Israeli novelist S. Y. Agnon "It is like an architect who asked for stone and they gave him brick; for he intended to build a temple, while they intended to build themselves a house to live in."[32]

This very activity—as in the slogan of being rebuilt while rebuilding the land—brought profound psychological shifts away from the dependence of Diaspora which, David Ben-Gurion noted, was "not merely political or economic; it is also moral, cultural, and intellectual, and it affects every limb and nerve of the body, every conscious and subconscious act."[33]

Joining a new social framework and a fully realized "normal" community of Jews brought short-run problems of adjustment and absorption but dissolved the problems of assimilation. Agnon describes an immigrant's feeling that now "he was in his own land, with his own people, with others like him, who shared many of his qualities and many of whose qualities he shared. He felt that he longer needed to strain to be like others, for he simply *was* like them, which had not been the case before."[34]

ZIONIST IDEOLOGY OR GALUT (DIASPORA) SUPERIORITY?

Jews remaining elsewhere, however, faced a new dilemma. If living in Israel was the highest expression of Jewish identity, what was their rationale for not being there? In practice, of course, people were tied to their lives, professions, languages, and families, integrated into the customs and mind-set of the society where they lived. Yet practical considerations did not altogether suffice to answer what was an existential issue. The Hungarian-born writer Arthur Koestler resolved the contradiction by arguing that the establishment of a state enabled a guilt-free full assimilation, "with an occasional friendly glance back and a helpful gesture" but joining fully "the nation whose life and culture they share, without reservation or split loyalties." Yet he ends this implication of liberation in disappearance with a hint—even down to the Christian imagery—that this step was a final act of surrender: "There must be an end to every calvary."[35]

While Israel generally attracted overwhelming support among Jews, Israel was abstracted to keep it at a distance, to ward off implications for one's own life, to protect the compromises worked out in the assimilation process. "What the Israeli does or thinks has no impact on Israel-Diaspora relations," said Professor Charles Liebman. "The American Jew plays out his relations with Israel in his own mind. It has very little to do with Israel."[36] Only a small proportion of American Jews visited the country, partly because unlike going to London, Paris or Rome, Asia or Latin America, this journey required an encounter with themselves, a potential threat to identity unlike any other destination.

An additional view, reflected by Alfred Mond's statement about a Jewish national home, was of Israel as refuge for Jews fleeing oppression in Europe, the Middle East, and, more recently, the USSR and Ethiopia. As such, it was insignificant in defining Jews who were successfully integrated as citizens in other places. This put the relationship to Israel in the familiar form of aid to endangered or impoverished communities always practiced by Jews.

Finally, while Jews could easily reject acts of their own society or government in the context of the political system—taking advantage of their psychic duality—intellectuals might see Israel's acts or very existence as involuntarily involving them in a far fuller degree of responsibility, undermining their own successful assimilation, and challenging the universal application of principles they prize. This view on the part of intellectuals could spark highly emotional reactions by those fearing Israel would make them hypocrites and wishing to parade their own independence and virtue. As one English professor put it, "I feel the daily horrors of Zionist treatment of the Palestinians, perpetrated in my name and with the financial support of my community, as a personal as well as a political tragedy. My ideology is of the old-fashioned Enlightenment sort that demands freedom and justice for everyone, not just for Jews."[37]

A strong reaction against the idea of someone else defining one's identity often leads to anger by those seeking to assimilate. When Jewish students protested the University of Pennsylvania's scheduling registration on Rosh Hashana, the Jewish provost replied that he saw no problem and accused the students of being too "sensitive" and "pushy" until he was overruled by the school's non-Jewish president. Since the provost considered himself sufficiently Jewish without commemorating any Jewish holidays, to say that Jews needed to do so contradicted his own sense of self. Some considered religious customs as primitive; others saw Jewish nationalism or even—like Asimov—the group's continued existence as retrograde.[38]

Alongside the debate about the meaning of Jewishness was that over the merit of Jewish life in Israel or in the Diaspora. A conversation between the chairman of the Conference of Presidents of Major American Jewish Organizations, Morris Abram, and Zeev Chafetz, an American who had emigrated to Israel, depicts this gap. Chafetz maintained that Israelis were like the football team down on the field, actually living and making Jewish history. Failing to note Chafetz's point, Abram agreed, asserting that American Jews were in the stands, watching and cheering them.

But in exercising their own choice not to be there, Diaspora Jews had to develop a rationale for doing so. Over a period of 1,800 years, Jews rarely ever physically returned to the land but considered themselves in an involuntary geographic exile. S. Y. Agnon said in his speech accepting the Nobel Prize, "Through a historical catastrophe—the destruction of Jerusalem by the Emperor of Rome. . .I was born in one of the cities of the Diaspora. But I always deemed myself as one who was really born in Jerusalem."[39]

Now, however, this sojourn became a voluntary exile. There were several arguments for defining one's home in terms of staying at home, including Israel's uncertain future, the Diaspora's creativity, America as a promised land, and Israel's shortcomings. Philip Roth has an Israeli character in *The Counterlife* say, "In the Diaspora a Jew like you lives securely while we are living just the kind of imperiled Jewish existence that we came here to replace. . . . We are the excitable, ghettoized, jittery little Jews of the Diaspora, and you the Jews with all the confidence and cultivation that comes of feeling at home where you are."

These ideas were justified, of course, by prejudgment. If American Jews had "confidence and cultivation," these were characteristics more expressed in the "non-Jewish" side of their character. American Jews who thought Israel too dangerous even to visit, for example, often lived in high-crime cities. The underlying reality was that they believed themselves not in exile but dwelling in the civilization that had formed them, even if—or especially if—their milieu was a local Jewish assimilationist version of the real thing.

This was the point made by novelist Saul Bellow: "The only life I can love, or hate is . . . this American life of the twentieth century, the life of Americans who are also Jews." Bellow wrote that he was told, "Only as a Jew in Israel . . . could I enter history again and prove the necessity and authenticity of my existence." But to do so, he continued, would actually invalidate his existence, "That would wipe out me totally."[40]

With partial assimilation as normative, to be at home was never to be at home, living a reflexive high-wire act of anxiety and marginalism: rage, anxiety, restlessness, insatiability, as well as alienation, skepticism, intellectual orientation, and moralism infused with passion. Adrienne Rich evoked this feeling in her poetry:

> By no means native, yet somewhat in love
> With things a native is enamored of—
> Except the sense of being held and owned
> By one ancestral patch of local ground.[41]

Yet the "ancestral patch" being rejected is as much that of one's own ancestors as the one belonging to those who are truly, unselfconsciously, native.

Henry Roth felt "like a foreigner" in Israel yet almost equally alienated in America. Living in a trailer, he wrote, "Here the land is not ours. The dwelling is, but the space isn't."[42] Philip Roth's Portnoy finds both his shiksa girlfriend and Israelis adjusted because they had a monolithic identity. Only he was not adjusted. An Israeli woman told him, "The way you disapprove of your life! . . . Everything is ironical, or self-deprecating."

He replies, "Self-deprecation is, after all, a classic form of Jewish humor."

"Not Jewish humor! No! Ghetto humor," she answers, tells him to go home, home into exile.

"Yes," Portnoy concludes, "I am a patriot too . . . only in another place! (Where I also don't feel at home!)"[43]

While Jewish life was certainly sustainable outside Israel—and existence was generally materially better and easier in America—it was also far more diluted and fragile there, and unsustainable without Israel. American Jewish life was entering a new era when the generations who remembered immigration or the Holocaust had passed, while intermarriage climbed and the number of adherents declined. Having secured its existence and absorbed new waves of migration, Israel was ready to enter its truly creative period.

In the 1930s, Koestler found Jews born in the land of Israel inferior to Diaspora Jews: "Their parents were the most cosmopolitan race of the earth—they are provincial and chauvinistic. Their parents were sensitive bundles of nerves in awkward bodies—their nerves are whip-cords and their bodies those of a horde of Hebrew Tarzans. . . . Their parents were intense, intent, overstrung, over-spiced—they are tasteless, spiceless, unleavened and tough. . . . In other words, they have ceased to be Jews and become Hebrew peasants."[44]

Such a judgment forgot that only a minority of Jews in Europe had been intellectuals. But Koestler found these young people contrary to his image of Jews based on the idea that security was creativity's enemy, whereas persecution and alienation bred spiritual or cultural achievement. He also knew the latter's cost as "that nervous over-strungness of exile and dispersion," "the racial inferiority complex," "the stink and filth and claustrophobia of the ghetto."[45]

This trade-off between suffering or assimilation in the Diaspora as the price of creativity was most frankly, shockingly confronted by Koestler, writing of contemporary events: In Buchenwald, Jews were being tortured. "Who would not swap all the formulae of Einstein" to save a single one? "But who, having completed the transaction, would rejoice about it?"[46]

Yet such human sacrifice was repugnant. Einstein himself rejected that argument. He wrote, "The best in a man can be brought out only when he belongs entirely to a human group. Hence there is grave moral danger in the position of the Jew who has lost contact with his own national group and is regarded as an alien by the group among which he lives. Often enough a situation of this kind has produced a despicable and joyless egotism."[47]

Similarly, antisemitism was not the key to Jewishness but merely an obstacle to living it. The end of effective antisemitism and acquisition of equality raises far more starkly the old choice between using this freedom to enhance a Jewish civilization or to escape. The era of assimilation moves toward completion as its fuel is exhausted, as Jews became either fully assimilated or normalized in a Jewish state, both outcomes jeopardizing an assimilationist Jewish culture and identity standing in between, pulled in the opposite directions of greater self-affirmation or disintegration.

Wrote Philip Roth, "The success of the struggle against the defamation of Jewish character in this country, has itself made more pressing the need for a Jewish self-consciousness that is relevant to this time and place, where neither defamation nor persecution are what they were elsewhere in the past."[48] It is perfectly sensible to have a strong Anti-Defamation League. It is ridiculous for antidefamation to be the cornerstone of Jewish identity and activity.

What makes it easier for the community to flourish also makes it harder for it to survive. Roth concludes, "The cry, 'Watch out for the goyim!' at times seems more the expression of an unconscious wish than of a warning: Oh that they were not there, so that we could be together in here."[49] Discrimination's collapse facilitates total assimilation, but fear of persecution often makes Jews strive harder and surrender more fully to achieve invisibility. Similarly, the end of obsessive fear about Israel's survival may reduce American Jewish support and activism on its behalf or for any Jewish cause. Tragically, the Shoah stands as an alternative symbol, sequestering Jewish civilization in a destroyed past rather than a vital future.

But if antisemitism can flourish in some parts of the world without Jews, it seems equally plausible that Jews can flourish without antisemitism. This adjustment must begin by understanding the victory that has been won, and spending energies no longer needed for defense on constructive activity both in the

Jewish state and among that portion of the Jewish people living in the United States.

NOTES

1. Theodor Herzl, *A Portrait for This Age* (New York, 1955), pp. 313–14.

2. Paul Mendes-Flohr and Jehuda Reinharz, *The Jew in the Modern World* (New York, 1980).

3. While writing this paper, I experienced this phenomenon twice in one day. A Jew living in New York said he disliked Israel because countries should not be based on religion. A politically sophisticated non-Jewish American asked why Israel should not stop being a Jewish state since most Israelis were secular.

4. Shlomo Avineri, *The Making of Modern Zionism* (New York, 1981), p. 115.

5. Quoted in Hannah Arendt, *The Origins of Totalitarianism,* (New York, 1973), p. 117.

6. This situation has posed especially interesting problems for Palestine Liberation Organization ideology. See Barry Rubin, *The PLO Between Anti-Zionism and Antisemitism* (Jerusalem: Hebrew University Sassoon Center, 1993).

7. *Washington Post*, June 27, 1991.

8. Ibid., July 28, 1990.

9. Charles Fleming, "Arnie's Army," *Spy* magazine, March 1992, p. 62.

10. Alan Dershowitz, *Chutzpah* (New York, 1991) p. 67; Ludwig Lewisohn, *The Answer* (New York, 1939), p. 233. In this era, American Jewish leaders often kept a low profile, arguing that to do otherwise was to encourage antisemitism. This situation reached tragic proportions in the failure of American Jews to do or say more about the fate of European Jewry under Nazi rule before and during the Shoah. Nonetheless, the preponderant guilt belongs not on American Jewish leaders and groups, who did less than they might have, but on the far more powerful set of wealthy, accomplished, and intellectual Jewish Americans who—with very few exceptions—did nothing at all because this served their own career and assimilationist interests.

11. Gershon Scholem, *On Jews and Judaism in Crisis,* (New York, 1976), p. 255.

12. Albert Goldman with Lawrence Schiller, *Ladies and Gentlemen, Lenny Bruce!!* (New York, 1975), pp. 475, 536, 647.

13. *Jerusalem Post*, February 2, 1992; the *Washington Post*, November 12, 1991.

14. Diane Jacobs, *But We Need the Eggs* (New York, 1982), p. 14.

15. Rachel Brenner, *Assimilation and Assertion: The Response to the Holocaust in Mordechai Richler's Writings* (New York, 1989), p. 125.

16. Jennifer Bailey, *Norman Mailer: Quick-Change Artist* (New York, 1979), p. 91.

17. Philip Roth, *Zuckerman Bound* (New York, 1985), p. 393.

18. This debate is analyzed in Barry Rubin, *Cauldron of Turmoil: America in the Middle East* (New York, 1992).

19. See Barry Rubin, "U.S.-Israel Relations and Israel's 1992 Elections," in Asher Arian and Michal Shamir, *Elections in Israel* (Albany, N.Y., 1994).

20. *Jerusalem Report*, April 23, 1992, pp. 31–32.

21. Ibid.

22. Ahad Ha-`Am, *Collected Essays* (New York, 1952), p. 248.

23. One might add that the most shocking negative stereotypes of Jews appear mostly in films made mostly by Jews, for example, *White Castle*.

24. Dershowitz, *Chutzpah*, p. 290.

25. Ibid., pp. 234–35.

26. Ibid., p. 3.

27. Philip Roth, *Reading Myself and Others* (New York, 1977), p. 149.

28. Ibid., pp. 131–32.

29. Shlomo Avineri, *Moses Hess, Prophet of Communism and Zionism* (New York, 1985), p. 220.

30. Jean Goodman, *The Mond Legacy* (London, 1982), p. 111.

31. Henry Roth, *Shifting Landscapes* (New York, 1987), p. 184.

32. S.Y. Agnon, *A Guest for the Night* (New York, 1968), p. 101.

33. Mendes-Flohr and Reinharz, *The Jew in the Modern World*.

34. S.Y. Agnon, *Shira* (New York, 1989), p. 547.

35. Arthur Koestler, *Promise and Fulfillment* (New York, 1949), pp. 332–35.

36. *Jerusalem Report*, February 27, 1992. Naturally, there are many exceptions to these and the following points.

37. Bruce Robbins in *PMLA* 107 (October 1992) 1283; see also 1280–82 and *PMLA* 108 (May 1993) 540–42.

38. Dershowitz, *Chutzpah*, p. 328.

39. Joan Comay, *Who's Who in Jewish History* (New York, 1974), p. 46.

40. Bellow's revealing title is "I Took Myself as I Was." *ADL Bulletin*, December 1976.

41. *A Change of World* (New Haven, 1951).

42. Henry Roth, *Shifting Landscapes*, pp. 224, 185.

43. Philip Roth, *Portnoy's Complaint* (New York, 1967), pp. 250, 264.

44. Arthur Koestler, *Thieves in the Night* (London, 1946), pp. 152–53.

45. Ibid.
46. Ibid., p. 154.
47. Albert Einstein, *About Zionism* (New York, 1931), p. 53.
48. Roth, *Reading Myself and Others*, p. 150.
49. Ibid., p. 149.

·7·

How Should We Think About Black Antisemitism?

GARY E. RUBIN

Gary Rubin is executive director of Americans for
Peace Now, and was formerly national affairs director
of the American Jewish Committee.

Gary E. Rubin examines the crucial nexus between black-Jewish relations
in America and black antisemitism, a relationship that is often confused,
with many in the Jewish community asserting that everything that is wrong
with black-Jewish relations has to do with antisemitism emerging from the
African-American community. Gary Rubin takes a hard look at this simplistic assertion; indeed, his essay is more an analysis of the state of the
relationship between blacks and Jews than it is of so-called black antisemitism. Rubin argues with the presumptions of simplicity. He tackles the
simplistic question "Are they or are they not antisemites?" and develops
an approach toward understanding an increasingly complex relationship, a
relationship that implicates, not so much antisemitism, but a range of public-affairs and public-policy issues.

J.A.C.

In writing about antisemitism among African Americans, it is
imperative to know exactly what we are trying to evaluate.
Antisemitism in general, and its manifestations among blacks in
particular, are emotion-laden topics with profound implications
for both the Jewish and African-American communities. Much of
what passes for analysis in this area is in reality academic-sound-
ing editorializing. To analyze the data carefully and to avoid the

pitfalls of polemics, we need to be clear about the questions we are asking and the methods that can satisfactorily answer them.

Anyone looking for prominent manifestations of black antisemitism will easily find them. Louis Farrakhan, Leonard Jeffries, the rioters in Crown Heights, and innumerable examples of less visible antisemites can be identified without difficulty and their activities described in meticulous detail. There would be no problem in providing an affirmative answer to the question "Do antisemites exist among African Americans?"

But that is not the key question. Our subject is not manifestations of antisemitism among American blacks, but black antisemitism. It is not nearly enough to cite and describe the ravings of individual bigots or to recount certain violent or hateful events if we want to study antisemitism among African Americans. For this investigation, we need to go beyond particular people and controversies to analyze the extent of antisemitism in the community as a whole and its implications for black-Jewish relations and for pluralism in the society in which both groups live.

To investigate this broader topic, this chapter poses four questions: What dangers do recent overt manifestations of African-American antisemitism present to Jews? How widespread are antisemitic attitudes among blacks and what place do they occupy in overall opinions of Jews? What larger social and ideological forces are influencing black and Jewish attitudes toward each other, and what effect do these trends have on antisemitism? And what are the practical effects of current attitudes of blacks and Jews toward each other and how can these outcomes be influenced by each community's actions?

I

To say that antisemitism exists in the African-American community is merely to state a banal truism. Antisemitism can be found among any identifiable group in the United States. A focus on blacks is justified by two further considerations. Black America is one of the chief places in the United States where visible and vocal antisemitism can still be observed. Moreover, the

151

African-American community is one of the only sites today where antisemitism is making a serious bid for communal acceptance and legitimacy. This danger is illustrated by three cases that have occurred in the past two years: Leonard Jeffries and academic bigotry, Louis Farrakhan and his search for respectability, and the communal consequences of the 1991 Crown Heights riot.

Leonard Jeffries, chair of the African-American Studies Department at the City College of New York, first came to intensive public attention through a speech he delivered at a state-funded conference in Albany in the summer of 1991. In that speech he attacked individual Jews in antisemitic terms and charged that Jews in the film industry systematically demean blacks.[1] Further investigation into Jeffries's writing and speaking revealed that he subscribes to a racial theory that holds that blacks are genetically superior to whites. When questioned about his views, Jeffries brushes off all criticism as racism aimed to discredit him as a black scholar.

Responding to the uproar caused by the airing of Jeffries's views, the Board of Trustees of the City University of New York voted to limit his normal three-year term as chair of the college's African-American Studies Department to one year. The board realized that his academic tenure could not legally be attacked or withdrawn so it decided to express its displeasure by limiting his chairmanship. For technical reasons, it chose to make its case on the basis of Jeffries's alleged poor stewardship of the department rather than over the content of his teachings. The courts overruled the board, reinstated Jeffries to his full term, and awarded him monetary damages. As of this writing, the legal aspects of the case are still unresolved as the prospect looms of further appeals.* The social and ideological import of the Jeffries affair are not in doubt, however. A racist with openly antisemitic views

---

*In a significant development in November 1994, the U.S. Supreme Court, in *Harelston* v. *Jeffries,* gave the City College a new chance to show that its demotion of Jeffries did not violate constitutional freedom-of-expression guarantees. The Court vacated an April 1994 Court of Appeals ruling that Jeffries's rights had been violated. The Supreme Court directed the Second Circuit Court of Appeals to reconsider the case (editor's note).

is continuing to teach at a large urban university and to head one of its major departments.

Moreover, Leonard Jeffries is not an isolated case. In the spring 1993 term at Wellesley College in Massachusetts, Tony Martin, a professor in the African-American Studies Department, taught as objective truth the Nation of Islam–produced book *The Secret Relationship of Blacks and Jews,*[2] which falsely identifies Jews as the major force behind the slave trade. When confronted with criticism, Martin charged that Jews were attacking him with racist motivation. The Wellesley administration made clear its abhorrence of Martin's views, but he still holds a tenured teaching position at the college.

No one knows the breadth of acceptance of Jeffries's or Martin's views among professors in African-American studies departments. Some of the most prominent leaders in this field, including Cornel West of Princeton and Henry Louis Gates of Harvard, have explicitly repudiated them.[3] But it is certain that through the medium of black studies, avowed antisemites are now teaching on American college campuses.

Of all major institutions, universities are the most critical for the success and security of American Jews. More than 90 percent of age-appropriate Jews acquire higher education and consider it essential to their social status. If an institution so indispensable to Jews becomes infused with antisemitism, their reaction will be strong indeed. Since the medium for the appearance of this hatred is black studies, Jews fear that African Americans could become the instrument for the academic legitimation of antisemitism in American life.

A similar concern underlies Jewish reactions to Louis Farrakhan. In a series of speeches that began to receive widespread public attention during the presidential campaign of 1984, Farrakhan has employed the classic antisemitic stereotypes of a powerful Jewish conspiracy aimed at subordinating blacks. His addresses typically draw thousands of listeners and consist of a popular self-help theme combined with denunciations of whites in general and Jews in particular. These events constitute one of the largest sites for the transmission of antisemitism today.

Farrakhan's antisemitism goes far beyond speeches, however. His Nation of Islam–produced book *The Secret Relationship*

Between Blacks and Jews, which charges that Jews played the major role in the slave trade, is widely distributed in the African-American community. *The Secret Relationship* is printed in academic style, including impressive-looking footnotes that lend it a surface credibility. This volume may be the single most effective piece of antisemitic propaganda produced in the United States since Henry Ford's *The International Jew* of the 1920s. In addition, Farrakhan supporters regularly speak at university campuses around the country, and his newspaper *The Final Call* is widely disseminated in inner-city areas.[4]

Farrakhan has not been satisfied with prominence as a visible but extreme black group leader. He has recently sought legitimation as a mainstream African-American voice. He asked for inclusion on the roster of speakers of the thirtieth anniversary march on Washington commemorating Martin Luther King's landmark "I Have a Dream" speech. Granting this request would have placed him among the core leadership of the civil rights movement. Only strong protests by Jewish members of the civil rights community prevented his participation. Less than three weeks after the march, on September 16, 1993, Farrakhan spoke to an audience of two thousand at a meeting of the Black Congressional Caucus Foundation on a platform that included black leaders in both Congress and the private sector. This entree to the mainstream could signal that Farrakhan's antisemitism (along with his antigay and antifeminist positions) does not disqualify him from leadership in one of America's most visible and powerful communities. Precisely what American Jews most fear—the mainstreaming of antisemitism—threatens to occur in this case.

This concern for the spreading of antisemitism is also evident in continuing Jewish reactions to the Crown Heights riot of August 1991. The passage of years has not blunted Jewish anger at the three days of uncontrolled physical attacks on the Jews of Crown Heights following a fatal auto accident in which a seven-year-old black child was killed by a car accompanying Rabbi M. M. Schneerson, the Lubavitcher "Rebbe," through the area. A trial resulted in the acquittal of an alleged murderer of a Jew killed during the attacks despite what appeared to be convincing evidence, and prospects for a successful retrial on federal civil rights grounds seemed uncertain at best. It appeared eminently possible that the most serious and damaging antisemitic rioting in American history, which occurred for three days without effective enforcement action from police or political authorities, would go entirely unpunished.[5]

The threat of Crown Heights becomes especially evident from an analysis of the demographics of the area. The neighborhood is home to Hasidic Jews and Caribbean-born blacks, neither of which group is typical of the Jewish or African-American population in the United States. Yet for many people, the Crown Heights riot became emblematic of black-Jewish relations, or at least of the dangers of what can happen if the relationship continues to undergo severe strain. The riot started as a Caribbean-Hasidic dispute, but it quickly escalated as American-born blacks from surrounding housing projects poured into the area. The experience demonstrated that angry black youth will join inner-city violence and vent their anger at Jews (crowds shouted, "Kill the Jews") when clashes occur.

Jeffries, Farrakhan, and Crown Heights represent something more than disturbing but isolated incidents of antisemitism. They demonstrate the danger that African-American antisemitism could spread from individual bigots to infect broad sectors of academia, the civil rights movement, and black residential areas. Gauging the reality of this threat requires a thorough analysis of African-American attitudes toward Jews.

II

Public opinion surveys of African-American attitudes toward Jews indicate a danger that the hatred represented by Farrakhan, Jeffries, and Crown Heights could indeed become widespread in the black community since a sizable base of antisemitic opinion exists there. At the same time, these surveys also show that substantial positive attitudes toward Jews are shared by many African Americans that could undergird the furthering of constructive relationships. Black opinion on Jews, in short, is complex and could move in a number of different directions.

Surveys covering the past four decades tend to show higher than average antisemitic attitudes among American blacks, especially on economic questions.[6] This trend remains in force in the latest studies. A 1992 national survey by Marttila and Kiley on behalf of the Anti-Defamation League finds that among Americans in general, 20 percent rate as "most antisemitic," 39 percent as "not antisemitic," and 41 percent are found to be in the "middle" on this measure. For African Americans, by contrast, 37 percent of respondents rated as "most antisemitic," 48 percent as "middle," and only 14 percent as "not antisemitic."[7]

Similarly, a 1992 survey of New Yorkers by the American Jewish Committee (AJC) found that an unprecedentedly high 47 percent of respondents in general took the position that Jews have "too much influence in New York City life and politics." This response was topped by black respondents, 63 percent of whom agreed with this statement.[8] The perception that Jews have too much power has traditionally been seen by many researchers as among the most accurate gauges of antisemitic attitudes in respondent populations.

These findings, which at first glance seem to indicate serious antisemitism, need to be examined more closely. For one thing, the percentages of "most antisemitic" among both blacks and whites represent declines from levels found in studies over the past three decades. Thus, while demagogues like Farrakhan and Jeffries were rising in visibility, the percentages of African Americans rating as highly antisemitic decreased. The bigotry of individuals did not necessarily represent a trend within the larger community.

Further, it is necessary to look closely at exactly what the designation "most antisemitic" actually means.[9] The ADL/Marttila survey consisted of eleven questions designed to indicate antisemitic attitudes. Respondents were asked whether they thought that Jews had particular economic, political, or social traits. If an individual responded with six or more replies deemed negative to Jews, he or she was counted as "most antisemitic." No or one negative response brought a rating of "not antisemitic," and two to five negative answers put a person in the "middle."

There has been some question whether some of the items on this "index of antisemitic belief" in fact identify negative attitudes toward Jews. The statement that Jews "stick together more than other Americans," for example, could have been endorsed by some respondents in an admiring way, especially in these times of communal breakdown and individual anomie. Yet, even if one accepts the ADL findings as largely accurate—and there is good reason for doing so—their implications for the study of antisemitism need further reflection.

The fact that a respondent could be classified as "most antisemitic" on the basis of six negative replies means that the same individual could have given positive replies about Jews on five of the eleven survey questions. Rather than being totally negative, this respondent may have been profoundly ambivalent about Jews, with negative feelings coexisting with positive opinions. The ADL's own report confirms the likelihood of this interpretation of the findings. The vast majority of respondents rated as "most antisemitic" gave six or seven negative answers; very few (2 percent of all respondents and one in ten of the "most antisemitic" group) gave ten or eleven antisemitic answers. Even those designated "most antisemitic," then, gave a number of positive responses on their attitudes toward Jews and should be more accurately classified as ambivalent than unrelievedly hostile.

This conclusion becomes even more convincing from a close analysis of the American Jewish Committee findings. The same sample that responds by 47 percent that Jews have too much influence in New York also shows by its responses that it admires Jews more than any other group in the city. In comparison to blacks, Hispanics, Asians, Irish, and Italians, respondents rank Jews first in being "intelligent" and "rich" and as least likely to be "prone to violence" or to "prefer to live off welfare." Jews rank second only to Asians as least likely to be characterized as "lazy."

Black respondents follow this pattern with some important exceptions. They outrank every other population but Hispanics in saying that Jews have too much influence in New York (63 percent of blacks give this response, 66 percent of Hispanics, and 31 percent of whites). At the same time, black respondents concur with others that Jews are intelligent, rich, not lazy, and not prone to live off welfare, though their level of agreement on these positive traits is slightly lower than that of respondents in general. Blacks also see Jews as more violent than do other respondents, but not by large margins. In sum, blacks follow the overall pattern of mixed positive and negative feelings about Jews, though their level of negative responses is slightly higher and their rate of positive answers somewhat lower.

One way to resolve the contradiction among respondents between the negative finding of high ratings for Jews having too much influence (even the 31 percent agreement to this characterization by whites exceeds the findings of previous studies) and the positive ratings on other traits is to question whether the "too much influence" response is indeed negative. It could be suggested that saying that Jews have substantial influence merely reflects power realities in the city or that other groups actually admire the power they perceive the Jewish community to have accumulated. This interpretation, however, ignores the wording of the question. It does not ask whether Jews have influence—which they surely do—but whether they have too much influence, a clear pejorative. Moreover, weight must be given to the fact that a response of "too much power" has historically been associated with antisemitism. Rather than seeing the "too much influence" response as part of a larger trend toward positive evaluations of Jews, it is more accurately understood as a negative response which, when placed in the context of the more positive findings, signals an ambivalent attitude toward Jews among both blacks and whites, with blacks somewhat more negative.

Two other findings from the AJC survey provide important insight into African-American attitudes toward Jews. When we think about one community's opinion about another, we usually assume that the surveyed group has a positive evaluation of itself and that whatever negative attitudes it may harbor toward others contrasts with its own positive traits.

This assumption does not hold for black respondents in the AJC survey. They state more negative opinions about New Yorkers in general than do average respondents, and also express problematic attitudes toward their own group. Black respondents are more likely than white to agree that blacks are likely to "prefer to live off welfare" and are "prone to violence." Black respondents exceed white by a margin of 53 percent to 43 percent in agreeing that in New York City, blacks "behave in a manner which provokes hostility." (On these questions, Asian and Hispanic respondents' negative replies exceed those of both blacks and whites.) To the degree that they give more negative responses than average about Jews, then, blacks are not singling Jews out, but rather following a pattern in which they provide unusually negative views about every group, including their own.

Moreover, several groups, including blacks, consider Jews to be part of the problem of intergroup relations, not just its victims. Jews self-evaluate very highly on whether they are "tolerant of other racial/ethnic groups," giving themselves a 4.6 rating on a seven-point scale on this measure. Others disagree that Jews are so tolerant. The sample as a whole gives Jews a 3.8 on this scale, with subgroups of respondents including 3.8 from blacks, 3.2 from Asians, and 3.8 from Catholics. Jews consider themselves much more tolerant than their neighbors believe them to be, a finding that must weigh heavily in evaluations of intergroup attitudes.

Finally, on black attitudes toward Jews, survey findings reveal a real possibility for change based on the social and economic conditions of African Americans. For several years, it was widely believed in the Jewish community that black antisemitism was unique among anti-Jewish sentiment in the United States because while measured antisemitism decreased among the general population as the income and education levels of respondents rose, among blacks it seemed to rise at higher levels of income and schooling. This perception was based on a misreading of a 1981 survey conducted for the American Jewish Committee by the firm of Yankelovich, Skelly and White. That study concluded that "in general, younger and better educated individuals are less likely to be anti-Semitic. However, among blacks, there is little relationship between age or education and anti-Semitism."[10]

On this point the 1992 ADL/Marttila survey is much more definitive. It clearly finds "a significant correlation between more education and less acceptance of antisemitic beliefs" among black respondents and an even stronger relationship between high occupational attainment among blacks and rejection of antisemitic attitudes. Black antisemitism, the ADL survey finds, is not some mysterious phenomenon fundamentally different from the attitude patterns of most Americans. Rather, it follows a familiar attitudinal path in which poorer and less educated people harbor more negative feelings toward others. As among other groups, the antisemitic attitudes of African Americans are subject to change through education and social mobility.

The ambivalent attitudes that surveys reveal blacks have toward Jews is not an unusual finding in intergroup relations. In fact, a close reading of the survey literature shows that Jews have similar mixed attitudes toward African Americans.

Studies show that Jews feel more warmly toward blacks than do other Americans and that they agree with blacks more often than others on specific public issues. But the relationship is not particularly close. On a measurement of group feelings devised by the National Opinion Research Center, Jews rated themselves as having "moderately favorable" feelings toward blacks; only 15 percent considered themselves closely identified with blacks. On issues, Jews exceeded other whites in endorsing black positions opposing segregation and favoring a strong governmental role in improving the economic position of blacks and other minorities.

On the other hand, Jews tend by substantial margins to oppose governmental actions they deem as unfairly favoring African Americans, such as busing to achieve school integration and affirmative action quota programs. Blacks tend highly to favor these vigorous governmental interventions. As public debate has centered more on strong public civil and voting rights programs, these disagreements between blacks and Jews have become more prominent and have affected the relationship as well as attitudes toward each other.[11]

Differences in African American and Jewish attitudes on issues fundamental to each also surface in the 1992 AJC survey. Among respondents as a whole, 55 percent agree that blacks in New York are discriminated against "a lot." This overall figure masks a sharp racial dichotomy. Seventy percent of black respondents believe that blacks are discriminated against a lot. By contrast, only 43 percent of Jews share this view, about the same as other white and Asian respondents. Since perceptions of discrimination are an important component of a group's self-image and evaluation of its status, this difference in evaluation of antiblack discrimination will likely have a substantial effect on mutual understanding and relations between African Americans and Jews.

Jewish respondents on the AJC survey rate blacks as comparatively more antisemitic than other groups. Thirty-one percent of Jewish respondents consider "most" or "many" blacks to be antisemitic, twice the rating they give to any other group. Conversely, only 15 percent of Jews responding to the survey said "few" blacks were antisemitic, fully ten percentage points below the next lowest group. Still, most respondents did not make a simple correlation between blacks and antisemitism; the plurality, 36 percent, said that "some" blacks are antisemitic.

On other evaluations of the characteristics of black New Yorkers, Jewish respondents did not differ appreciably from other whites. They joined with Irish and Italian respondents in rating blacks comparatively negatively on being lazy, prone to violence, preferring to live off welfare, and not being intelligent. On the other hand, the AJC survey did not ask questions about positions on social policy issues on which other studies have shown Jews to be much closer to blacks than other groups. Moreover, it must be kept in mind that this survey covered only New York City; its relevance to attitudes in the rest of the country is unknown.

What emerges from this review of recent surveys is a complex and volatile picture. No simple generalizations can be made about African-American and Jewish attitudes toward each other. Blacks say Jews have too much influence, but also hold admiring views of them. Jews tend to support blacks on more issues than do other groups, though substantial disagreement remains between them, and to feel moderately close to blacks although they share other groups' negative opinions about them. These attitudes may contradict each other, but they coexist.

The attitudinal climate exists for both growing tension and coalition building. Demagogues can exploit points of conflict that truly exist between the two communities, but there is also potential readiness for outreach that can be activated. How this welter of attitudes affects actual relations between African Americans and Jews will depend very much on the development of events in the social and political arenas.

III

If attitudes exist in both the African-American and Jewish communities that could promote greater tension or further cooperation, what larger social forces will influence relations between the two communities? In terms of antisemitism, what social trends will create the conditions for its expansion and what are the conditions most conducive to arresting it?

Mutual suspicion and hatred grow with increasing social isolation. Groups in regular contact that cooperate on public issues know each other too well to succumb to easy and hostile stereotyping. They may have serious substantive disagreements, but their familiarity will prevent the rise of the belief in the evil or perverted nature of the other since these negative characterizations will be contradicted by daily experience. Moreover, to the degree that a coalitional strategy produces benefits to each community, there is a concrete interest among groups to promote a positive working relationship and avoid the tension that could impede the realization of joint goals.

Hatemongers like Jeffries and Farrakhan thrive in an atmosphere of isolation. Jeffries's racial theories of white inferiority and Jewish conspiracy could not be sustained in the normal interchange of rigorous academic discourse. To promote his views, Jeffries depends on the separation of his African-American Studies Department from the rest of the university. Any attempt to apply mainstream scholarly standards must be parried by the charge of racism. Jeffries, to survive, must answer only to his self-serving evaluative criteria and shut out the rest of the world.

Similarly, Louis Farrakhan's demagoguery depends on social isolation in order to thrive. His classically antisemitic ravings against Jewish power have no basis in reality and can only be believed to the extent that there is no contact with Jews to contradict his outlandish statements. In the same way, the charge contained in *The Secret Relationship Between Blacks and Jews* that Jews controlled the slave trade can only be sustained to the extent that its backers and their audience are insulated from generally accepted standards of truth which if applied to their work would prove them wrong. By contrast, disadvantaged blacks living at the margins of society would be comforted by the theory that their plight is due to someone else's conspiracy.

If social and intellectual isolation breeds the conditions of hatred, current trends in the United States are not encouraging. In residential patterns, changes in social status, political beliefs, and issue goals, the separation of African Americans from whites in general and Jews in particular remains pronounced. The conditions for substantial antisemitism are in place.

In their study of Atlanta, presumably one of the most racially enlightened cities in the country, Gary Orfield and Carole Ashkinaze illustrate the extent of African-American isolation. Not only is the inner city of Atlanta cut off from regular interaction with other, largely white sectors of the city, but when blacks earn higher incomes and move out of the core inner city, they do so to largely segregated suburbs. Residential separation remains in force at every level of social status.[12]

This residential separation has profound social consequences. Segregation means that blacks and whites attend different schools. Indeed, according to Orfield and Ashkinaze, black leadership accepted separate schools in return for greater control over the educational system. Since white schools in the suburbs receive more resources and offer a more college-oriented curriculum, more of their graduates acquire higher education, thus perpetuating inequality in future generations. A similar dynamic applies in the occupational sphere. Higher-level jobs are more plentiful adjacent to white areas, so that residential separation reinforces economic inequality.

As a result of these trends, African Americans in both the city and the suburbs live separately from whites, have lower average incomes, reside in worse housing, attend poorer schools, are subject to more crime, have access to fewer jobs, and see less opportunity for their children than do whites. Their isolation is profound. These conditions form the optimal breeding ground for the growth of extreme ideologies like those promoted by Jeffries and Farrakhan.

Isolation is found in other areas as well. The political sphere, for example, is often perceived as the arena where black and Jewish interests most coincide and where cooperation is most evident. Indeed, the 1992 elections continued a long-term trend for Jews and African Americans to vote in similar ways in presidential and congressional contests. Moreover, both groups have shown a greater-than-average tendency to back liberal candidates and issues and to support the cause of social equality. Still, these coalitional trends mask basic divergences. While Jews and blacks espouse similar values, they understand terms such as "liberal" and "equality" quite differently.

Steven M. Cohen's 1988 survey of Jewish, black, and other political opinion confirmed the widely held view that Jews, though at a declining rate, and African Americans are disproportionately likely to describe themselves as liberals and Democrats. Moreover, they are substantially more willing than other groups to back liberal positions such as support for social welfare programs, reductions in defense spending, and opposition to cuts in domestic expenditures. As noted above, however, the two groups diverge on more active forms of governmental intervention. For example, Cohen found substantial black support and Jewish opposition for "giving preference" in hiring blacks.[13]

Significant differences also exist on other dimensions of liberalism. Jews take very liberal positions on social issues such as support for church-state separation, reproductive rights, the rights of gay men and lesbians, and opposition to curbing the expression of pornography. African Americans, by contrast, are relatively socially conservative on these issues and tend to back positions more in line with the majority of Americans. For Jews, positions on social questions are an essential part of liberalism, whereas these issues are far less important to the liberalism of blacks, who tend to define their political stance more in terms of welfare and jobs issues.

There is also a significant difference on the meaning of equality. According to studies conducted by the National Research Council, blacks place primary emphasis in government action on the achievement of social equality. Their goal is not merely the freeing of the individual to compete equally in society but the attainment of substantial equality among groups. Underlying this goal is the conviction that economic inequalities are not primarily the result of individual talents or deficiencies but the consequences of structural unfairness that systematically disadvantages African Americans. Since the causes of inequality are thought to be social, the remedies must relate to advancement of the group as a whole, not merely the freeing of individuals from discrimination. This definition of equality underlies black support for programs such as school busing and affirmative action quotas.[14]

Jews, by contrast, support an activist government precisely to free the individual to compete without discrimination in a free society. Jews will back government spending for education, health care, and job training because they see these initiatives as enhancing the capacity of individuals to realize their own potential according to their talents and merits. The emphasis on equality is on the freeing of people from discrimination, not on giving any group a special edge on achievement. Therefore, Jews oppose by large margins government programs they perceive as unfairly advancing the interests of whole groups rather than individuals, such as school busing and affirmative action quotas. In short, both Jews and African Americans see equality as a high value and want government to promote it, but Jews believe that equality must center on the individual while blacks hold that this value can only be accomplished on the group level in this society.[15]

Jews are the most liberal of all white Americans. Yet on fundamental issues like the very meaning of liberalism and equality, they fundamentally differ from African Americans. This divergence poses the danger that blacks might become as isolated in America on political and ideological issues as they are residentially and economically. As noted above, if this growing isolation continues, it could provide fertile ground for the spread of extremist and antisemitic movements and views such as those of Jeffries and Farrakhan. Social separation would facilitate the expression of antisemitic opinions that, as we have seen, exist in the black community.

IV

Are trends toward social, political, and economic isolation in the African-American community inevitable, with the necessary result that blacks will increasingly feel alienated from mainstream society and adopt extremist and antisemitic ideologies? Or are there countervailing trends that could enhance the identity of black citizens with other Americans and further mutual respect and understanding? What kinds of actions on the part of Jews and African Americans can avoid the dangers of polarization and promote pluralism?

In a recent landmark essay, the noted historian Arthur Hertzberg argued against the widespread conception that antisemitism stems from a basically irrational hatred of Jews that is fundamentally impossible to explain but will always exist. Instead, Hertzberg points to impressive evidence that anti-semitism is associated with low levels of income and education and asserts that it can be countered by programs that further social stability by advancing the interests of minorities. Hertzberg's view presents a clear challenge to American Jewry. Rather than simply bemoaning antisemitism, the community can actively counter it by addressing the social conditions of poverty and isolation in which it flourishes.[16]

The 1992 ADL/Marttila poll lends powerful support to Hertzberg's argument. As noted above, for years many Jewish analysts believed that contrary to the trend in other groups, antisemitism among blacks increased as the income and education levels of respondents rose. As blacks attained the characteristics of mainstream American life, this interpretation held, they became more susceptible to unreasoned behavior such as antisemitism.

The ADL survey shattered this conceptualization. African Americans, like everyone else, become less prone to antisemitic attitudes as their incomes and education rise. The previous view described antisemitism among blacks as an essentially irrational phenomenon. It had no relation to education and was therefore not vulnerable to programs designed to counter it. But if, as the ADL survey indicates, antisemitism among African Americans follows well-known and understood patterns, effective initiatives can be mounted, especially those that break down African-American isolation and promise social and educational mobility.

The assumption behind this argument is that acculturation to mainstream American life and values reduces ethnic and racial hatred, including antisemitism. To the degree that people feel they have a real stake in this society, including an opportunity to advance in its social and economic systems, they will adopt its pluralistic values. There is a real stake for Jews and the society at large in promoting the mobility of African Americans.

But, as noted above, there are powerful forces in African-American life leading to communal separation. Social deprivation, poor education, lack of occupational opportunity, residential segregation, and other ills make difficult the achievement of the acculturation that encourages the adoption of mainstream values

and reduces hatreds such as antisemitism. Demagogues like Farrakhan and Jeffries feed off the frustration this isolation generates
to legitimate separatist ideologies.

Still, there exist important countervailing forces among
African Americans that are striving for the realization of full
opportunity and the integration of a proud black community in a
pluralistic American society. The most significant site for current
black advancement is the political arena. In 1992, in no small
part as a result of the enforcement of the Voting Rights Act of
1965, blacks increased their representation in Congress by 50 percent, to thirty-nine members. While many were elected from
overwhelmingly black areas and did not need to work with others to gain office, once in Congress the necessity to function
coalitionally will inevitably assert itself since working to build a
legislative majority is the only path to Congressional success.

At the same time, increased African-American representation
will doubtless secure support for issues high on the black agenda.
Other representatives will seek out the greater numbers of blacks
to join their coalitions and in doing so will have to pay heed to
the interests of African Americans. The same dynamic will play
out in state legislatures and city councils, where blacks have also
made impressive gains. Moreover, with their increased political
power, African-American officials will relate to leaders of other
communities as equals, rather than being put in the position of
accepting help from powerful patrons as was the case in the past.
Increased participation in American electoral politics, in short,
will inevitably produce the kind of working relationships that
build partnerships and discourage bigotry.[17]

Which direction black America will pursue, isolation or integration, or what portion of its population will choose either path,
is uncertain. The serious social problems facing the community,
and the resulting skepticism that America will provide a fair
chance for mobility, are real. The chances for progress through
political power and the rise of the black middle class present an
alternative vision for the future. Which perspective emerges as
more powerful will have a telling impact on the potential for
antisemitism to spread in the African-American community or to
continue its declining path.

Outside communities such as Jews can have only limited

impact on the direction of these debates among African Americans. But to the extent that bigotry declines with increasing social opportunity and acculturation, it is very much within the Jewish interest to participate in coalitions seeking greater opportunity for minority populations. More generally, to the extent that countering hatred requires acculturation to American pluralistic values, Jews have a strong stake in playing a vigorous role in America in defense of pluralism and the social and educational policies that further it. Yet the Jewish community is increasingly divided on whether it wants to pursue this agenda, for it is now split along lines not dissimilar to the debate just described among African Americans.

In recent years, the Jewish community's pubic agenda has increasingly turned inward. In the 1960s, Jewish organizations could be found in the forefront of campaigns for civil rights, social welfare, employment opportunity, and other broad social issues. In contrast, today the bulk of current Jewish effort is concentrated on a more narrow and internal set of concerns, such as promoting the interests of Israel, rescuing endangered Jewish communities abroad, combatting antisemitism, and seeking to assure Jewish continuity. In many ways, this more focused agenda speaks to critical Jewish needs; only a foolish community would ignore its own survival issues. The question, however, is whether in pursuit of the narrow agenda it is necessary or wise to jettison vigorous Jewish action on broad social issues.

This turning away from the broad domestic agenda has hurt the Jewish community's capacity to combat antisemitism in two ways. First, as noted above, antisemitism flourishes in an atmosphere of isolation. The more groups know each other, the less the opportunity exists for unchecked stereotypes to grow. If Jews have a legitimate concern about antisemitism in any community, the rational response is not to withdraw from contact, which will only exacerbate the bigotry, but to reach out to members of targeted groups who can be influenced in a positive direction. In the black context, this strategy would mean consistent relationships with African-American elected officials and national and local leaders but no interaction with followers of Farrakhan or Jeffries, whose hateful doctrines would only receive legitimacy from contact with mainstream Jewish groups.

This point applies just as aptly to the Jewish community as well. To the extent that Jews withdraw from arenas where they come into contact with other groups, stereotypes and bigotry toward others will grow in the Jewish community. The 1992 AJC survey shows that significant negative attitudes toward minorities already exist among New York City Jews. Jews are not immune to the general principle that isolation produces bigotry and tension.

Jewish withdrawal to a solely internal agenda hurts the fight against antisemitism in another way. Broad opposition to bigotry depends on acculturation to American pluralistic values. The viability of pluralism depends, in turn, on the committed participation by all groups in addressing the problems of a society they all share. If Jews withdraw from concern with pressing social problems, they will be harming the pluralistic ethos of the country and thereby weakening the most effective barrier the society has for combating all forms of bigotry, including antisemitism.

Of course, fighting antisemitism is not the only or even the primary motivation Jews should have in taking an activist stance on social issues. There must be a fundamental conviction that action in this area is the right thing to do and that policies that are backed will be effective in responding to human needs. Nor should this agenda be perceived in conflict with internal survival issues. Jewish continuity will only be assured if young Jews witness Jewish values in action in areas like urban policy.

But it is important to understand that Jewish actions have an impact on the direction of antisemitism. Gauging African American antisemitism requires an analysis of trends in the black community and their potential implications for Jews. But it is also necessary for Jews to look closely at the effects of their own behavior on intergroup relations and to take actions most conducive to the promoting of pluralistic values. No group can escape responsibility for combatting all forms of hatred and for building a more understanding society.

NOTES

1. The text of Jeffries's speech is reprinted in *New York Newsday,* August 19, 1991, pp. 3, 25–29.

2. *The Secret Relationship Between Blacks and Jews*, vol. 1 (Boston: Nation of Islam, 1991).

3. Henry Louis Gates, Jr., "Black Demagogues and Pseudo-Scholars," *New York Times*, July 20, 1992, p. A15; Cornel West, "On Black-Jewish Relations," in *Race Matters* (Boston: Beacon Press, 1993), p. 78.

4. *Louis Farrakhan: The Campaign to Manipulate Public Opinion* (New York: Anti-Defamation League, 1990); Kenneth Stern, *Farrakhan and the Jews in the 1990s* (New York: American Jewish Committee, 1992).

5. Richard Girgenti, *Report to the Governor on the Disturbances in Crown Heights*, 2 vols. (Albany: New York State Division of Criminal Justice, 1993); Kenneth Stern, *Crown Heights: A Case Study in Anti-Semitism and Community Relations* (New York: American Jewish Committee, 1991).

6. Jennifer Golub, *What Do We Know About Black Anti-Semitism?* (New York: American Jewish Committee, 1990); Gary Marx, *Protest and Prejudice* (New York: Harper & Row, 1969).

7. *Highlights from an Anti-Defamation League Survey on Anti-Semitism and Prejudice in America* (New York: ADL, 1992).

8. Carolyn Setlow and Renae Cohen, *1992 New York Intergroup Relations Survey* (New York: American Jewish Committee, 1993). Some of the conclusions in this chapter are based on the raw data for this survey.

9. The following analysis draws heavily from Gary E. Rubin, "A No-Nonsense Look at Anti-Semitism," *Tikkun*, May–June 1993, pp. 46–48, 79–81; and Milton D. Morris and Gary E. Rubin, "The Turbulent Friendship: Black-Jewish Relations in the 1990s," *Annals of the American Academy of Political and Social Science*, November 1993, pp. 42–60.

10. "Anti-Semitism in the United States, vol. 1, the Summary Report," Yankelovich, Skelly and White for the American Jewish Committee, July 1981, p. 26.

11. Tom W. Smith, *Jewish Attitudes Toward Blacks and Race Relations* (New York: American Jewish Committee, 1990).

12. Gary Orfield and Carole Ashkinaze, *The Closing Door* (Chicago: University of Chicago Press, 1991).

13. Steven M. Cohen, *The Dimensions of Jewish Liberalism* (New York: American Jewish Committee, 1989).

14. Gerald David Jaynes and Robin M. Williams, Jr., eds., *A Common Destiny: Blacks in American Society* (Washington, D.C.: National Research Council, National Academy Press, 1989), p. 214.

15. Smith, *Jewish Attitudes*.

16. Arthur Hertzberg, "Is Anti-Semitism Dying Out?" *New York Review of Books*, June 24, 1993, pp. 51–57.

17. Morris and Rubin, "Turbulent Friendship," pp. 53–56.

·8·

Antisemitism and the Far Right: "Hate" Groups, White Supremacy, and the Neo-Nazi Movement

DANIEL LEVITAS
Daniel Levitas, former executive director of the Center
for Democratic Renewal, has written extensively on
extremist political and social movements.

Antisemitism has long played a pivotal role in the formation of ideologies that inform the activities of extremist and "hate" groups. Daniel Levitas's essay, using right-wing hate groups as paradigmatic, probes the ideology of extremism. Levitas makes the point that the "radical right" is not monolithic, even as they share common attributes, and he highlights the differences between diverse hate groups. Indeed, the 1995 terrorist bombing of the Oklahoma City Federal Building highlighted the often-nuanced differences between "militias" and other groups of the far right. While there are in fact links between many in the militia movement and adherents of Nazi and "Identity" groups, Oklahoma City demonstrated that one need not be an antisemite to be a murderer.

Levitas moves from the history of the Ku Klux Klan to the contemporary "hate" manifestations of organized extremist groups. With respect to counteraction, his expressed view is that whatever legislative and judicial vehicles are at the community's disposal ought be used in combatting hate crimes, and that such counteraction is effective. In this regard, the reader is invited to compare the somewhat more skeptical view of Marc D. Stern, "Antisemitism and the Law," chapter 18.

J.A.C.

White supremacist and neo-Nazi hate groups are commonly thought of as politically marginal yet sensationally violent. They are, however, part of a larger social movement whose impact greatly exceeds the sum of all its parts. The influence of this movement is felt far beyond the ranks of those involved: the 25,000 hard-core activists and the 150,000 to 200,000 supporters who buy literature, attend rallies, or make donations.

The movement is also significant because it acts as an intellectual and spiritual repository for many of the flaws of American society such as slavery, manifest destiny, nativism, Jim Crow laws, and segregation. Like a virus that replicates within its host, hate groups have an opportunistic relationship to society. They survive by preserving and generating *ideas* inimical to democracy and thrive by introducing them into the body politic.

Antisemitism and racism have historically been a driving force behind the movement, pushing hate groups into often violent conflict with the accepted norms of what constitutes a pluralistic society. Over the past fifteen years, hatred of lesbians and gay men has also taken center stage on the far right agenda.

Whether based in the Midwest, North, or South, hate groups share a common antisemitic and racist philosophy as well as a murderous hatred of lesbians and gay men, nonwhite immigrants, Communists, and agents of "ZOG"—an imagined "Zionist Occupied Government." In their view, the government of the United States is in the thralls of an international Jewish conspiracy which has disenfranchised and debased the white majority through affirmative action, forced integration, and "race mixing."

The Ku Klux Klan still parades in hoods and sheets by day and pursues time-honored traditions of cross burning and racist terrorism by night. Violent skinheads and neo-Nazis strive to provoke a race war and plot to overthrow the government while instructing their members in the virtues of underground guerrilla warfare they call "leaderless resistance." The Populist Party has chosen electoral politics as its arena of activism.

Antisemitism manifests itself in different ways among different groups. In the rural heartland, so-called Christian Patriots and Constitutionalists view Jews as agents of an international banking conspiracy responsible for the perceived illegal and unconstitutional activities of the Federal Reserve. These advocates of "Christian Common Law" preach tax resistance and speak of the illegitimacy of Fourteenth Amendment citizens, that is, those slaves emancipated at the end of the Civil War and guaranteed their rights by Constitutional amendment.

For neo-Nazis and traditional national socialists, Jews are parasitic culture-destroyers who must be exterminated along with other racial and ethnic minorities. Believers in the racist theology of Christian Identity think Jews are satanic impostors, racial minorities are subhuman, and they themselves are the true descendants of the lost tribes of Israel. In the South, Jews are seen as Bolshevik social engineers who have forced integration upon an embattled white minority. Regardless of their view of Jews, diverse hate groups share the same goal of reinventing the United States in the image of the country as it never was: a white, Christian republic.

Unlike thirty or sixty years ago, when Klansmen yearned to return to the days of Jim Crow segregation or revive the unreconstructed South, today's advocates of white supremacy look to the future and the opportunity to create a *new* nation by politics, agitation, and armed insurrection.

Hate groups are both classically reactionary, favoring ultraconservatism as an antidote to the perceived evils of liberalism, and downright revolutionary when it comes to their view of the state, which they hope to dismantle.

In their disdain for feminism, immigration, affirmative action, and equal rights for lesbians and gay men, hate groups are a lot like traditional conservatives. Antisemitic ideas are present in both camps, just as they exist across the broadest spectrum of political thought, from left to right. The fact that practically all hate groups view traditional conservatives with contempt does not negate these underlying similarities.

What distinguishes the far right from most ultraconservative groups and religious fundamentalists, however, is more than extra zeal for their commonly held convictions. White supremacists and neo-Nazis want to go beyond simply asserting Western, cultural, "traditional" family values. They want to *exterminate* their opponents. Ultraconservatives are content to establish their hegemony by subjugating their opposition.

Although antisemitism is certainly present in the ultraconservative movement and religious right, it is of a different type than that on the far right. Conservatives, such as the late president Richard Nixon, may hold antisemitic stereotypes, ascribe certain "racial" characteristics to Jews, or act punitively against individuals because they are Jews, but this antipathy does not extend to either a desire or a plan to attempt a second Final Solution. This dividing line—between the institutionalized racism, ethnocentrism, and homophobia of ultraconservatives and the annihilationism of the far right—is a key factor that distinguishes one from the other.

Equally significant, and disturbing, are the occasional bridges laid across this divide by the affinity of some ultraconservatives for Holocaust revisionism and other virulent strains of antisemitism. The distinction between ultraconservatism and the far right also becomes blurred when some religious fundamentalists call for the execution of homosexuals.

In its broadest context, social antisemitism includes both personal prejudices and political movements. The former can sometimes be measured quantitatively with opinion polls, while the latter can be assessed, at best, only through qualitative means, such as examining the growth or decline of far-right groups.

Although hate groups are by no means alone in their ability to inject antisemitism and racism into mainstream political debates, this phenomenon is one of the important aspects of the far right and is something unlikely to be revealed by opinion polls or other quantitative means.

It is important to point out that hate groups have not gone unchallenged. Religious, civil rights, and nonprofit advocacy organizations have organized against them, aided hate-crime victims and proposed solutions ranging from campus speech codes to stiffer jail terms for perpetrators of hate crimes. Police departments, city councils, state legislatures, Congress, and the U.S. Supreme Court also have responded to hate-group activity, often in conflicting ways. Many of the proposed remedies have sparked fierce debate, particularly among civil libertarians, liberals, and antibigotry activists.

THE KU KLUX KLAN

Since its founding in Pulaski, Tennessee, in December 1865, the Ku Klux Klan has used vigilantism and violence to attack its opponents, real and imagined. Its tools have been the hood, the gun, and the rope, its pastimes night riding, cross burning, and murder. From 1865 until 1872, the Klan raised a guerrilla army throughout the South to intimidate newly freed slaves, defeat African-American suffrage, and sabotage Reconstruction. By the time the Klan was formally disbanded in 1869, following congressional probes and mass arrests, it had largely accomplished its goal of restoring pre–Civil War "law and order" to the South.

During the Klan's second era, which was inaugurated with a 1915 cross burning at the top of Georgia's Stone Mountain, the organization's slogan became "100 percent Americanism." The Klan was still steeped in white supremacy, but it added antisemitism and hatred of Catholics to its agenda as well.

Although some were content to take the Klan's rhetoric at face value, the Klan's war against immigration, communism, and labor unions was also a surrogate battle against the Jews, who were regarded as alien Bolsheviks determined to corrupt America through liberalism. Of course, the Klan also despised Irish and European immigrants, and its nativist rhetoric was aimed at them too. In addition, the Klan ostensibly opposed dope, bootlegging, prostitution, and adultery.

The anti-Jewish and anti-Catholic tenets of Protestant fundamentalism were a powerful force behind the rise of the 1920s Klan, and it has been estimated that as many as 40,000 ministers joined the hooded order during this period.[1]

The rebirth of the Klan was linked to one of the most notorious antisemitic incidents in American history. In 1915, Leo Frank, the Jewish owner of a Marietta, Georgia, pencil factory, was convicted of the rape and murder of fourteen-year-old Mary Phagan, one of his employees. Frank's trial was conducted in an atmosphere of antisemitic hysteria, and the evidence against him was biased and inconclusive. (Eighty-one years later, on March 11, 1986, Frank was posthumously pardoned by Georgia governor Joe Frank Harris in response to a campaign by the Atlanta Jewish Community Relations Council, the National Jewish Community Relations Advisory Council, the Anti-Defamation League, and other Jewish groups.)

Frank was abducted from a prison farm soon after his conviction and lynched by a mob calling themselves the Knights of

Mary Phagan. They rallied to the cry "End Jewish Interference in Georgia." Col. William Simmons, a former circuit-riding minister and the founder of the revived Ku Klux Klan, took note of the breadth and depth of this antisemitic sentiment when, three months after the lynching, he recruited members of the Knights to sign the first Klan charter.

As explained by Elizabeth Tyler, co-owner of the Southern Publicity Association, which had been retained by Simmons to coordinate Klan membership recruitment and public relations efforts, Jews were upset about the Klan because they knew it "[taught] the wisdom of spending American money with American men."[2]

Another indicator of the tenor of those times could be found in the widespread distribution of *The International Jew: The World's Foremost Problem*, a rewrite of the antisemitic tract *The Protocols of the Elders of Zion*. *The International Jew* was first serialized in 1920 by Henry Ford in the pages of his newspaper *The Dearborn Independent*, and half a million copies were put into circulation in the United States. The Klan also reprinted its own bound edition of the *Dearborn Independent* articles.

As a mass movement, the Klan was a great success. It recruited three to four million members and elected numerous governors, U.S. senators, and congressmen. The Klan also played an instrumental role in pressuring Congress to pass a succession of laws restricting immigration, culminating with the Immigration Acts of 1921–1924. In this way, the long arm of the Klan reached forward across history. Its impact was felt by those Jewish refugees fleeing Hitler's armies and concentration camps who were unable to enter the United States because of the immigration quotas established with the support of the Klan nearly a generation before.

The Klan fell on hard times in the 1930s, due to a combination of factors. First, it was severely weakened by a succession of internal rivalries and lawsuits between competing factions. Second, a portion of the political terrain it had occupied was seized by newer groups promoting fascism and Nazism. Third, the momentum of the New Deal and the liberalism of the Franklin D. Roosevelt administration captured the hearts and minds of millions of Americans and provided an alternative to the race-baiting and isolationism of the Klan. Lastly, the Klan was a victim of its own success. After passage of the Immigration Act of 1924, the Klan had accomplished one of its major objectives and it became more difficult to rally support around the immigration issue. The Klan's forays into politics, while often successful, also led to organizational faction fights and galvanized external opposition.

Of course the Klan did not disappear. While its activities paled in comparison to those of the previous decade, it still zealously pursued floggings and murder. The Klan focused its energies on combatting FDR, the New Deal, and the "twin evils" of unionism and communism, which had recently arrived in the South.

In the late 1930s, some Klan leaders began talking to the pro-Nazi German American Bund about a merger. The alliance culminated in an embarrassing debacle in August 1940, when hundreds of Klansmen and their supporters rallied with 800 members of the German American Bund at the Bund's 200-acre camp near Andover, New Jersey. The event provoked an uproar in the press and in Congress, prompting the formation of the Dies Committee, which later became the House Un-American Activities Committee (HUAC). Although the Dies Committee displayed more interest in harassing labor unions and hunting down Communists, some of its revelations were damaging to the Klan.

This was not the first time the Klan had established links with supporters of Nazi Germany. Seventeen years earlier, in 1923, Rev. Otto Strohschein, a naturalized American citizen and Klansman, formed the German Order of the Fiery Cross in Berlin with the goal of "ridding the country of undesirables by fighting the Jews."[3] Although Hitler eventually eliminated the order, as he did all secret societies not directly under the Nazi party's control, German fascists and American Klan groups expressed their mutual admiration for one another in various communiqués across the Atlantic for almost two decades.

The Klan and the Bund were not the only organizations in the United States that admired Hitler and endorsed the Nazi campaign against the Jews. Hundreds flourished. Some of the leaders became household names, including William Dudley Pelly, Rev. Gerald Winrod, and Rev. Gerald L. K. Smith, founder of the Christian Nationalist Crusade. Other groups such as Charles Lindbergh's America First Committee camouflaged their antisemitism in the rhetoric of isolationism and received the endorsement of ardent Jew-haters such as Rev. Charles Coughlin, the famed "radio priest."

America's entry into the Second World War further eroded support for the Klan, however, and by 1942 the organization had only ten thousand dues-paying members. A 1944 tax bill levied by the Internal Revenue Service on income and profits earned by the Klan during the 1920s finally brought the lingering second era of the KKK to a close.

An Atlanta obstetrician, Dr. Samuel Green, led the organization's postwar revival in 1946. However, it took another decade before the third-era Klan emerged full force. Beginning in the late 1940s, a growing union movement in the South, combined with more frequent challenges to segregation, gave the Klan plenty to rail against.

After the U.S. Supreme Court declared segregated public schools unconstitutional in *Brown* v. *Board of Education* on May 17, 1954, the Klan had yet another reason to step up its attacks on civil rights activists, sympathetic whites, and anyone else it believed was behind the communist plot to bury Jim Crow. One 1959 report attributed 530 acts of violence to the Klan in the five years following the Brown decision.[4] The list included six murders, twenty-nine shootings, forty-four beatings, and forty-five bombings, of which four targeted Jewish temples or community centers in Miami, Jacksonville, Nashville, and Atlanta. The third-era Klan was well underway.

With the passage of the 1964 Civil Rights Act and the 1965 Voting Rights Act, it became apparent that the Klan had failed to stop the civil rights movement. By 1972, the Klan had faded almost entirely from public view, and in 1974 the Federal Bureau of Investigation estimated Klan membership at an all-time low of 1,500. However, that same year, a twenty-four-year-old history graduate from Louisiana State University named David Duke ushered the Klan into its fourth era.

Duke recruited on college campuses, rode the television talk-show circuit, and traveled to South Boston during the busing crisis of 1975. His media-savvy approach helped the Knights of the Ku Klux Klan quickly recruit 3,500 members. Duke was a different breed of Klansman, but it was more than his penchant for fancy suits and mass media that set him apart. Ideologically speaking, Duke was a National Socialist first and a Klansman second. His genius was in recognizing how the trappings of the Klan—and America's fascination with them—could be used successfully to pursue an essentially Nazi agenda.

Duke did not disappear into obscurity like so many Klan leaders who had their fifteen minutes of fame before him. Instead, he patiently focused his efforts on the electoral arena. In 1975, Duke won 33 percent of the vote in his bid for the Louisiana State Senate, campaigning as a moderate conservative. He ran again in 1979, polling 28 percent of the vote. Duke continually refined his approach, achieving spectacular success in campaigns for U.S. senator and Louisiana governor a decade later.

In 1978, Bill Wilkinson, a former ally of Duke's, took center stage. Wilkinson had formed his own group, the Invisible Empire Knights of the Ku Klux Klan, and his incendiary rhetoric and violence attracted headlines and scores of new recruits. By 1979, Klan membership in several different factions had risen to 11,500, the highest level in more than a decade.

THE RESURGENCE OF THE RIGHT

The revival of the fourth-era Klan took place within the context of a broader resurgence of more sophisticated far-right groups. Although many organizations often competed with one another, a new emphasis was placed on coalition building and the exchange of ideas. Individual leaders began to look beyond the narrow boundaries of their organizations and see themselves as part of a larger social movement.

Throughout the 1980s, the far right worked hard to create a mass base among certain key constituencies, and it achieved significant results. Large numbers of dispossessed farmers and rural residents became convinced that an international Jewish banking conspiracy was behind the farm crisis. Thousands of white youth joined the skinhead movement while others participated in racist, reactionary, and homophobic activities on college campuses.

The movement contained distinct military, religious, political, and intellectual components, as it does today. Paramilitary training camps mushroomed, prompting dozens of states to enact restrictive legislation. Christian Identity theology flourished in a wide swath, cutting diagonally across the country from the Pacific Northwest through the Great Plains and Midwest and onward to the Southeast. In 1984 Klansmen, neo-Nazis, and others were joined together by the far-right Liberty Lobby to create the Populist Party, an amalgam of racists and antisemites who attempted to use the legitimacy of electoral politics to spread their message of hate. Academic racists joined with Holocaust deniers to support the Institute for Historical Review (IHR), another brainchild of the Liberty Lobby's founder, Willis Carto.

THE KLAN/NAZI UNDERGROUND

Philosophically, the driving force behind the resurgence of the far right in the late 1970s was a growing belief that more radical, revolutionary measures would be required if the white supremacist movement was ever going to accomplish its goals.

When Jim Crow was the law of the land, the Klan had prided itself on being a "law and order" organization. Now that segregation was struck down, some Klan groups adopted a more militant outlook and allied themselves with Nazi groups or openly embraced national socialist ideas. A few called for the violent overthrow of the government.

These developments were brought home dramatically in 1979 with the fatal shooting of anti-Klan, Communist Workers Party marchers in Greensboro, North Carolina. On November 3, a caravan of forty Klansmen and Nazis opened fire on the protestors and in eighty-eight seconds five were dead, nine others wounded. An all-white, all-Christian jury acquitted the shooters, despite the fact that the massacre was recorded by television cameras in its entirety.

The attack was orchestrated by a coalition of hate groups under the banner of the United Racist Front and was the product of numerous planning meetings between Klansmen and neo-Nazis. Harold Covington, a leader of the National Socialist Party of America, was one of the principal strategists behind the Front.

One year later, in 1980, he won 54,000 votes in a bid for North Carolina attorney general.

In 1979, Richard Butler, a Christian Identity preacher and former California Klansman, convened the first Aryan Nations World Congress on his twenty-acre encampment in northern Idaho. By 1982, the congress had become an annual event, attracting up to three hundred Klansmen, neo-Nazis, Christian patriots, and Identity adherents from the United States and abroad, radicalizing participants.

Similar gatherings were held in Michigan at the farm of Robert Miles, a former insurance company executive, organizer for George Wallace, and Klansman. Miles had also served six years in jail for planning to firebomb empty school buses in 1971 as a protest against busing. Ironically, Miles termed his gatherings the Sanhedrin, after the council of Jews held in ancient times.

After several years of talking, people were finally ready for action. In 1983, Miles and Louis Beam, another former Klan leader, began publishing the *Inter-Klan Newsletter and Survival Alert*, an underground newsletter that advocated armed revolution as an alternative to public rallies and other ways of building mass support for the white supremacist movement. "The vast majority of the White Race [sic] will . . . oppose the Klan and any other racial movement. . . . It is . . . pure fantasy to imagine the Klan as a broad based movement that will . . . affect peaceful political change. . . . There should be no doubt that all means short of armed conflict have been exhausted," they wrote.[5] It was in the *Alert* that Miles and Beam first declared that this new strategy of revolutionary activities inaugurated the arrival of the fifth-era Ku Klux Klan.

In *Essays of a Klansman* (1983), Beam argued that if the Klan was to be successful in the fifth era it would have to return to the principles of clandestine terror that had served it so well during the 1860s.

Beam published a point system which ranked the effectiveness of "proposed acts against the enemy," depending on whether the victims were government decision makers, federal court judges, civil rights leaders, or "street people." Those who carried out acts against the "control center" earned one point, becoming an "aryan warrior," while those who acted against "White Jewish

Demonstrators [sic], agitators, communists, Negroes, Mexicans, or 20 million other non-whites" were rated only as "cannon fodder" or mere "assailants."

It was these various writings, and the ideas behind them, that helped spark the formation of the neo-Nazi terrorist group the Order, also known as the Bruder Schweigen or Silent Brotherhood. The blueprint for the Order also was laid down in more detail in a book published in 1978, *The Turner Diaries* by William Pierce, a former assistant professor of physics at Oregon State University and founder of the neo-Nazi National Alliance. As a vehicle to disseminate Pierce's personal political views, the novel told the story of Earl Turner and his futuristic band of neo-Nazi revolutionaries and their war against "race-mixers," homosexuals, the FBI, and the Pentagon. The book played a key role in spreading Nazi ideology across the far right.[6]

Among those who joined the Order were former Klansmen, Christian Identity followers, and neo-Nazis. Their first meetings took place in the summer of 1983 at the Aryan Nations compound in Idaho. Beginning in December that year they committed a series of crimes including bank robbery, murder, armored-car robberies that brought them $6 million, and counterfeiting. Their most prominent victim was Jewish talk-show host Alan Berg, who was gunned down in the garage of his home in Denver, Colorado, on June 18, 1984. In April 1985, twenty-three Order members were indicted on racketeering charges. By year's end, all had pled guilty or been convicted and were sentenced to lengthy prison terms.

By the mid-1980s, there were several dozen Klan factions operating throughout the United States and the most influential leaders had adopted a decidedly militant stance. For example, Glenn Miller's White Patriot Party (WPP) became one of North Carolina's most vocal proponents of revolutionary white supremacy. The paramilitary WPP had 1,500 members at its peak and often marched in camouflage fatigues, several hundred strong, behind signs saying "Wake up whitey! End Federal Oppression. Expose Zionist Empire." Members displayed stiff-armed salutes to accompany their cries of "white power." At the same time, other, more traditional Klan groups stayed the course and denounced their Nazified brethren.

Although the rank-and-file members of the Order had been prosecuted successfully, the government still wanted to crack down on those who had masterminded the violence. In 1987, the Justice Department indicted Butler, Beam, Miles, and seven others on charges of seditious conspiracy to overthrow the government of the United States. After a three-month trial in 1988 in Fort Smith, Arkansas, the ten defendants were acquitted by an all-white jury. The trial was an embarrassing setback for government prosecutors.

THE SKINHEAD MOVEMENT

At the same time as the Klan/Nazi underground was taking shape, gangs of racist, neo-Nazi youth known as skinheads first made their presence known in the United States. The skinheads had originated in Great Britain as an offshoot of various youth subcultures including the punk rock music scene, and by the early 1970s many were involved in neofascist organizations like the British National Party. In 1986, the Atlanta-based Center for Democratic Renewal (formerly the National Anti-Klan Network) counted 300 racist skinheads in the United States. By 1991, the number had increased tenfold to 3,500 in more than thirty-five cities.

At first the skinheads operated largely independent of other hate groups. A significant generation gap existed between the hard-drinking, rowdy, often drug-using skinheads and their older counterparts in the white supremacist movement. The skinhead emphasis on Nazism was also a source of conflict between them and some of the more traditional Klan groups which didn't yet share Louis Beam's philosophy.

It was not long, however, before the skinheads joined forces with other white supremacists. Religion and theology provided key avenues for interaction. Butler organized special events to attract skinheads, particularly those interested in Christian Identity. One such event, the "Aryan Youth Congress," was held on the Idaho compound in 1989 on the 100th anniversary of the birth of Adolf Hitler.

Other skinheads who were less interested in Identity—or who

favored Odinism and Paganism instead—linked up with Tom Metzger's White Aryan Resistance (W.A.R.). Metzger had served under David Duke as the Grand Dragon of the California Knights of the Ku Klux Klan in the late 1970s. In 1980 he made headlines after winning the Democratic nomination for Congress from California's Forty-third District. In addition to promoting Norse mythology and nature worship, Metzger preached a particular brand of neo-Nazism known as the "third position," which emphasized class consciousness and the need for white workers to struggle against both capitalism and communism.

Metzger and his son John organized the "White Student Union" to recruit racist youth at college campuses and on the streets. In 1987, the Aryan Youth Movement/White Student Union newsletter spoke of creating "a new wave of predatory leaders among Aryan Youth." "Our enemies understand only one message: that of the knife, the gun and the club on the campus or in the streets," it continued. "We shall continue to encourage 'sporadic incidents' . . . across America . . . while simultaneously rebuilding the hunter-killer instincts in our youth."

The following year, in November 1988, an Ethiopian student living in Portland, Oregon, named Mulugeta Seraw was bludgeoned to death by a group of skinheads linked to Metzger and W.A.R. Seraw's brutal death sparked a public outcry and led to a $12.5 million judgment against Metzger after the Montgomery, Alabama–based Southern Poverty Law Center (SPLC), together with the Anti-Defamation League, sued him in civil court on behalf of Seraw's surviving family.

Metzger's racist propaganda was circulated widely among the skinheads, and a telephone hot line operated by W.A.R. served as a communications center for neo-Nazi youth. Other Metzger associates, such as Dennis Mahon, formerly of the White Knights of the Ku Klux Klan, reached out to skinheads by organizing various "Aryan Fests" which featured racist music by day and paramilitary training at night.

Under the leadership of Thom Robb—himself an Identity minister—the Knights of the Ku Klux Klan made its first concerted attempt to reach out to the skinhead movement in January 1987, at the Knights' annual anti–Martin Luther King holiday rally in Pulaski, Tennessee. Skinheads were a visible presence at

the Pulaski rallies in subsequent years. The Knights also recruited Shawn Slater, a skinhead from Aurora, Colorado, who ran a
mail-order music business dedicated to promoting the British
Nazi band Skrewdriver and the sale of neo-Nazi paraphernalia.

Other groups that developed links to skinheads included the
Confederate Knights of America, based in North Carolina; the
National Socialist German Workers Party—Overseas Division
(NSDAP-AO), led by Gary Rex Lauck, of Lincoln, Nebraska; and
the Tennessee-based Christian Guard.

Skinheads committed a total of at least thirty-five murders
from December 1987 to October 1993, and hundreds, perhaps
thousands, of assaults. Judged by Louis Beam's point system, the
skinheads who carried out these attacks were hardly "Aryan warriors." Their targets were usually chosen at random and included
people of color, lesbians and gay men, the homeless, synagogues
and other Jewish institutions, as well as fellow skinheads.

However, the brutality of these incidents, combined with a
series of more overtly political skinhead crimes, did contribute to
the revolutionary atmosphere that Klan leaders like Beam sought
to create.

In 1992 a group of skinheads associated with the Aryan
National Front (ANF) based outside Birmingham, Alabama, were
convicted for stealing military hardware, including M-16 rifles
and explosives, from Fort Benning, Georgia. Arrested along with
them was Bill Riccio, a longtime white supremacist and former
Invisible Empire Knights of the Ku Klux Klan organizer. ANF
skinheads were also convicted of the 1992 murder of a homeless
African-American man in Birmingham.

In July 1993, the FBI arrested eight neo-Nazis around Los
Angeles who called themselves the Fourth Reich Skinheads. Six
of those arrested were under the age of twenty-three. They were
charged with trafficking in weapons and bombs and planning to
murder black motorist Rodney King (whose videotaped beating by
police officers sparked riots in south-central Los Angeles in 1992)
to provoke a race war. In addition to plotting a Sunday morning
machine-gun attack on one of the area's largest black churches,
they planned to send a letter bomb to a local rabbi.

Some of those involved in the plot had been members of the
racist, antisemitic, and anti-Christian Church of the Creator

(COTC). Initially, many skinheads were drawn to COTC because it provided them with boxes of literature which they distributed anonymously in suburban and working-class neighborhoods. With the headline "RAHOWA" (an acronym for "Racial Holy War") blazoned across its masthead, the COTC newspaper generated instant media coverage and controversy which the skinheads loved.

COTC also operated a "ministry" to imprisoned skinheads and other incarcerated white supremacists, notably youths. Like the prison ministries operated by Richard Butler and Robert Miles, COTC targeted inmates associated with the Aryan Brotherhood, a white prison gang whose motto is "Kill to get in, die to get out."

Just two weeks after the arrests of the Fourth Reich Skinheads, the Sacramento, California, and Tacoma, Washington, offices of the National Association for the Advancement of Colored People (NAACP) were firebombed. Three skinheads linked to both COTC and the neo-Nazi American Front were arrested for the Tacoma bombing.

The skinhead movement was attractive to young people in part because it was peer-based and rejected adult interference. Unlike the Klan youth auxiliaries of the late 1970s, which never really recruited beyond the families of Klan members, skinhead groups operated independently, even though they sometimes acted in concert with the philosophies and wishes of a handful of older mentors.

The skinhead movement also became significant because it was truly unique. While nearly all the hate groups of the 1980s and '90s traced their origins to an earlier political incarnation or movement, the skinheads were the most original development on the far-right scene.

The skinhead movement emerged just when other far-right groups were becoming more revolutionary. And the violent fervor of groups like the Order induced the skinheads to militancy which brought in more members and further radicalized the climate for far-right organizing. Although some established Klan groups tried to distance themselves from skinhead violence, fearing civil lawsuits or criminal prosecutions, their disclaimers were usually more rhetorical than heartfelt.

At the same time as the skinheads radicalized the larger movement, their activities also heightened long-simmering political tensions between those on the far right who still hoped to impact the mainstream and those who preferred to pursue the path of revolution.

The far right's emphasis on recruiting youth—whether in the streets or on campus—made its mark in the 1980s, and will be felt in succeeding generations, as skinheads and college students come of age and continue their political activities. This phenomenon underscores the need for new and more effective curricula dealing with issues of racism and bigotry as well as continued expansion—and improvement—of Holocaust education efforts.

CHRISTIAN IDENTITY THEOLOGY

There was more to the increased militancy of the far right, however, than simply a new affinity for Nazism. According to Leonard Zeskind, former research director for the Center for Democratic Renewal and a national expert on hate-group activity, it was the religious beliefs of Christian Identity that provided the necessary theological rationalization for much of the racist and antisemitic violence during the past decade.

Identity proponents such as Richard Butler taught that the "Anglo-Saxon-Celtic" people were the true descendants of the lost tribes of Israel and that Jews were satanic because they were the product of the sexual union of Eve and the Devil. Blacks and other racial and ethnic minorities were "pre-adamic": mistakes by God before the creation of the perfect white race. People of color were referred to as "mud people," because they were manufactured from the earth, as opposed to whites, who were formed from divine materials.

British or Anglo-Israelism, as Identity was originally called, was developed by Richard Brothers, a delusional eighteenth-century religious fanatic who had proclaimed himself a direct descendent of King David and rightful heir to the British throne. In 1785 he was committed to an asylum.

With the publication of tracts such as *Our Israelitish Origin* by John Wilson in 1840 and *Identification of the British Nation with Lost Israel* by Edward Hine in 1871, Anglo-Israelism spread throughout Britain.[7] The religion was first popularized in the United States in 1928 by Howard Rand, a Bible scholar, lawyer, and one-time Prohibition candidate for Massachusetts attorney general, who started a small Anglo-Israelite group in Haverhill, Massachusetts. In 1953, Rand's slick, multicolored hate sheet, *Destiny*, was being sent to 15,000 subscribers in the United States.

Although Anglo-Israelism was not always antisemitic and racist—some believers argued that Jews should be recognized as "kin"—its earliest proponents in the United States, including Rand, W. J. Cameron, and Wesley Swift, were inveterate racists. Many had direct links to quasi-fascist organizations.[8]

Christian Identity was significant because it transcended the mere anti-Judaism of Protestant fundamentalism and offered a new, more virulent brand of antisemitism. Like fundamentalism, this antisemitism was deeply rooted in Scripture, but it also offered an explicitly racial theory of the Jews.

The emergence of Christian Identity also owed a certain allegiance to the Eugenics movement, which had taken shape more than one decade earlier. The publication of such works as *The Passing of the Great Race* (published in 1916 by Charles Scribner's Sons) by Madison Grant—then the chairman of the New York Zoological Society—and Klansman Lothrop Stoddard's *The Rising Tide of Color* (published by Scribner's in 1920) contributed significantly to the popularization of racial antisemitism, a theme echoed by Christian Identity.

In addition to providing religious justification for far-right violence, Christian Identity was significant because it promoted cohesion among disparate elements of the far right. Neo-Nazis, Klansmen, Christian patriots, and other white supremacists, who often disagreed about many aspects of movement organizing, were able to establish a common bond through their shared faith. Identity also provided a useful entree into many communities that would have otherwise rejected groups espousing Nazism or white supremacy. This was especially true in the rural Midwest and Great Plains, where many people were recruited into the far right through innocuous Christian Identity "bible study" sessions, which replaced overt appeals to antisemitism and race hatred.

Although no reliable figures exist for the total number of

Identity believers in the United States, it is possible there are as many as 40,000 adherents. This figure does not include the relatively large membership of other, more "mainstream" British Israelite groups, such as Herbert W. Armstrong's Worldwide Church of God—an Anglo-Israelite sect that eschews racism and antisemitism—which had 100,000 followers in North America in the mid-1980s.

THE NORTHWEST MOUNTAIN REPUBLIC

Of all the regions of the country, Identity established its heaviest concentration of followers in the isolated, rugged terrain of Washington State, northern Idaho, and western Montana. By the early 1980s, the region had also become home to the Aryan Nations and a handful of other, lesser-known far-right groups.

In 1986, Richard Butler and Bob Miles suggested that white supremacists from across the nation should relocate to Idaho, Washington, Montana, Oregon, and Wyoming. Their scheme was seconded by other leaders, but not by all. Those who supported the idea called their plan the "Northwest Territorial Imperative," and dreamed of seceding from the "mongrelized" United States to establish a five-state "Northwest Mountain Republic." While the plan did not spur large numbers of movement activists to relocate, the region was still regarded as something of a safe haven by hate groups. In addition to those who responded to Butler's call, the geographic isolation of the Northwest made it particularly attractive to many on the far right who wanted to drop out of mainstream society and avoid taxes and other forms of government intrusion.

Among those who fit the latter description were two Christian Identity followers from Iowa, Randy and Vicki Weaver, who moved to northern Idaho in the mid-1980s. Their experiment with self-sufficient living and far-right politics came to a bloody end in August 1992, after an eleven-day standoff with two hundred federal agents.

The impasse began when a federal marshal, William Degan, was killed in a gun battle with the Weavers and a family associate, twenty-four-year-old Kevin Harris. Degan had been conduct-

189

ing surveillance on the mountain ridge in an attempt to enforce an arrest warrant issued for Randy Weaver for allegedly selling illegal firearms to a government agent three years previously. Weaver had failed to appear at a 1991 court hearing and had vowed never to be taken alive. Police and federal agents used tanks, earth-moving equipment, remote-controlled surveillance machines, and a helicopter in a futile effort to dislodge the Weavers from their cabin on top of Ruby Ridge.

By the time it was over, three people were dead, including Degan, Vicki Weaver, and the couple's fourteen-year-old son. The event made national headlines and galvanized Klansmen, Christian patriots, and skinheads across the country.

Eventually, Populist Party presidential candidate James "Bo" Gritz negotiated the surrender of Weaver and Harris, who had also been severely wounded. Weaver and Harris were acquitted of murder charges related to the shooting of Marshal Degan in July 1993. In addition to highlighting the murderous potential of Christian Identity believers, the Weaver standoff was significant in at least three other respects.

First, it demonstrated the tremendous depth of local support that the Christian Patriot movement had cultivated in the region. For eighteen months, from February 1991 until August 1992, the Weavers held out in their cabin without electricity or telephone while being regularly supplied with food by a network of friends, neighbors, and supporters. After Weaver surrendered, Identity leaders and far-rightists organized the United Citizens for Justice to press for murder indictments against federal authorities.

Second, the acquittal of Weaver and Harris demonstrated that the criminal justice system could not always be effective in prosecuting even the most extreme far-rightists, especially in cases where jurors thought the government was using strong-arm tactics. Like the 1988 sedition acquittals in Fort Smith, Arkansas, the trial of Weaver and Harris was a debacle for government prosecutors. In the eyes of the media and the jurors, the white supremacists had become the victims and government agents were the criminals.

Third, the siege revealed the media savvy of the far right. It also demonstrated certain weaknesses within the media itself. Weaver consciously chose terms like "white separatist" to avoid the negative connotations associated with white *supremacy*, and the hundreds of journalists who descended on Idaho to report on the siege dutifully described him as such. Virtually no mention was made of the family's Identity beliefs or of the fact that Weaver had attended Aryan Nations meetings at the group's Hayden Lake compound.

Key activists worked the courtroom on a full-time basis during the trial, arranging interviews for Weaver and spoon-feeding information to the press. Ironically, this tactic was borrowed straight from the political trials of leftists and civil rights movement activists. The result was overwhelmingly positive coverage in the local press. Newspapers that might have condemned groups like Aryan Nations never criticized the Weavers or examined their beliefs closely. Instead, they placed all the blame for the confrontation on the federal agents.

THE ELECTORAL ARENA

In contrast to the violent, clandestine activities of the military wing of the far right, other sectors of the movement sought to use the very visible arena of electoral politics to gain support for their message and organizations. Unlike the political efforts of the Klan in the 1920s, however, these attempts were rarely designed to win a voting majority, although in some instances they came surprisingly close. Instead, far-right political campaigns were used intentionally to provide a platform for the dissemination of racism, antisemitism, and homophobic bigotry.

In other instances, such as the campaigns waged by Lyndon LaRouche and his surrogates, the political process was also viewed as part of a larger strategy to destabilize mainstream institutions—such as the Democratic Party—that were believed to hold together the center of political power.

LYNDON LAROUCHE

For almost three decades, Lyndon LaRouche has engaged in political activities that have been chameleonlike in their shifts from left to right; however, he has been consistent in creating and elaborating conspiracy theories that contain a strong dose of anti-semitism.

LaRouche's National Caucus of Labor Committees (NCLC) was founded in the late 1960s and drew its initial support from former members of various left-wing groups such as Students for a Democratic Society and the Progressive Labor Party. LaRouche quickly moved to the right, establishing alliances with organizations like the Ku Klux Klan and the Liberty Lobby. He set up dozens of front groups in the United States, Latin America, and Europe—all of them dedicated to promoting elaborate conspiracy theories and LaRouche's peculiar brand of antisemitic, neofascist ideology.[9]

LaRouche made his first bid for president in 1976. His campaigns in 1980, 1984, and 1988 netted a total of more than $1.7 million in federal matching funds. LaRouche even campaigned from federal prison in 1992, when he was serving time for a 1988 conviction for loan fraud and tax evasion. Although LaRouche never drew more than a minute fraction of the national vote in any presidential campaign, his electoral strategy was successful in several respects.

LaRouche's followers succeeded in winning significant numbers of low-level positions within some local Democratic Party structures. For example, in the March 1984 Democratic primaries near Chicago, the LaRouchians won fifty-seven suburban county committee seats, including all thirty-one seats in DuPage County. LaRouche's National Democratic Policy Committee (NDPC) claimed they ran 114 candidates in Illinois that year.[10]

In perhaps the best-known incident of LaRouchian electoral manipulation, two LaRouche-sponsored candidates, Janice Hart and Mark Fairchild, won the March 1986 Illinois Democratic Party primary nominations for secretary of state and lieutenant governor, respectively. This stunning upset forced Adlai Stevenson III, the party's chosen gubernatorial candidate, to withdraw from the ticket. Stevenson, who had otherwise been expected to mount a strong campaign, ended up running as an independent and lost.

LaRouche pursued a "tripartisan strategy" of running candidates for public office as Republicans, Democrats, or independents. Congressional districts with very small numbers of either registered Democrats or Republicans were targeted because the party with the fewest registered voters usually didn't run a candidate. This left the political field open to the LaRouchians. After winning in these uncontested primaries, the LaRouche candidates went on to certain defeat in the final election, but not before they had created political and media havoc and secured an effective platform for their ideas. LaRouche delighted in the turmoil these efforts caused within both political parties, particularly the Democratic, and he viewed this strategy as a kind of political guerrilla warfare.

LaRouche's electoral efforts were also successful because they broke new ground for other far-right groups such as the Populist Party, which copied his approach.

DAVID DUKE, RALPH FORBES, AND THE POPULIST PARTY

Formed in February 1984, the Populist Party disguised its neo-Nazi agenda by nominating former Olympic athlete Bob Richards as its first presidential candidate. Among the key figures behind the party were Robert Weems, a former state chaplain for the Mississippi Invisible Empire Knights of the Ku Klux Klan; Ralph Forbes, a Klan activist and Christian Identity minister; and A. J. Barker, a former state organizer for the National Association for the Advancement of White People. Behind them all was the shadowy figure of Willis Carto, founder of the antisemitic Liberty Lobby and a leader on the far right since the 1950s.

The Liberty Lobby's biweekly tabloid, *The Spotlight*, trumpeted the cause of the Populist Party to its 100,000-plus subscribers and the 20,000 members of its "board of policy."

Beginning in 1987, the Populist Party pursued the same tripartisan strategy as LaRouche, running candidates as Democrats, Republicans, and Populists. The most successful efforts were the campaigns of former Klan leader David Duke. As Leonard Zeskind summarizes in *Ballot Box Bigotry: David Duke and the Populist Party*, "[Duke] entered the Democratic Presidential primaries, announcing his candidacy in June 1987. He ran for President in the 1988 general election as the candidate of the Populist

Party. At the end of the year he switched again, running as a Republican for the Louisiana statehouse. He won."[11]

Duke used each campaign to build support for the next. First, he won approximately 41,000 votes in five states in the March 1988 "Super Tuesday" Democratic presidential primaries; 25,400 of them in Louisiana. Then he ran as a Populist in the November 1988 general election and received 45,878 votes in eleven states (of which 18,555 were cast in Louisiana). Three months later, in February 1989, Duke successfully translated the media visibility, grassroots support, and campaign skills he had acquired from these two previous campaigns into victory in his bid for Louisiana state representative.

Duke did not sever ties to the Populist Party after his election to the statehouse. In March 1989 he was the featured speaker at a meeting of the party in Chicago, an event attended by other well-known Klansmen and neo-Nazis.

In November 1989, Duke announced his intention to run for the U.S. Senate against incumbent J. Bennett Johnston. Despite publicity about the sale of Nazi and racist literature from his legislative office in Metairie, Duke polled a remarkable 44 percent of the vote in the election the following year, and won 60 percent of all votes cast by whites.

On January 4, 1991, Duke launched his fourth bid for public office in three years, this time for governor of Louisiana. After he edged out incumbent governor Buddy Roemer, and came in second in a three-way primary on October 19, public opposition intensified. Up to that point most people were content to simply ignore Duke and hope he would go away.

The exception was the Louisiana Coalition Against Racism and Nazism (LCARN), a political action committee dedicated solely to defeating Duke that was chartered by leaders of the Christian and Jewish communities. Anti-Duke campaigners of various stripes, including both Democrats and Republicans, were actively involved.

On November 16, less than a month after the primary, former governor Edwin Edwards defeated Duke 61 to 39 percent in the general election.

Although a sizable minority of whites were galvanized to vote against Duke by LCARN—and by the vociferous last-minute opposition of business leaders, the media, and state elected officials—the majority (55 percent) still supported him. In addition to the 45 percent of whites who voted against Duke, the key factor in his defeat was record black voter turnout.

After the 1991 gubernatorial election, few people beyond LCARN wanted to examine what it was that had captured the hearts and minds of Duke supporters. Many observers preferred to judge him by conventional political standards, which dictated that Roemer had defeated Duke in a landslide. According to other analysts, Duke's electoral strength was a mere "fluke."

In fact, Duke's 700,000 votes in the 1991 gubernatorial campaign (and 600,000 votes in the 1990 Senate campaign) were a stunning success. In addition, 14,322 people made financial contributions to the 1991 campaign, 6,775 of whom lived outside Louisiana, thereby helping Duke compile a lucrative list of potential supporters for future efforts.

The atmosphere at Duke campaign rallies, where as many as 500 to 1,500 people would gather, was electric. Whenever Duke discussed crime and welfare, it was clear his message was about blacks. When Duke railed against the "Eastern establishment" and the "liberal media," he was talking about Jews. Copies of *The Spotlight* were distributed throughout the crowd.

Duke masqueraded as a conservative Republican but was unable to avoid publicity about his bigoted beliefs and ties to racist and antisemitic groups. In his 1990 and 1991 campaigns, the publicity was so extensive that it is fair to say that most of those people who voted for him did so knowing full well his Klan beliefs and his past associations. In fact, many Duke supporters may have voted for him *because* of these beliefs and affiliations rather than in spite of them.

Overall, Duke's fifteen-year experiment with electoral politics was a pioneering success. Time and again he won, in spite of the electoral defeats.

Duke inspired others, like his 1988 presidential campaign manager Ralph Forbes, to follow in his footsteps. On May 29, 1990, Forbes, a former American Nazi Party captain, won an astounding 46 percent of the primary vote campaigning as a Republican for lieutenant governor of Arkansas. He lost to a conservative African American, Muskie Harris, in a runoff election one month later. Forbes's loss was due to some of the same factors that had contributed to Duke's defeat in 1991, specifically opposition from business leaders and the media.

The Populist Party's 1992 presidential candidate was retired lieutenant colonel James "Bo" Gritz, a decorated Vietnam War veteran and, for a short time, Duke's 1988 vice presidential running mate. Gritz made it on the ballot in nineteen states and polled slightly under 100,000 votes, but received negligible support outside his Western base of Idaho, Arizona, and Utah. As a testament to Duke's cultivation of Louisiana's fertile political soil, however, Gritz picked up 19,289 votes there.

Gritz's 97,754 votes were nearly four times the number polled by LaRouche in almost as many states, and 17,159 more than the 80,595 that the New Alliance Party—a left-wing political cult that once had ties to LaRouche—candidate Lenora Fulani counted in forty states and the District of Columbia.

By 1992, the Populist Party had fallen into disarray because of faction fights and lawsuits. Gritz's performance was respectable, however, considering that 1992 was also the year conservative maverick H. Ross Perot polled nearly 20 million votes running for the White House, no doubt drawing considerable support from voters who might otherwise have supported one of many third parties, including the Populists. Gritz set aside his electoral ambitions in 1993 and concentrated on building his political base within the Christian Patriot movement in the Pacific Northwest.

Although contemporary political campaigns by the far right have never come close to matching those of the second-era Ku Klux Klan, the impact of these electoral efforts has been felt both inside and outside the movement. Unlike a cross burning conducted by several dozen Klansmen in a cow pasture, or the violence of groups like the Order, the political campaigns of Lyndon LaRouche, David Duke, Ralph Forbes, Bo Gritz, and others provided a vehicle for the mass dissemination of antisemitism and racism.

The campaigns also brought in hundreds of thousands—and, in the case of LaRouche, millions—of dollars that would otherwise have been inaccessible. As Zeskind points out in *Ballot Box Bigotry*:

According to the Federal Election Commission, Duke raised and spent $406,569 between June 2, 1987, and December 31, 1988, for his bid in the Democratic primaries. The Populist Party National Committee raised and spent an additional $136,172 between September 27, 1988, and the end of the year.... Although the total—$542,741—is small by major party standards, it is a considerably larger campaign budget than that of any other white supremacist organization.[12]

In the simple act of declaring their candidacy for public office, white supremacists and neo-Nazis legitimized public discussion of their issues in a way that no sidewalk rally or television talk show ever could.

THE POSSE COMITATUS, CHRISTIAN IDENTITY, AND THE CHRISTIAN PATRIOT MOVEMENT

Henry L. Beach was a retired dry-cleaning businessman when he founded the Posse Comitatus (Latin for "power of the county") in 1969 in Portland, Oregon. He was once a member of William Dudley Pelly's quasi-fascist Silver Shirts. Beach instructed his members to charter independent groups, each composed of a minimum of "seven male Christians," and to make their existence known to the local sheriff, who supposedly represented the highest legal authority in the nation.

Beach taught that America was not a democracy and that the nation had been established as a "Christian Republic." The Constitution was solely derived from a divinely inspired Bible, and most laws passed by Congress and the state legislatures were unconstitutional. "Christian Common Law" was promoted as an alternative legal system.

Beach and the Posse focused their antigovernment rhetoric with particular zeal on the income tax and the Federal Reserve banking system, believing them both to be products of a fictional international Jewish conspiracy. In this way, the Posse injected an explicitly antisemitic tone into the debate about both taxes and monetary policy that had long been simmering among conservatives and far-rightists of all stripes.

Because of their strongly held antitax beliefs, Posse members increasingly became involved in conflicts with the authorities. In 1974, Thomas Stockheimer, a leader of the Wisconsin Posse, was convicted of assaulting an IRS officer.

By 1976, an FBI investigation identified seventy-eight Posse chapters in twenty-three states and estimated between twelve thousand and fifty thousand hard-core members.

As interest rates rose to double digits and the farm economy worsened at the end of the 1970s, the Posse grew, particularly in the rural Midwest and Great Plains. This trend continued into the next decade, and the number of illegal tax protestors increased more than threefold, from 17,222 in 1980 to 57,754 in 1983, according to the Internal Revenue Service.[13]

The significance of this chapter in the history of the contemporary far right cannot be overstated. Beginning in the mid-1970s and continuing over the short span of a decade, the once politically marginal Posse Comitatus succeeded in winning widespread acceptance for its ideas. By introducing right-wing tax protestors to hard-core proponents of Christian Identity theology and synthesizing the two ideologies, the Posse Comitatus contributed greatly to the formation of the Christian Patriot movement. Of the total 25,000 activists in the white supremacist movement counted by Leonard Zeskind in 1992, approximately 15,000 were Christian patriots. Ninety thousand to 120,000 people made donations, purchased literature, or sympathized with this particular aspect of the movement.

Unlike its counterparts in the Order and the Aryan Nations, which had eschewed mass organizing in favor of white revolution, the Christian Patriot movement was able to cultivate a mass following. This did not diminish the violence of individual Christian Patriots, however, especially in conflicts with law enforcement. By the mid-1980s, several widely publicized incidents had occurred:

• On February 13, 1983, Gordon Kahl, a farmer and Posse Comitatus member, shot and killed two federal marshals outside Medina, North Dakota, who were trying to serve him a warrant for outstanding income taxes. Although there was widespread media coverage about the run-in with the sixty-three-year-old "tax protestor," only the most thorough reporters explained the relevance of Kahl's Christian Identity beliefs. Kahl died four months later in a shootout in Arkansas after a nationwide federal manhunt.

• On October 14, 1984, Nebraska farmer Arthur Kirk died in a shootout with a state highway patrol SWAT team outside his home near Grand Island. While on the phone with a police negotiator, Kirk claimed Israeli foreign intelligence—the Mossad—was out to get him. "There's a big move on to try to subvert the Constitution, to change the whole thing. Communism, that isn't Communism, it's Judaism," he said.

• Five-year-old Luke Stice and James Thimm, twenty-five, were brutally murdered in 1985 by fellow members of a Posse Comitatus/Christian Identity group living on a farm near Rulo, Nebraska. The group had approximately twenty members, and an arsenal of guns and ammunition had been accumulated in preparation for a coming "race war."

In the wake of bad publicity surrounding these and other incidents, many Christian Patriots stopped referring to themselves publicly as the Posse Comitatus. Dozens of new groups emerged, all of which shared the same far-right beliefs, but they chose new names such as the National Agricultural Press Association (NAPA), the Patriots Information Network, Barristers Inn, and the Golden Mean Team. The LaRouchians also tried to penetrate rural areas, attending farm meetings and protest rallies, distributing literature and seeking new recruits.

The growth of the Posse Comitatus in the late 1970s coincided with the emergence of the American Agriculture Movement (AAM) in 1977, which organized tens of thousands of farmers to lobby Washington, D.C., for higher farm prices and changes in Carter administration farm policies. They arrived first by plane and pickup truck in 1978, and then by tractorcade the following year.

The antisemitism and conspiracy theories of the Christian Patriot movement were taken up by a core group of AAM activists who popularized them further. This trend eventually provoked a debilitating split inside AAM which featured heavily in the organization's ultimate demise.

Although there was a brief lull in 1980–81, farm protests took off again in 1982, this time spearheaded by liberal farm and rural advocacy groups. Farm crisis hotlines were established in more than a dozen states, and grassroots meetings attracted hundreds throughout the farm belt. Electoral activity surrounding the 1984 presidential election galvanized progressive rural activists in the political arena.

But far-right organizers were still leading farmers down a different path. Lobbying for farm policy reform and building coalitions with inner-city congressional leaders were not high on their agenda. Liberal farm groups decided they had to combat the rural radical right for two reasons: First, they had deep ethical and moral concerns about the racism and antisemitism of the far right. Second, they correctly judged that the far right was a threat to their efforts to recruit farmers to progressive political action.

In 1985, ABC television's *20/20* program had broadcast a hard-hitting story about antisemitism in the farm belt. The segment, entitled "Seeds of Hate," focused on the propaganda, recruitment activities, and violence of rural far-right organizations and their links to more well-known hate groups such as the Aryan Nations.

The broadcast was not simply the result of good investigative reporting. As early as 1983, liberal farm groups like PrairieFire Rural Action in Des Moines, Iowa, had teamed up with national organizations like the Center for Democratic Renewal (CDR) to funnel information about the far right to media outlets like the *New York Times* and National Public Radio. "Seeds of Hate" was a direct outgrowth of these efforts. PrairieFire and CDR also organized training sessions to help farm leaders combat the Christian Patriot movement.

In 1985, the American Jewish Committee released a comprehensive report on the farm crisis and the rural radical right. Jewish community leaders throughout the Midwest also became involved, sponsoring forums on the farm crisis and joining efforts to expose and counter hate groups in the farm belt.

One indicator of the penetration of the far right in the farm belt was revealed in February 1986 when the Anti-Defamation League of B'nai B'rith (ADL) released the results of a Lou Harris poll of rural Iowans and Nebraskans. Thirty-five percent put heavy blame for the farm crisis on "an international Communist conspiracy" and twenty-eight percent blamed the Trilateral Commission, a persistent bogeyman of the far right. Twenty-seven percent agreed with the claim that "farmers have always been exploited by international Jewish bankers who are behind those who overcharge them for farm equipment or jack up the interest on their loans."

Probing the level of antisemitism further, Harris found that 42 percent of those surveyed agreed with the view that "Jews should quit complaining about what happened to them in Nazi Germany." An equal number believed the charge that "when it comes to choosing between people and money, Jews will choose money." And 27 percent felt that "Jews have too much power in America."

In analyzing the results, Lou Harris and Associates wrote:

One can argue, of course, that the 27 percent [of respondents who blamed "international Jewish bankers" for the farm crisis] are not simply more than about one in four rural residents of these pivotal midwestern farm states, but that it also means that the residue of seventy-three percent are not prepared to make such a charge against Jews. However, it must be pointed out that any phenomenon which affects over one in four residents must be viewed as a mass phenomenon, even if it is not massive. Put another way, one does not have to venture far into either state to find an abundant number of people who are prepared to lay some of the real blame for the plight of farmers on international bankers, and many of these clearly are thought to be Jewish.[14]

After 1989, when the farm crisis no longer made national headlines, the geographic focus of far-right organizing shifted from the Midwestern states of Iowa, Wisconsin, Illinois, and Minnesota to the Great Plains and Northwest.

COUNTERING HATE GROUPS AND HATE CRIMES:
LAW ENFORCEMENT, LITIGATION,
AND LEGISLATION

The activities of the Klan in the late nineteenth century prompted the federal government to pass a series of civil rights laws broadly known as the "Ku Klux Klan Acts." Some (codified at 18 U.S.C. 241–247) impose criminal penalties on those who deprive persons of their federally protected civil rights. Others (codified at 42 U.S.C 1981–1985) authorize civil actions for monetary damages.

Although some civil rights activists feel these statutes have not lived up to their full potential, these laws remain one of the most effective litigation tools for countering hate-group activity.

For example, in 1980 the National Anti-Klan Network and the Center for Constitutional Rights (CCR) launched a federal civil rights lawsuit against three Klansmen who had injured five African-American women in a shooting spree in Chattanooga, Tennessee. The lawsuit was based on the Ku Klux Klan Acts and was the first such suit filed in the twentieth century. Two years later a jury found all three Klansmen liable and fined them $535,000.

Subsequent lawsuits brought by the Southern Poverty Law Center (SPLC), also based on these Reconstruction-era statutes, succeeded in winning large damage awards which bankrupted entire Klan organizations, such as the Invisible Empire in 1993. The SPLC filed other, equally successful lawsuits based on contemporary civil statutes and won money damages against other Klan groups such as the United Klans of America and individual white supremacists such as Tom Metzger.

In addition to the Ku Klux Klan Acts, new laws were passed in response to each resurgence of hate-group activity. In the 1920s and again in the late 1940s and early 1950s, state legislatures and city governments passed antimask laws and other measures targeting the Klan.

Although the Federal Civil Rights Act of 1964 and the Voting Rights Act of 1965 were not aimed specifically at the Klan, they had the effect of outlawing many of the discriminatory activities that Klan members instigated or supported. Other civil rights–era legislation such as the Fair Housing Act provided an avenue for prosecuting hate groups and their members.

In response to paramilitary training by Klan groups in the late 1970s and early 1980s, state legislatures enacted a variety of restrictive measures. These, and other older laws regulating paramilitary activity, provided a new avenue for civil rights advocates to combat hate groups.

In 1982, the SPLC brought suit successfully against the Knights of the Ku Klux Klan on behalf of the Vietnamese Fisherman's Association based upon an obscure Texas law outlawing private armies. SPLC lawyers also went after the military arm of Invisible Empire Knights of the Ku Klux Klan, the Klan Special Forces, and succeeded in shutting down several training camps it operated in Alabama. An SPLC suit against the White Patriot Party in North Carolina in 1984 resulted in a consent decree barring the WPP from engaging in further paramilitary training. When the WPP violated the decree in 1986, its leaders were found guilty of contempt of court and the organization disbanded.

Escalating hate crimes in the 1980s prompted state legislatures to enact a patchwork of laws that provide for mandatory hate-crime data collection by the authorities, mandatory police training about bias crime, and stiffer jail terms for individuals who commit crimes motivated by bigotry. As of 1992, forty-six states and the District of Columbia had some form of hate-crime legislation on their books.

Although it is impossible to determine whether these laws have actually deterred hate crime and hate-group activities, their enactment communicates a message about what conduct is or is not socially acceptable.

It is when hate groups plunge into the murky waters of constitutionally protected speech and political activity, organizing rallies and demonstrations, that these laws have the least impact, however. In fact, when a conflict exists between these First Amendment rights and the Fourteenth Amendment rights of persons entitled to equal protection under the law, the courts have generally leaned toward protecting hate groups rather than shielding their victims. This is sometimes true in situations involving actions as well as words.

In a 1992 decision, *R.A.V.* v. *City of St. Paul*, the U.S. Supreme Court ruled that cross burnings were a form of protected speech. The case stemmed from a nighttime cross burning conducted by three white youths in front of an apartment occupied by an African-American family. The youths were prosecuted under a city ordinance outlawing hate crimes which the Supreme Court ruled unconstitutionally vague. In his majority opinion, Justice Antonin Scalia argued that the burning cross was intended to convey a particular political message and that, by outlawing such acts, the ordinance was trampling on free speech. This reasoning was used two years later, in May 1994, by the New Jersey Supreme Court when it invalidated a 1981 state hate-crime statute similar to the St. Paul city ordinance.

In a dissenting opinion to *R.A.V.*, Justice Harry Blackmun wrote, "I see no First Amendment values that are compromised by a law that prohibits hoodlums from driving minorities out of their homes by burning crosses on their lawns, but I see great harm in preventing the people of St. Paul from specifically punishing the race-based fighting words."

In subsequent criminal prosecutions of cross burners brought by the civil rights division of the U.S. Department of Justice, some defendants have used the *R.A.V.* decision in their defense, but none have been acquitted. That is probably because the prosecutions have been brought under the old Ku Klux Klan Acts, specifically Title 18 USC Sections 241 and 245, whose legal basis is better defined than the St. Paul city ordinance which was poorly conceived and drafted.

In a 1993 decision, *Mitchell* v. *State of Wisconsin*, the U.S. Supreme Court upheld the constitutionality of a Wisconsin law which provided enhanced penalties for hate crimes. The reasoning in *Mitchell* also was used by the New Jersey Supreme Court in 1994 to uphold a 1990 statute providing harsher penalties for criminals who choose their victims based on race, religion, or other personal characteristics.

The effectiveness of the early anti-Klan statutes and subsequent state legislation has varied greatly with the circumstances of individual cases. Certainly, when all-white, all-Christian juries weigh the fate of those accused of hate crimes, the potential for bias is high, as occurred in the state trial for the 1980 murders in Greensboro, North Carolina.

When the social and political climate appears permissive to hate groups, escalating violence is usually also the result, as was the case with the Klan through much of the Jim Crow years.

It was with this in mind that the National Anti-Klan Network and eight victims of racist violence sued the Reagan administration Justice Department in 1983 for its failure to prosecute hate violence. The Klanwatch Project of SPLC concurred with the Network's analysis of the Reagan administration to a degree, observing that the administration's policies, "rightly or wrongly, are perceived by Klansmen and other racists as signals for escalation of attacks on minorities and for a retreat back to segregation, white supremacy and other evils of the past."[15]

Conversely, when the will to prosecute is strong, these laws have usually proven effective in bringing the perpetrators to justice.

Although far-right groups often resort to violent, criminal activities, even the most vigorous legal sanctions will have only a limited effect on the movement as a whole. Like a balloon squeezed at one end, the more pressure that is applied to groups engaged in illegal activities, the greater the tendency for the movement to expand in a legal, political direction. David Duke's political campaigns of 1988–91 can certainly be seen in this context.

Although private civil actions against hate groups and their leaders—such as those brought by CCR and SPLC—have been very successful, victims of hate crimes rarely pursue civil remedies because these lawsuits are extraordinarily expensive. Lawyers also are unwilling to take these cases because they know the financial resources of hate groups are limited and plaintiffs rarely recover even a fraction of what the court awards.

Nevertheless, publicity surrounding a relatively small number of high-profile cases brought by SPLC has had a chilling effect on some hate groups, forcing them to moderate their rhetoric if not their actions. In the case of the Invisible Empire (IE), SPLC legal action helped exacerbate internal tensions in the group over whether or not to allow skinheads at IE events. Those who opposed the skinheads on ideological grounds were able to use the threat of legal liability for skinhead violence to bolster their arguments that the organization should sever its ties with neo-Nazi groups—which it did.

Whether articulated as "leaderless resistance," the "fifth-era Klan," or underground, guerrilla warfare, there will always be those on the leading edge of the far right who preach revolution and leave a trail of bodies in their wake. They will not accomplish their goal, but their martyrdom and continued activities will inspire a steady stream of the most violent—and committed—recruits. This has been a defining tendency of the far right since the first days of the Ku Klux Klan, and will continue well into the future despite government prosecutions, civil suits, and the like.

Racism, homophobia, antisemitism, xenophobia, white nationalism, and isolationism form the ideological foundation of the white supremacist and neo-Nazi movement. These ideas are not marginal to life in the United States, but exist in a state of dynamic tension with those alternative values of pluralism, tolerance, and democracy that also form the basis of the American experience.

Conventional attitudes toward the far right are shaped heavily by the mainstream media and the voices of America's liberal and centrist intellectual elite. While the violence of hate groups is usually taken seriously, the political agenda of the white supremacist movement is not clearly understood.

Most historians and social scientists agree that the Ku Klux Klan of the 1920s exerted significant influence on politics and social relations, locally and nationally. Similarly, there is a consensus about how the terroristic violence of white supremacists in the 1950s and '60s acted as a mechanism of social control to preserve white dominance and prevent black people from asserting their constitutional rights. There is far less agreement, however, about the degree to which present-day hate groups are a relevant political or social force.

In fact, the far right is often described as an assortment of alternately threatening and entertaining social misfits beholden to outlandish conspiracy theories and visceral race hatred who dress in white sheets and Nazi paraphernalia. Their activities are not usually portrayed as the foundation for a credible political movement, yet their ideas *have* constituted a solid basis for political action for generations, both here and abroad.

The notion of the "authoritarian personality" drives much of the debate surrounding the search for an archetypical hatemonger. Explanations for why people join hate groups are often couched in psychological shorthand, and involve discussions of broken homes and alienation rather than a thorough analysis of the role—and attraction—of racism in society.

While it is certainly true that people join hate groups for a variety of reasons, more credence should be given to the notion that people join because they are attracted to the very *ideas* of white supremacy and antisemitism that the groups espouse.

As long as outdated stereotypes about hate groups and their followers dominate public perceptions, those who should oppose the far right will continue to underestimate the situation and will refrain from allocating sufficient resources to deal with it.

The numbers of people involved in hate groups will wax and wane, but each resurgence—like the campaigns of David Duke—brings with it new opportunities to disseminate bigotry throughout the electorate. Issues like gay and lesbian rights and fear of immigrants will continue to be a powerful organizing tool for the far right, and have significant potential to draw support from the political mainstream.

Although groups like the Ku Klux Klan have historically posed a more direct physical threat to African Americans, the very existence of hate groups also threatens the safety and security of the Jewish community. Bigots attack and deface Jewish institutions and places of worship at the same time as they assault other minority groups and attack democracy.

In response to hate-group activity, the Jewish community has traditionally reached out to the leadership of other racial, ethnic, and religious communities and developed relationships with opinion makers, public officials, and the media. However, combatting the far right also requires the creation of grassroots coalitions of common interest that can gather up a wider array of social and political forces and diverse constituencies—teachers, union members, rank-and-file clergy, and so on.

Historically, the far right's success or failure has been greatly affected by the nature of the opposition that has been arrayed against it—whether in the form of pre–Civil War abolitionism, the antifascism of the Roosevelt era, or the civil rights movement of the 1950s and '60s. The same dynamic will be at work in the future. The growth—or decline—of the far right will be determined by whether, how, and to what degree a political movement capable of challenging the values and ideology of bigotry can be galvanized into action.

NOTES

1. See Wyn Craig Wade, *The Fiery Cross: The Ku Klux Klan in America* (New York: Simon & Schuster, 1987), p. 171.

2. Quoted in David A. Chalmers, *Hooded Americanism: The History of the Ku Klux Klan* (Durham, N.C.: Duke University Press, 1987), p. 33.

3. Wade, *Fiery Cross*, p. 266.

4. Chalmers, *Hooded Americanism*, p. 349.

5. Leonard Zeskind, "The Klan Tries to Enter New Era," *The Hammer* 9 (Spring 1985), 20–25.

6. For more information about William Pierce, his ideology and background, see Leonard Zeskind, "State of the Union," *Searchlight* magazine, London, 218 (August 1993), 20–22.

7. British Israelism underwent its mid-nineteenth-century revival at approximately the same time as European ideas about Jews were undergoing a profound transformation. In 1844, Christian Lassen, a professor at Bonn, was the first scholar to propose a specifically racial distinction between "Semitic" and "Aryan" peoples, where previously the distinction that had been made was purely a linguistic one. This view was further popularized by the French writer and diplomat Count Arthur de Gobineau, who published his *Essai sur l'inegalité des races humaines (Essay on the Inequality of the Human Races)* at about the same time (1853–55). From the late 1700s onward, the emerging sciences of anthropology, ethnology, archeology, and zoology all gave impetus to the quest to divine the "racial groupings" of humanity, including the "racial characteristics" of the Jew. These "scientific" inquiries ultimately formed the basis for the Eugenics movement.

8. For a brief but thorough and fascinating history of British Israelism in the United States, see Ralph Lord Roy, *Apostles of Discord* (Boston: Beacon Press, 1953), pp. 92–117.

9. For a more substantive account of LaRouche's antisemitism, see Dennis King, "The Jewish Question," in *Lyndon LaRouche and the New American Fascism* (New York: Doubleday, 1989), pp. 38–46.

10. For a thorough analysis of LaRouchian electoral strategy, see ibid., pp. 103–11.

11. For more information on the Populist Party and David Duke, see *The Populist Party: A Fraud by America's Racists and Anti-Semites* (Atlanta: Center for Democratic Renewal, 1984); and *Ballot Box Bigotry: David Duke and the Populist Party* (Atlanta: Center for Democratic Renewal, 1989). For a thorough chronology of the career of David Duke, see *The Politics and Background of David Duke*, 5th ed. (New Orleans: Louisiana Coalition Against Racism and Nazism, December 1991).

12. As quoted on p. 12 of Zeskind, *Ballot Box Bigotry.*

13. See James Coates, *Armed and Dangerous: The Rise of the Survivalist Right* (New York: Hill and Wang, 1987), p. 111.

14. See Louis Harris, Study No. 864002, *A Study of Anti-Semitism in Rural Iowa and Nebraska* (New York: Louis Harris and Associates, February, 1986).

15. As cited in Wade, *Fiery Cross*, p. 392.

·9·

Political Antisemitism: What Can We Learn from the David Duke Exit Polls?

MARK MELLMAN

Mark Mellman, a survey research analyst, heads
Mellman-Lazarus-Lake, a Washington, D.C.,
polling firm.

Mark Mellman's note on the exit poll data on the 1991 Louisiana gubernatorial race, in which former Klan official David Duke garnered 55 percent of the white vote, is an analysis of a classic example of a situation
in which voters will support a racist and antisemite not *because* of his or
her racist views, but *despite* that person's racist views.

J.A.C.

Is a supporter of a bigoted candidate necessarily a bigot? Put differently, does a vote for a bigot indicate a voter's desire for racist
policies? To ask these questions is to invite controversy. Declaring that voters may support racists for nonracist reasons may
seem to excuse evil. It should not. Rather, it should reveal a
frankly more frightening possibility—that voters could bring upon
themselves great tribulations for more mundane reasons.

The 1991 Louisiana gubernatorial elections between Edwin
Edwards and David Duke illustrate the point and provide a laboratory within which to explore a variety of theories about the rise
of racist candidates. Edwards, the only Democrat and a former
governor known for high living and corruption, advanced to the
runoff with nearly united support from the black community. He
gained 34 percent of the total vote. Duke, a Nazi, received 32 percent, gaining his berth in the runoff with support from white vot-

ers divided between him and Republican Buddy Roemer. It set up one of the strangest and most important contests in contemporary American politics. The line of the day was that while David Duke was the only person in Louisiana that Edwin Edwards could beat, so Edwards was the only person *Duke* could beat.

Edwin Edwards faced the electorate as a deeply flawed candidate. First, many thought him a crook. By 54 to 37 percent, Louisianans believed he was not "a man of integrity." Only 31 percent saw the former governor as moral, while 56 percent thought that word did not describe him. Sixty-one percent thought he did not set a good example. Among white voters, evaluations of Edwards along the honesty dimension were even worse. Only 25 percent thought him a man of integrity, while 70 percent believed he lacked integrity. Indeed, the bumper sticker that popped up across the state among anti-Duke voters read: "Vote for the crook—it's important."

A second key Edwards flaw was his image as a typical politician at a time when voter resentment toward politics as usual was beginning to build. More than seven in ten voters (73 percent) thought he was "too much of a politician." By 59 to 26 percent, voters believed he was too close to special interests. Nearly two-thirds (64 percent) thought he "represented the political establishment." Again, these negative evaluations were even more striking among white voters.

Finally, Louisiana voters believed that Edwin Edwards did not share their values or represent their point of view. Sixty-eight percent saw him as a tax-and-spend politician. Only 19 percent thought he would do a good job holding down taxes, while 70 percent gave him negative evaluations in this sphere. Only 35 percent believed Edwards shared their values, and only 38 percent believed he reflected their point of view on the issues.

It is worth belaboring these numbers primarily to understand just how poor a reputation Edwards had among his putative constituents. When asked to recall how he had done as governor last time he served, 26 percent gave Edwards positive ratings while 69 percent offered negative evaluation of his earlier term. Here too, white voters were harsher in their judgments, with a mere 17 percent offering positive ratings and 80 percent professing negative ratings.

Of course, few had high regard for Duke. Only 35 percent thought him to be a man of integrity and only 36 percent saw him as moral, yet Duke was seen as much less of a politician, more as a representative of middle-class interests, and less of a tax-and-spend politician. As with Edwards, only 26 percent offered positive evaluations of Duke's tenure in the state legislature.

It is instructive to examine how well Louisiana voters thought each candidate represented the interests of various constituencies. As Figure 1 indicates, most white Louisianans believed Duke represented no one's interests "very well." The largest number (but only 27 percent) said Duke represented people like them. By contrast, almost no whites (8 percent) thought Edwards represented their interests, whereas a large number (44 percent) saw the former governor as a representative of big business and the wealthy. Edwards was also thought to represent the interests of blacks.

Edwards's flaws notwithstanding, how could anyone support a former Nazi and Klan leader in an election for governor without associating themselves with those philosophies? In Duke's case, the answer was clear: people believed he had changed. Just a few weeks before the election, voters were evenly divided (44 percent each) between those who thought Duke had changed and those who believed he had not (see Figure 2). Nearly all of those who were supporting him held the view that their candidate was no longer a Nazi and a Klansman (see Figure 3). Duke's strategy was designed to reinforce this viewpoint. He labeled his Nazi association a "youthful indiscretion." More important, he used religion to buttress this claim, maintaining that he had been "born again." It was this religious rebirth that provided the "new" David Duke with a certificate of authenticity. Duke's campaign leaned heavily on the notion of the "new" David Duke.

Naturally, the campaign against him sought to unmask Duke. Two elements were critical components of the effort in the closing weeks of the campaign. First, a group of fundamentalist ministers who interviewed Duke publicly proclaimed his conversion experience to have been false. They argued that Duke had in fact not been "born again." He was thus the same old Nazi. Shortly thereafter, a tape-recorded interview emerged in which Duke claimed he would in the future hide his Nazi affiliation in order to be more acceptable to voters. This tape recording was put into a TV commercial and run hundreds of times in the closing days of the campaign. Obviously the spot was designed to demonstrate that Duke had not changed but was only trying to defraud the electorate.

These twin efforts had the desired effect. By election day 59 percent of voters believed Duke had not changed, while 37 percent believed he had (see Figure 2). Among those who believed Duke had not changed his beliefs, Edwards won 91 to 9 percent. Put differently, only 5 percent of Louisiana voters thought Duke had the same views he had as a Klan leader and yet voted for him.

However, this does not indicate the absence of racism in Louisiana—though it was not perhaps of the old Jim Crow variety. What has been called "symbolic racism" is a fact of political life in Louisiana. We used three questions to tap this view of racial hostility (see Figure 6). Forty percent of whites agreed with the view that "blacks have pushed too far too fast." Of these, 53 percent supported Duke, while only 25 percent were voting for Edwards at the time of our poll. Just under four in ten whites (39 percent) agreed that "blacks have too much control over our government." Of these, 58 percent supported Duke while 23 percent expressed support for Edwards.

Thus, while only 7 percent of whites supported Duke while believing him to be a Nazi, about 40 percent expressed a hostile attitude toward blacks. A definitional debate about what constitutes racism is far beyond the scope of this report. Suffice it to say there is some difference between Nazism and a belief that blacks have pushed too far too fast, though the latter clearly reflects significant hostility toward blacks.

It has been suggested by some that racism and antisemitism go hand in hand. At least in Louisiana, symbolic bigots did not seem to flock together. Fifteen percent of blacks and 13 percent of whites agreed that "Jews have too much influence over our government." This hostility toward Jews was at a much lower level than anti-black feelings. Moreover, individuals do not seem to necessarily share hostility toward both groups. Of those who believed that Jews had too much governmental control, about half (52 percent) felt that way about blacks, while 44 percent of those who criticized excessive Jewish power did not believe blacks exerted too much influence. Attitudes toward the two groups are not completely coincident.

Students of bigotry often point to economic dislocation as a primary cause of racist voting patterns. The Louisiana results do not support this approach. As Figure 4 indicates, only 29 percent of Duke voters believed their family's economic situation had gotten worse over the preceding four years. An almost equal number (27 percent) thought their financial situation had improved. The bulk of Duke voters (44 percent) perceived no change in their economic situation.

Response to another exit poll question sums up several of the arguments of this brief analysis.

The largest number of Duke voters (39 percent) cited government corruption, for which Edwards was infamous, as the prime determinant of their vote. Just over a quarter (27 percent) focused on the state's economy. Just over one in ten Duke voters (12 percent) admitted that racial issues were a key factor in their vote. Thus about 5 percent of Louisiana voters admitted supporting Duke because of his racial views, about the same percentage who voted for him while believing he had not changed those views. By contrast, Edwards voters overwhelmingly cited the economy or Duke's views on racial issues as the prime determinant of their vote. (See Figure 5.)

Too many Louisianans, including 55 percent of whites, supported David Duke in his bid for governor. Yet most of them thought Duke had changed his views and many were reacting against a candidate whom they viewed as a corrupt representative of big business and the wealthy. Had voters not come to realize that Duke was in fact an unreconstructed Nazi, they would have made a terrible mistake. But it would probably have been a mistake and not a conscious attempt to install a Nazi governor in Louisiana. Fortunately, in our democracy voters usually see through to the truth and make wise choices.

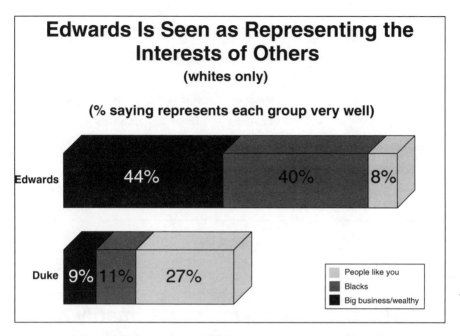

Figure 1.

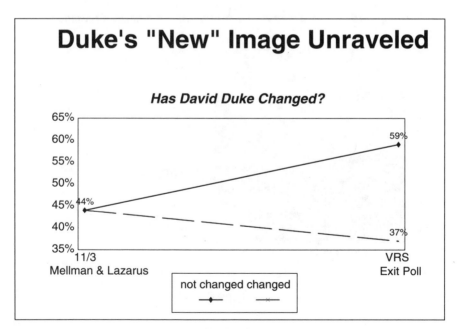

Figure 2.

Perceptions of Duke's Change of Heart Were Central to Vote

	Mellman & Lazarus 11/3		VRS Exit Poll	
	Edwards	Duke	Edwards	Duke
Believe Duke Has Changed	16%	84%	13%	87%
Believe Duke Has Not Changed	73%	8%	91%	9%

Figure 3.

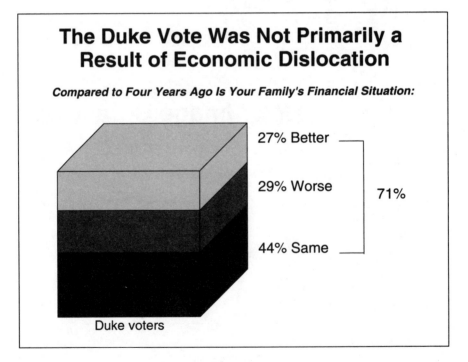

The Duke Vote Was Not Primarily a Result of Economic Dislocation

Compared to Four Years Ago Is Your Family's Financial Situation:

27% Better

29% Worse   71%

44% Same

Duke voters

Figure 4.

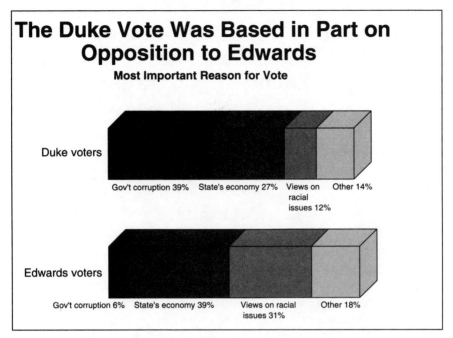

Figure 5.

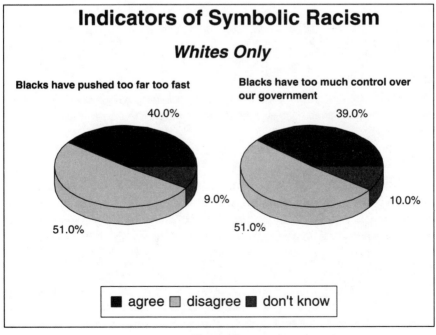

Figure 6.

·10·

Antisemitism in the Christian-Jewish Encounter: New Directions as We Enter the Twenty-first Century

A. JAMES RUDIN

A. James Rudin, a rabbi, is the national interreligious
affairs director of the American Jewish Committee and
the author of *Israel for Christians: Understanding
Modern Israel.* He is also the coeditor of *A Time to
Speak: The Evangelical-Jewish Encounter, Evangelicals
and Jews in an Age of Pluralism, Evangelicals and
Jews in Conversation,* and *Twenty Years of Jewish-
Catholic Relations.*

Rabbi A. James Rudin develops two approaches to the Christian-Jewish
dialogue. On the one hand, the Christian religious sources of antisemitism—in fact, arguably the major taproots of antisemitism—have not
as yet been fully examined. These sources of antisemitism persist even in
the 1990s. In large measure because of the emotive power that drives
much of religion, theologically based antisemitism has been hard to eradicate.

At the same time, Rudin reports, since the end of World War II there
have been systematic efforts on the part of most national and international
church bodies, and many Christian leaders, to explore and take steps to
counteract antisemitism. The vehicles for these activities are examination
of Christian Scriptural text, community and more recently seminary education, revisiting the liturgy, and exploration of theology. "There has been
more progress in Christian-Jewish relations over the past twenty years
than in the previous two thousand," Rudin said in 1985—commemorating
the twentieth anniversary of the issuance of the Vatican II document *Nostra Aetate* ("In Our Time") that rejected Christian antisemitism and defined
a new relationship between Catholics and Jews—and this progress is most

evident in the repudiation of antisemitism, at least formally, by Christian bodies.

J.A.C.

Christian-Jewish relations in the United States are the most dynamic, robust, and ongoing of any in the world. And these extensive and intensive interreligious programs present a new and important forum for combatting one of the world's oldest pathologies, religious or theological antisemitism. While the issue of constitutional protections is addressed elsewhere in this volume, I offer a brief analysis of the American Constitution as a vehicle for explaining the extraordinarily positive Christian-Jewish relationships that exist today in the United States.

As a direct result of the religious strife in Europe, especially the Thirty Years War and the Inquisition in Spain and Portugal, as well as the excesses committed both in Great Britain and in the American colonies against religious dissenters and minorities in the seventeenth and eighteenth centuries, the framers of the Constitution of the United States, especially James Madison, took great care to provide specific guarantees for religious freedom and liberty.

The concluding clause of Article VI of the Constitution reads:

... no religious Test shall ever be required as a Qualification to any Office or public Trust under the United States.

Immediately following the Constitution's ratification in 1787, ten Amendments were added—the "Bill of Rights." The First Amendment deals in part with religion:

Congress shall make no law respecting an establishment of religion, or prohibiting the free exercise thereof; or abridging the freedom of speech, or of the press; or the right of the people peaceably to assemble, and to petition the Government for a redress of grievances.

The third American president, Thomas Jefferson, was also an ardent champion of individual religious liberty. Indeed, it was Jefferson who first spoke of a "wall of separation" between religion and the American Government. In 1776 Jefferson wrote:

The care of every man's soul belongs to himself. . . . No man has the right to abandon care of his salvation to another. No man has the power to let another prescribe his faith. . . . The essence of religion consists in the internal persuasion of belief.[1]

In 1808, at the end of his presidency, Jefferson wrote to a group of Virginia Baptist leaders:

We have solved by fair experiment, the great and interesting question whether freedom of religion is compatible with order in government, and obedience to laws. . . . everyone [can] profess freely and openly those principles of religion. . . .of his own reason. . . .and inquiries.[2]

Constitutional guarantees, and more than two centuries of religious pluralism in the United States, have helped establish a strong foundation for religious liberty. They have also provided a legal mandate for positive interreligious relations in the United States, and have acted as a shield against official, government-sponsored antisemitism. But the Constitutional guarantees did not, and of course could not, end *religious* antisemitism.

This exceptional emphasis on religious liberty by the Constitution's framers and by America's early political leaders is especially impressive when we recall that there were probably only five thousand Jews in the United States in 1787, out of a total population of some three million, most of whom were Protestant Christians.

Jefferson, Madison, and their colleagues could easily have designated Christianity as the official religion of the United States, but they consciously chose not to do so. The founders of the American republic meant to separate the institutions of church and state and to prohibit the establishment of religion. In effect, they provided the Constitutional basis, if not the theological basis, for religious pluralism and positive interreligious relations, and at the same time they validated a pattern of religious acceptance and accommodation.

Under the law, no religious group can become the favored or "established church," and all faith communities in the United States are free to mount campaigns to win the hearts, souls, and purses of the American people. For Jews, this meant that from the start, no one church or religious group could seize or control the organs of governmental power, establish itself as the official religion, and carry out campaigns of discrimination aimed at non-established religious groups, namely Jews and other minorities. The American model as advocated by Madison, Jefferson, and others, was of course a welcome change from the often bitter anti-semitic Jewish history in Europe.

America has been a fertile ground for Christian-Jewish relations because it has no collective national memory of the Middle Ages, the Crusades, the Inquisition, the many religious wars of Europe, the Protestant Reformation, or the Roman Catholic Counterreformation. As a nation, there was no direct historical legacy from the dark and painful European past, a past often filled with bloody intra-Christian battles and anti-Jewish pogroms. This historical reality, often little noted on either side of the Atlantic, has had an extraordinary impact upon America's religious life, Christian-Jewish relations, and the presence of antisemitism.

To put it in business parlance: America early on deregulated religion and by so doing has allowed hundreds of faith communities to exist in freedom. It is estimated that there are nearly 270 separate Protestant denominations alone in the United States, along with Roman Catholic, Eastern Orthodox, Jewish, Muslim, Hindu, Buddhist, and a host of other religious groups.* This voluntary arrangement regarding religion has never been neat or efficient, but it has been relatively free of government interference or control.

But it has only been since the end of the Second World War, and the Holocaust, that positive Christian-Jewish relations and the active campaign against religious antisemitism has begun to accelerate in both quantity and quality. For example, in 1948 at its meeting in Amsterdam, and as a direct result of the Holocaust, the World Council of Churches (WCC), representing 325 Christian church bodies in 140 countries, publicly for the first time condemned antisemitism.

In 1965, the Second Vatican Council's declaration *Nostra Aetate* ("In Our Time"), adopted by the world's 2,200 Roman

---

*Indeed, it has been estimated that there are as many as 1,200 religions, sects, and faith groups in the United States. (Editor's note)

Catholic bishops, gave the Christian-Jewish encounter even greater impetus. This landmark statement declared that the death of Jesus "cannot be blamed upon all the Jews then living, without distinction, nor upon the Jews of today." The Catholic Church, it went on, "deplores the hatred, persecution, and displays of anti-Semitism directed against the Jews at any time and from any source."[3]

Reflecting their commitment to improved relations with the Jewish people, the Vatican, the World Council of Churches, and two American church bodies, the National Council of Churches (NCC) and the National Conference of Catholic Bishops (NCCB), have all established offices on Christian-Jewish relations. The NCCB is composed of America's Roman Catholic bishops who lead the 58 million Catholics in the United States, and the NCC's thirty-two member denominations represent 48 million American Christians, both Protestant and Eastern Orthodox.

The NCCB's Christian-Jewish Relations Office began its work in 1967 and the NCC's office was inaugurated in 1974. Some American Protestant denominations have professional staff members who are also engaged in this effort, and several major U.S. Jewish organizations, including the American Jewish Committee, the Anti-Defamation League of B'nai B'rith, and the Union of American Hebrew Congregations, have interreligious affairs departments. The range of interreligious cooperation is vast, encompassing numerous shared concerns: antisemitism, immigration and refugees, arms limitation, aiding the poor and the homeless, bioethical questions, religious liberty, human rights, racism, sexism, ageism, world hunger, AIDS, crime, drugs, preserving family life, and a host of other issues. There are Christian-Jewish associations in Israel, Latin America, and Europe as well.

Basic to all Christian-Jewish relations are three issues. First is the persistence of antisemitism among some Christians, and the long Christian record of the "teaching of contempt" toward Jews and Judaism that helped provide the theological climate for the Shoah, the Holocaust. The Shoah was the culmination of centuries of anti-Jewish teachings and practices.

The American Baptist Churches, a major Protestant denomination, has designated Yom Hashoah, the Holocaust Remembrance Day that is commemorated each April, as part of their official ecclesiastical calendars. In addition, some churches also observe the dates of November 9 and 10 in memory of the Nazi Kristallnacht pogroms in 1938.

Annual Holocaust commemorations are increasing in many American churches, and in April 1994 there was a formal and official Holocaust Commemoration Concert at the Vatican at which time Pope John Paul II spoke with eloquence about the evils of the Shoah:

> We are gathered ... to commemorate the Holocaust of millions of Jews.... This is our commitment. We would risk causing the victims of the most atrocious deaths to die again if we do not have an ardent desire for justice, if we not commit ourselves, each according to his own capacities, to ensure that evil does not prevail over good as it did not millions of the children of the Jewish people ... do not forget us.[4]

Many Christian leaders and scholars are actively addressing the issue of antisemitism, and are urging that all areas of church life be purged of anti-Jewish material. This includes teaching materials, textbooks, preaching aids, hymnals, seminary curriculum, and liturgy. The greatest advances have been achieved in religious textbooks and liturgy reform, but much more work remains in the vital area of seminary education.

In 1972 the Southern Baptist Convention, the largest Protestant denomination in the United States numbering some fifteen million members, adopted a resolution condemning antisemitism. The resolution concluded:

> Southern Baptists covenant to work positively to replace all anti-Semitic bias with the Christian attitude and practice of love for the Jews, who along with all other men are equally beloved of God.[5]

In 1991 the Episcopal Church's General Convention adopted a resolution that deplored:

> anti-Jewish prejudice ... in whatever form or on whatever occasion and urge its total elimination from ... the Episcopal Church, its individual members, its various units.[6]

And the United Methodist Church at its 1972 General Conference adopted an extensive resolution on Christian-Jewish relations that included these sections:

> ... Christians must also become aware of that history in which they have deeply alienated the Jews. They are obligated to examine their own implicit and explicit responsibility for the discrimination against and the organized extermination of Jews, as in the recent past [the Holocaust]. The persecution by Christians of Jews throughout centuries calls for clear repentance and resolve to repudiate past injustice and to seek its elimination in the present. . . .

> ... the Christian obligation to those who survived the Nazi holocaust, the understanding of the relationship of land and peoplehood . . . suggest that a new dimension in dialogue with Jews is needed . . . in such dialogues, an aim of religious or political conversion, or of proselytizing, cannot be condoned . . . there is no tenable biblical or theological base for anti-Semitism.[7]

Pope John Paul II declared in 1985 that

> Anti-Semitism . . . has been repeatedly condemned by the Catholic teaching as incompatible with Christ's teaching. . . . Where there was ignorance and . . . prejudice . . . there is now growing mutual knowledge, appreciation, and respect.[8]

In 1987 both the General Assembly of the Presbyterian Church (U.S.A.) and the General Synod of the United Church of Christ (UCC) adopted important and potentially historic statements on Jews and Judaism. The UCC was the first major American Protestant church to affirm that "Judaism has not been superseded by Christianity," and that "God has not rejected the Jewish people." The UCC publicly acknowledged that

> The Christian Church has throughout much of its history denied God's continuing covenantal relationship with the Jewish people. . . . This denial has led to outright rejection of the Jewish people . . . and intolerable violence. . . . Faced with this history from which we as Christians cannot, and

must not, disassociate ourselves, we ask for God's forgiveness.[9]

The Presbyterian statement, in the form of a church study paper, made a similar theological point and specifically called upon Christians to "repudiate" the historic "teaching of contempt" for the Jewish people and their religious tradition. The statement also cautioned Presbyterians "when speaking with Jews about matters of faith to acknowledge that Jews are already in a covenantal relationship with God." The Presbyterian statement affirmed "the continuity of God's promise of land [Israel] along with the obligations of that promise to the people of Israel."[10]

Both the United Church of Christ and Presbyterian statements reflect the growing trend among many Christians to come to terms with Jews and Judaism on a theological level as well as on a personal basis. These two leading Protestant denominations have provided important building blocks to develop a new and deeper relationship with the Jewish people.

In 1971, the Lutheran Council in the U.S.A., representing the three largest Lutheran denominations in the country, issued an excellent statement on Christian-Jewish relations, calling for mutual respect and understanding between the two faith communities.

Because Martin Luther's later writings are filled with particular hostility to Jews and Judaism, the Church Council of the Evangelical Lutheran Church in America (ELCA), the largest Lutheran body in the United States, in 1994 adopted a remarkable resolution that explicitly repudiated the anti-Jewish writings and teachings of Luther.

In the long history of Christianity there exists no more tragic development than the treatment accorded to the Jewish people on the part of Christian believers. . . . Lutherans . . . feel a special burden in this regard because of certain elements in the legacy of the reformer Martin Luther and the catastrophes, including the Holocaust of the twentieth century, suffered by Jews in places where the Lutheran churches were strongly represented. . . .

In the spirit of that truth telling, we . . . must with pain acknowledge also Luther's anti-Judaic diatribes and violent recommendations of his later writings against the Jews. . . . We reject this violent invective . . . we express our deep and abiding sorrow over its tragic effects on subsequent generations . . . we particularly deplore the appropriation of Luther's words by modern anti-Semites for the teaching of hatred toward Judaism or toward the Jewish people. . . . We recognize in anti-Semitism a contradiction and an affront to the Gospel . . . and we pledge this church to oppose the deadly working of such bigotry, both within our own circles and in the society around us. Finally, we pray for . . . increasing cooperation and understanding between Lutheran Christians and the Jewish community.[11]

This significant action by the ELCA represents an important trend that is currently underway within many Christian bodies. It may be impossible to amend or eliminate the anti-Jewish elements in the New Testament, the writings of the Church Fathers, and in other Christian teaching materials that have been used to foster antisemitism. However, those elements can be officially repudiated and placed within a historical context that greatly reduces their potential to influence negatively today's Christians.

The 1994 ELCA Church Council statement on Luther's teachings about Jews and Judaism is especially helpful in this area. The Lutheran statement acknowledged a special responsibility to improve Christian-Jewish relations because the Holocaust took place in areas of significant Lutheran influence in Europe.

Almost from the beginning of Christianity a clear separation existed between East and West. Over time Western Christianity became centered in Rome and spread to Spain, Portugal, Britain, France, Germany, and Poland. Eastern Christianity's center became Constantinople, the "second Rome," and it extended to much of Greece, the Middle East, Asia Minor, the Balkans, Romania, and Russia. Eastern Orthodox Christians did not accept the claims to spiritual primacy of the Bishop of Rome, the Pope, and in 1054, there was a permanent break, "The Great Schism," between Western and Eastern Christianity.

Byzantine rulers such as Justinian (527–565) closely linked church and state, and a rich mixture of faith and culture emerged.

The rise of Islam in the East placed exceptional pressure on Eastern Orthodoxy, and in 1453 Constantinople (Turkish name Istanbul) fell to the Muslims.

More than three million Orthodox Christians, mostly Greek and Russian, live in the United States, along with other Orthodox communities including Arab, Serbian, Coptic, Armenian, Ukrainian, Rumanian, Syrian, and Albanian churches. And even though Eastern Orthodoxy is the majority Christian expression in modern Israel, most American Jews know little about the Orthodox churches or the long and complex Jewish history that took place within the Byzantine Empire. While most of the Jews who lived in Byzantium were Sephardic, many American Jews of Ashkenazi background trace their family roots to countries with large Orthodox Christian populations, such as Russia, Romania, Ukraine, Serbia, and Bulgaria.

As in the West, the record of theological antisemitism is a mixed one. Bulgaria saved much of its Jewish population from the Nazis during World War II. At the same time the record was extremely dismal in Russia, Romania, and Ukraine, all centers of Orthodox Christianity, even under Communism.

But it would be an error to irrevocably link Eastern Orthodoxy with antisemitism. In 1993, Ecumenical Patriarch Bartholomaios I, the spiritual leader of Orthodox Christians, sent a warm personal greeting to an international conference of Orthodox Christian and Jewish leaders that was held in Athens, Greece. The patriarch, who resides in Istanbul, declared that Orthodoxy "has never encouraged racist ideas and theories .'.. such as the persecution and genocide of people who belonged to a different culture or worshipped God in a different way."[12]

In 1568 an earlier ecumenical patriarch, Metrophanes, also condemned attacks against Jews, declaring, ". . . do not oppress or accuse anyone falsely; do not make any distinctions or give room to the believers to injure those of another belief."[13]

All too often future Christian clergy receive little or no accurate instruction about Jews and Judaism, the Jewish roots of Christianity, the Shoah, modern Israel, or the continuing pathology of antisemitism. Christian seminaries render a grave disservice to their students by omitting or giving short shrift to these critical subjects.

Of special concern in any analysis of theological antisemitism are performances of "Passion plays" that often foster potent anti-Jewish portraits and attitudes. Passion plays are dramatic presentations depicting the life, trial, and death of Jesus. Traditionally sponsored by churches or religious communities, these plays are increasingly often strictly commercial productions.

The National Conference of Catholic Bishops has issued guidelines warning that Passion plays can convey harshly negative images of Jews and Judaism. The world-famous Oberammergau Passion play, performed every ten years in Bavaria, Germany, has been the subject of numerous critical studies by both Christian and Jewish scholars.

But of equal concern are the many Passion plays performed annually in the United States. These plays attract large audiences including Sunday school students and Christian educators. The plays are dramatically powerful sources for reinforcing antisemitic attitudes and stereotypes. This is particularly true since the plays are frequently understood by audiences as the "gospel truth." That is to say, they are biblically accurate rather than the product of the sometimes vivid imaginations of the various playwrights. Because of these issues, many Christian leaders in the United States have been deeply involved in analyzing Passion plays, and in seeking the removal of all anti-Jewish dramatic material from them.

Old negative antisemitic stereotypes of Jews as a people "cursed and punished by God" remain embedded in Christian teaching and preaching along with the image of the exiled "wandering Jew." Scholars have identified a variety of unchallenged and uncorrected dualism at work within many churches: the Christian "God of love" versus the Jewish "God of wrath"; the "New" Testament versus the "Old" Testament; the "New Israel" (the Church) versus the "Old Israel" (the Jews); liberating Christian "grace" versus suffocating Jewish "law"; the loving "people of Jesus" versus the deceitful "people of Judas." All these false comparisons often transmit to Christians a highly negative image of Jews and Judaism that contributes to religious antisemitism.

A second central issue, following antisemitism, in the contemporary Christian-Jewish encounter is the nexus of mission, witness, conversion, and proselytization, all of which are fundamental themes in Christianity. Many Christian-Jewish conferences have grappled with these themes and some useful definitions and clarity have emerged. The Christian mission to the Jews, that is, the active campaign to convert Jews to a particular form of Christianity, is perceived by most Jews as the ultimate form of theological antisemitism.

In much of Jewish thought and collective experience, the Christian mission and missionaries are inextricably linked with antisemitism since the paramount aim of such missionary activity is the literal elimination of both Jews and Judaism from the world scene. In any study of antisemitism, it is important to recognize that aggressive Christian missionary efforts aimed at Jews represent an attempt to end Jewish life in the world.

"Mission" is a shared religious term that is usually interpreted in different ways by each faith community. Jewish self-definition includes the mission to spread the message of the one God, ethical monotheism, to the entire world. "On that day the Lord shall be One and God's name shall be One" (Zechariah 14:9). Jews are to be a "light to the nations" (Isaiah 42:6), but the Jewish mission has historically been free of coercion and religious "triumphalism," a term meaning that one particular religious tradition has gained spiritual victory and domination over all others.

Jews have historically experienced the Christian mission in highly negative, antisemitic ways. For centuries, Jews were the victims of forced conversions, medieval disputations, expulsions, and death at the hands of those Christians who sought to "bring the Jews to Christ." For over a thousand years in Europe the Jews were an oppressed minority within a Christendom that did not permit religious freedom as we know the term today. European Jews lived, until the Enlightenment, in social, economic, and religious conditions that were humiliating and crushing.

Even in modern times the Jewish people are often confronted by coercive Christian missionaries who see Jews solely as candidates for conversion, and view Judaism as an incomplete religion. Because of this long historical record of Christian contempt and hostility toward Jews and Judaism, the term "mission," whatever its earliest theological roots, is universally regarded by Jews as an antisemitic attack upon their sacred history, and upon a perfected and authentic religion.

The "religious right" is active once again in the United States, and is led primarily by evangelical Christian leaders, many of whom actively seek the conversion of the Jewish people to their particular brand of Christianity. It is the classic Christian "mission."

Although the religious right's agenda is mostly political, some of its leaders are, as the manifesto of the Coalition for Revival's manifesto asserts, "working to Christianize America and the world."[14] Although it is sometimes hard to cite explicit antisemitic statements in the carefully crafted rhetoric of the religious right, many Jews and Christians perceive the presence of traditional religious antisemitism within the movement. For example, the Rev. Pat Robertson, a prominent religious right leader, has written:

> The liberal Jews have actually forsaken Biblical faith in God, and made a religion out of political liberalism. . . . If someone attacks abortion-on-demand or asks for prayer in the schools, the liberal Jewish community reacts as if this stand were somehow anti-Semitic. They have anti-Christian liberalism intermingled with Judaism to such a degree they can't distinguish anymore.[15]

Indeed, the call for a "Christian America" by the religious right is understood by many to be a form of classic antisemitism because such an America would exclude Jews from full participation in the society. The establishment of a "Christian America" would not only fly in the face of the fundamental principles of the Constitution and the Bill of Rights, it would also contradict more than two hundred years of shared history, legal precedents, and a tradition of religious pluralism. As articulated by some religious right leaders, a "Christian America" would violate the American commitment to both democratic government and religious liberty, and would be a clear signal that non-Christians, including American Jews, are less than full citizens.

At the same time, leaders of the religious right are strong public supporters of Israel. Much of that support is based upon specific Christian theological doctrines involving apocalyptic and "End of Days" theology prophecies.

Fortunately, a growing number of Christian theologians are repudiating the dark antisemitic side of Christian history and teaching. These theologians are publicly repentant for Christianity's past injustices against Jews, and increasingly, they emphasize the Jewish roots of Christianity.

The late William S. LaSor, professor of Bible at Fuller Theological Seminary in Pasadena, California, a leading evangelical institution, has written:

> Just as I refuse to believe that God has rejected this people (Romans 11:1), and that there is no longer any place for Israel in God's redemptive work or in the messianic hope, so I refuse to believe that we who were once not his people, and who have become his people only through grace, can learn nothing from those who from of old have been his people.[16]

In 1973 Dr. Billy Graham, the leading Christian evangelist of the twentieth century, publicly criticized the excesses of the key 1973 Christian evangelistic campaign. Citing the New Testament book of Romans, Chapters 9–11, Graham declared:

> I believe God has always had a special relationship with the Jewish people. . . . In my evangelistic efforts, I have never felt called to single out Jews as Jews. . . . Just as Judaism frowns on proselytizing that is coercive, or that seeks to commit men against their will, so do I.[17]

Today many Christians see "mission" and "witness" in a different light than in centuries past. They now make a distinction between the two: mission is usually insensitive and coercive, but witness is the living out of one's faith without attempting to proselytize or convert another person. For such Christians, witness is free of hidden agendas or subliminal messages: "You are my witnesses, says the Lord" (Isaiah 43:12).

The third critical theme in Christian-Jewish relations is the State of Israel. The emergence of Israel in 1948 has compelled Christians and Jews to examine themselves in a new light, as they seek possible theological meaning from the rebirth of the Jewish state in the Middle East. As a result, Israel must be at the center of any meaningful Christian-Jewish encounter.

One of the positive results of the Christian-Jewish dialogue has been a commitment by members of both communities to work for the security and survival of the State of Israel. Jews have prayed for thousands of years: "Next year in Jerusalem!" The verse "If I forget thee, O Jerusalem, let my right hand forget her cunning" (Psalm 137) forms a central commitment of Judaism. The words "Zion" and "Jerusalem" appear hundreds of times in the Bible.

Many Christians understand and even share in the redemptive meaning of Israel. Along with Jews, they are aware that Israel, like any other nation-state, is not free of imperfections and defects. Yet many Christians are deeply stirred by the rebirth— some might even say the resurrection—of a democratic Jewish state and by the specter of Jews from 120 countries "returning to Zion."

The Rev. Edward H. Flannery, one of the architects of Christian-Jewish relations in the United States, who served as the first executive secretary for Catholic-Jewish relations for the National Conference of Catholic Bishops, has declared:

> In view of the ceaseless persecutions visited upon Jews so often by Christians throughout the centuries, and because of their scattered state throughout the world, it is the Christian, above all, who should rejoice at the upturn in the Jewish people's fortunes in our time that has brought them back to their ancient homeland. The return to Israel can only be seen as the righting of a historic wrong.[18]

In 1980 the National Council of Churches (NCC), representing thirty-two Protestant and Eastern Orthodox denominations, adopted a policy statement on the Middle East that still remains the NCC's most authoritative position on the subject. The statement affirmed Israel's right to exist as a "Jewish State," while it also recognized the Palestinians' right to self-determination.

The National Council of Churches warned against the temptation to scapegoat Israel by employing a "double standard" when judging Israel:

> The NCC ... recognizes the need to apply similar standards of judgment to all countries in the Middle East in questions of human or minority rights, and to resist singling out only one nation for particular focus without due recognition of other continuing human rights problems throughout the region.[19]

The NCC also clearly recognized that ancient theological antisemitism exists within some Middle Eastern churches, and is being used for contemporary political purposes:

> ... the theological differences that still exist within the Christian community over ... the continuing role of the Jewish people ... some theological positions, when combined with the political dynamics of the area could be understood as what the West would call anti-Semitism ... seeds of religious alienation can be carried through the churches themselves.[20]

A prominent Evangelical scholar, Professor Marvin R. Wilson of Gordon College in Wenham, Massachusetts, has described his own understanding of the State of Israel:

> ... the remarkable preservation of Israel over the centuries and her recent return to the land are in keeping with those many biblical texts which give promise of her future. But my concern and support for Israel only begins with predictive prophetic texts; it does not end there. The more relevant prophetic texts ... are those which speak to Israel's present situation by calling men and nations to practice justice, righteousness, kindness, and brotherhood in their dealings with one another.[21]

On the last day of December, 1993, representatives of the Vatican and Israel signed an accord in Jerusalem that opened the way for full and formal diplomatic relations between the Holy See and the Jewish state that were established in June 1994. This welcome event ended decades of controversy and removed a major impediment to Catholic-Jewish relations throughout the world.

In 1987, on the eve of Pope John Paul II's trip to the United States, the Vatican had publicly declared that there were no theological barriers to full relations with Israel. The Vatican ruled out religious antisemitism as a possible obstacle to such relations. Instead, the Holy See insisted that diplomatic relations with the Jewish state was a strictly political matter between two nation-states.*

The accord signaled the normalization of relations not only between the two signatories, but also between Roman Catholics and Jews throughout the world. By its action, the Vatican sent a clear signal to Israel's enemies that the Roman Catholic Church recognizes Israel as a permanent and legitimate member of the international family of nations.

These general themes—antisemitism, the Holocaust, mission and witness, and the State of Israel—are central to Christian-Jewish relations. But it is also important to discuss how Christians and Jews actually relate to one another.

There are millions of people of faith who live behind the various pronouncements and declarations on antisemitism and inter-religious relations. How do people really encounter one another? And what are the implications of these encounters for anti-semitism?

Since the conclusion of the Second Vatican Council in 1965, there have been more positive Catholic-Jewish encounters than there were in the first 1,900 years of the Roman Catholic Church. Since 1965 many important and far-reaching Catholic statements have been promulgated. Catholic bishops in Latin America, the Netherlands, Belgium, France, Switzerland, Germany, and Brazil (the country with the world's largest Catholic population) have all issued strong statements going beyond *Nostra Aetate* in calling for improved relations with Jews, and these

---

*A more likely explanation for the Vatican's reluctance to normalize relations with the State of Israel was the concern of Rome for the well-being—indeed the fate—of Christian communities in Arab lands. (Editor's note)

statements have included sharp condemnations of all forms of antisemitism.

Until the liberating force of the Second Vatican Council and *Nostra Aetate*, the Catholic Church was locked into a self-imposed ghetto, a barrier against the modern world. The council broke down those walls, or, to use Pope John's striking imagery, the Church opened a window to the world.

Both Jews and Catholics suffered because of this self-imposed ghetto. Jews often suffered with the loss of their lives because of antisemitism whereas Roman Catholics often suffered a spiritual deprivation. Victim and victimizer—both suffered, albeit in very different ways.

It must always be remembered that prior to the Second Vatican Council, most Christian-Jewish dialogues were Protestant-Jewish in nature. Indeed, I can testify to my own experience as a young American Jew growing up in Virginia. In those years, the 1940s and '50s, a Presbyterian or Episcopalian minister spoke in my family's synagogue once a year, and our rabbi, himself a German-born refugee from Nazi antisemitism, spoke annually in a neighboring church.

Although Virginia, as part of the American South, was filled with many evangelical Protestant churches, our rabbi rarely if ever exchanged pulpits with them. But it was this Protestant-Jewish relationship, tentative as it was, that constituted almost all of what passed for Christian-Jewish relations in those years. This fact should not be devalued or underestimated, but rather the pioneering effort immediately after World War II should be remembered with deep appreciation in the ongoing struggle against antisemitism.

And it must always be recalled that Protestants, in whatever denomination or faith community, remain the Christian majority in the United States. And while Jews are regularly engaged in programs and encounters with Roman Catholics and increasingly with Muslims, it was the Protestant community that was an early innovator in interreligious work in America.

American Jews and members of "mainline" Protestant churches—those bodies affiliated with the National Council of Churches and the World Council of Churches such as the Episcopal Church, the United Methodist Church, the Presbyterian

Church, the American Baptist Churches, the United Church of Christ, and the Disciples of Christ—are somewhat similar in their socioeconomic status within American society. Until recently, if you asked the "average Jew"—assuming there is such a person—precisely which Christian church or group that person knew the best, the answer would often be a Protestant group.

But a strange thing is happening in "mainline" Protestant-Jewish relations in the United States. The top-level leadership of some Protestant churches maintains a tepid to cold attitude toward the State of Israel, but the "grass roots," millions of regional and local Protestants, remain strongly supportive of the Jewish state.

This bifocal approach on the part of Protestants vis-à-vis Israel is replicated in other sharp intra-Protestant differences involving many theological, sexual, social, and cultural issues. A few years ago some leadership elements within the Presbyterian Church (U.S.A.) proposed a statement on human sexuality that took radical new positions. But at the Presbyterian General Assembly the statement was bitterly attacked by the rank-and-file membership, and the sexuality declaration was not passed. There are other such instances, although on different issues, within many of America's leading Protestant churches.

On the other hand, as a direct result of Professor Reinhold Niebuhr's teaching during the 1940s and '50s at Union Theological Seminary in New York City, most mainline Protestant churches have abandoned active conversion campaigns specifically aimed at the Jewish community. And such churches generally do not formally participate in mass evangelistic campaigns that are usually sponsored by other, more theologically conservative Protestant churches.

To turn the coin over, Jews find enormous support for Israel among evangelical leaders as well as from those in the church pews. Evangelicals represent the single largest Christian body of support for Israel. That support is, of course, warmly welcomed by both American Jews and Israelis, and one clearly remembers that in 1980 the Israeli prime minister, Menachem Begin, presented a major award to Dr. Jerry Falwell, a prominent Evangelical leader.

At the same time, many within the evangelical community

have not followed the Niebuhrian lead and abandoned Jewish evangelism, and in a bizarre twist, some of the same evangelicals who publicly support Israel with fervor are sometimes also directly involved in missionary activities aimed at Jews. Some evangelical churches even grant free space and moral support to the deceptive "Jews for Jesus" and other so-called Hebrew Christian groups.

The situation is nuanced: almost all American church bodies have publicly condemned and repudiated antisemitism. However, if American Jews seek strong public support for Israel, they will turn first to the large evangelical community. This community, estimated to number some 50 million people, still seeks to convert Jews. This is a legitimate Christian activity considered an act of antisemitism by most Jews.

If these same American Jews seek coalition partners in the Protestant community on a host of social justice issues, including gun control, sexual equality, pro-choice on abortion—what is generally called the "liberal agenda"—they will turn instinctively and historically to the mainline Protestant churches, which have often been highly critical of Israeli policies and actions.

A word about the black Protestant churches in the United States. Twenty years ago there was a strong movement among many Protestants to form a large "United Church." There was much enthusiasm for bringing the various mainline churches into union. But there was also strong opposition to such a proposal, and the black churches especially were wary of a "megachurch" that might mean an end to their distinctiveness. The proposed United Church never became a reality, and the black opposition was a key factor in the outcome.

The black churches then and now represent the one universally trusted institution in the entire black community. The church remains with its people in America's inner cities. And, as was the case with the synagogue in much of pre-1939 Eastern Europe, the black church remains a central political, cultural, and social focus of the community. It is no accident that so many black civic and political leaders are ordained ministers. Jesse Jackson, John Lewis, Benjamin Chavis, Ben Hooks, Andrew Young, and Carl McCall are notable examples.

And the black church, despite its many problems, still remains the one place where blacks can be totally "at home" with their own traditions and style of worship; again the analogy with the synagogue is obvious. For Jews, the most direct means of relating to the 23 million–plus black Americans on almost every issue is through the church.

Jews and blacks have each been a "victim people." In a twist of history, Jews, victims of antisemitism, and blacks, victims of racism, are bound together in the shared agony of victimization.

While blacks, quite understandably, favor a liberal social agenda, the black clergy is generally theologically conservative and male-oriented. So as with everything else in life, things are never as simple as they might first appear. Yet, positive black Protestant-Jewish relations are essential to both communities.

There is one special area in the battle against antisemitism that needs an extraordinary effort from both Jews and Christians, and that is the development of a "theology of pluralism." Because much of religious antisemitism is based upon a triumphalistic Christianity, a theology of pluralism would radically change that centuries-old Christian self-perception. A theology of pluralism would compel many Christians to reexamine the ancient canards against Jews and Judaism that have historically been employed to discredit the religion of the "Elder Brother," that is, of Judaism. An intense debate is currently underway in many Christian churches centering on this critical question of religious pluralism.

Because of the singular history and tradition of American society, Jews and Christians live together in a pluralistic society in this country. Yet that pluralism, which has been a hallmark of the United States, is like a tender, frail plant that needs constant nurturing if it is to survive and grow stronger.

Dr. Martin E. Marty, a distinguished scholar of religious history and a Lutheran, has correctly warned:

Now the West is uncertain. All kinds of forces are filling the vacuum. . . . Here [in the United States], not many get killed, but they hate each other. The lucky thing about America is we live in such a mixed-up pattern. In the rest of the world, groups are mostly on one side of the hill or the other. It's not hard to see who to shoot.

Here, you don't know where to shoot. Shoot a feminist, it might be my wife. Shoot a Hispanic, it might be my foster daughter. Shoot a Jew, it might be my colleague. Shoot a gay, it might be a best friend. . . . The rest of the world never made the move to our style of rationality.[22]

A significant step would be for Jews and Christians to plumb the spiritual depths of their traditions in order find the theological foundations for religious pluralism. It is not enough that we live together as faith communities; rather, our faiths must sustain and anchor our shared existence in a pluralistic setting. Unless that happens, the cruel winds of antisemitism, religious bigotry, and extremism, combined with economic turbulence, could spell disaster for the interreligious efforts that have already shown such promise. Our best and most creative theological minds are urgently needed for this critical task.

Former French president Charles de Gaulle, speaking in another context, once summarized his country's situation when he declared that "France does not have permanent friends; it has, instead, only permanent interests." Substitute the words "Jewish people" for "France" and one has an accurate description of the current state of Christian-Jewish relations within the United States. One fact clearly emerges from this general overview of antisemitism and Christian-Jewish relations: there is today a strong commitment within both communities to strengthen the existing relationship.

The Christian-Jewish relationship has already borne rich fruit as well as controversy, and the future will be no different. Jews and Christians will come together on shared concerns, especially the efforts to oppose antisemitism, while of course remaining fully faithful to their unique religious traditions.

They will also differ, not only over theological tenets, but over a host of other concerns as well. Yet they have both come too far to abandon the dialogue at this late date. The English poet Robert Browning, in his poem "Rabbi Ben Ezra," wrote: "Grow old along with me, the best is yet to be." The toxic impact of religious antisemitism will be eradicated as the dialogue matures and deepens.

NOTES

1. Saul K. Padover, *The Complete Jefferson* (New York: Duell, Sloan, & Pearce, 1943), pp. 943–44.

2. Ibid., pp. 538–39.

3. Eugene J. Fisher, *Seminary Education and Christian-Jewish Relations* (Washington, D.C.: National Catholic Educational Association, 1988), pp. 85–86.

4. Catholic News Service, *Origins* 23: 45 (April 28, 1994), 780.

5. Marc H. Tanenbaum, Marvin R. Wilson, and A. James Rudin, eds., *Evangelicals and Jews in an Age of Pluralism* (Grand Rapids, Mich.: Baker Book House, 1984), p. 40.

6. Episcopal Church, *Distinction Between Criticism of Israel and Anti-Jewish Prejudice*, Resolution D122, 70th General Convention, Phoenix, Ariz., 1991.

7. United Methodist Church, *Bridge in Hope: Jewish-Christian Dialogue*, General Conference, Atlanta, Ga., 1972, pp. 4–7.

8. Eugene J. Fisher, A. James Rudin, and Marc H. Tanenbaum, eds., *Twenty Years of Jewish-Catholic Relations* (New York and Mahwah, N.J.: Paulist Press, 1986), p, 17.

9. United Church of Christ, *The Relationship Between the United Church of Christ and the Jewish Community*, UCC General Synod XVI, Cleveland, Ohio, 1987.

10. Presbyterian Church in the U.S.A., *A Theological Understanding of the Relationship Between Christians and Jews*, 199th General Assembly, Biloxi, Miss., 1987.

11. Evangelical Lutheran Church in America, *The Declaration of the Evangelical Lutheran Church in America to the Jewish Community*, Chicago, Ill., April 18, 1994.

12. International Jewish Committee for Interreligious Consultations–Eastern Orthodox Churches, *Joint Communiqué*, Athens, Greece, March 1993.

13. Ibid.

14. Lori Forman, *The Political Activity of the Religious Right in the 1990s* (New York: American Jewish Committee, 1994), p. 11.

15. Pat Robertson, *The New Millennium* (Irving, Texas: Word Publishing, 1990), pp. 291–93.

16. Marc H. Tanenbaum, Marvin R. Wilson, and A. James Rudin, eds., *Evangelicals and Jews in Conversation* (Grand Rapids, Mich.: Baker Book House, 1978), p. 93.

17. Marc H. Tanenbaum et al., *Evangelicals and Jews in an Age of Pluralism*, p. 39.

18. A. James Rudin, *Israel for Christians: Understanding Modern Israel*, (Philadelphia: Fortress Press, 1983), p. 124.

19. Ibid., p. 135.

20. Ibid., p. 126.

21. A. James Rudin and Marvin R. Wilson, eds., *A Time to Speak: The Evangelical-Jewish Encounter* (Grand Rapids, Mich.: Eerdmans Publishing Company, 1987), p. 172.

22. Martin E. Marty, *Modern American Religion, Vol. 2: The Noise of Conflict* (Chicago: University of Chicago Press, 1991), pp. 1–14.

·11·
Denial of the Holocaust:
An Antisemitic Political Assault

KENNETH S. STERN
Kenneth Stern is program specialist in antisemitism
and extremism for the American Jewish Committee.
He is the author of *Holocaust Denial* and, most
recently, of *Loudhawk: The United States Versus the
American Indian Movement.*

Kenneth S. Stern's essay tackles a topic that has received much media
attention, so-called Holocaust revisionism, the denial of the Holocaust as
a vehicle for antisemitism. Stern takes the issue of Holocaust denial
beyond the question of education and public awareness—important factors, to be sure, if we factor in recent data that suggest that significant
numbers of Americans do not know very much about the Holocaust—to
the realm of Holocaust denial as a political phenomenon.

The question remains, as it does with respect to any extremist antisemitic rhetoric, of how much impact denial of the Holocaust has on the
American body politic. Have the "deniers" succeeded in their efforts aimed
at converting Americans to their antisemitic cause? The answer is no. The
danger of Holocaust denial, however, lies not in the number of those who
adhere to this form of antisemitism, but in the fact that Holocaust denial
is an example of an antisemitic manifestation heretofore considered
extremist or "fringe," in which efforts are being made toward introduction
into mainstream institutions of the society, in this case higher education
and the media. Further, the actual witnesses to the Holocaust—the survivors—are a dwindling cadre. As their numbers diminish, as they are no
longer to deliver personal testimony to the reality of the destruction of
European Jewry, antisemites will seize upon Holocaust denial with greater
fervor as a vehicle for their anti-Jewish agenda. This reality suggests that

the most effective strategy for the future in combatting Holocaust denial lies not in the point-by-point refutation of the "deniers," but in enhancing oral history and other educational projects on the Holocaust.

J.A.C.

Holocaust denial is no more about the Holocaust than the medieval claim that Jews poisoned wells was about water quality. Throughout history, antisemitic canards have influenced people to understand their world through the scapegoating of Jews. Poisoners of wells. Killers of Christ. Murderers of Christian children whose blood is drained to make matzah. Secret conspirators who run the world. The hidden hand behind the slave trade. As Judge Hadassah Ben Itto, president of the International Association of Jewish Lawyers and Jurists noted, "They don't replace each other, these lies; the list becomes longer all the time."[1] Holocaust denial is not only one of the more recent lies, it is also one of the most sophisticated.

Holocaust denial began before the Holocaust ended. Various German SS officers, knowing that the end was near, fled to South America, the Arab states, and elsewhere. Shortly after the war a few tracts appeared, attempting to distort history. In 1949 a French concentration camp survivor, Paul Rassinier, wrote *Monsonge d'Ulysse*, casting doubt on the Nazis' intention to kill Jews and on the number of Jews killed. In 1962 an American isolationist, Harry Elmer Barnes, wrote a pamphlet entitled *Blasting the Historical Blackout*, claiming that the Germans expelled from Czechoslovakia and Poland after the war suffered a fate "far more hideous and prolonged than those of the Jews said to have been exterminated in great numbers by the Nazis."

The first major Holocaust-denying work appeared in 1976, when Arthur Butz, an American professor of electrical engineering at Northwestern University, wrote *The Hoax of the Twentieth Century.* He acknowledged that Jews were persecuted by the Nazis, but denied that they were exterminated. Gas chambers, he alleged, were used merely for delousing. Many who had not heard of Holocaust denial before heard about it through the controversy surrounding Butz.

By 1978, professional antisemites, white supremacists, and

neo-Nazis began to understand the potential usefulness of Holocaust denial. The Holocaust was the central moral albatross of Nazism. Exalting the Holocaust as a positive event in human history was not a way to make friends or influence people. To deny the Holocaust would not only cleanse the image of Nazism, it would also empower supernationalistic, xenophobic, antisemitic political groups by making them believe they were the maligned victims of a suppressed truth.

In 1978 Willis Carto, the central force behind a network of antisemitic enterprises such as the Liberty Lobby and the Noontide Press, opened a new organization called the Institute for Historical Review (IHR). The IHR held its first conference in 1979. The white supremacists, neo-Nazis, and Klansmen who attended were enthralled by what was called "Holocaust revisionism." Yes, Jews were discriminated against in Germany, but they were not exterminated. Yes, there were concentration camps, but no gas chambers. Yes, the pictures of Jews in the camps at the end of the war were disturbing, but the Allies, not the Nazis, were to blame because they destroyed rail lines, leaving people to die of starvation and typhus. "Yes," stated with enough truth to sound believable, followed by a distorted "but" designed to flow from that truth.

Holocaust "revisionism," the attendees quickly understood, was to look like a serious, scholarly pursuit. It hijacked the name of "revisionist" from the school of real historians who, after World War I, tried to explain the events of that war through new perspectives. And by publishing a scholarly looking journal, the *Journal of Historical Review*, and holding conferences, the IHR made every effort to mask its unadulterated pro-Nazi, antisemitic agenda. Only the hard-core members would know that they could purchase Holocaust-denial material along with antisemitica and material glorifying Hitler and the Third Reich, including tapes of Luftwaffe marches and of Hitler's "best" speeches of 1933.

Holocaust denial fit well into the antisemitic and profascist agenda of hard-core antisemites. It was crafted in the mold of a prosecutor's dream: crime, motive, and opportunity. The "crime" was the Jews' inventing the story of the Holocaust. The "motive" was legitimacy for the state of Israel and reparations from Germany.[2] The "opportunity" was the old antisemitic canard of Jewish control of the media and of Hollywood. Since these building blocks of Holocaust denial were cross-pollinating, if anyone—even someone who did not see the world through an antisemitic lens—bought the premise of the allegation, the rest made perfect sense. For neo-Nazis and white supremacists, Holocaust denial fit into their preconceived notions of the power and evil of Jews.

By the early 1990s, the IHR had become the spine of the international Holocaust-denying movement, featuring speakers from around the world at its conferences and distributing books, tapes, a journal, and other material in many languages all over the globe. The material carefully used enough truth, and played on peoples' ignorance of the details of the Holocaust, to sound credible.

The Anne Frank diary was a hoax, they claimed, because writing had been found on the manuscript in ballpoint pen, a 1951 invention.

The Nuremberg trials were a fraud, they claimed, a kangaroo victors' court that extracted confessions from German soldiers through torture.

The gas chambers were never used to kill people, they claimed, because the gas used, Zyklon B, left a residue called "Prussian blue." More Prussian blue was found on the chambers for killing lice than those allegedly used for killing people. How could that be? People are bigger than lice. In any case, Zyklon B is an explosive gas. How could it have been used in gas chambers, which were next door to crematoria? How could there be pictures of Nazi guards smoking outside of the gas chambers?

The crematoria, they contended, were for people who died from "natural" causes, not extermination. Modern crematoria require five hours to consume one body. How could 1940s-era crematoria have accommodated the necessary number of corpses if these were extermination camps?

Imagine an eighteen-year-old, with little historical sophistication, who hears these claims. They appear to raise reasonable questions. The deniers—who have presented questions such as these in advertisements designed for college newspapers and through other means—then ask, why can't these matters be "debated"? What is there about the Holocaust that is unique, that it cannot be discussed between opposing schools, "extermination-ists" and "revisionists"? Is it not important that questions like these be answered? Why won't the "exterminationists" debate? What are they afraid of? Is the Holocaust some societally sanc-tioned "truth" that is off-limits to discuss? Who made this so?

In modern times, antisemitism has functioned best when it is catalyzed by conspiracy theories, including the preposterous proposition of the *Protocols of the Elders of Zion*—that a few Jews, meeting secretly, control all the important events in the world. Holocaust denial feeds from the same trough of conspira-cy, but provides a seemingly more rational basis for its lunacy. No one can deny that tremendous propaganda is generated during a war, or that throughout history the winners get to write *their* ver-sion of events. Jews, therefore, need not have entirely "invented" the Holocaust—they may just have believed wartime propaganda and then, through their control of the media and Hollywood, made the story part of the generally accepted view of people worldwide.

Holocaust denial, therefore, builds on and improves the old-line antisemitic canards of Jewish power and control. In its own insular dementia, it makes perfect sense, and any challenge to it is dismissed as the work of evildoers who are trying to reassert their "big lie," that the Nazis exterminated Jews.

History teaches that any form of bigotry must not be ignored, even if it is "silly." All bigotry is palpably absurd, but that has not stopped people from believing it and political movements from using it. If "silly" hate can become empowering, all the more reason to take Holocaust denial seriously, since denial blends enough truth with its pseudoscience and pseudohistory to seem logical. Furthermore, the "logic" of Holocaust denial has a new currency in the post-Communist world.

World War II was the central defining event of the last half-century, especially in Europe. In its wake, Communism was imposed on Eastern Europe, and relationships between the West-ern European nations were realigned. The horror of extreme nationalism, of race-based ethnic stereotyping, of hatred becom-ing an acceptable part of state ideology, of the logical end point of antisemitism, became understood lessons of the Holocaust.

With the end of the cold war, the newly free countries of Eastern Europe have been throwing off the old Communist party line (which never included the extermination of Jews in its version of World War II history), and reestablishing their claims of national sovereignty. Many of the last non-Communist national heroes were leaders of the Nazi puppet regimes. In the Ukraine and elsewhere, people we call war criminals are having statues erected and streets renamed in their honor. This redefinition of history, inevitable as it may be, plays right into the hands of the Holocaust deniers.

Beyond Eastern Europe, repaint World War II without the Holocaust and what do you get? Perhaps a war between competing systems that each had their demerits—capitalism, fascism, Communism. Perhaps just an ugly phase of history, just as Stalin's USSR was an evil part of history. Without the gas chambers and the Holocaust, Nazi Germany is relativized into just another troubling part of human history. That, too, is good for the agenda of the deniers.

Imagine our eighteen-year-old again. What does it matter if he or she believes that the events of his or her grandparents' youth were not as is generally accepted? If World War II and the Holocaust were the defining events of the last half of the twentieth century, and an untrue understanding of those events was *imposed* on Europe, all political formations and actions for the last five decades have been based on false assumptions. Asylum policies, programs that promote pluralism and democracy and oppose xenophobia and nationalism-run-wild, are all suspect as manifestations of control by outside forces—meaning either by Jews or, in some cases, by Americans (seen as controlled by Jews). The profascist political agenda of the deniers is well served by the combination of the passage of time and the need for European countries to redefine themselves in the aftermath of the cold war.

And even when outright denial of the Holocaust is not at play, the relativizing of the Holocaust aids the deniers' agenda by blurring the unique aspects of the Holocaust. There are sites of former concentration camps in Europe that note that internees were kept there from the late 1930s until the late '40s. Not mentioned is that the first occupants were the victims of the Nazis, and the later residents the Nazi victimizers captured after the war.

Nazism and fascism become blurred as yet another dark period of European history.

What has been the impact of Holocaust denial in the United States? With the exception of one minor election in New Jersey in 1994 and a few other crackpots who have run, no one has campaigned for office on a platform of Holocaust denial. Although many media outlets have pandered to the Holocaust deniers by giving them airtime without knowing how to expose their Nazi connections or the manner in which their lies are constructed, no major news group has proclaimed that the Holocaust never happened. Even though a few untenured lecturers have taught Holocaust denial from time to time (until discovered and fired), there are no colleges or universities where denial of the Holocaust is taught in the curriculum.[3] Yet key American institutions—politics, the media, the campus—have had difficulty dealing with Holocaust denial.

David Duke in Louisiana provides an example. Duke's denial of the Holocaust was well known. Yet in his statewide races for senator and governor in the early 1990s, he garnered nearly 700,000 votes and between 55 and 60 percent of the white vote. Undoubtedly, very few voted for Duke because of his Holocaust denial. Yet for many, denial of a major twentieth-century tragedy involving Jews was seen as quirkiness, not as a character defect disqualifying him from elective office. "Oh that David," no doubt some said, "yeah he has this crazy thing about the Holocaust, but we like him because. . . ."[4]

Talk radio and tabloid television have also given airtime to Holocaust deniers. Some hosts will exploit any bizarre issue in order to pump up ratings. Others honestly think they can expose the deniers, but do not do the massive amount of preparation that is necessary to accomplish that. Sometimes survivors are invited to give "balance," but more often than not the deniers appear more even-toned because, of course, the survivors are incapable of debunking the deniers' lies, such as pseudoscientific claims about the operation of the gas chambers.

The campus has been the most aggressively pursued target of the Holocaust deniers. Bradley Smith, who is media director of he IHR, sends prepaid Holocaust-denying ads to college newspapers under the auspices of a front group that he calls the "Committee for Open Debate on the Holocaust." Many campuses have turned down his ads, but others, including Brandeis University, have accepted his text for publication. Some who accepted did not notice the content of the ad before printing it; others (many with Jewish editors) made an editorial decision to print it. Some operated under a misguided understanding of the First Amendment.[5] And still others believed that surrounding the ad with other material, or running it as a guest column, or donating the proceeds to the U.S. Holocaust Memorial Museum, was the proper thing to do.[6]

While running denial ads suggests that college journalists are no more sophisticated than radio and television talk show hosts when it comes to exposing and debunking bigotry, one exception is the *Skidmore News*. Jens Ohlin, the editor in chief, was approached by Smith to run an ad. Ohlin originally planned to do so, but after speaking with members of the campus, survivors, Jewish organizations, and others, he not only refused the ad, he turned the question around. In a sixteen-page supplement to the April 21, 1994, issue, *Skidmore News* asked, "Why are Holocaust Deniers Targeting College Campuses?" Ohlin answered with a quote from Bradley Smith, spoken at a California meeting in 1991. "I don't want to spend time with adults anymore," Smith said. "I want to go to students. They are superficial, they are empty vessels to be filled."

By exposing Smith's agenda and organizational connections through interviews with survivors, historians, and students, and with a full-page letter from Skidmore's president, David Porter, the *Skidmore News* not only created a model for dealing with Smith's ads, but also set a standard for student journalism. (President Porter's letter had said that "to deny the Holocaust is to deny history itself. . . . I urge all members of our community to think carefully about the motives behind such an ad and about the practice of targeting college campuses for distribution of such material.")

Rather than taking the easy way out by printing the ad and hiding behind the false front of the First Amendment, the staff of the paper worked frenetically over two weeks, collecting material and interviewing scores of people. They demonstrated how hard work produces good journalism.[7] Unfortunately, too many other young editors do not understand the carefully packaged hate that Holocaust denial is, or the bizarre conclusion that is its logical outcome: that American, German, British, French, and all other historians in the world would have to be part of a massive conspiracy to hide the "truth" about World War II.

For many reasons, Holocaust denial could very well become the conduit for much of the next century's antisemitism. First, memory is a powerful antidote to lies. People who lived through World War II remember the true character of Nazi Germany and the condition of European Jewry after the war. Liberators and survivors alike can be brought into classrooms and interviewed on television and in college newspapers, communicating personal experience that grabs the mind because it also grabs the heart.[8] But soon the witnesses will be gone, and the power of someone saying "this is what happened to me" will no longer exist.[9]

Second, the collective memory of the Holocaust will be further removed as generation succeeds generation. Current events become history, become parents' history, then grandparents' and great-grandparents' history. No matter how important or traumatic, history loses currency with each succeeding generation. World War I is remembered today, correctly, as an extreme example of cruelty in warfare—but its memory does not have the impact on day-to-day living that it had in the 1920s and '30s. For Jews, the destruction of the Temple two millennia ago is still remembered, as is the Inquisition five hundred years ago, but they cannot have the same imprint on this generation as they did on those whose lives were touched by these events. The Holocaust, as a unique episode in human history, will of course be remembered, but as human history it cannot avoid the organic transformation of time. As memory is affected by the passage of people and time, it allows a clearer field for those who would distort events for political and bigoted purposes.

Third, the Holocaust deniers have large sums of money at their disposal. In addition to money from their supporters and some foreign sources (including some Arab nations), Jean Edison, the granddaughter and heiress of Thomas Edison, left a bequest of at least $10 million[10] which is being used to promote Holocaust denial.

Fourth, Holocaust denial has become the accepted ideology of the far-right, neo-Nazi, profascist groups. It is the ideological glue that allows them, despite their various differences, to share a common understanding of history and of what that history says about the future. It is helpful to them to believe that the post–World War II world was built on the foundation of a lie (that fascism and Nazism were evils to be rejected).

History teaches that we ignore mass-based ideologies of hate at our peril. Already these forces have pushed some mainstream political parties in Europe (especially in Germany) to accept part of their agenda: restrictions on the liberal asylum laws that followed World War II. Certainly, the mainstream parties are not being prodded to give credence to the anti-foreigner policies of the far-far right because they doubt the Holocaust. But that they have been influenced by these groups and co-opted some far-right issues means that the extremist groups are seen as having some political legitimacy. The extremist groups are not denying the Holocaust because they have a fetish about a few pages in the history books that they think historians have gotten wrong, and that they want to correct. These people want power, and Holocaust denial is a major conduit for their broader violent, bigoted, anti-semitic, and antidemocratic agenda.

Fifth, denial of the Holocaust will be aided by the increasing relativizing of the Holocaust. The entire stream of human history is polluted with stories of genocide and hatred, and it serves no purpose to attempt to rank suffering or count tears. Each genocide was unique, and it is precisely because of that uniqueness that we must learn from each of them, whether it be the enslavement of blacks or the slaughter of American Indians or the mass murder of Armenians or the Nazis' attempted annihilation of world Jewry.

But while the Holocaust was not a species outside of the human experience in bigotry, to label it as just another example of that indulgence is to distort it. For example, Americans built camps for Japanese-Americans during World War II, and that too was a horrible reflection of prejudice. But there is no comparison, as some would make, between an internment camp in the American West and Auschwitz. One was a temporary warehouse of human beings, the other a manufacturing plant designed to produce corpses.

What was unique about the Nazi genocide was that it took place in a "modern" and "enlightened" society that, during the course of war, had difficult choices to make. Should this train be used to transport soldiers and weapons and supplies to fight the war, or to bring Jews and Gypsies and gays and Communists and others to camps, many of which were no more than factories of death? Uniquely in human history, the latter choice was uniformly made.

When the relativizers try to rob the Holocaust of that uniqueness, to make it just another chapter in the interminable story of man's inhumanity to man, the necessary conclusion of their "logic" is that there is no longer any need to understand how the Nazi Holocaust came about, and how it worked. Those who want to merely turn the Holocaust into another generic volume on a large shelf of human misery make it easier for those who want to remove the volume outright.

Combining with all these factors is the historical attraction for antisemitic canards. Some sequels are more successful than the original, and Holocaust denial—because of its play on memory and history, and its political usefulness—has the potential to be even more disastrous to people's views of Jews than the Jewish "conspiracies" posited in the *Protocols of the Elders of Zion*, since it feeds off those fantasies and brings them to a new, and current, height.

If Holocaust denial has the potential to be a force for antisemitism and dangerous political movements, how should it be combated now, when it is still in its infancy?[11]

First, it cannot be ignored. Only twenty years ago many people suggested that the United Nations resolution equating Zionism with racism should be ignored because it was absurd. But soon the definition of Zionism as racism crept into placards in parades, statements of speakers on campuses, into law books, dictionaries, and on television. At San Francisco State University, Jewish students were told that they should not be allowed to run for student government because, as Jews, they were Zionists and, as Zionists, racists, and racists should not be allowed to seek election. Racist canards grow, especially when planted by those with a political purpose. They do not wither and die on their own.

Holocaust denial plays on lack of knowledge, antisemitic images, and political agendas. It must therefore be combated in all of its aspects.

There are those who suggest that combating Holocaust denial is a matter of education, and to a degree it is. Deniers play on ignorance, and therefore education is an essential component of the fight against denial. But while it is necessary, it is not sufficient. Some suggest that knowing history will ensure that history, or something that smells very much like it, cannot be repeated. But human history proves otherwise. Hitler knew of the Armenian genocide by the Turkish government in the early part of the twentieth century. That knowledge did not stop him from designing a program of genocide; it gave him inspiration. Today, images of "ethnic cleansing" in the former Yugoslavia resonate with those who understand the Holocaust. But the world allows this 1990s genocide to occur because other "interests" are perceived as more important than putting an end to the slaughter.

Knowledge is essential, and so educational programs and museums (such as the excellent U.S. Holocaust Memorial Museum in Washington, D.C.) and Holocaust centers and oral histories and conferences and books and research are all important. But they are not enough.

Holocaust deniers must be exposed for what they are, and their lies for how they are crafted. They cannot be "debated," for at this stage that is all the deniers crave, the legitimacy of debate. A debate presupposes that there are two "sides," each with a legitimate viewpoint, and that there is agreement on a common set of ground rules to discuss their honest differences. Deborah Lipstadt, author of *Denying the Holocaust: The Growing Assault on Truth and Memory*, says that to debate deniers is like "trying to nail Jell-O to a wall. They lie, they fabricate." Furthermore, it is common practice to refuse to debate hatemongers. Jewish organizational representatives will not meet with Nazis, Ku Klux Klan members, David Duke, or Louis Farrakhan because to do so suggests that their hatred is somehow not so serious, when it is really beyond the pale of what is acceptable. To debate deniers is to give them what they want—an image that allows them to hide their hatemongering behind a facade of pseudoscience and pseudohistory. Of course, refusal to debate the deniers allows them to suggest that the "exterminationists" have something to hide. But the response is easy: credible historians debate the Holocaust all the time—just not with Nazis.

Because the deniers hide behind credible scholarship (they suggest that any revision or new insight by the real historians proves that their inquiries are just as valid), it is important that people know the networks of white supremacy, Nazism, and fascism through which they operate. By and large, the people behind the Institute for Historical Review have demonstrable neo-Nazi ties and Nazi affections.

It is also essential that their lies be exposed, not as debate, but so that people can understand how easily they take a partial truth and use it to distort reality. Take, for example, the claim that Anne Frank's diary was a fraud because a copy of the manuscript had writing in ballpoint pen, a 1951 invention. What the deniers don't say is that this writing consisted of emendations made later by her father, and that the original edition of the diary was published in 1947.

Or take the matter of the gas chambers and the properties of Zyklon B gas. The deniers say that there was more Prussian blue residue of the gas on the delousing chambers than on the killing chambers, and that this should not be. What they do not say is that the person who wrote this report for them, Fred Leuchter, was indicted and convicted in Boston for practicing engineering without a license (his credentials were only a B.A. in history). Nor do they say that, because people were actually killed in the chambers much quicker than lice, there was less time for the gas to adhere to the walls, and thus to produce any residue. Nor do the deniers—who point out the explosive properties of the gas and pictures of Nazi guards smoking nearby—mention that it was deadly to humans at .03 grams per cubic meter, used to kill people at 12 to 20 grams per cubic meter, but explosive at only 67.2 grams and above.

As the deniers craft new lies out of the minutiae of the day-to-day operation of the extermination plans and practices of Nazi Germany,[12] research must be done regarding to each and every new lie, again not as debate, but as exposure of their lack of credibility and methods of deceit.

In addition to education and exposure of the deniers and their handiwork, a more difficult but probably more important need is to combat their political agenda in its entire range. Holocaust denial is an ideological lubricant for the growing forces in the post-Communist era who want to make the world—especially Europe in the twenty-first century—have some of the more devastating and brutal attributes of twentieth-century fascism. Holocaust denial does not exist in a vacuum; it is a political phenomenon which uses antisemitic canards as building blocks. A successful strategy to combat it requires an acknowledgment that the entire structure is problematic, not just those parts that defame the dead.

NOTES

1. Kenneth S. Stern, ed., *The Effort to Repeal Resolution 3379* (New York: American Jewish Committee, 1991), p. 41.

2. Deniers never note that reparations work the other way—compensating survivors, not the dead. If there were an incentive to play with numbers for financial gain, it would be to *reduce* the number of dead and increase the number of survivors, not the other way around.

3. Contrast this with the extreme racist Afrocentrists, like Leonard Jeffries of the City University of New York and Tony Martin of Wellesley, who are tenured and teach antisemitic pseudoscience and pseudohistory in the classroom.

4. Patrick Buchanan, who ran for president in 1992, also dabbled around the edges of Holocaust denial. He questioned the workings of the gassing mechanisms at Treblinka based on a bizarre observation that children had survived being trapped in a Washington, D.C., tunnel contaminated with diesel fumes, and wrote of the "so-called Holocaust Survivor Syndrome" and the "group fantasies of martyrdom and heroics."

5. The First Amendment to the United States Constitution guarantees freedom of speech and of the press. It means that no one can tell the press what to print or not to print, nor can government prohibit the Holocaust deniers from offering ads or printing their own newspapers. But the right of Mr. Smith to offer an advertisement puts no obligation on a paper to run it. Newspapers routinely reject ads they find obscene, libelous, factually inaccurate, or against their view of public policy (cigarettes, ROTC). A newspaper, like a person, has a right to define its own character, and to cultivate a reputation that it can distinguish between historical fact or hateful fiction.

The proper role of the First Amendment regarding the decision to run an ad is parallel to the role of the Sixth Amendment regarding a lawyer's decision to take a client. The Sixth Amendment mandates that people charged with serious crime have a right to counsel; it does not require that every lawyer take every case.

6. The United States Holocaust Memorial Museum has a policy of refusing donations designed to "assuage the guilt" of college editors who have accepted Holocaust-denying ads.

7. The American Jewish Committee provided a copy of the *Skidmore News* to every library on every four-year campus in the United States, for reference as a "good" model.

8. Jens Ohlin, writing about the process through which he first decided to print, then decided to reject and expose a Holocaust-denying ad, wrote:

> As we prepare to go to press, students are still approaching me asking why I will not print the advertisement. I tell them a story. I tell them about how last weekend I listened for two hours as the father of a good friend recounted his experiences at Auschwitz. His mother and father were exterminated during the Holocaust and he did manual labor at Buchenwald. He was 14 at the time.
>
> It was the first time he had spoken in such detail about the Holocaust. I looked straight in his eyes, and I knew then what my decision about the ad was going to be.
>
> I tell anyone who asks me why I won't print the advertisement about that interview. If they looked in his eyes, they wouldn't print the ad either. If they would, then they simply are not human. *Skidmore News*, April 21, 1994, Special Supplement, p. 2.

9. Oral and video history projects are important cataloguers of this information, but cannot replace the ability to look someone in the eye.

10. See Doreen Carvajal, "Civil War Rages Among Holocaust Revisionists," *Los Angeles Times*, May 8, 1994, p. A1. See also Herb Brin, "'Revisionists' Blow Fuse with Edison Legacy," *San Diego Heritage*, May 20, 1994, p. 1.

11. Attitudinal surveys suggest that Holocaust denial is a relatively small, but potentially growing, phenomenon. In 1994 less than 2 percent of Americans were hard-core Holocaust deniers. Yet, there is great ignorance about the Holocaust itself. While 85 percent of Americans say they know what the term refers to, in one poll only 24 percent, when asked to define the Holocaust, gave completely correct answers. Furthermore, many Americans believe that the extent of the Holocaust has been exaggerated—for example, a 1993 telephone survey in Georgia showed nearly 20 percent saying that while they "believe the Holocaust was a real event. . .the number of people killed by the Nazis was probably nowhere near six million," and nearly another 19 percent stating that they were "not sure whether the Holocaust did or did not occur."

Data from Europe show more awareness of the facts of the Holocaust (24, 33, 35, and 59 percent of Americans, British, French, and German respondents gave completely correct definitions of the Holocaust respectively). Nonetheless, there is both a massive level of ignorance of the Holocaust and a direct correlation between such knowledge and resistance to denial. Ignorance, too, must be a matter of concern. See Tom Smith, *Holocaust Denial: What the Survey Data Reveal* (New York: American Jewish Committee, 1994).

12. Regarding the crematoria, Yehuda Bauer writes, "[T]he incinerators at Auschwitz were built to cremate nine corpses per hour. There were forty-six ovens and, at peak times, fifty-two, which were in operation ten to twelve hours per day. Thus there was a *potential* possibility of cremating 4,043,520 corpses during the two years the incinerators were operational." For complete references exposing the deniers' claims, see Kenneth S. Stern, *Holocaust Denial* (New York: American Jewish Committee, 1993), pp. 58–81.

·12·
Women and Antisemitism

LETTY COTTIN POGREBIN

Letty Cottin Pogrebin is a founding editor of *Ms.*
magazine and the author of seven books, most
recently *Deborah, Golda, and Me: Being Female and
Jewish in America.*

The matter of antisemitism in the feminist movement was more than
merely a footnote to American social history, as Letty Cottin Pogrebin's
"Anti-Semitism in the Women's Movement" dramatically demonstrates.
This venue for antisemitism came from a variety of sources: the Israeli-
Palestinian problem, expressed as anti-Zionism; an invisibility of Jewish
realities, and an ignoring of Jewish concerns, in feminist consciousness;
anti-Jewish slurs, sometimes deriving from internalized oppression—Jewish
self-hatred—the classic example being the "Jewish American Princess" or
"JAP" joke; misunderstanding of and misplaced emphasis on the patriar-
chal aspects of Judaism; and the troubled relationship between blacks and
Jews in the late 1960s.

"Anti-Semitism in the Women's Movement" first appeared in the June
1982 issue of *Ms.* magazine, and had both immediate and lasting impact.
The effect of the publication of Pogrebin's seminal article was to give sanction and voice to Jewish women all over the country to speak out about
and against antisemitism in the feminist movement. As Pogrebin later
explained:

> It allowed Jewish women to ventilate suppressed anger and bit-
> terness and make a positive claim on their Jewish identity; it

exposed some feminists' anti-Semitic feelings and inspired movement activists to analyze this behavior constructively in workshops
and conferences, and to confront antifeminist vultures who
swooped down to declare the Women's Movement dead just
because I had discovered gangrene in one hand.

"The problem came out of the closet," Pogrebin said, in recalling in
1994 her 1982 essay, "and was addressed with the same seriousness
as was racism. Jewish women realized that they had a *legitimate* voice.
Jewish women could say, 'I am not just a feminist; I am a feminist and a
Jew.'"

Although Jewish feminists were engaged in activism outside the mainstream of the women's movement in the early 1970s, Pogrebin gave legitimacy to pursuing a Jewish agenda within the mainstream of the movement. An entire Jewish feminist movement was thus re-created, in which
a positive agenda has been pursued, and in which Jewish women do not
view themselves only as victims.

Pogrebin's essay raises a number of questions for today, less with
respect to overt antisemitic manifestations and more in terms of "Jewish
negativity and shame [that] are flourishing" as mechanisms by which people can distance themselves from virulent expressions that do take place.
With respect to "JAP baiting," discussed at length by Pogrebin, the etiol-
ogy of this antisemitic manifestation has as much—probably more—to do
with anti-woman animus (and from Jewish men as well) as with anti-Jewish feeling. It's a complicated phenomenon. But Pogrebin is clearly on the
mark when, in discussing this and other issues, she asserts, "Sexism and
anti-Semitism are interactive hatreds."

Reprinted here is a coda to "Anti-Semitism in the Women's Movement," as it appeared in a chapter entitled "Special Jewish Sorrows:
Women and Anti-Semitism" in Letty Cottin Pogrebin's book *Deborah, Golda,
and Me: Being Female and Jewish in America* (Crown Publishers, 1991).

J.A.C

Since that long-ago day on the beach in Winthrop when I discovered my parents' lies, nothing has left me feeling quite as
shocked and vulnerable as the discovery of anti-Semitism among
feminists whom I had regarded as clear-thinking allies and cru-
saders for social justice. Even worse, in a way, was the overwhelming evidence of *Jewish* denial, *Jewish* self-hatred, and the

flight from Jewish identity that I had uncovered in my interviews with feminists who were Jews by birth.

I began to recognize in many Jewish activists the Rosa Luxemburg syndrome—the tendency to ignore our "special Jewish sorrows" as if they are somehow too self-serving. I too began to question what accounts for the phenomenon of a group so capable of compassion for others but only of contempt for its own. In this respect, Jews in general closely resemble women in general. Traditionally, both women and Jews have been reluctant to confront our persecutors: women are afraid to rile the men in our lives; Jews, to provoke the Gentile. We are good at self-criticism. We are better at fighting for the rights of others—workers, children, Central Americans, boat people, other minority groups—than standing up for "our own."

What happened with the *Ms.* readers' letters is a good case in point. Of the twenty or so that were critical of my article, several were from women who took issue with me for singling out blacks, a few were from spiritualists defending the goddess-worshipers, one or two promoted anti-Zionism or the Palestinian cause, and a few were from Movement loyalists who faulted me for breaking ranks and publicly criticizing the Movement. My editorial colleagues decided to print three letters which they introduced with the following editors' note:

> Letty Cottin Pogrebin's article . . . drew one of the largest reader responses of any article ever published in *Ms.* The overwhelming majority of the letters expressed support of Letty Pogrebin for taking on a topic of such complexity, gratitude for an analysis that challenged their own assumptions, and relief that someone had named for them a problem that had brought pain to their own lives. . . . For the anti-Semitism forum, we have chosen to expand the discussion by publishing three longer letters expressing points of view challenging arguments in Pogrebin's analysis. We hope that these critiques will serve the original purpose of a continuing dialogue on this important issue.

This troubled me. *Ms.* had never initiated a "continuing dialogue" on racism, nor had we felt the obligation to publish disproofs of black women's claims of racism, but somehow the existence of

anti-Semitism was open to argument. The first letter was a rebut-
tal from novelist Alice Walker; the second was from the spokes-
woman of a Palestinian Rights Organization. But the third published letter was the most disturbing. It was a group effort signed
by ten *Jewish* academics and it began: "We do not wish to deny
the validity of others' experiences, but we suspect that the charge
of anti-Semitism in the Women's Movement is exaggerated."
After acknowledging that "anti-Semitism in any form is impermissible" and "anti-Semitism did taint" the U.N. Conference,
and "a couple of Pogrebin's examples from Third World women's
literature do support her argument," the professors concluded,
"We see these examples as atypical." They excused the debacle of
Copenhagen as a phenomenon of "international diplomacy, where
imperialist and anti-imperialist politics prevail over autonomous
feminist discourse." And they asked that the anti-Semitism of
black feminists be understood in the light of "the relevant history [of] the contradictory and sometimes tormented relationships
of Jews and blacks in the United States."

Men and women also have a long history of "tormented relationships," yet feminists do not soft-pedal our critique of male
sexism or let "understanding" of our shared history dictate a tolerance for misogyny. I am well aware of the historical relationship but rather than excuse black anti-Semitism because of it, I
believe that our shared history results in higher expectations on
both sides.

Finally, the group letter accused Jewish women of "disproportionate concern with anti-Semitism in the Women's Movement,"
attributing it "to the recent focus on racism." In other words,
they claimed Jewish women were playing me-too with black
women: "An assertion of Jewish identity and a focus on anti-
Semitism allows many Jewish feminists to participate in the politics of the oppressed."

For ten first-rate Jewish intellectuals to interpret other Jews'
testimonial evidence as a bid for attention—or for that matter, for
any feminist to ignore another woman's felt experience of humiliation and ridicule—struck me as selective feminism, or Rosa
Luxemburg–ism at its worst. Would the academics have charged
"exaggeration" had eighty Asian-American women recounted
their experiences with anti-Asian bigotry in the Women's Move-

ment? Would Japanese, Chinese, Korean, Filipino, and Vietnamese women be accused of asserting their ethnic identity just to get in on "the politics of the oppressed"? Or wouldn't they have been heard—and wouldn't the women's community have responded with mea culpas from every quarter? That ten Jewish women had refused to hear the special Jewish sorrows of other women struck me as a danger signal.

I picked up similar signals in some of the unpublished letters from other Jewish women who beat up on themselves and other Jews rather than engage the anti-Semites. One condemned her fellow Jews as Philistines and capitalist oppressors, never crediting the Jewish social reformers who pioneered in the settlement house movement, labor union movement, civil rights movement, antiwar movement, not to mention the Women's Movement. Some letter writers said they had grown up believing Jews to be uniformly overprivileged; they didn't seem to know there are Jewish working classes or Jewish old people living in poverty, not country clubs. They thought Jewish suffering had faded away like the photographs of their immigrant ancestors on the Lower East Side. Even sophisticated political activists were ignorant of how recently Jews had been banned from restricted communities, victimized by Jewish quotas in universities, corporations, and law firms, and attacked by "respectable" anti-Semites on the radio and in public life. They never wondered (or noticed?) why such a disproportionate number of political activists are Jews, or what might have impelled so many Jews to work in social justice movements, and especially in feminism. Could it be something in their Jewish upbringing or heritage that led them to doggedly pursue justice for women? With all the energy devoted to feminist theory and analysis, these movement women seemed uninterested in how the Jewish ethical system, with its profound emphasis on justice, might have informed their politics.

Most troublesome, in my view, were the many admissions of Jewish collaboration or silent complicity in the face of personal experiences with anti-Semitism. Like many of the women I had surveyed for my article, the Jewish letter writers revealed their ethnic shame, or should I say lack of ethnic pride. Feminists who felt ashamed had chosen to dissociate themselves from the negative stereotypes firmly imprinted in their minds. Rather than identify as Jews, they had preferred to count themselves as feminists, anarchists, leftists, Marxists, civil rights workers, defenders of minorities and oppressed peoples. They did not recognize in their own denial of Jewish oppression proof of the impact of anti-Semitism. Nor did they perceive the irony of feminists struggling to fortify one dimension of their being, the female, while leaving another dimension, the Jew, repressed, and humiliated.

Things have changed since my article was published in 1982. An affirmative Jewish feminism has flourished in secular contexts about which I shall say more in the next chapter. But while thousands of women have claimed or reclaimed their Jewishness in proud, positive ways, Jewish negativity and shame are also flourishing. At this writing, some women shy away from Jewish identification in order to distance themselves from the Israeli government's sometimes brutal repression of the *intifada*. More commonly, others want to dissociate themselves from the JAP stereotype, and its pernicious by-product, "JAP baiting," a form of hate speech, which has lately inspired menacing outbursts of anti-Semitism, especially on college campuses.

News reports document a growing number of incidents of virulent JAP baiting directed at Jewish women by men and women, non-Jews and Jews. JAP baiting is the one hate crime of which men are never the victims. It takes many forms, from vulgar jokes to verbal assaults to symbolic acts of violence, but the target is always female. At schools in what some call the "Oy Vey League"—Syracuse, Boston, American, Cornell, Miami, Ithaca, George Washington, Maryland, and Pennsylvania universities—whole stadiums shout "JAP! JAP! JAP!" while shaking their fingers at well-dressed Jewish women in the stands at sporting events. Slogans like ZAP-A-JAP or SLAP-A-JAP are scrawled on walls or emblazoned on T-shirts. Catcalls and graffiti say, "JAPs suck!" and "Frigid JAP bitch." At American University, two male students sponsored a contest to find the "Biggest JAP on campus." At Syracuse, areas where Jewish women students live are called JAP havens. The SDT sorority is translated "Spend Daddy's Trillions." Other schools label certain locations "JAP-Free Zones" or "Bagel Beach" (where the JAPs get their tans).

Much of JAP baiting is sexually denigrating; some of it

implies sexual and physical violence. One T-shirt says, MAKE HER PROVE SHE'S NOT A JAP; MAKE HER SWALLOW. Another asks, HAVE YOU SLAPPED A JAP TODAY? Posters mimicking the Ghostbuster symbol show a diagonal line through a woman holding a Visa card and a can of Tab soda, under the headline, BACK OFF BITCH. I'M A JAP-BUSTER! The Cornell University "humor" magazine published a chilling feature called "JAPS-B-GONE: A Handy Info Packet for the Home Exterminator," which instructs users on how to kill a JAP.

Logically, there's no difference between "Kill a JAP" and "Kill a Jew" since women who are called JAPs are also Jews, yet few Jewish people react to JAP "joking" with anything like the horror and outrage that would accompany the first T-shirt that said HAVE YOU SLAPPED A JEW TODAY? or BACK OFF YID, I'M A JEWBUSTER!

The young Jewish women who have been under attack have reacted with understandable humiliation and fear. Some say they have been so stigmatized and denigrated by JAP baiting that they are often considered—and consider themselves—unworthy of a Jew's love or a Gentile's friendship.

"At Passover, I always wanted to ask 'The Fifth Question: How come my brothers don't go for Jewish girls?'" said a Los Angeles woman who is quoted in *The Invisible Thread*, Diana Bletter's book of interviews and personal profiles.

A student from a Jewish community on Long Island admitted in another interview how painfully self-conscious she has become about her appearance, origins, and ethnicity:

> When I attend college next year, I plan to dress conserva-
> tively. But I'm worried that even if I wear well-tailored,
> nonflashy clothes, people might still label me as a JAP. . . .
> I'm nervous that when I walk into the dorm, my future
> roommate might look at me and think, "Oh, no, a Jewish
> girl from Long Island."

Some defenders insist that what is under attack is the JAP "image," a certain way of dressing or speaking that can describe a Jew and a non-Jew alike. But the point is that the image or condition under attack is being defined *as* Jewish. Constant usage of this negative association desensitizes people to the power of name calling and creates a seemingly "rational" excuse to defame or harm Jews. Not so long ago we saw chilling evidence of where this excuse can lead: JAP hatred provided a Jewish man with his murder defense. Steve Steinberg claimed that his wife, Elana, was a "spoiled, overindulged brat—the stereotypical Jewish-American Princess." He said her excessive shopping drove him crazy, so he stabbed her twenty-six times. In 1981, an Arizona jury acquitted him.

Sexism and anti-Semitism are interactive hatreds. That JAP baiting is as hurtful to Jews as to women remains true even though JAP caricatures often are created by Jews and joked about by Jews—including Jewish women. The JAP idea seems to be the dumping ground for a lot of garbage from everybody with a problem—non-Jews who hate Jews, men who hate women, Jewish men who hate Jewish women, and Jewish women and men who hate themselves. Male novelists, screenwriters, comedians, or "innocent" tellers of JAP jokes seem to be projecting their own Jewish self-hatred onto the JAP character. By attacking Jewish women, they can believe they are attacking *women* and not the Jewishness they despise in themselves. The woman who collaborates in this game may unconsciously hope to deflect attention from her own Jewishness or femaleness onto the JAP target, thereby asserting that she is a better class of Jew or woman—as if to say, "That girl is one of them, but I'm not."

Jews who JAP bait, and Jews who trivialize JAP baiting, reveal that they do not consider an attack directed solely and specifically at Jewish women to be an attack on The Jews. Yet JAP harassment has been a climate-setter for other kinds of anti-Semitism, from Nazi regalia at fraternity parties, to vandalized campus sukkah structures, to Holocaust denial, to anti-Semitic speakers like Louis Farrakhan being invited to many universities, to the physical intimidation of Jewish students.

Most Jews who laugh at JAP jokes have little understanding of the cumulative impact of incessant negative imagery on a Jewish woman's sense of herself, and on the whole culture's view of Jewish women. But sociologists are beginning to document how JAP bashing contributes to Jewish intermarriage by influencing more and more Jewish men to disdain and avoid Jewish women. Psychologists have begun to chart its corrosive effect on the self-esteem of Jewish girls. And Jewish feminists are hammering home the idea that the JAP stereotype is driving Jewish women away from their identity and their community.

"I grew up thinking that being Jewish meant shopping in malls, hating nature, and talking about non-Jews as 'the goyim,'" says a Jewish woman from Virginia in *The Invisible Thread.*

> I thought that being a young Jewish woman meant being a Jewish American princess, and being an older Jewish woman meant marrying a short dumpy man and playing Mah-Jongg. Since I didn't feel like either kind of woman, I thought there was no place for me among Jews. Those stereotypes chased me away from Judaism.

Such sentiments—and I hear many of the same things when I speak before Jewish audiences—leave me more concerned about the impact of *Jewish identity resistance* on the Jewish future than about the long-term effects of Christian anti-Semitism. In 1989 there were 1,432 incidents of anti-Semitic vandalism, harassment, threats, and assaults, the highest level in the United States since the Anti-Defamation League first began compiling statistics eleven years before. But while the ADL counts incidents of swastika graffiti and bomb threats, they do not keep track of the number of Jewish women who are being damaged, and "chased away from Judaism," by the deprecations of the JAP stereotype. It is not enough for Jews to be *anti*-anti-Semitic, we must also be pro-Jewish—and that means being pro–Jewish women.

·13·

Antisemitism on the Campus: Challenge and Response

JEFFREY A. ROSS AND MELANIE L. SCHNEIDER

Dr. Jeffrey A. Ross is the director of the Department
of Campus Affairs/Higher Education of the Anti-
Defamation League. Melanie L. Schneider is the
former director for campus and community
consultation of the National Jewish Community
Relations Advisory Council. She is now the New York
director of the Federation of Reconstructionist
Congregations and Havurot.

A number of dramatic manifestations of antisemitism have occurred in recent years at American colleges and universities. Jeffrey A. Ross and Melanie L. Schneider offer a comprehensive review and analysis of campus-based antisemitism and the campus as a vehicle for antisemitic expression. Emerging from Ross and Schneider's essay is a picture of the increasing use of the campus as a forum for the expression of antisemitism by off-campus groups and individuals (such as Holocaust deniers and African-American extremists, as is explored in other chapters in this volume). Jeffrey Ross characterizes campus antisemitism "not as antisemitism on the campus but as antisemitism coming *to* the campus from off the campus, and then going *from* the campus *to* the larger society."

Among the issues addressed by Ross and Schneider are the question of multiculturalism and the ongoing debate surrounding this sensitive educational issue; the impact of the media in portraying a level of campus antisemitism greater than the reality of antisemitism on most campuses around the country; and the issue of Jewish identity and Jewish functional literacy in terms of the impact of whatever antisemitism that may indeed exist on Jewish students, and the efficacy of student counteraction of antisemitism.

Finally, Ross and Schneider are clear on one significant point: the world has turned over many times since the era in which antisemitic discrimination *was* the reality for most Jews in the world of academia. While anti-Jewish discrimination may not have completely disappeared from the academy, discrimination is not the issue in any discussion of late-twentieth-century campus antisemitism.

J.A.C.

College and university campuses have emerged in the 1990s as one of the major sites for the introduction and dissemination of antisemitism into American society. Increases in the scope and depth of bigotry brought to campus can be seen in the activities of off-campus groups which use the college or university as a platform (Holocaust deniers, the Nation of Islam), of antagonistic student groups, and of some faculty who import hatred into their curriculum (Tony Martin, Leonard Jeffries). This activity is compounded and, to a degree, made possible by many of the trends in academe that are included under the otherwise well-intentioned phenomenon of multiculturalism. They include pressures to modify traditional academic standards in admissions, faculty hiring, and curriculum development as campuses are subject to politicization and made to respond to claims of group entitlements.

Paradoxically, these disturbing trends have emerged at the same time that American colleges and universities have witnessed an unprecedented flowering of Jewish achievement. Through the early 1960s, many institutions of higher education employed discriminatory quotas to limit Jewish academic em-ployment and student admissions. Those institutional barriers have since fallen. Jews are now well represented among the faculty and administrative leadership as well as among the student body at the most prestigious American institutions of higher education.

American Jews are among the most highly educated groups in American society. More than 90 percent possess a college education and 60 percent have some graduate-level training. Jews, who number less than 2.5 percent of the total U.S. population, make up nearly 5 percent of the nation's undergraduate student population. Approximately 10 percent of America's college and university professors are Jewish. A significant number of Ivy League and other elite universities that previously excluded Jews now have Jewish presidents. Programs and departments of Judaic studies have proliferated and have been legitimized in the academic world during the past twenty years.

Jews have flourished so well in this academic meritocracy that they have become highly visible as Jews, even though a number of Jewish academics are ambivalent about their Jewishness. This notoriety has produced both security and insecurity. While well established, respected, and comfortable in academe, many Jews are afraid that their gains may prove to be temporary. Antisemites have argued that Jews are disproportionately overrepresented in academic and administrative positions to the detriment of other groups.

Headlines in the general and Anglo-Jewish press have provided an impression that antisemitism and related issues of bigotry on campus are more prevalent than they actually are. The public impression is undoubtedly more alarmist than the actual situation warrants. Several studies suggest that most Jewish college students feel safe and secure. The media provide more coverage to negative than positive trends.

Nonetheless, many Jewish students, faculty, and staff have come to perceive themselves as subject to attack as Jews on a variety of American college and university campuses. They face challenges for which they lack adequate strategic experience and tactical resources. Among the issues confronting them:

1. The Jewish community has experienced outbreaks of antisemitism originating on campus and from off-campus groups that seek to exploit on-campus tensions. In recent years, a consistently increasing number of recorded antisemitic incidents have taken place on college and university campuses throughout the United States. In 1992, the Anti-Defamation League's annual *Audit of Anti-Semitic Incidents* showed that acts of antisemitism on campus increased at an annual rate of 12 percent even though such incidents in American society as a whole declined by 8 percent. The number of reported incidents rose once more at a 7 percent rate in 1993. Overall, from 1988 to 1993, they increased by 126 percent.

Manifestations of antisemitism on campus have included a concerted campaign by Holocaust deniers, "JAP" baiting, campus appearances by extremist and antisemitic speakers, and numerous instances of vandalism, harassment, and even physical assault. Indeed, the campus has become one of the major sites in which antisemitism is expressed and subsequently transmitted into the general society.

2. The college and university Jewish community feels isolated from the larger Jewish community and is unsure of the commitment of the organized community to Jewish life on campus. As a result there has been an increase of feelings of vulnerability to campus antisemitism. Up to now, the larger Jewish community has never been willing or able to provide a set of strategic priorities or to focus resources on this problem.

3. The campus Jewish community lacks adequate strategic and tactical perspectives for defining a Jewish response to multiculturalism. There is a legitimate Jewish interest in broadening the traditional curriculum so as to promote increased scholarly attention to the profound three-thousand-year-old Jewish experience. The Jewish experience in America is an important case of minority adaptation that deserves serious scholarly study. The recent dramatic growth in academic Judaic studies programs is one positive response to these concerns. Nonetheless, the Jewish community needs to develop an understanding of the inherent tendencies within some variants of multiculturalism toward separatism and ideological extremism. It must identify and develop a strategy to deal with increasingly politicized curricula; standards of political correctness; the abandonment of academic criteria in many hiring, tenure, promotion, and resource allocation decisions; the growth of demands for ascriptive group entitlements, which often lead to discrimination against Jewish groups; and the opening up of the campus to well-paid forays by extremist leaders and spokesmen.

4. Anti-Israel sentiment, although considerably reduced in intensity since the late 1980s, still smolders on campus. It has been found in the actions and pronouncements of student groups, in the teaching of many faculty members, in written course materials, in articles and opinion pieces in the campus press, and in appearances by speakers biased against Israel and Zionism. It reflects a problem that has not been fully resolved with the dramatic progress in the peace process that publicly emerged in Sep-

tember 1993. The campus Jewish community still searches for effective ways to combat anti-Israel propaganda and agitation in addition to finding ways of effectively making the case for Israel on campus.

5. College and university campuses have become increasingly diverse in recent years. Jews on campus have not been adequately equipped to come to grips with this diversity and to define their place as Jews within it. They and others are unclear about their status. Are they a distinct minority group or are they part of the white majority? Jewish students and academics need to develop strategies and tools for intergroup outreach and dialogue.

FLASH POINTS:
ANTISEMITIC MANIFESTATIONS ON CAMPUS

Antisemitism on campus is rarely experienced as a continual phenomenon. Rather, it is experienced in the form of flash points in which a great deal of emotion and activity are concentrated. Such flash points can be the result of either organized and political or unorganized and apolitical activity.

Incidents of individual harassment such as threatening telephone calls and notes, swastikas placed on the doors to dormitory rooms, and ethnoreligious taunts generally occur in the context of interpersonal disputes that happen occasionally on campuses and other sites where people live in close proximity. Visible ethnic and religious differences provide weapons of hurt to the protagonists in such disputes, allowing for a process of escalation that can soon get out of control, leading to the emergence of a potential intergroup conflict out of an interpersonal one. The occurrence of such incidents is unpredictable and the short-run damage that can result may be severe. ADL data indicate that the frequency of such incidents (or at least those that are reported) has increased in recent years.

Nonetheless, these are the types of incidents that are generally handled well by campus authorities and judicial mechanisms, sometimes with the cooperation of local law enforcement agencies, and to which the community relations bodies of the Jewish community on and off campus have generally rendered effective assistance. While emotions and fears can be intense, the impact of these events is temporary and relatively few people are directly affected.

While one should not underestimate the very real pain experienced by the victims of such antisemitic incidents, it should be noted that most of these occurrences are sui generis in nature and do not seem to be related to larger patterns of events. The flash points that are much more troubling and have wider community-level impact are those that reflect the activity of organized anti-semitic forces with a politicized agenda. Such groups have been increasingly successful in using manufactured controversy on campus as a relatively cheap and extremely cost-effective mechanism for bringing wide attention to themselves and communicating their message to both specific constituencies and the general society off campus. Two cases in point have been the campus campaigns waged by Holocaust deniers and by antisemitic extremists from within the black separatist community, including but not limited to representatives of the Nation of Islam.

Holocaust Denial*

Holocaust deniers, centered in the California-based Institute for Historical Review (IHR) and such offshoots as Bradley Smith's Committee for Open Debate on the Holocaust (CODOH), have seen themselves as the ideological vanguard of and as missionaries from the hate movement to the wider public. From its very beginnings, the "Holocaust Revisionist" movement has sought ways in which it could pitch its message to a mainstream audience. The college and university campus became a focus of this effort as far back as the 1970s. The IHR made an effort to attract and encourage rogue academics like Northwestern University's professor of electrical engineering Arthur Butz—author of an early and influential Holocaust denial volume, *The Hoax of the Twentieth Century*. The IHR itself produces a quasi-academic journal,

*See also Kenneth Stern, "Denial of the Holocaust. An Antisemitic Political Assault," chapter 11 in this volume. (Editor's note)

The Journal of Historical Review, complete with copious foot-notes, charts, graphs, and ponderous prose, and seeks to distrib-ute it among academics. Deniers such as Michael Hoffman, active at Cornell in the 1980s, frequented college campuses (although he had no student, faculty, or staff status).

In the winter of 1991, Bradley Smith pioneered a new tactic of campus manipulation that brought—and yet brings—the Holo-caust denial movement its greatest success. Starting at North-western University, he submitted a full-page, paid Holocaust denial advertisement to the campus newspaper. The newspaper printed his ad, generating much controversy and discussion, even producing speaking engagements for Northwestern's Professor Butz, whose profile in Evanston has been generally low-key. Most of all, from Smith's point of view, the episode was given wide coverage in the Chicago-area news media.

Encouraged, Smith submitted his ads to more campus news-papers in the fall of 1991, beginning with the University of Michi-gan. During the 1991–92 school year, he succeeded in getting the ad published in approximately nineteen campus newspapers among more than sixty journals to which it was submitted. Pro-tracted and emotional public debate was stimulated on the cam-puses where the ad was rejected as well as in those schools where it was published. By the end of that year, Smith's campaign no longer had as much novelty and surprise on its side and Hillel, ADL, and other Jewish community bodies had succeeded in blunting much of its impact. Smith declared victory and put his effort largely on hold during the 1992–93 academic year, targeting only two campuses of the University of Texas and getting his ad published on both.

With a newly revised advertisement attacking the legitimacy of the U.S. Holocaust Memorial Museum, Smith, during the school year of 1993–94, succeeded in having his materials pub-lished as ads, letters, or Op-Ed pieces in newspapers on thirty-one campuses. His success encouraged Canadian Holocaust denier Ernst Zundel to create his own ads that were published on half a dozen American campuses (Canadian law prevents such materials being published on campus newspapers in that country).

Largely through this campaign, Holocaust denial emerged from the lunatic fringe onto the wider societal agenda.

Smith counted on the on-campus controversy produced by his ads—whether published or not—to generate a news story that would be covered in the mainstream press and on TV, giving him a multiplier of free publicity. When Smith's advertisement was published in the campus newspaper at Brandeis University in December 1993, the resulting controversy was covered in the *New York Times* and the *Washington Post* and given a full-page article in *Time* magazine. The ad at Brandeis cost less than $250 (the check was never cashed as the editors donated it to the U.S. Holocaust Memorial Museum, which refused to accept it).

A similar controversy at New York's Queens College in February 1994 was featured in a lead story on CBS's highly rated newsmagazine program *60 Minutes.* This coverage led to a full one-hour program on the *Donahue Show* featuring Smith and his colleague, David Cole. The editors at Queens who printed Smith's ad also refused to accept the nominal advertising fee, even though the episode had netted Smith millions of dollars worth of free publicity. As a result of these moves, Holocaust denial became an issue of wide public discussion as well as of much concern in the Jewish community. It was in public view, both on and off campus, as never before. It is hardly surprising that Steven Spielberg, for instance, felt compelled to describe his film *Schindler's List* as an answer to Holocaust denial.

The Nation of Islam

The hate-group tactic of using the campus as a springboard to the greater society was largely pioneered by the Nation of Islam and other extremist elements within the black community. Throughout the 1980s and into the '90s, such figures have become regular features of the campus lecture circuit.

Louis Farrakhan turned his attention to college and university campuses in the late 1970s, soon after he began his revival of the Nation of Islam after the death of its founder, Elijah Muhammad. The campuses provided an audience of young black people who were increasingly estranged from both white society and formal black leadership during the Reagan era. Fees from campus appearances proved to be a regular, lucrative source of personal and institutional funding. Most of all, planned campus appearances generated prolonged intergroup controversy that attracted increasing media coverage. This coverage allowed Farrakhan and other extremist figures to achieve a prominence that would not have been available had their appearances been confined to inner-city locations.

Maintaining and manipulating controversy proved essential to generating the campus invitations (mostly for events sponsored by campus black organizations), the fees increasing, and the TV cameras rolling. The more controversial the speaker, the "sexier" and greater the demand, which in turn extended the coverage he received. Early on, it was found that antisemitism embedded in a generalized theme of radical black empowerment was a surefire ticket to success.

Thus, not only Farrakhan but others such as Kwame Toure (who was the former 1960s black radical Stokeley Carmichael), rap musician Professor Griff, and one-time Chicago politician Steve Cokeley took their message of "Jewish evil" to the nation's campuses. They were soon joined by rogue academics such as Leonard Jeffries of the City College of New York and Tony Martin of Wellesley College.

These speakers developed a litany of antisemitic charges that they repeated on each of their many campus appearances. They offered the proposition that Jews were singularly responsible for the African slave trade; that Jewish control over Hollywood had lent itself to the making of films degrading to blacks and justifying the forced supression of black aspirations; that Israel was a white, racist, colonial settler society oppressing Palestinian (and Muslim) people of color; that Jews in American urban areas systematically cheated and mistreated blacks; and that the original children of Israel described in the Bible were black, making today's white Jews little more than interlopers and impostors. Even the charge that AIDS was deliberately spread into the black community by Jewish doctors injecting the HIV virus into black babies was given a hearing on campus.

By the late 1980s, Farrakhan's public persona was softened and his rhetoric became more restrained. This outward change resulted in his growing acceptance into the mainstream of the black community. As Farrakhan increasingly played the role of statesman, his lieutenants appeared on campuses throughout the country preaching the old harsh, extremist, antisemitic message. Thus, the Nation of Islam could communicate to its younger followers the message that the organization had not changed despite its leader's altered role. It also allowed the Nation of Islam to remain in the public eye.

Chief, though hardly unique, among Farrakhan's tribunes on campus was Khalid Abdul Muhammad. Throughout the early 1990s, in appearances on campuses such as Queens College and Columbia University, he developed a reputation for heated rhetoric. In late 1993 he burst into the consciousness of the larger society through an inflammatory and viciously antisemitic address he delivered at Kean College in New Jersey. Further campus appearances (such as at the University of Florida, Trenton State, the University of North Carolina at Greensboro, Howard University, and SUNY at Buffalo), even after Farrakhan seemingly disavowed his Kean College speech and formally demoted him, resulted in national headlines and an outpouring of speaking invitations.

While Bradley Smith and Holocaust deniers have no on-campus constituency to speak of, black extremists enjoy a support structure among a politicized minority of black students. They often dominate black fraternity leadership and especially black student unions. Such organizations have access to student programming funds and have the power to set an agenda through their choice of speakers. In this manner, they provide the Farrakhans, Muhammads, Toures, and others with a national platform.

In order to understand more fully the context of these developments, one needs to examine the larger ongoing controversies concerning multiculturalism and Afrocentrism on campus and their impact upon the on-campus Jewish community. While antisemites tactically use the campus as a springboard to gain wider publicity, it is the Jewish community on campus that must live with the consequences.

MULTICULTURALISM ON CAMPUS

Multiculturalism continues to be an emotionally charged issue for many ethnic groups, including Jews. Its meaning and intent, however, have been understood differently depending upon whose definition is used, and upon whose agenda is being addressed. Some observers, including Professor Molefi Kete Asanti, chair of African-American studies at Temple University, have defined multiculturalism as "infusing the curriculum with Afrocentrism, thus giving it new life." Alternatively, Diane Ravitch, assistant secretary for education during the Bush administration, stressed that multiculturalism ought to incorporate the experiences of different ethnic groups. The texture and expression of multiculturalism varies from campus to campus, and may involve each of the aforementioned qualities.

Other observers, however, such as Dr. Jack Salzman of Columbia University, have noted that multiculturalism is less of an educational issue than one of power and politics in both academic and nonacademic campus pursuits. There is a limited, and in fact, shrinking pie of resources directed to academic, enrichment, social, and cultural activities within the university. To be sure, various ethnic groups, people of color and Jews alike, are vying to maintain their current portions, or to secure larger slices of that pie.

Some strongly Jewishly identified members of the campus community have expressed concern that administrators and others attempting to create a more multicultural campus environment have disregarded Jewish issues and sensitivities. While administrators and faculty may be fulfilling their mandate to recognize the experiences of those who have been marginalized, oppressed, or underrepresented in positions of power or influence, these well-intentioned attempts at recognizing diversity often leave Jewish culture, contributions, and interests out of the multicultural equation.

Professor Martha Ackelsberg of Smith College has noted an invitation that she received to the opening of the new multicultural collection of the Smith library. Not only did the collection omit representing Jewish cultural traditions, but the opening was scheduled for the first day of Rosh Hashanah. Ackelsberg brought these observations to the attention of the university administration, which had "simply not considered" the Jewish calendar and substantive experience. The administration, however, was responsive to Professor Ackelsberg's request, and the date of the event was changed.

Professor Edward Alexander of the English department cited an earlier example from the University of Washington. This example involved a Task Force on Ethnicity meeting to finalize a proposal that would compel every student to devote one quarter of the required humanities and social science credits to ethnic studies. Alexander recounts that the task force denied "most favored minority status" to such candidates as Italian and Irish Americans. The task force went on to oppose the inclusion of Jews because they are not "people of color" and have not suffered from institutionalized discrimination in this country.

Finally, a Duke University document entitled "Duke's Vision" discussed multiculturalism as one of the principles of the school's educational mission. In this connection, Duke requires all incoming freshmen to attend a diversity training seminar. One striking example of a strangely inappropriate reference to Jews was included in a quiz which included the following true or false statement: "Jewish students should support all the policies and actions of Israel." As Edward Alexander notes, there is no parallel statement saying "black students should support all the policies and actions of the African National Congress."

Over the past five years, with varying degrees of seriousness, the Jewish campus community has been searching for its role regarding multiculturalism. Instinctively, Jews realize that this movement may be a natural home for Jewish life and culture. At the same time, the multicultural agenda has been promoted by other ethnic minorities whose members have sometimes considered Jews to be in the category of white and successful, and therefore undeserving of representation in this movement. Some in the Jewish community are concerned that multiculturalism may undermine principles of shared American values and underscore group differences. Indeed, American Jews have become educationally, politically, and economically successful by living in a culture that minimizes the focus on ethnic and religious group differences.

Still, rather than searching for a constructive role within multiculturalism, too many in the Jewish community have retreated from asserting their rightful place in the multicultural agenda, claiming that Jews are unwelcome at the multicultural table. It does not seem to serve Jewish interests to abandon this increasingly important arena.

Alternatively, some campus groups and observers have found a niche and are working constructively to shape the Jewish role within multiculturalism. Some groups, including members of Hillel and campus-based Jewish community relations councils, view multiculturalism as an opportunity to promote Jewish identity in the stew of ethnic, racial, and religious diversity. Brooklyn College, home to nineteen different ethnic student communities, in 1990 established a Multicultural Action Committee (MAC). Hillel at Brooklyn College, and later its campus-based Jewish Community Relations Council, initiated the inclusion of Jewish representatives on the MAC. Jewish culture and heritage is now presented at cultural celebration festivals, at forums on minority concerns, and at programs that educate about diversity, although some black community activists, speaking at such events, have resorted to open expressions of antisemitism (most recently at a MAC-sponsored conference held in May 1994).

There was one example of a creative Jewish response to multiculturalism. In 1991, a Jewish Student Press Service symposium, in cooperation with the Jewish Theological Society and a number of human relations agencies, focused on multiculturalism, Jews, and the campus. One goal of this conference was to discover and define the role of multiculturalism within Judaism and Jewish life. In addition to using multiculturalism as a vehicle to deepen one's understanding of Jewish identity, the event sought to probe important questions such as: Are Jews a minority? What is the connection between Jewish studies and the "canon," that body of significant literature and works? Is multiculturalism a politically correct cover for expressions of antisemitism or anti-Zionism?

At a 1992 National Jewish Community Relations Advisory Council plenary session forum, Gary Rubin, former national affairs director with the American Jewish Committee, described American Jews as being in a high state of anxiety over multiculturalism. Rubin presented his vision of a pluralistic multiculturalism that encompasses the experiences of many different groups while seeking the common ground, concerns, and values shared by all groups in American society. He and others advocated that the canon, or body of significant literature and works, should strive to be as inclusive as possible. "The more racial, religious, gender and other experience it covers, the better grasp we will have of the world," said Rubin. This notion is based on the premise that "people of one background can learn from the experiences and great works of another."

Colleges are now introducing courses focusing on ethnic literature and ethnic history, where contributions from many different groups are considered important for teaching students of all backgrounds. With this development and others that reflect an inclusive multiculturalism, one can hope for dynamic intergroup coalitions working for the common good of all members of society, individual group respect, and improved intergroup relations. This vision stands in sharp contrast to the comparative victimization, politicization, inflated fear, assault on common standards, special pleading, and competing claims for legitimacy that have emerged in connection with extremist variants of multiculturalism.

The Jewish community's anxiety over multiculturalism seems to have calmed a bit, not because we have learned to successfully find our place within multiculturalism or have come to recognize its value, but because the Jewish community may now have a more focused perspective. We have a better understanding of the impact of multiculturalism in relation to the values and practice within universities. In addition, leaders in the Jewish community are focusing their attention inward and addressing issues of identity building as well as productive intergroup relations.

Afrocentrism

In the midst of multiculturalism, one finds the emergence of an antisemitic form of Afrocentrism, touted most notably by Professor Leonard Jeffries, chairman of the black studies department and professor at City College of New York. Jeffries has been among the most outspoken proponents of a multiculturalism that is truly an antisemitic form of Afrocentrism. Jeffries's message, discussed earlier, has raised legitimate concern as he has traveled the national campus speaking circuit, reaching thousands of students and attracting negative attention from Jewish students and others in the campus community.

The lasting impact of Leonard Jeffries's version of antisemitic Afrocentrism, while difficult to assess, has been greatest among

African-American undergraduate students exposed to his views at an important juncture in their education and personal development regarding attitudes toward other groups. While Jeffries may have enjoyed popular attention from African-American student organizations, he has not been accepted in scholarly circles. Prior to his notoriety, however, he was sought out and served on an influential New York State commission developing a curriculum for multicultural education in New York public schools. Jeffries's impact on academics, faculty colleagues, and serious thinkers regarding multiculturalism can be assessed as marginal as his racism, antisemitism, and sloppy academic habits have been exposed.

Antisemitic Afrocentrism has come under further fire since the spring of 1992, when Professor Tony Martin of Wellesley College required for his course an antisemitic book developed, published, and distributed by the Nation of Islam entitled *The Secret Relationship Between Blacks and Jews*. Based on selective misquotations and fraudulent pseudoscholarship, the book purports to illustrate the singular Jewish historical responsibility for the transatlantic slave trade. Martin was criticized by fellow academics (including leading Afro-American Studies scholars such as Henry L. Gates, Jr., Cornel West, and his own department chairman, Selwyn Cudjoe), as well as by administrators and Jewish organizations, but has maintained his teaching post.

The Martin furor has sparked intense debate over the boundaries of academic freedom, scholarship, and institutional responsibility. Academics such as Edward Shields, a professor at the University of Chicago, stated that "the notion of academic freedom has been turned on its head. He should be removed not because of his anti-Semitic speech but because his scholarship is garbage." Professor Guy Rogers, a Wellesley history professor, further illustrates this point, stating that "Wellesley has a mission and responsibility that has to do with education. You can't wrap yourself in the First Amendment and teach that the world is flat." When Martin self-published his own antisemitic diatribe, a slim volume entitled *The Jewish Onslaught*, the president of Wellesley College issued a widely released public letter of censure.

Now well known due to media coverage, Martin has gone on, like Jeffries, to become a sought-after speaker for black student union–sponsored lectures on campuses around the country. Along with Jeffries, Chicago's Steve Cokeley (who maintains that AIDS is deliberately spread into the black community by Jewish doctors who inject the HIV virus into black infants), and the Nation of Islam's Khalid Abdul Muhammad, Martin was a featured speaker in a five-hour hate marathon sponsored by the student-led Unity Nation, held at Washington's Howard University in April 1994, which was widely covered in the press and broadcast over C-Span.

Reverend Louis Farrakhan and his deputy Khalid Abdul Muhammad—in addition to Martin, Jeffries, Cokeley, Toure, and other noted antisemites—are often invited as speakers to campus as part of multicultural programs, particularly during Black History Month. In November 1993, in one such case, Khalid Abdul Muhammad appeared at Kean College in New Jersey and spewed vicious hate at Jews, Catholics, gays, and others and called for violence against whites. All the while, administrators failed to forcefully condemn their messages, leaving the unfortunate impression that such utterances are an accepted part of multicultural expression.

Political Correctness

"Political correctness," a term that originally came into vogue as playful self-criticism by those on the political left, has reemerged with greater seriousness to describe a campus culture that does not tolerate open discussion of ideas. Critics of the current culture on some campuses charge that "political correctness" characterizes a campus atmosphere where many groups' claims or interpretation of history cannot be challenged. Among the list of issues that have been deemed politically incorrect is visible support for Israel. It is in this arena that the rhetoric and charges of cultural imperialism and racism have been hurled at Jewish students who display their support of Israel. While anti-Zionism is most certainly a serious form of antisemitism, it should be noted that many charges of political correctness and the presence of campus "thought police" are often wildly inflated. Increasingly, charges of political correctness are viewed as code for attacks on the political left by conservative academics and their organizations on the political right.

WHO HAS RESPONDED AND HOW?
WHAT DYNAMICS ARE AT PLAY?

While support from the general Jewish community's community relations and defense organizations is an important resource for confronting and responding to campus antisemitism, the primary players have been, and must continue to be, organizations of the campus Jewish community, the Hillels and Jewish student organizations which represent the Jewish community on campus. In the end, it is they who are directly effected and will have to live with the fallout and consequences of antisemitism and its response. Even so, empowering the campus community, through the provision of specific resources and the sharing of expertise to best address antisemitism, has been and continues to be an appropriate role for the general Jewish community.

With increased experience in confronting a rather steady flow of extremist speakers with an antisemitic message, Jewish student groups have become increasingly sophisticated in their response. Generally, there are several important dynamics at play when Jewish student groups and their supporters consider appropriate responses to speakers with an antisemitic message. First, there is the students' need to *do* something, to feel as if they are effective, to maintain self-esteem and self-respect. Most important, identified Jewish students, angered by these messages, want to project the image and convey their message that Jews will not stand idly by in the face of antisemitism. After centuries of prejudice of the worst kind, contemporary American Jews rightly feel that it is incumbent upon them to effectively confront antisemitism where it exists.

The imperative to act, however, must be informed by consideration of the most effective action. On campus, one particularly effective tactic has been to place antisemitism as a discrete form of hate within the context of bigotry and racism that effect other societal groups. This is often difficult to accomplish in a moment of outrage and hurt. Among the most effective responses have been coalitions of students and faculty who have come together to decry an antisemitic act or statement and to condemn bigotry in all its forms. Prejudice reduction programs such as the Anti-Defamation League's Campus of Difference project, used on more than two hundred campuses, have also proved important in promoting systemic change toward a more respectful campus environment.

A snapshot of a response to a visit by Kwame Toure to Oberlin College illustrates the potential risk of proceeding with dramatic, high-visibility responses to antisemitism that may be ill-conceived. Jewish students who attended Toure's speech were prepared to stand up at the mention of his first antisemitic remark. The Jewish students were dressed in T-shirts that read "Stop the Hate." When they stood, disrupting Toure's speech, Toure focused vitriolically on the Jewish activists, who were then shouted down by the now enraged black students attending the event.

It is unclear as to whether a majority of those in attendance subscribed to Toure's racism or antisemitism. However, it is clear that the silent protest of the Jewish students enabled him to generate a hostile reaction from the audience. This outcome left some Jewish students feeling proud of their courage, yet intensely alone and terrified by the experience. Obviously, there were other methods of addressing Toure's antisemitism that did not involve direct confrontation in a vulnerable and losing situation where a practiced demagogic speaker could use them to his own advantage.

Experienced students have learned that public confrontation of an antisemitic speaker can have the opposite of the desired outcome. Often it generates more attention than a speaker could have garnered on his own. Thus, national and local agencies such as Hillel, the National Jewish Community Relations Advisory Council (NJCRAC), and the Anti-Defamation League (ADL) have encouraged students to time public statements and events of protest for *before* or *after* the appearance of extremist speakers, or to opt for a more nuanced approach such as monitoring the event with a prepared statement for the press. Such statements clearly acknowledge the right of free speech and expression, yet repudiate the message of hate. Other approaches include handing out leaflets at the door of an event, so as not to create increased a priori publicity for an antisemitic speaker.

Among the preferred approaches recommended by Jewish community relations professionals and others are rallies that include members of other minority and ethnic groups. Here coalition partners send collective messages against hate and bigotry of any form. Among the groups that have joined Jewish students in rallying against followers of Louis Farrakhan and Leonard Jeffries are Italian-American, Asian-American, and gay and lesbian students. In the ideal campus setting, a rally of this kind would not be the first opportunity where Jews and others worked together. However, such rallies and projects have been the geneses of further productive intergroup relations.

Jewish campus groups and their supporters have also developed public statements in response to antisemitic incidents. These statements accompany behind-the-scenes discussions which educate campus influentials such as the newspaper staff, student government, and administrators. These statements and discussions have been helpful in responding to antisemitic incidents and remarks.

In recent years, the submission to campus newspapers of Holocaust denial literature developed by Bradley Smith and his antisemitic Committee for Open Debate About the Holocaust have raised particularly thorny issues regarding freedom of expression and editorial judgment. While some naive campus journalists have considered the printing of Holocaust denial material as part of their obligation to uphold freedom of expression, the campus Jewish community has sought to inform those in the campus media that their obligation is to exercise good judgment and high editorial standards. Just as most campus journalists would not consider printing an overtly sexist or racist advertisement filled with lies and distortions, they should exercise the same judgment when it comes to one with antisemitic content.

In the case of visiting speakers with an antisemitic message, the challenge to university administrators has been to strike a balance between preserving campus freedom of expression on the one hand and countering bigotry and antisemitism on the other. University administrators sometimes oppose or resist running the risk of stifling free expression by interfering with a group's choice of whom to invite to speak on campus. Indeed, groups ought to be free to invite anyone they wish. However, administrators have a responsibility to speak out against hateful speech that insults members of the campus community. This is an ongoing issue, generally not remediable by such quick fixes as campus conduct or antibias codes which have come to the fore in the early 1990s. Though well-intentioned, narrowly drawn codes have been attacked for inhibiting free speech and thereby creating more problems than they solve.

The efficacy and constitutionality of campus antibias codes were examined by both the ADL National Commission and the NJCRAC in 1990. These organizations did not endorse the codes as an effective means for lessening intergroup tension. The most effective measure against "bad speech" in the view of the ADL and NJCRAC is not to limit speech but to counter it with "good speech" and to implement programs which foster intergroup understanding and prejudice reduction.

THE IMPACT OF CAMPUS ANTISEMITISM

While it is safe to say that the vast majority of Jewish students feel comfortable on most college campuses, antisemitism, as is the case with all forms of hate and bigotry, is a pathological feature of our societal and campus landscape. Where it occurs it is potentially hurtful and damaging. Unlike antisemitism in the general community, campus antisemitism exists in a self-contained community where students live, work, and learn in close proximity to one another. Jewish college students are unable to easily turn away and separate themselves from antisemitic situations and individuals.

There are, however, different factors related to one's Jewish identity that play a role in how Jewish students may experience antisemitism on campus. This discussion involves several, if not more, categories of students. Among them are those for whom being Jewish is a marginal part of their identity. These students may be described as disinterested and rather apathetic regarding their Judaism. A second category includes those who may be Jewish activists, completely involved in Jewish affairs and very strongly identified. For them, Jewish life centers around a set of causes and political involvements. A third category consists of those who have a strong, well-rounded, and varied Jewish identity.

Many Jewish students who might describe themselves as "just

Jewish," and for whom Judaism is a marginal part of their identity, may not be tremendously effected by campus antisemitism. For these students, the college years are about academics, career definition, and socializing. In short, they are Jews who are concerned with the business of being a college student and not being identified as Jewish. They may feel very secure on campus and may not be effected by campus antisemitism, if it exists, because they may be oblivious to it.

For a second group of students, those who come forward as Jewish activists and who possess strong Jewish identities, campus antisemitism, where it exists, may play a large part in shaping their college experience. While it seems ironic that the most Jewishly identified students may in fact feel most insecure on campus, this paradox grows out of the fact that the antisemitism that exists greatly effects them. They are on the front lines, responding to the crises, representing the Jewish community, and countering antisemitism when and where it exists. On campuses that have experienced numerous visits by speakers with an antisemitic message, and where courses and professors may have an anti-Israel bias, these students may feel beleaguered as the result of regularly dealing with campus antisemitism.

The third group may have the most balanced and healthy Jewish experience on campus. These are students who have a varied and full range of Jewish experiences and education from which to draw support for their experiences of antisemitism. In addition, they may be involved in a range of other campus pursuits providing them with a broader experience of life as a Jewish college student on a given campus. These are the students who, while Jewishly educated and identified, are not completely focused and preoccupied by campus antisemitism where it exists.

Jewish education stands out as a factor intrinsically related to college students' experience of campus antisemitism. The university environment is one that values education. Therefore, the clear lack of Jewish education among otherwise well-educated and bright young people becomes an important factor. Many Jewish students are ignorant with regard to Israel and Jewish education, which they do not experience in any other area. The discomfort this lack of knowledge produces causes many young people to further distance themselves from organized Jewish life.

The uneducated Jewish student, if he or she does not opt out of Jewish life, is sometimes profoundly affected by antisemitism and responses to anti-Jewish hate on campus. For example, a rally to protest antisemitism or the appearance of a Louis Farrakhan on campus becomes a salient or "peak" Jewish experience for the student who does not participate in Jewish events or holidays throughout the year. Obviously, this reflects a Judaism that is out of balance, and certainly not what the Jewish community would regard as a "positive Jewish experience."

The void in Jewish education, however, did not suddenly occur when Jewish students landed on the college campus. Its roots generally lie with parents who, if they did provide any Jewish education for their children, most likely did not assign a high enough priority on reinforcing it at home.

It is reasonable to conclude that without a full palette of Jewish education and experiences to comprise a young person's Jewish identity, antisemitism may rise as a primary shaper of fragile Jewish identities. A Jewish identity that includes aspects of education, celebration, spirituality, and a sense of history and peoplehood provides the balance and support to respond to antisemitism when it arises, and to place it in context.

IS WHAT WE SEE ON CAMPUS A HARBINGER OF THINGS TO COME?

In today's campus community, increasingly characterized by greater diversity, ethnic tension, and a heightened sensitivity to bigotry of all kinds, antisemitism is a small but significant part of the stew. As mentioned earlier, antisemitism and other forms of hateful expressions are raising important campus discussions regarding guidelines for civility, boundaries of freedom of speech, adherence to truth, and academic honesty. This debate has also brought to the fore university administrators' responsibility to maintain an environment conducive to learning and exploration, and where all members of the campus community feel secure.

Perhaps the most important question with which to conclude this discussion of campus antisemitism is whether or not it is a harbinger of future developments with regard to antisemitism in

America, or if trends on campus exist as a discrete set of circumstances which cannot be compared with the general society. The answer here is very Jewish, both yes and no.

The university is both a reflection of the general society *and* a laboratory where life provides insight into future societal trends. There it is possible to perceive the direction and impact of future intergroup relations in America, as well as the impact of campus antisemitism on tomorrow's public policy.

It should be underscored, however, that the campus is different from the community in that it is an artificial, planned, intense environment where idiosyncratic scuffles can easily become heated debates. This tension is fueled on those campuses that regularly receive visits from speakers with an antisemitic message, resulting in a painful experience for Jewish students. The general community's reaction to antisemitism which occurs on campus, however, is complicated. While antisemitism of any kind, anywhere, is upsetting and makes us angry, some in the general community would want to protect our young people and tend to think that the campus ought be an island free from intergroup tension. Clearly it is not. Perhaps this instinctual reaction to campus antisemitism, combined with the knowledge that Jewish students are living in these sometimes hostile environments, has resulted in a communal "gevaltism" and overemphasis on campus antisemitism.

Having noted the distinctions between campus and community, we return to the question of whether antisemitism on campus is a harbinger of future trends in the general community.

The college years are a time in life when young people are experimenting with their adult identities, beliefs, and values. As today's university campuses are more ethnically diverse than most American communities, the college experience represents the first time in which many students are placed in a heterogeneous environment with others of different ethnic, religious, and racial groups.

Tense and hostile college experiences in which students feel as though they are under siege, disrespected, or in fierce competition for scarce resources play a role in the future of American public policy and life in the general community. These interactions of antisemitism and other forms of hate and racism may result in bigoted and polarized feelings which accompany students into the "real world," once they assume positions of power and responsibility in communities.

There is, however, a hopeful side to this picture. The college years have the potential to provide a laboratory for improved intergroup relations in American society. Sharing classroom and dormitory experiences, opportunities for coalitional work on issues of mutual concern, as well as creative venues for learning about various cultures and faiths can help to build positive relationships that accompany students when they graduate.

To be sure, there is an interplay between the academy and the community. The trends that occur in one arena ultimately affect the other, and we have seen significant social movements and ideas which sprang from the university. It is not a cliché to note that today's college student is tomorrow's community leader. The atmosphere within the university setting, often the most racially and socially integrated experience of one's life, may in fact predict the nature of intergroup relations within society, if not future trends in antisemitism.

Unlike the period before the 1960s, Jews do not suffer from institutionalized discrimination in higher education in America. The most important portals have already been crossed in this regard. Jews are now found in relatively large numbers among students, faculty, and administrators at the most prestigious colleges and universities in this country. Judaic studies are now represented in the curriculum as never before.

A 1992 study at the University of Massachusetts, however, indicates that 40 percent of all Jewish students reported experiencing antisemitic harassment during their undergraduate years. While ADL and other data point to an increasing number of incidents on a growing number of campuses in recent years, there is much that we do not know about the current state of antisemitism on campus. In particular, we lack reliable survey data on attitudes among college and university students. Without such data, we cannot easily judge whether the reported incidents are isolated flash points or indicators of a larger, more widespread pathology.

Many of the issues found on campus reflect not so much hard-core antisemitism as intergroup conflict over scarce resources for curricula, admissions, financial aid, student programming, and so forth during hard economic times. Repeated battles over such issues as affirmative action involve tangible differences in historical memory and perceived group interests. Adversaries should not be automatically equated with antisemites. Such controversies, if handled creatively, can lead to a positive learning experience on all sides, which may bode well for the future of intergroup relations.

Nonetheless, it cannot be denied that the 1980s and '90s have witnessed a true increase in the incidence of antisemitism on campus. This increase is compounded by the inability or unwillingness of campus administrators to deal effectively with it. While most Jews on campus undoubtedly feel secure as individuals, those who care about their Jewish identity have come to feel more vulnerable as Jews.

Part of this vulnerability is due to the seeming exclusion of Jewish concerns from much of the multicultural agenda. Many Jews on campus feel that the protections afforded to minorities by the culture of political correctness do not include them. They are often excluded from a circle of civility on campus, which leaves them as targets.

Jews have suffered an increased attack on campus in recent years as part of a general assault on difference and diversity. Blacks, Asian Americans, Latinos, Native Americans, gays and lesbians, and others have all experienced growing levels of bigotry. When one group is subject to assault, all become vulnerable.

Nonetheless, there is something special about the Jewish condition on campus, which makes it different from the experience of others. Much of it is due to the organized and politicized nature of the assault. The antisemitic hate movement has chosen the campus as a focus for its activities, as a cost-effective site from which the attention of the larger society can be gained. This struggle on campus is of the greatest consequence. It is likely to intensify in the coming years as more off-campus groups try to penetrate the campus. Much hinges on the outcome.

PART FOUR

ISSUES IN CONTEMPORARY ANTISEMITISM

·14·

The New Antisecularism:
Right for the Jews?

MARK SILK

Mark Silk is a staff writer for the Atlanta *Journal-Constitution*. He is the author of *Spiritual Politics: Religion and America Since World War Two* and *Unsecular Media: Making News of Religion in America*.

Mark Silk uses the 1990s phenomenon of the resurgent religious right as a vehicle for exploring how people think about religion in the United States. The nexus of fundamentalism, political rhetoric, church-state separation, antisemitism and Jewish security, and democratic pluralism is fertile territory for Silk's analysis of religion's rhetoric and impact in late twentieth-century America.

Silk characterizes the religious right as "antisecularist," and this usage makes sense. The term "fundamentalism" has been used in the religious-political context to gather any number of religious movements into some sort of political religion. Fundamentalism imputes a traditionalism that is not always true or valid; some "fundamentalist" groups are in fact new political entities. "Antisecular" may therefore be a formulation that better characterizes the phenomenon and collection of groups and individuals. (Indeed, many "neoconservatives" have joined the antisecular ranks. Their interest in religion, we may infer from Silk, derives from purely instrumental reasons—a particular social agenda—rather than from the intrinsic reasons of religion itself.)

Further, antisecularism suggests, at least to this reader, some of the anger and distress in America. In post–Cold War America, in an era that has seen some significant ideological collapse, antisecularism may be the salient ideology. Silk's discussion of this ideology—from his staring point of the celebrated correspondence between the Christian Coalition's Pat

Robertson and Anti-Defamation League official Abraham Foxman, to his peroration to the reader on the purpose of the "religion clauses" of the First Amendment—leads ineluctably to the answer to his question "Is anti-secularism 'right for the Jews'?" Jews, Silk asserts, as a religious minority, appropriately "cast their lot with the secular public square of contemporary America," thereby guaranteeing that their (and everybody else's) religious expression will be protected.

J.A.C.

In June 1994, the Anti-Defamation League of B'nai B'rith flung a gauntlet at the feet of the most potent political-religious force in American society since the heyday of the civil rights movement. In a 193-page report, written by staff member David Cantor, the venerable Jewish defense agency made out a case that politically active evangelical Protestantism had become a menace to the republic.

The Religious Right: The Assault on Tolerance and Pluralism in America forswore anti-Christian bigotry and acknowledged the right of Evangelical Christians to politick for their values, "like anyone else."[1] While calling attention to a number of antisemitic pronouncements and a bona fide antisemite or two, the report did not charge the religious right as a whole with antisemitism. Neither did it omit to mention the movement's record of strenuous support for the state of Israel (albeit by way of a theological agenda that envisaged the ultimate conversion of the Jews).

But in a *tour d'horizon* of groups and activists, the report adduced example upon example of hostility toward those who did not share their social views, political agenda, or preferred lifestyle. What made this hostility dangerous, the ADL contended, was that it was joined to an effort to undermine the Constitutional separation of church and state. Rather than being one voice among many in the noisy play of American politics as usual, the religious right was an "exclusionist" movement seeking "to restore what it perceives as the ruins of a Christian nation by seeking more closely to unite its version of Christianity with state power."[2]

The report's primary object of attention was Pat Robertson, proprietor of the Christian Broadcasting Network, sometime

Republican presidential aspirant and launcher of the grassroots lobbying organization the Christian Coalition. Not only was Robertson the religious right's preeminent figure, but as leader of the Christian Coalition, he seemed most capable of turning rhetoric into a political reality of some kind. It was, unquestionably, a dark rhetoric, filled with anger and resentment. Evangelical Christians, Robertson claimed, were victims of a bigotry "more terrible than anything suffered by any minority in our history." A cunning conspiracy of antireligious leftists and internationalists had managed to banish Christian concerns beyond the pale of American public life. "They have kept us in submission because they have talked about separation of church and state. There is no such thing in the Constitution. It's a lie of the left, and we're not going to take it anymore."[3]

Robertson, when the Cantor report appeared, did not turn the other cheek. In a "Dear Abe" letter to ADL national director Abraham Foxman dated June 22, he called the portrayal of himself "an inconceivable breach of trust." Then he catalogued the acts he had performed as "one of the strongest friends of the Jewish community in the entire world": hundreds of thousands of dollars from the Christian Broadcasting Network for the United Jewish Appeal, the resettlement of Russian Jews, and other Jewish causes; personal lobbying efforts against arms sales to Israel's Arab adversaries and in favor of the pardon of the convicted spy Jonathan Pollard. He noted that he had received various honors from American Jewish organizations and Israeli government officials.

Why, then, had Foxman launched this assault against him? Referring to a recent telephone conversation with the ADL leader, Robertson quoted him as saying that elected officials "cannot in any way be influenced by their religious beliefs." This, Robertson wrote, was "a radical secularism" contrary to the history of "ordered liberty" in Western civilization and democracy in America. He concluded by denouncing the report's "false charges" of antisemitism, yet insisted that "no amount of slander and vituperation" would shake his support for Israel and the Jewish people.[4]

Foxman responded on July 14 in a "Dear Pat" letter, pointing out that the ADL report had called neither Robertson nor the Christian Coalition antisemitic. He quoted the report's recognition of both the right of evangelical Christians to pursue their views politically and the importance "to a healthy democracy" of their doing so. But he reiterated the concern about Robertson's criticism of "separation of church and state." The next day, Robertson sent off the following brief reply:

> I read your answer, and it is painfully obvious that you are a deeply troubled individual who has somewhere along the way lost your Judaic roots only to seek in radical secularism what only God can give you.
>
> Please know, Abe, that I will pray earnestly that you may indeed meet personally the God of Abraham, Isaac and Jacob, and that His blessing will be upon you.

On July 18, Foxman shot back:

> Save your prayers for yourself. I haven't lost my Judaic roots—but it's just like you to decide for others what their spiritual needs are or should be.
>
> I have met my God of Abraham, Isaac and Jacob, and do not need your guidance, prayers, or intervention.
>
> May God be with you.

By the end of July, the Christian Coalition was in the field with *A Campaign of Falsehoods: The Anti-Defamation League's Defamation of Religious Conservatives*, a twenty-nine-page effort to point out inaccuracies and misrepresentations in the ADL report. Furiously assailing the report, it nonetheless took a restrained approach to the church-state question. There was, it said, a "lively debate" about the role of religion in American public life and the meaning of the First Amendment. The Christian Coalition supported religious freedom for all. During his 1988 presidential campaign, Robertson had declared his belief in the separation of church and state.[5]

On August 2, in a paid advertisement in the *New York Times* headlined "Should Jews Fear the 'Christian Right'?" seventy-five Jewish (neo) conservatives accused the ADL of using "insinuation and guilt by association" to impeach those "whose only crime seems to be the seriousness with which they act on their Christian convictions." The separation of church and state was not the same thing as "the elimination of religious values and concepts from political discourse." Judaism was not "coextensive" with liberalism, "as the ADL seems to suggest." On the all-important issue of support for Israel, the ADL had violated the Jewish principle of *Hakarat Hatov*—"the duty to acknowledge the good done to us."[6]

The next day, Foxman wrote Robertson a letter apologizing for two factual errors in *The Religious Right* and assuring him of the ADL's "good faith." Robertson responded by accepting the apology, and reiterated his support for Israel and Jewish interests. The tempest, it seemed, had passed. In passing, however, it illuminated not only a shifting political fault line within the Jewish establishment but a challenge to the traditional Jewish embrace of strict church-state separation.*

Publication of *The Religious Right* represented a certain political repositioning on the ADL's part. During the first decades after its founding in 1914 the agency had been accustomed to see the greatest religious threat to Jewish interests in conservative Christianity, whether Protestant or Roman Catholic. But in the years since World War II the focus of concern had gradually shifted. Jews, at home in American society as never before, no longer seemed to have much to fear from domestic antisemitism, which survey after survey showed to be in sharp decline. Israel was another matter. Institutionally, the Roman Catholic and mainline

*Robertson's stance vis-à-vis the Jews occasioned another, briefer tempest six months later, when *The New York Review of Books* published an article attacking his 1991 bestseller, *The New World Order* (February 2, 1995, 21–25). The article, by Michael Lind, argued that Robertson's portrayal of a world-wide conspiracy of freemasons, communists, and international bankers partook of classic antisemitism, albeit Robertson never actually mentioned that various of his banker bogeymen were Jews. After the *New York Times* columnist Frank Rich picked up the charge, Robertson issued a statement of self-defense denying that his book was antisemitic. Saying "I deeply regret that anyone in the Jewish community believes that my description of international bankers and use of the phrase 'European bankers' in my book refers to Jews," he offered his "sincere regrets" if his statements had been "misunderstood." He then reiterated his strong support for Israel and attacked criticisms of his book as "specious objections" brought forward by "the radical left" (*New York Times*, March 4, 1995). Whatever one makes of this apologia, it is certainly true that Robertson chose to fish in some very dirty waters.

Protestant churches had never been enamored of the Jewish state; especially since the Six-Day War, they had sent no small amount of criticism in its direction. On the Christian left, expressions of hostility were even more vociferous. All this stood in marked contrast to evangelical Protestantism, which supported Israel in the belief that the ingathering of Jews in the Holy Land betokened the millennium.

In their 1974 volume *The New Anti-Semitism*, the ADL officials Arnold Forster and Benjamin Epstein directed attention to enmity among Christian clergy of the center and the left, not the right.[7] Their successor, Nathan Perlmutter, went further. In *The Real Anti-Semitism in America*, which appeared two years after the emergence of the religious right during the 1980 election campaign, he and his wife, Ruth Ann Perlmutter, called upon the Jewish community to abandon its long-standing alliance with liberal Protestantism in favor of the fundamentalists, despite their more exclusivist theology.

> Christian-professing religious attitudes, in this time, in this country, are for all practical purposes, no more than personally held religious conceits, barely impacting the way in which Jews live. Their political action, as it relates to the security of the state of Israel, impacts us far more meaningfully than whether a Christian neighbor believes that his is the exclusive hot line to "on high."[8]

In the 1980s, the ADL itself looked after Israel's security by monitoring the news media's coverage of the Israeli invasion of Lebanon, the Intifada, and other events in the Middle East for signs of anti-Israel bias. Vigilance against left-liberal criticism of Israel was, moreover, an element in a larger effort by conservative Jewish intellectuals to persuade American Jews to replace their customary liberal sympathies with a social and economic agenda closer to that of Ronald Reagan. Under the circumstances, the intensity of the reaction to *The Religious Right*, on the part of both Robertson and the signers of the *New York Times* ad, can be put down to shock that the ADL had abrogated their entente cordiale.

The ADL's willingness to take on the religious right doubtless had something to do with the accelerating peace process in the

Middle East; it was no longer so important to subordinate domestic concerns to the cause of Israel's security. And those concerns were on the rise. The hard-edged rhetoric of the 1992 Republican convention, notably from Pat Buchanan and Robertson himself, had given many Jews *agmas nefesh* and *brenen in hartzn*—that anxious Yiddish feeling of heartburn, of burning in the guts. In addition, ADL regional offices reported that the Christian Coalition was running "stealth" candidates for various local offices, with unsettling agendas that included restoring prayer in public schools.

It is worth recalling that "Christian" has historically been a code word for "anti-Jew" on the extremist right, from Father Coughlin's Christian Front in the 1930s to Gerald L. K. Smith's Christian Nationalist Crusade, still active in the 1970s, to the Christian Identity ideology of today's Aryan Nations.[9] Rightly or wrongly, the Christian Coalition could not help stirring up these associations. In this respect, it differed from the first membership organization of the religious right, Jerry Falwell's Moral Majority, which always represented itself as seeking adherents regardless of faith. But whatever the nomenclature, American Jews as a whole resisted the efforts to invite them into an evangelical alliance. As the historian Naomi Cohen noted somewhat wistfully, "While their continued security and well-being should theoretically allow more flexible responses, the mindset fashioned by historical precedents still conveys an image of the New Christian Right as a clear-and-present danger."[10] The ADL report was, among other things, an articulation of popular Jewish concerns.

But was the Jewish community right to continue to identify its interests with a strict interpretation of the separation of church and state? Although *The Religious Right* made a point of acknowledging the contributions of religion to the national debate, church-state separation remained its lodestar. Its articulation of this position may have fallen well short of what anyone outside the Robertson camp would have regarded as "radical secularism." Nevertheless, religious rightists were not the only ones arguing that contemporary separationism had gone too far.

The argument received its defining metaphor in 1984 from the Lutheran pastor (shortly to become Catholic priest) and longtime religious activist Richard John Neuhaus, whose *The Naked Pub-*

lic Square was a tract for the times that blamed secularism for all the discontents of American culture.

> The point is that the widespread exclusion of religiously grounded values and beliefs is at the heart of the outrage and alienation (to use a much overworked term) of millions of Americans. They do not recognize *their* experience of America in the picture of America purveyed by cultural and communications elites. At the heart of this nonrecognition—which results in everything from puzzlement to crusading fever—is the absence of religion.[11]

In his book on the 1988 presidential election, *Under God*, the Catholic man of letters Garry Wills portrayed Democratic candidate Michael Dukakis as an avatar of political secularism, and blamed the Democrats' failure on their "divorce" of politics from religious values.[12] In *Hollywood Vs. America* (1992), the Jewish movie critic Michael Medved (who subsequently signed the *New York Times* advertisement) contended that the "negative attitude toward Judeo-Christian believers is so pervasive and so passionately held in Hollywood that some producers will use every opportunity to express their contempt."[13] In *The Culture of Disbelief* (1993), a book warmly embraced by President Clinton, the Episcopalian law professor Stephen L. Carter indicted American elite culture generally with casting religious points of view into outer darkness.[14]

There is some evidence that, during the 1980s, this view of Americans as a religious folk oppressed by a secularist elite became widespread throughout the country, at least among the religiously committed. For example, in a 1989 survey of religion reporting and readership, most people interviewed in four Philadelphia congregations felt the press had "some sort of a 'bias' against religion."[15] By contrast, in the early 1960s comments about newspapers and magazines in religious journals were, according to one study, "largely neutral."[16] To be sure, ever since the Great Awakening there has been a tendency in American culture to charge elites with irreligion. But through most of the twentieth century, it had been generally assumed that the educated classes were merely the leading edge of a society that was becoming more secularized throughout.[17] Now, with religion apparently in the ascendant not only in America but also in the Muslim world and behind the former Iron Curtain, the assumption of ineluctable secularization could no longer be sustained. Indeed, the main religious story line for the end of the twentieth century has been that people of faith are leading a counterrevolution against a morally impaired secular society. Arguably, the most potent ideology of the post–Cold War era is antisecularism.

University of Chicago law professor Michael McConnell, a leading ideologist, blames American-style secularism on political liberalism, which he sees as having evolved since the eighteenth century from religion-friendly to religion-hostile. Thus, freedom *of* religion grew less important than freedom *from* religion, and "neutral" came to mean "secular"—"as if agnosticism about the theistic foundations of the universe were common ground among believers and nonbelievers alike." In the postmodern age religion is fine, says McConnell, but only as long as it is kept within the cloister of private life.[18]

In a more utilitarian spirit, the historian Gertrude Himmelfarb (also a signer of the *Times* advertisement) defending nationalism against its internationalist critics, calls upon religion to succor the nation-state in the course of a defense

> So we should be inspired to seek a nationalist remedy for the diseases most incident to nationalism. . . . And among these remedies (as both Toqueville and the Founding Fathers recognized) is religion itself—or, rather, a plurality of religions, religions that tolerate one another and that are themselves not merely tolerated but respected, and not merely as a private affair but as an integral part of public life.[19]

Presumably, religion can be considered a "nationalist remedy" only if it enjoys some kind of quasi-official status in public life. What has motivated the antisecularist reaction, of course, is the apparent undermining of such status—whether through removal of prayer in public schools, the legalization of abortion, or the social legitimation of homosexuality.

Perhaps because of the absence of an established church, Americans have long been susceptible to interfaith religious activity, whether for the sake of spiritual revival, moral reform, or general principles. The idea that radically different faiths share a common cause was the impetus for the country's first great ecumenical gathering, the 1893 World's Parliament of Religions in Chicago, whose organizer issued a call to "unite all Religion against irreligion . . . to present to the world . . . the substantial unity of many religions in the good deeds of the religious life."[20]

The immediate antecedents of America's current antisecularism, however, lie in the years just after World War II, when democratic values seemed pale and feckless in comparison with the seemingly dynamic and inspirational creed of Communism. What was needed were the combined spiritual resources of religion—Protestant, Catholic, Jewish, Mormon—to undergird the cause of democracy and strengthen America's moral fiber. The "Judeo-Christian tradition" came into widespread use as the watchword of the needed faith, the enlistment of which into national service was symbolized by public acts such as the inclusion of the phrase "under God" in the Pledge of Allegiance.[21]

During the Cold War, the mobilization of a popular religious front against an outside foe helped bring Jews firmly within the spiritual fold; anticommunism was good for the Jews. But in post–Cold War America, the religious crusade has been directed against domestic opponents of public religion, and this has placed Jews in something of a dilemma. As Naomi Cohen points out, "Since official acknowledgement of religion meant at bottom a favored position for the majority religion, Christianity, Jews committed themselves to an open-ended defense of strict separationism and sought through legislation and the courts to prevent state favoritism toward religion in general and Christianity in particular."[22]

This fact has not escaped the notice of religious rightists, nor have they been afraid to single out "liberal Jews" as incarnations of their separationist bogey. Pat Robertson himself has made a habit of distinguishing Orthodox Jews (good) from liberal ones, who may be attacked for "their on-going attempt to undermine the public strength of Christianity."[23] Given the preponderance of the non-Orthodox over the Orthodox, such pronouncements have fallen somewhat ominously on Jewish ears. Should we pull in our horns and reconsider our long-standing enthusiasm for separation of church and state?

Yes, says Irving Kristol, the intellectual lion of neoconservatism (and another signer of the *Times* ad): "Well, perhaps this is a time for questioning whether more is better, and even whether what has been 'good for the Jews' will continue to be so." American society will become "more Christian, less secular"; the wall of separation between church and state will grow "more porous." Anticipating no substantial upsurge in antisemitism, with a certain satisfaction Kristol foresees that Jews will be led to become less "militant" in their "insistence on secular society."[24]

But is the discreet course the right course?

For starters, the antisecularist case cannot be regarded as proven. Notwithstanding the claims of Robertson, McConnell, et al., the removal of certain religious trappings from the public square has come about not from irreligion so much as from the need to take religious pluralism seriously. Protestant control over public education led Roman Catholics to establish their own school systems in the nineteenth century. Recitation of the Lord's Prayer at the beginning of the public school day could only prove obnoxious to observant Jews. Were those the good old days?

Nowadays, support for religious freedom appears to be stronger than ever. When the Supreme Court weakened its standard for upholding religious free-exercise claims in *Smith* v. *Employment Division* (1990), Congress was persuaded to reverse the decision by the broadest coalition ever to back a religion bill, extending from the Christian Coalition to the American Civil Liberties Union and People for the American Way, and including organizations from all segments of the Jewish community. As coalition members were very much aware (and as was later proved by Clinton administration policies), the Religious Freedom Restoration Act protected religion in the public square as much as it did private religious expression. To be sure, it is assuredly no easy matter to determine where unconstitutional establishment leaves off and protected free exercise begins. But to consider the current state of religion law as radically secularist seems absurd.

First Amendment boundary disputes are, of course, only part of the story. At the heart of the antisecularist complaint is the conviction that American society has become a kind of moral Walpurgisnacht; that, deprived of religion's authoritative prescriptions of right and wrong, it has fallen prey to all manner of corruption and idolatry. Religion—often, again, under the rubric of the Judeo-Christian tradition—is required to restore public virtue and good order.

Religious history does not inspire confidence that this can do the trick. Less than a century ago, evangelical Protestants waged wars against alcohol, dancing, theatergoing, prostitution, and gambling—none of which has enlisted the public zeal of their present-day descendants. A little earlier, Northern and Southern Evangelicals were bitterly divided on the morality of slavery. Over the centuries, there has been no single Judeo-Christian policy on (for example) war, the taking of interest, divorce, abortion, plural marriage, women's rights, or (despite Leviticus) homosexuality. In short, infusing public life with religion—even Judeo-Christian religion—is unlikely to mark out a clear moral path.

It is, however, likely to make democratic politics more difficult and acrimonious. Religiously based values are one thing; turning government into an arena for holy war is quite another. Civil society is predicated on some measure of tolerance and respect for those who disagree. Even if intended as no more than pep-rally hyperbole, the religious right's ugly denunciation of perceived enemies and its vehement antiseparationist rhetoric have threatened real mischief, not only for the legislative process but in the public square generally.

Much of the religious encounter in America takes place in a place that is neither strictly private nor fully public—that is, in the broad territory between governmental institutions and the nexus of individual, family, and house of worship. Gray areas there may be, but there are also boundaries that are crossed at peril. When the president of the Southern Baptist Convention publicly declares that God does not hear the prayers of a Jew, or the governor of Mississippi expresses the view that America is a Christian nation, it is a violation of the unstated rules of public religious discourse. These rules even affect religious broadcasting, as the experience of the interfaith cable television network Faith and Values shows.

Faith and Values came into existence as Vision Interfaith Satellite Network (VISN) in the wake of the scandals involving televangelists Jim Bakker and Jimmy Swaggart in 1987. The impetus came from Tele-Communications, Inc., the nation's largest cable company, which sensed a market for mainline religious fare, and in short order Roman Catholic, Greek Orthodox, Unitarian, Jewish, Mormon, and an array of Protestant bodies signed up for airtime. Then, in October 1992, VISN entered into a channel-sharing arrangement with ACTS, the eight-year-old cable network of the Southern Baptist Convention.

The merger with this manifestly multireligious enterprise created a small storm of criticism from Southern Baptists, for many of whom "interfaith" meant something quite different from what it means elsewhere. As Darrell Robinson of the Baptists' Home Mission Board put it, "We have an interfaith witness program that deals with cults and false religion. The chief concern was that ... Southern Baptist programs were interrelated with programs that we were opposing and exposing the heresies of."

But unbeknown to the critics, ACTS itself had, from its inception, embraced a live-and-let-live interfaith policy similar to VISN's. As ACTS executive vice president Richard McCarthy said, "A pastor in his pulpit might say that Muslims and Jews don't have any hope of getting to heaven. But we would not want him to say it on ACTS." Why not? There are truths that can be pronounced in the privacy of one's home or church that civility or public relations forbids even conservative Southern Baptists from saying on the public airwaves. Even the very conservative Southern Baptist Convention was not about to attack Judaism or Islam (or Roman Catholicism) publicly as false religions, or to let such attacks go forth under its aegis. And so the criticism of the VISN/ACTS merger died away.[25]

It is the separation of church and state that keeps theological differences from turning the public square into a religious combat zone. Those differences, it should be recalled, are often profound, and for Jews they have had many bad consequences. Not surprisingly, Jewish specialists in interfaith dialogue have worked hard over the years to persuade their Christian colleagues not only to cease blaming Jews for the death of Jesus but to acknowledge the continued legitimacy of the Jewish covenant and thus abandon efforts at conversion. They have applauded Christian theologians who have been willing to blame Christianity for antisemitic persecutions culminating in the Holocaust.

For all that, it is simply the case that the Christian Bible often turns to anti-Jewish polemic.[26] In the words of one Christian theologian:

> If we freely *criticize* Christian *tradition* in terms of its response to Judaism, can we *exempt* the *New Testament* from that critique? And so do not we, too, often resort to an artificial rescue mission which amounts to intellectual dishonesty, artificially softening the clearly anti-Jewish statements of the New Testament rather than coming to terms with them (italics in original).[27]

Whatever liberal theologians decide to make of such statements, asking those who believe in the inerrancy of Scripture to disown them may be asking too much. Jews, for their part, are not ashamed of rejecting the idea of a Gentile covenant with God by way of Jesus. So, in the spirit of true pluralism, should they be able to accept the fact that many Christians believe that Jesus is the only way to salvation, that the Christian covenant supersedes the Jewish one, that evangelism among the Jews is a legitimate performance of the Christian enterprise. And even if professions of philosemitism and abjurations of proselytizing are wrested from Bible-believing Christians, what of other minority faiths? A visit to any evangelical bookstore will yield present-day polemics against Mormons, New Agers, Scientologists, and so on.

There are, in sum, many reasons for Jews not to kowtow to those who would desecularize the public square. This is not to say that every fight is worth fighting or that every slope is a slippery one. A mandatory moment of silence at the beginning of the school day need not make someone a stranger in a strange land. Student-led Christian prayer piped in over a school intercom very well may.

It is a staple of antisecularist rhetoric that the religion clauses of the First Amendment were intended to prevent government from interfering with religion, not to exile religion from public life. It is far more accurate to say that they were designed to protect religious minorities from suffering at the hands of a government acting on behalf of a religious majority. To the extent that Jews remain a distinctive religious minority, they are right to cast their lot with the secular public square of contemporary America—a civil society where one's religion, freely practiced and freely expressed, entitles one to no special consideration, positive or negative, from the state. Taking pluralism seriously demands no less.

NOTES

1. David Cantor, *The Religious Right: The Assault on Tolerance and Pluralism in America* (New York: Anti-Defamation League, 1994), p. 3.

2. Ibid., p. 1.

3. November 1993 address, quoted in Cantor, *Religious Right*, p. 4.

4. This and subsequent Robertson-Foxman correspondence from ADL and Christian Coalition files.

5. *A Campaign of Falsehoods: The Anti-Defamation League's Defamation of Religious Conservatives* (Chesapeake, Va.: Christian Coalition, July 28, 1994), pp. 20–21.

6. *New York Times*, August 2, 1994.

7. Arnold Forster and Benjamin R. Epstein, *The New Anti-Semitism* (New York: McGraw-Hill, 1974), pp. 79–90.

8. Nathan Perlmutter and Ruth Ann Perlmutter, *The Real Anti-Semitism in America* (New York: Arbor House, 1982), p. 156.

9. See Mark Silk, *Spiritual Politics: Religion and America Since World War II* (New York: Simon & Schuster, 1988), p. 41; Forster and Epstein, *New Anti-Semitism*, p. 298.

10. Naomi W. Cohen, *Natural Adversaries or Possible Allies? American Jews and the New Christian Right* (New York: American Jewish Committee, 1993), p. 45.

11. Richard John Neuhaus, *The Naked Public Square: Religion and Democracy in America* (Grand Rapids, Mich.: Eerdmans Publishing Co., 1984), p. 99.

12. Garry Wills, *Under God: Religion and American Politics* (New York: Simon & Schuster, 1990), p. 242.

13. Michael Medved, *Hollywood Vs. America: Popular Culture and the War on Traditional Values* (New York: HarperCollins, 1992), pp. 64–65.

14. Stephen L. Carter, *The Culture of Disbelief* (New York: Basic Books, 1993).

15. Stewart Hoover, Barbara M. Hanley, and Martin Radelfinger, *The RNS-Lilly Study of Religion Reporting and Readership in the Daily Press* (Philadelphia: Temple University School of Communications and Theater, 1989), p. 30.

16. J. Daniel Hess, "The Religious Journals' Image of the Mass Media," *Journalism Quarterly* 41 (1964), 107. On religion in the news media, see

Mark Silk, *Unsecular Media: Making News of Religion in America* (Urbana and Chicago: University of Illinois Press, 1995).

17. See, for example, Hornell Hart, "Changing Social Attitudes and Interests," in *Recent Social Trends in the United States* (New York: McGraw-Hill, 1933), pp. 412–14.

18. Michael W. McConnell, "'God Is Dead and We Have Killed Him!' Freedom of Religion in the Post-Modern Age," *Brigham Young University Law Review*, 1 (winter 1993) 174, 184. McConnell criticizes recent interpretations of the First Amendment's religion clauses, arguing in a "postmodernist" vein that they depend on an unsustainable distinction between public and private religion. Yet he acknowledges at the same time that a public-private distinction is "utterly indispensable to a theory of religious freedom" (p. 184).

19. Gertrude Himmelfarb, "The Dark and Bloody Crossroads Where Nationalism and Religion Meet," in her *On Looking Into the Abyss* (New York: Alfred A. Knopf, 1994), p. 120.

20. Quoted in Richard Hughes Seager, ed., *The Dawn of Religious Pluralism: Voices from the World's Parliament of Religions, 1893* (LaSalle, Ill.: Open Court, 1993), p. 5.

21. Silk, *Spiritual Politics*, pp. 90–99. See also Mark Silk, "Notes on the Judeo-Christian Tradition in America," *American Quarterly* 36: 1 (spring 1984) 65–85.

22. Cohen, *Natural Adversaries*, p. 2.

23. Quoted from Robertson's *The New Millennium* in Lori Forman, *The Political Activity of the Religious Right* (New York: American Jewish Committee, 1994), p. 24.

24. Irving Kristol, "The Future of American Jewry," *Commentary*, August 1991, pp. 25–26.

25. *Atlanta Journal-Constitution*, April 3, 1993.

26. See Egal Feldman, "American Protestant Theologians on the Frontiers of Jewish-Christian Relations, 1922–82," in David A. Gerber, ed., *Anti-Semitism in American History* (Urbana and Chicago: University of Illinois Press, 1986), pp. 363–85; also Egal Feldman, *Dual Destinies: The Jewish Encounter With Protestant America* (Urbana and Chicago: University of Illinois Press, 1990), pp. 206–46.

27. J. Christiaan Beker, "The New Testament View of Judaism," in James H. Charlesworth, ed., *Jews and Christians: Exploring the Past, Present, and Future* (New York: Crossroad, 1990), p. 64.

·15·

Antisemitism in America:
A View from the "Defense" Agencies

ABRAHAM H. FOXMAN

Abraham H. Foxman is the national director of the
Anti-Defamation League.

The conspicuous role of national Jewish "defense" organizations—primarily the "Big Three," the Anti-Defamation League, the American Jewish Committee, and the American Jewish Congress—together with the activities of well over a hundred Jewish community relations councils around the country, reflects the activism that has characterized the response of Jewish groups to public affairs matters, including antisemitism, particularly in the post–World War II era. In Abraham H. Foxman's essay the activities of the Anti-Defamation League of B'nai B'rith (ADL), the most visible of the Jewish community relations and defense agencies, serve as an exemplar of American Jewish communal intervention in the monitoring and counteraction of antisemitism.

Foxman catalogues a range of antisemitica in his essay, and reviews the responses of his agency to these manifestations. Particularly valuable for any student of antisemitism—and to any professional in the field of counteraction—are his analysis of political antisemitism and of the dramatic, and highly effective, tactic of the ADL in responding to the antisemitism of Nation of Islam spokesman Khalid Abdul Muhammad in 1994. The response to Muhammad illumined the use of basic tactics and techniques in the combatting of racist rhetoric.

Foxman's description of the activities of the organized Jewish community does raise a number of questions. Most generally, the essay poses the question of the appropriate place of antisemitism on the Jewish communal agenda. During an era in which the contours of the Jewish communal agenda are changing, priorities are shifting, and dollars are shrinking, many community professionals and leaders question the expenditure of funds earmarked for the counteraction of antisemitism. Foxman makes a good case for such expenditure. His case, however, is largely premised on the assumption that the security of American Jews rests on counter-ing the activities of antisemites and other bigots. What *is* best for enhanc-ing Jewish security—or, for that matter, the security of any minority group? Chasing after antisemites? Or working to improve societal conditions through an advocacy of social and economic justice? Or ensuring consti-tutional guarantees, most centrally the separation of church and state? Or all of the above?

Another question suggested by this chapter concerns prejudice-reduc-tion programs. ADL's "A World of Difference," described here, is a com-prehensive program aimed at combatting bigotry and fostering intergroup understanding in the school, the workplace, and other societal venues and institutions. But it has not been proven that these programs, which have been a favored vehicle of many human relations agencies since the 1950s, have been effictive. Indeed, many of the data on attitudinal anti-semitism, tracking *generational* rather than *individual* decreases in anti-semitism over the past fifty years, suggest that the Jewish and other com-munities need to carefully examine their commitment to this approach.

Foxman concludes his analysis with a valuable observation about the consensus that has developed over the years with respect to the strate-gies and tactics used by Jewish groups in monitoring and counteracting antisemitism. This consensus—and it is a broad one, transcending ideo-logical, political, social, and religious differences among Jewish groups—lies at the root of effective communal activity in this area. In sum, Fox-man's message is clear: the Jewish community in America in the post-Holocaust era is organized effectively and appropriately to combat antisemitism, whatever questions exist with respect to strategy and tac-tics. The strength of the consensus to monitor antisemitism, to speak out, to engage in counteractive methods, may very well be the most valuable contribution of the organized Jewish community.

J.A.C.

Antisemitism is a protean hatred. For almost two thousand years Jews were attacked as killers of Christ; Jews were said to poison the wells of medieval Europe; to perform ritual murder; to worship "our father, the devil," as the Gospel of John narrates.

(Contemporary Christianity has, of course, repudiated these teachings.) In more modern times, societal crises have prompted demagogues to identify Jews alternately as the driving force behind industrial capitalism, international Communism, or both. Jews have been portrayed as hidden economic parasites draining the blood of nations and communities, and as an elitist cabal secretly plotting and controlling world events. In these schemes, Jews have been blamed for the world wars, the assassination of President Kennedy, the AIDS virus, the Gulf War, even the depletion of the ozone layer.

Beneath each of these notions is a conception of Jews as inherently distinct, inherently alien, and antagonistic to other religious, ethnic, and national groups. Certainly this assumption— backed by the pseudoscience of "racial hygiene," designed to verify these differences—laid the foundation for the murderous Nazi propaganda of "the eternal Jew." In the United States, such a conception of Jews has echoed uncomfortably through the years in the rhetoric of Henry Ford, Father Coughlin, and Louis Farrakhan.

This depiction of Jews similarly animates an obsession with Jewish power and American-Jewish support for Israel. For the antisemite, Jews work against America's national interests and for their own benefit when they support Israel. By the grammar of antisemitism, Israel becomes a political embodiment of Jewish self-interest, the individual Jew a personification of the general "Zionist menace."

Because historically antisemitism has taken many forms, the organized Jewish community's evaluation of and response to this threat—spearheaded in the United States since 1913 by the Anti-Defamation League (ADL) and engaged in by other "defense" agencies of the community, such as the American Jewish Committee and the American Jewish Congress—has had to be comparably versatile. In addition to the ADL's long-standing commitment to studying and reporting on avowedly antisemitic hate groups, we have attempted to measure the general public's susceptibility to anti-Jewish attitudes and behavior.

For example, since 1978, ADL has published an annual audit of antisemitic incidents in the United States. Similarly, in 1992 ADL commissioned the polling firm Marttila and Kiley to conduct the third major survey in three decades on antisemitism in America.

These studies reveal a number of significant trends. The 1992 public opinion survey, for example, indicates that hard-core anti-semitic beliefs have declined among Americans—from a total of 29 percent of the population in 1964 to 20 percent today. This figure nonetheless translates to a population of nearly 40 million American adults currently holding deeply ingrained prejudice against Jews.

Furthermore, some anti-Jewish attitudes have actually increased in the past 30 years. There has been a steady rise in acceptance of the notion that Jews have too much power in the United States—from 11 percent in 1964 to 31 percent in 1992. In just the last decade, the percentage of Americans who believe Jews in this country are more loyal to Israel than to the United States has risen from 30 percent to 35 percent. (Other, more personalized beliefs, such as the suggestion that Jews are less honest or "too shrewd" in business, have declined sharply since the 1960s.)

The 1992 survey also indicated that Americans over the age of sixty-five are twice as likely as those under sixty-five to be considered most antisemitic. This finding suggests two trends: that the decline in hard-core antisemitic attitudes is likely to continue with the passing of older Americans and the concurrent influx of younger, more tolerant citizens into the adult population; and that attitudes toward Jews among older Americans themselves have improved over their lifetime. The study further indicates that the most likely subgroups with antisemitic beliefs are those with high school educations or less, and blue-collar and semiskilled workers.

A particularly troubling finding of this survey, consistent with previous polls, is the significantly greater receptiveness of African Americans to antisemitic views compared to white Americans—though, as with the general population, antisemitism among blacks has declined demonstrably since 1964. Beyond this basic conclusion, however, the 1992 survey once again refutes the mistaken but widespread belief that college-educated blacks are more antisemitic than are less-educated blacks. African Americans with professional or managerial positions are significantly more likely to reject antisemitism than are blue-collar and semiskilled African Americans. African Americans, additionally, are the *only* subgroup for whom regular contact with Jews resulted in a decrease in anti-Jewish attitudes.

The 1992 study also refuted other conventional assumptions about American antisemitism. For example, religious beliefs appear to have little impact on antisemitism: the incidence of ingrained prejudice against Jews varies negligibly between Catholics and Protestants, between regular churchgoers and occasional worshippers. Political and economic disaffection, likewise, triggered only a slight increase in the susceptibility to anti-Jewish beliefs. To the extent that antisemitic attitudes endure in this country, blaming their persistence simply on a stagnant economy or cynicism toward the political process is too facile.

The one factor that most strongly affects an individual's acceptance of antisemitic stereotypes is the presence of other racist, xenophobic, and intolerant ideas.[1] Thus, the seeds of antisemitism are much more likely to sprout from inner beliefs—an individual's personal values or view of other people—than from external influences or pressures.*

Given the basic fact that antisemitic attitudes have declined among the general population in recent decades, why do so many Jews—as is the case with many members of other minority groups in America—sense that the climate of bigotry is worsening, that the tolerance which sustains our multicultural society is currently imperiled? One factor that may explain this belief is the steady increase in antisemitic incidents over the past few years.

ADL's 1993 audit, for example, recorded 1,867 antisemitic acts in forty-four states and the District of Columbia—an 8 percent increase over the 1992 total, and the second highest total in the audit's fifteen-year history. Dividing the types of incidents into acts of vandalism and personal harassment, the latter category—comprising threats, assault, and verbal abuse—rose 23 percent over the 1992 total. For the third straight year, these incidents outnumbered acts of vandalism, 58 percent to 42 percent. Such

---

*For a comprehensive review of the survey data, see Renae Cohen, "What We Know, What We Don't Know About Antisemitism," chapter 3 in this volume. (Editor's note)

personal, "in-your-face" incidents have risen 245 percent since 1986. Incidents on college campuses (122) similarly increased 7 percent over 1992, and have doubled since 1987.

The data are clear: although antisemitic attitudes have declined over the past generation, the willingness of hard-core antisemites to act on their prejudice through direct confrontation with Jews has increased. Further contributing to the sense that Jews, and pluralism itself, are under siege has been the occurrence of several dramatic incidents in recent years.

The most significant of these events, of course, was the tragic rioting in Crown Heights, Brooklyn, in August 1991. The riots began when Gavin Cato, a black child, was accidentally killed by a car driven by a Hasidic Jew. Later that evening, Yankel Rosenbaum, a rabbinical student with no connection to the accident, was fatally stabbed by a gang of black youths who reportedly shouted, "Kill the Jew!" Over the following three evenings, rocks were hurled at a synagogue and at Jewish homes; bands of young people shouted anti-Jewish epithets and "Heil Hitler!"

Yankel Rosenbaum was murdered, not because he was involved in something, or because he had done something, but because he was a Jew—plainly and simply that. There was nonetheless a curious silence, at first, from too many in the Jewish community and the general public about this murder. An uncomfortable color-consciousness perhaps motivated this self-imposed restraint: had Yankel Rosenbaum been murdered by a gang of white youths, Jews justifiably would have been up in arms. But here the community quietly listened to the outpourings of sociological explanations. Jews were slow to anger.

It became apparent, however, that the Jews of Crown Heights were cowering in their homes; the city was bombarded with shrill anti-Jewish choruses emanating not only from the streets but from black-oriented radio stations and newspapers. The *Amsterdam News*, New York's leading black paper, published headlines such as "Many Blacks, No Jews Arrested in Crown Heights" and "Racial Double Standard Causes Unrest, Activists Say." These statements not only rationalized and condoned antisemitic unrest, but possibly incited it.

Beyond such blatant rabble-rousing, many in the media pontificated about systemic inequities and the frustration of blacks in

Crown Heights—both surely exist, but in no way can they legitimate terrorizing and killing Jewish neighbors. A bizarre moral equivalency emerged in the interpretation of the riots; the accidental death of Gavin Cato was equated with the brutal lynching of Yankel Rosenbaum.

Outrage continues to smolder among Jews at this murder, still unresolved three years later. In that time, other events have reinforced the fear that entrenched antisemitism and bigotry among the young can easily ignite almost unimaginable brutality.

In July 1993, for example, federal and local police agents arrested eight individuals with ties to three white supremacist groups—the Fourth Reich Skinheads, White Aryan Resistance, and the Church of the Creator—in Los Angeles. The eight individuals were charged with attempting to instigate a race war by conspiring to assassinate leaders of the African-American and Jewish communities. In addition, they had planned to bomb the largest black church in Los Angeles, and were arrested on the day that the conspiracy ringleader, Christopher Fisher, began preparing a letter bomb to send to an Orange County rabbi. During the arrests, police seized pipe bombs and machine guns, racist paraphernalia including Confederate and Nazi flags, and a framed portrait of Adolf Hitler.

Only eleven days after the arrests in Los Angeles, police in Salinas, California, arrested two skinheads from Washington State. During a search of their car, authorities uncovered three pipe bombs, four loaded shotguns, military apparel, ammunition, wigs, climbing gear, white supremacist propaganda, and a page from a Portland, Oregon, telephone book listing Jewish agencies and synagogues. Under questioning by the FBI, one of the skinheads confessed to bombing an NAACP office in Tacoma, Washington. He also stated that his group, which included a third skinhead arrested the same day in Seattle, had planned to attack Jewish and African-American institutions, military installations, gay and lesbian social places, and radio and television stations.[2]

Another indelible event in the record of contemporary bigotry occurred on November 29, 1993, when Khalid Abdul Muhammad, then serving as national spokesman for the Nation of Islam (NOI), delivered a speech at New Jersey's Kean College in which he drew upon virtually every antisemitic myth and slander in history:

[T]he Jews said to Jesus, we be not born of fornication. We have one father, even God. You know how they're quick to say that. One people, one planet, hell, you didn't want to share it with us until it got all out of whack. Until you had messed up the ozone layer. Until you had destroyed much of the rain forest. Until you had tampered with the delicate balance in nature. . . .

Jesus was right. You're nothing but liars. The Book of Revelations is right. You're from the synagogue of Satan. . . . Who is it sucking our blood in the Black community? A white imposter Arab and a white imposter Jew.[3] Right in the Black community, sucking our blood on a daily and consistent basis. . . .

We found out that the Federal Reserve ain't really owned by the Federal Government. . . . It's owned by the Jews. . . . I don't care who sits in the seat at the White House. You can believe that the Jews control that seat that they sit in from behind the scenes. They control the finance, and not only that, they influence the policy making. . . .

Muhammad's diatribe ventured further afield to malign gays and lesbians, Catholics, the handicapped, and women. He also argued that whites in South Africa be given "twenty-four hours to get out of town, by sundown. . . . If he won't get out of town by sundown, we kill everything white that ain't right . . . in South Africa. We kill the women, we kill the children, we kill the babies . . . we kill 'em all."

Because Khalid Abdul Muhammad had made these same remarks at college campuses across the country for over a decade, and because this speech was made at a time when the Nation of Islam was being embraced by members of the Congressional Black Caucus and the leaders of the NAACP, the Anti-Defamation League felt compelled to speak out. On January 16, 1994, the ADL placed a full-page advertisement in the *New York Times* (and later in other papers) reprinting parts of Muhammad's tirade and stating, without further elaboration, "Minister Louis Farrakhan and the Nation of Islam claim they are moving toward greater moderation and increased tolerance. *You decide."*

The ad generated an unprecedented response: an extraordinary coalition of journalists, members of the clergy—Jewish, Catholic, Protestant, and Muslim—civil rights leaders (both black and white), elected officials, even the vice president of the United States, emerged to denounce the bigotry emanating from NOI. As Cynthia Tucker, the editorial page editor of the *Atlanta Constitution*, commented, "The act of publicizing something that is vile and offensive and bigoted is, in fact, an old and respected civil-rights tactic." Using this strategy enabled us, for the first time in recent memory, to make antisemitism a major issue in the African-American community, one which black leaders recognized as having an impact on the moral stance against racism.

It is important to note that a consensus developed within the Jewish community, and among its agencies, with respect to the strategic approach toward counteraction of antisemitism—that of publicizing the offensive statements of the racist and antisemite without editorial comment—represented by the ADL ad. The strategy of public education has long been recognized by the organized Jewish community as most efficacious.

That struggle, of course, is not over—Khalid Abdul Muhammad continues to tour the country making his hate-saturated speeches on behalf of NOI. Louis Farrakhan, in spite of his refusal to repudiate antisemitism and intolerance, remains a force to be reckoned with in African-American cultural and political life. But ADL's advertisement reestablished in the general public's mind the centrality of antisemitism to the Nation of Islam; there has been little talk, since January, of a "moderated" or "reformed" NOI. More important, through the response to the ad, the Jewish community has now been able to identify dozens of new allies, from all corners of the public square, in its battle against bigotry.

Other manifestations of antisemitism require different kinds of responses. Skinhead and other hate-motivated violence, specifically, requires law enforcement counteraction, as well as exposure. In this regard, ADL has been in the forefront of civil rights groups in educating law enforcement about the danger posed by extremist organizations. We have also worked for decades on devising legislation to curtail extremist activities which endanger public safety. We have cooperated as well with other organizations in securing civil damages from groups whose members have committed racially motivated crimes.

For example, last year in Illinois, Jonathan Haynes was arrested for the murder of a plastic surgeon whom he had targeted to "condemn bleached-blond hair, tinted blue eyes, and fake facial features brought by plastic surgery. This is the time that we . . . stop feeding off Aryan beauty." (Haynes made this statement in court, after having confessed to this murder and to the 1987 murder of a San Francisco hairdresser for the same reason.) After Haynes's 1993 arrest, ADL was able to provide authorities with copies of correspondence between Haynes and a now-deceased Holocaust denier, with a letter advertising Haynes's Nazi-inspired artwork, and with letters written by Haynes published in the periodicals of the group White Aryan Resistance. Convicted in March 1994, Haynes currently sits on death row.

In other hate-crime cases, ADL has been responsible for helping prosecutors secure increased sentences, by drafting model legislation to distinguish these crimes—motivated by hatred toward entire groups—as exceptional assaults against not only the individual victim but society as a whole. Since 1981, ADL model legislation, designed around this "penalty enhancement" concept, has been adopted by more than half the states in the union. Some form of legislation designed to redress bias-motivated crimes has been adopted by forty-six states and the District of Columbia.[4] In the 1993 case *Wisconsin* v. *Mitchell*, the U.S. Supreme Court upheld the constitutionality of the penalty-enhancement approach embodied in ADL's model legislation.

Prior to our model hate-crime legislation, ADL had drafted model laws to prohibit paramilitary training by extremist groups. In the 1950s we similarly advocated "anti-mask" laws to prevent Ku Klux Klansmen from concealing their identities while engaging in acts of terror and intimidation. In addition, ADL has joined with the Southern Poverty Law Center (SPLC) in their efforts to secure civil damages from hate groups whose members engage in criminal conduct. In 1987, ADL provided SPLC counsel Morris Dees with a key piece of evidence in his civil suit against the United Klans of America, then the largest KKK faction in the country.

As a result of this suit, sparked by the 1981 lynching of a black teenager by United Klans of America members, the SPLC secured a $7 million judgment against the group, effectively destroying it. Again in 1993, ADL provided SPLC with evidence in their suit against the Invisible Empire Knights of the KKK. In his settlement with SPLC, the leader of this Klan faction agreed to disband his group. In 1990, ADL served as cocounsel with SPLC in a civil suit against Tom and John Metzger, leaders of White Aryan Resistance. This suit resulted in a $12.5 million judgment against the two for their role in inciting neo-Nazi skinheads to murder an Ethiopian immigrant in Portland, Oregon.

All of these efforts are crucial counteractive measures, but they each respond to extremist behavior *after* incidents and hate crimes have occurred. How do Jewish defense agencies respond to the climate which fosters bigotry and antisemitism? Particularly, what can be done in response to the fact that, in spite of the decline of antisemitism among younger generations, America's youth remain the most likely perpetrators of hate-motivated violence, and the primary targets of antisemitic propaganda?

One approach aimed at combatting nascent prejudice is ADL's A World of Difference Institute. This education and diversity training workshop seeks to combat bigotry and foster intergroup understanding in the school, the community, the workplace, the campus, and within law enforcement agencies. Its objectives include helping individuals identify biased or stereotypical beliefs they may harbor about other groups; providing techniques and strategies to challenge prejudice and discrimination; and equipping participants with the skills to successfully live and work within a pluralistic environment.

Begun as a pilot program in 1985, ADL's A World of Difference Institute has now trained more than 110,000 elementary and secondary school educators; more than 70,000 employees in over 100 corporations, small businesses, and government agencies; and diversified groups of students and staff at more than 400 college campuses. Internationally, A World of Difference Institute has conducted anti-bias training workshops in Berlin, Rostock, and Bremen, Germany—at the invitation of the German government—and has worked with middle managers from South Africa and educators in Moscow. Literally millions of people around the world have been reached by the program, and educated in the values it fosters.

Young people nonetheless continue to be at risk from demagogues and hatemongers, and college campuses especially remain focal points for anti-Jewish campaigns. The most pernicious of these efforts has been the series of newspaper advertisements purchased by Bradley Smith's Committee for Open Debate on the Holocaust (CODOH). The first of these ads claimed to question not the fact of Nazi antisemitism, but merely whether this hatred resulted in an organized killing program. A more recent ad has questioned the authenticity of the U.S. Holocaust Memorial Museum in Washington, D.C., alleging that the museum provides no concrete evidence that gas chambers were used for mass murder in Hitler's concentration camps.

Advertisements such as these have appeared in student newspapers since 1991 on more than three dozen college campuses—including campuses with large Jewish populations, among them Brandeis University and New York's Queens College. Though there is no evidence that these ads have persuaded large numbers of students to doubt the settled record of events which comprise the Holocaust, their publication has generated acrimony and has frequently caused friction between Jewish and non-Jewish students.

This is precisely the intent of the advertisements: by attacking the facts of the Holocaust, and by framing this attack merely as an unorthodox viewpoint or a challenge to "open debate," the ads subtly encode traditional antisemitic images of Jews as controllers of academia and the media, and Jews as exploiters of non-Jewish guilt. These beliefs, of course, bear comparison to the preachings which brought Hitler to power in prewar Germany.

The Holocaust-denial campaign is perhaps the most disturbing antisemitic activity on college campuses today. It reflects the efforts of increasingly sophisticated antisemites to exploit three tendencies in the contemporary culture: (1) widespread ignorance of history, even among otherwise well-educated young people; (2) a misunderstanding of the meaning and practice of free speech and a free press; and (3) the credulity toward and acceptance of conspiracy theories, reflecting an inability to distinguish legitimate scholarship from reckless speculation.

ADL and other Jewish groups have responded to this phenomenon by intensifying our efforts to educate young people about the Holocaust. In 1977 ADL founded the Braun International Center for Holocaust Studies to serve as a public education and research facility. The center's activities include developing and implementing curriculum guides for schools, conducting workshops and seminars for educators, producing and distributing books, films, exhibits, and media programs, and sponsoring public conferences and symposiums. The Center also publishes *Dimensions: A Journal of Holocaust Studies*, and maintains a resource library.

On college campuses, ADL professional staff have lectured about Holocaust denial to students and educators, and have provided background information on Smith and his cohorts to student editors and administrators. We have additionally produced two publications, *Hitler's Apologists: The Anti-Semitic Propaganda of Holocaust "Revisionism"* and *Holocaust Denial: A Pocket Guide*, to enable students to make informed responses when confronted with Smith's propaganda.

Comparably hateful propaganda, unfortunately, is even more pervasive among black antisemites on college campuses. Student groups at many colleges continue to sponsor and enthusiastically receive representatives of the Nation of Islam, as well as other African-American demagogues, such as Steve Cokeley, the leading proponent of the theory that Jewish doctors created the AIDS epidemic by injecting black babies with the virus, and Kwame Toure (formerly Stokely Carmichael), whose standard applause line for over a decade has been "The only good Zionist is a dead Zionist."

Student editors and journalists at black-oriented publications have also indulged in antisemitism. In 1991, for example, a reporter for the UCLA student publication *Nommo* wrote that *The Protocols of the Learned Elders of Zion*—the most notorious anti-Jewish forgery in history—"present information which some believe confirms the theory that so-called Jews have plotted to control the world economically." The article also defined Jews as a "small group of european [sic] people who have proclaimed themselves God's 'chosen' by using an indigenous African religion, Judaism, to justify their place in the world."

In October 1993, an article appeared in the student newspaper of New York's LaGuardia Community College, *The Bridge*, which stated, "Jews don't own the United States but some act as if they do.... Jews immigrated here after over 4.5 million [sic] were

killed in Hitler's concentration camps. If it wasn't for the presence of an all-Black army unit, many more Jews would have died
... their race was almost extinct. Now they are trying to 'extinct'
Blacks out of everything, including existence."

Although campus officials denounced the article as inflammatory propaganda, the student who wrote it was not reprimand-
ed. In fact, he was promoted to the post of news editor. The editor who published the article was also promoted to editor-
in-chief. Similarly, a City University journalism professor, Alisa
Solomon, wrote in the *Village Voice* that she had shown her students the offending article, asking if they would have published
it. She wrote, "More than half said yes, arguing that they didn't
see anything objectionable in the piece even if they disagreed
with it ... they *could not tell* that the article was anti-Semitic
[emphasis in original]."[5]

In May 1994, a student at the University of Akron, Ohio,
wrote in a Kent State campus publication, *UHURU,*

> Jews have undoubtedly been victims in their own history,
> but ... Jews have exercised ... an inordinate or dispro-
> portionate role in the decimation, defilement, cultural col-
> onization, enslavement and genocide of many of the
> world's people up until today.... Don't be fooled by the
> facades and affectations, for they have not behaved like
> friends ... to African, Arab or Native-American people.
> These are the works of those who should be described as
> enemies of our people, our children, and our future.

Most of the specific charges made against Jews in the
UHURU article first appeared in a Nation of Islam publication,
The Secret Relationship Between Blacks and Jews. This book,
which essentially accuses Jews of instigating and dominating the
Atlantic slave trade, has become, in the words of Harvard Professor Henry Louis Gates, "the bible of the new anti-Semitism."[6]
(ADL has published an analytical response to *The Secret Relationship,* titled *Jew-Hatred As History;* it has been distributed to
thousands of students, educators, and journalists across the country.)

At least one African-American studies professor, Wellesley
College's Tony Martin (known previously as an authority on the

black nationalist leader Marcus Garvey), has adopted *The Secret Relationship* as a class textbook. When Jewish and non-Jewish faculty members—including the chairperson of his own department—as well as members of the Boston Jewish community objected to the choice of this book, Martin produced an antisemitic screed of his own, *The Jewish Onslaught*. Since publishing this book, Martin has toured college campuses promoting its litany of Jewish wrongdoing.

A more famous academic mining the same vein as Professor Martin and NOI's Historical Research Department is Professor Leonard Jeffries, who achieved notoriety in 1991 for delivering a speech at the Empire State Black Arts and Cultural Festival in which he blamed "rich Jews" for controlling the colonial slave trade.[7] He further described the existence of a "conspiracy, planned and plotted and programmed out of Hollywood [by] people called Greenberg and Weinberg and Trigliani and whatnot" to denigrate African Americans in the movies. He added that "Russian Jewry had a particular control over the movies, and their financial partners, the Mafia, put together a financial system of destruction of Black people. It was by design, it was calculated."

Jeffries, like Martin, has delivered variations of this oration—along with his frequently noted beliefs that an abundance of the skin pigment melanin accounts for what he claims is the superior intellect and physical prowess of black people—before college audiences around the country. He also presided over an April 1994 lecture sponsored by the Black African Holocaust Council, a Brooklyn group associated with the Nation of Islam, at which a video was shown denying the existence of gas chambers at Auschwitz. The video is distributed by the Institute for Historical Review, the leading Holocaust-denial organization, and has been promoted by Bradley Smith.

The City University of New York (CUNY), where Jeffries serves as chairperson of City College's black studies department, responded to the professor's 1991 speech by not renewing his term as department chair. Jeffries challenged the decision in court, and was ordered reinstated in 1993. That decision was also appealed, and the U.S. Second Circuit Court of Appeals upheld the professor's reinstatement, ruling against City College in April 1994. In July 1994 the New York State Attorney General asked the United States Supreme Court to review the appeals court ruling. (ADL and other Jewish organizations have filed amicus curiae briefs supporting CUNY's as yet unsuccessful appeals.)

Of greater ultimate significance than Jeffries's legal victory, however, is his success in reaching the hearts and minds of college students. How can one explain the appeal of such noxious ideas to college-educated audiences? One factor noted previously in the spread of myths about Jewish control of the slave trade, obviously, is the woeful lack of understanding most students have of history—what the historical record states, and how scholars come to understand these events.

Most Americans, black or white, know nothing about their own history, and know nothing about the history of persecution and degradation that brought Jews to this country. As Alisa Solomon and Eric Breindel have pointed out, many seem to lack, also, an understanding of what antisemitism is. If the Nation of Islam's—or Leonard Jeffries's—exaggerations and distortions of Jewish involvement in slavery reach students before a truthful account of events, then those students, unless they possess an unusual sense of intellectual curiosity and rigor, are lost; they are captive to Farrakhan's and Jeffries's version of history.

With Holocaust denial, it is again the ignorance of student journalists that is being exploited. Though there is no evidence that any of the editors who have published Bradley Smith's advertisements believed the calumny contained in them, most have defended their decision on grounds that not publishing the ads would violate the spirit of the First Amendment. These students never seem to realize that the First Amendment gives them, as editors, the right to decide exactly what goes into their newspaper. The First Amendment does not compel an editor to publish an ad; rather, it prevents the *government* from dictating what will or won't go into a publication. (ADL's reports on Holocaust denial elaborate on this distinction.)

Both Holocaust denial and NOI's slave-trading myths, of course, are conspiracy theories; their purpose is not to identify occasional plots which have caused historical incidents, but to cast a "vast" or "gigantic" conspiracy as the single motivating factor in world events. Though ostensibly dealing with singular occurrences, their intent is to seduce an audience to a specific way of looking at Jews' interaction with history. Thus, the editor of one Holocaust-denial publication wrote in the inaugural issue of his journal that "Talmudic Jewry is at war with humanity. Revolutionary communism and International Zionism are twin forces working toward the same goal: a despotic world government with the capital in Jerusalem."

Conspiracy theories of this sort appear to be the vanguard of antisemitic ideology today, just as "anti-Zionist" rhetoric was twenty years ago, or pseudoscientific theories about the Jewish "race" dominated the antisemitism of the Nazis. One reason for their appeal to professional hatemongers is the currency of other conspiracy theories in the popular culture. After the scandals of Watergate and Iran Contra alerted the public to the possibility of governmental covert action, the fear that world events have spun beyond the control of ordinary citizens (because control of the society has fallen to sinister forces) fueled the popularity of works such as Oliver Stone's film *JFK* and Pat Robertson's best-seller *The New World Order*.

If segments of the population are really willing to believe that President Kennedy was killed by the military-industrial complex because he was too soft on Communism, or that a secret group of Bavarian Freemasons has controlled the secular left for more than two hundred years, then it is not hard to imagine some of these same people falling for the lies of Bradley Smith or the fabrications of Louis Farrakhan and Leonard Jeffries. All of these conspiracy theories share the core feature that the "research" which supports them—little more, in fact, than a compendium of anecdotes divorced from their original context—is rigged to arrive at predetermined conclusions, not historical revelations or insights.

Indeed, some conspiracy theories in general circulation owe their genesis to extremist hate propaganda. Lyndon LaRouche, the demagogue known for years for his twisted theories linking the drug epidemic, AIDS, world "underpopulation," and international financial crises to Jews—particularly ADL[8]—as well as the Trilateral Commission, the British monarchy, the KGB, the International Monetary Fund, the Congress of Vienna, the Freemasons, and Henry Kissinger (among others), also made strenuous efforts to popularize the "October Surprise," a supposed 1980 plot instigated by the Reagan campaign to ensure the presidential candidate's election by delaying the release of American hostages in Tehran. This lurid tale gained such popularity that only a congressional investigation put the theory to rest.

LaRouche associates were also responsible for the assertion that the U.S. Drug Enforcement Administration, which supposedly "controlled" a European drug-smuggling route, had allowed terrorists to commit the bombing of Pan Am 103 over Lockerbie, Scotland. This fantasy found its way into court—where the LaRouchean testimony was discredited—when Pan Am's insurers used the scenario to argue that the airline's lax security was not to blame for the catastrophe. Reports of the trial inspired a cover story in *Time* magazine devoted to the LaRouche-inspired conjecture.

Liberty Lobby, the nation's largest antisemitic propaganda mill, has similarly joined the JFK conspiracy craze by publishing *Final Judgment,* a book which purports to expose "how the CIA, the Mossad and the Meyer Lansky Crime Syndicate collaborated in the murder of John F. Kennedy. . . . The book also presents new revelations which now show that the so-called 'French connection' to the JFK assassination is, in reality, the Israeli connection. . . . [The book] brings forth new material which links former President George Bush to the JFK conspiracy." Of course, Liberty Lobby's chief counsel, Mark Lane, had already written a JFK conspiracy book titled *Plausible Denial;* the organization's mania for conspiracies, however, appears to be inclusive enough to assimilate both theses.[9]

The effort of hate groups to use such outlandish ideas to lure the gullible into accepting their agendas, or at least part of them, is easy to understand. Less explicable, and more indicative of the worsening climate of intolerance, is the disturbing tendency of too many responsible citizens to rationalize or ignore antisemitism and antisemites when they emerge in the mainstream.

Take, for example, the recent political campaigns of David Duke. When the former Klansman and neo-Nazi unsuccessfully ran for the U.S. Senate in 1990, and for governor of Louisiana in 1991, he carried the majority of white votes in both elections; in the governor's race he reportedly won two-thirds of the white fundamentalist vote.

This is not to suggest that every Duke supporter was an overt antisemite or Nazi sympathizer. The findings of ADL's 1992 survey, as well as the personal experiences of most of Louisiana's small Jewish population, would refute such a charge. Duke skillfully manipulated voter discontent toward blacks, the federal government, and the Louisiana political establishment. By thus appealing to voters' other prejudices, he was able to convince those voters to cast a blind eye toward his virulent hatred of Jews.*

Given the evident popularity Duke enjoyed among white evangelicals, the role that the Reverend Billy McCormack, the state director of the Christian Coalition and at the time an influential member of the Louisiana Republican Central Committee, played during this period is particularly troubling. On September 23, 1989, McCormack and his associates on the Central Committee tabled a motion to censure then state legislator Duke. The state party never repudiated Duke during his term as legislator, despite the unanimous condemnation of the Republican National Committee, and despite the fact that Duke was known to be selling racist and antisemitic hate propaganda from his legislative office.

When interviewed by the *Los Angeles Times* in November 1990 about Duke, McCormack suggested that the former Grand Wizard posed no greater a threat to America than "the Jewish element in the ACLU." He added that Duke was "saying some things that are very true, and that's the reason he's getting as many good marks as he's getting." Because some of Duke's political positions apparently echoed McCormack's, McCormack was willing to defend Duke. He did so even though in defending Duke, he not only ignored the twenty-year record of one of America's leading hatemongers, but also indulged in antisemitic scapegoating of his own.

A similar trend emerged from the 1992 presidential campaign of the political commentator Pat Buchanan. For a figure in the political mainstream, Buchanan has compiled a disturbing record of antagonism toward Jews and other American minorities. He has accused Israel and the American Jewish community of fomenting the Gulf War; he has offered unsettling praise for Hitler's "great courage . . . oratorical powers . . . extraordinary

*See Mark Mellman's analysis of the Duke vote in chapter 9 of this volume. (Editor's note)

gifts . . . [h]is genius"; he has defended nearly every suspected Nazi war criminal investigated by the Office of Special Investigations; he has questioned the settled history of the Holocaust; he has offered apologies for South African apartheid; he has expressed fear that immigration will render whites a minority in America; he has called for a "religious war" to remake America as "a Christian country."

The source of Buchanan's antipathy toward American pluralism differs from Duke's totalitarianism. Duke's covert Nazism is premised on a doctrine of "Aryan" supremacy: whites are genetically, if not divinely, entitled to rule the world. Or, as he expressed it in 1987, "I sincerely believe that the future of this country, civilization, and planet is inseparably bound up with the destiny of the white race."

Buchanan's philosophy is culturally, not racially, derived. As the conservative commentator Irving Kristol described it,

> Pat Buchanan is seeking to shape the conservative movement along reactionary lines. And behind him there has formed a curious coalition of what have been called "paleo-conservatives"—i.e., conservatives of the 1930s–1950s vintage. . . . [T]he basic thrust of this mini-movement is, in a profound sense, radical and antipolitical. These people really do want to turn the clock a long ways back. . . . Only a revolution can turn a society's clock back to any substantial degree, and the "paleos" may have revolutionary enthusiasm but nothing of great interest to say to the live human beings who constitute the American public.[10]

Christian triumphalism can be described as the motivation for Buchanan's reactionary politics. As he told the Christian Coalition at the September 1993 Road to Victory conference, "Our culture is superior because our religion is Christianity and that is the truth that makes men free." This statement reportedly received the loudest ovation of the entire conference, attended by more than two thousand people. Though such a statement cannot be considered in the same vein as David Duke's megalomaniacal rhetoric, it offers a vision of America in open conflict with contemporary and historical reality, a vision with little or no regard for Jews or other religious minorities.

Nationwide, Buchanan and his "mini-movement" received some three million votes in the Republican primary season. That voters could cast their ballots for a man so lightly committed to the ideals of American democracy, or the equality of its citizens, is deeply troubling. Of even greater concern, however, is the reaction Buchanan's public record has received from fellow conservatives and fellow journalists.

William F. Buckley, for instance, wrote of Buchanan in the December 1991 *National Review*, "Here was a Gentile who said things about Jews that could not reasonably be interpreted as other than anti-Semitic in tone and in substance. . . . As far as I can tell . . . Buchanan's reach is as extended today as in the fall of 1990, when he was suggesting that . . . only satellites of Israel favored military action against Iraq."

Six weeks later, however, Buckley himself was endorsing Buchanan as a "tactical vote" against President Bush in the New Hampshire primary. If Buckley was alarmed—at least with respect to Buchanan's remarks concerning the Gulf War—that Buchanan's reach extended so far, how could he nonetheless promote Buchanan, even out of grievance toward Bush, and thereby extend the columnist's reach even further?

Subsequently, at the Republican National Convention in Houston, Buchanan delivered perhaps the most divisive speech before a national audience in recent memory. He was greeted with cheers on the Astrodome floor. Only after the Republican defeat in November did the speech receive widespread criticism from within the party. To date, Buchanan remains a respected and prominent member of the journalistic community, capable of exerting a significant influence on the conservative movement in the coming years. His continued acceptance as a pundit and political strategist represents a dismaying indifference to—or at best rationalization of—intolerance within the mainstream political community.*

*Jewish groups were hesitant to identify Buchanan as an antisemite until an incident on March 2, 1992, when, at a campaign rally in Marietta, Georgia, Buchanan told a group of Jewish protesters that his rally was "of Americans, by Americans, and for the good old U.S.A." The American Jewish Congress subsequently branded Buchanan "as genuine and authentic an antisemite as they come." (Editor's note)

One finds even more dismaying the flirtation the Nation of Islam has carried on with the political mainstream for the past several years. It would of course be erroneous to suggest that every individual who has embraced Louis Farrakhan has become by association an antisemite. Indeed, the popular reception the Nation of Islam (NOI) has received typically has stressed the group's anti-drug work in inner-city neighborhoods and its focus on black self-reliance—programs and beliefs, in fact, not dissimilar from countless less-publicized organizations not tainted by intolerance—and has attempted to minimize the group's long-familiar record of antisemitism.

Thus, in the name of community empowerment, the U.S. Department of Housing and Urban Development in 1992 began awarding contracts worth millions of taxpayer dollars annually to the NOI Security Agency, which has patrolled federal housing projects throughout the country. (The NOI's record as a security group is decidedly mixed; while the agency's contracts have been renewed at some projects, they have been fired from others.) Federal and city funds have also been awarded to Washington, D.C.'s Abundant Life Clinic, run by NOI Health Minister Abdul Alim Muhammad, M.D., to treat AIDS patients.[11] These subsidies have been awarded despite NOI's well-established homophobia, its endorsement of various AIDS conspiracy theories involving Jewish doctors and the federal government, and the fact that Muhammad's AIDS treatment—low-dose oral alpha interferon—has been tested in the United States, Canada, Germany, and Uganda, and found to have no significant medical effect against the disease.

Such contracts have helped validate an organization whose stated mission is utterly at odds with American multiculturalism and democracy. Of equal concern are the personal contacts, noted previously, which Farrakhan has developed with a number of leading African-American politicians over the past decade. These activists have repeatedly stated that they have embraced Farrakhan, not in support of his bigotry but in pursuit of greater black unity and coordination against the common threats facing their community.

The search for unity is understandable. Nonetheless, African-American leaders must recognize that the embrace of an unrepentant hatemonger inevitably discourages others—women, gays and lesbians, Latinos, Asians, as well as Jews—from attempting to form a broader social and political coalition with African Americans. Such a coalition is essential because the problems currently affecting the African-American community—crime, violence, unemployment, drugs, disease, and despair—are not just black problems, they are *American* problems. Every citizen has a stake in their solution, because every citizen has a stake in the common destiny of the nation.

It is vital for all citizens to not only confront Farrakhan and other demagogues—black and white—but to offer solutions to the problems facing American society. Or, as Professor Julius Lester recently expressed the challenge in *Dissent* magazine:

> It is not Farrakhan's speech that should be silenced; rather, we—blacks, Jews, and whites—must be given—must create—something else to listen to, namely a narrative that gives us all an image in which we can see, not only ourselves as belonging to the good, but each other, too. What might that narrative be? Perhaps it is one some blacks and some Jews and others tried to create in the sixties, a narrative that saw as the good not race, but community. . . .
>
> Farrakhan offers an ugly and hateful vision. . . . It is time we offered an alternative. If we do not, we cede moral authority to those who, in their self-hatred, hate us all.

The agencies of the organized Jewish community in the United States have a mandate to counter antisemitism. The defense agencies of the community continue to exercise their appropriate functions of monitoring, measuring, and counteracting antisemitism. There has developed, over the years, a broad consensus with respect to the strategies and tactics employed in carrying out these activities. The Anti-Defamation League, for its part, contributes to this narrative by speaking out against all forms of antisemitism, racism, and intolerance. ADL's research and fact-finding departments continue to alert the public to the hazards of prejudice and the activities of hatemongers. Our A World of Difference Institute will continue to educate teachers and students, employers and employees, to surmount obstacles to tolerance and diversity in an increasingly pluralistic environment. ADL's legal affairs department, often in concert with other agencies, drafts amicus curiae briefs and model legislation to protect civil and religious liberties, and to establish constitutionally viable punishments for extremists whose bigotry and hate motivates them to engage in criminal activities.

In sum, the formulation adopted from ADL's 1913 statement of purposes could well serve as a motto for all Jewish organizations: "to stop the defamation of the Jewish people . . . to secure justice and fair treatment to all citizens alike."

NOTES

1. ADL confirmed this finding with a June 1993 survey, also conducted for the League by Marttila and Kiley, on racial attitudes in the United States. This second study concluded that education (or lack thereof) is the most important predictor of racially prejudiced attitudes, and that a high correlation exists between intolerance and xenophobia generally, and anti-black racism specifically. Among the most prejudiced group (29 percent of the population), neither political ideology nor party affiliation proved a consistent predictor of racial prejudice, though ideological liberals and moderates were more likely to fall in the least prejudiced group (45 percent of the population). The only significant difference between the two studies concerned the relationship of age to prejudice: antisemitism steadily declined among younger Americans, but racism was higher among Americans aged 18 to 29 (31 percent), than those aged 30 to 49 (23 percent).

2. The latter two conspiracies signify a disturbing new trend among neo-Nazi skinheads to act upon more ambitious and organized violent schemes either by working with or taking inspiration from older, more established hate groups. Although neither of these incidents resulted in a loss of life, since June 1990 there have been more than two dozen murders committed by racist skinheads—in the preceding three years there had been only six. These homicides have included the stabbing death of a homeless black man in Alabama; the firebombing of a gay white man and lesbian black woman in Oregon; the stomping death of a fifteen-year-old Vietnamese immigrant in Texas; and the robbery and stabbing of an eighty-three-year-old woman in Florida by her own skinhead grandson. Neo-Nazi skinheads currently number approximately 3,500, affiliated with more than 160 gangs, in over 40 states. In the year since these two plots were uncovered, skinhead hatred and violence have shown no signs of abating.

3. This was not the first instance in which Khalid Abdul Muhammad had attacked Arabs. According to Peter Noel, writing in the February 15,

1994, issue of the *Village Voice*, Muhammad in 1992 appeared on the New York radio station WLIB with a member of a rival Black Muslim sect. There, he attacked his opponent for having "become not just a white man's nigger but now . . . the Arabs' nigger." He also referred to Arabs as "the rusty, dusty, dirty desert Arabs," and reportedly blamed the Prophet Muhammad for the terrible conditions of the world today—a remark blatantly blasphemous to traditional Islam.

4. The current exceptions are Nebraska, South Carolina, Utah, and Wyoming.

5. When Bradley Smith's ads first appeared in 1991, the student editor-in-chief at Cornell's *Daily Sun* also defended the decision to run the piece on grounds that it "did not overtly slur Jews." His defense prompted Eric Breindel, an editor for the *New York Post*, to write, "Those who deny that the mass murder of European Jewry by Hitler and his collaborators took place commit an unspeakable outrage against Jewish history, Jewish memory and Jewish humanity. If they aren't anti-Semites . . . then there's no such thing as an anti-Semite."

6. Minister Farrakhan, responding on the *Arsenio Hall Show* to Professor Gates's characterization of the book, stated, "You know a bible, a bible should never be denigrated. The word of God should never be denigrated." The issue for Minister Farrakhan thus was not his book's antisemitism, but Professor Gates's use of the term *bible!*

7. It is important to bear in mind that in contrast to Professors Martin and Jeffries, a number of African-American scholars and academic leaders— Cornel West, Orlando Patterson, Randall Kennedy, and Henry Louis Gates at Harvard, Selwyn Cudjoe at Wellesley, Russell Adams at Howard University, Roger Wilkins at George Mason University, the feminist scholar Bell Hooks, and United Negro College Fund Director William Gray—have been at the forefront in denouncing black antisemitism.

8. Vintage antisemitism from LaRouche includes his bizarre analysis of *The Protocols of the Learned Elders of Zion:* "The fallacy of the 'Protocols of Zion' is that it misattributes the alleged conspiracy to Jews generally, to *Judaism.* A corrected version of the 'Protocols' would stipulate that the evil paths cited were actually the practices of . . . B'nai B'rith" (*New Solidarity,* December 8, 1978). LaRouche's particular obsession with ADL stems from the league's exposure of his group's antisemitism during the 1970s and the assistance we provided prosecutors in their successful tax, loan, and mail fraud case against the organization. The conviction resulted in LaRouche receiving a fifteen-year federal sentence in 1988, from which he was paroled in January 1994. ADL's recent publication *Paroled: The LaRouche Political Cult Regroups* discusses the many facets of LaRouche's organization, its philosophy, and its campaign against ADL.

9. Moreover, L. Fletcher Prouty, a retired Air Force colonel who has been interviewed on Liberty Lobby radio programs and has served on Liberty Lobby's "Populist Action Committee," reportedly was the model for "Mr. X," Donald Sutherland's character, in Oliver Stone's *JFK*.

10. William F. Buckley, *The Search for Anti-Semitism* (New York: Continuum), 1992, p. 126.

11. In addition to his work with the Abundant Life Clinic, Dr. Muhammad is NOI's leading contact with the LaRouche organization. In the 1980s, Muhammad participated in a Paris meeting on AIDS called by a LaRouche front group. In the fall of 1992, he collaborated in a series of meetings and rallies with LaRouche representatives to denounce ADL as "the new Ku Klux Klan"—an ironic designation, considering the fact that LaRouche has been associated with members of the "old" Ku Klux Klan. The most recent of these rallies attended by Dr. Muhammad took place on April 13, 1994, at Baltimore's Morgan State University.

·16·
How Jews Use Antisemitism

ARTHUR HERTZBERG

Arthur Hertzberg has been professor of history at
Columbia University, and is now visiting professor of
humanities of New York University. He is the author
most recently of *The Jews in America: Four Centuries
of an Uneasy Encounter.*

Arthur Hertzberg offers, within a historical context, a sharp counterpoint
to Abraham Foxman's observations on the role of the organized Jewish
community in counteracting antisemitism.

J.A.C.

Studies of antisemitism have almost invariably included a
question for both Jews and Gentiles: In your view, how virulent is antisemitism? The answer is strikingly different. In the
United States more than three-quarters of American Jews think
that antisemitism is a serious threat; at least nine out of ten Gentiles believe that Jew-hatred is residual and vanishing. In the former Soviet Union, in a study done in 1990, four out of five Jews
predicted antisemitic violence that year, but only 2 percent of the
non-Jews thought that pogroms were possible. In actual fact, the
Jews were wrong—there was no violence—but that did not belay
their fears. Jews in the former Soviet Union continue to answer
the poll takers that they regard antisemitic violence as a present
danger.

This striking difference in perception is not the only anomaly
in the recent history of antisemitism. The overt reaction by

American Jews to the Holocaust was strangely delayed for twenty-five years. The opening of the death camps at the end of the Second World War in 1945 was a major cause for the outburst of energy and passion throughout the Jewish world for the creation of the State of Israel. But for the next two decades American Jews avoided remembering the Holocaust for what it was, the most terrible expression of antisemitism in all of Jewish history. Few wanted to hear the accounts by the survivors of the death camps of the horrors they had experienced. Large interest in the Holocaust appeared only in the 1970s, when a younger generation that had been born after 1945 was coming to maturity. Books without number were published, and widely read, describing the horrors. Courses about the Holocaust became the staples of religious schools in the synagogues, and of the Jewish studies programs which were burgeoning in the colleges and universities. Holocaust centers and memorials were created in every Jewish community of some size. Why did it take so long for the Holocaust to be remembered, not obliquely, as a prime reason for the labors for Israel, but directly, as the climactic event in the long history of antisemitism?

These two recent events—the continued sensitivity of Jews to antisemitism even as it has been lessening, and the long wait by American Jews before they confronted the Holocaust—are both part of a larger story. It is the question of the significance of antisemitism in modern Jewish history. By this I do not mean the impact of Jew-hatred on Jews, for that negative story has been told many times and in great detail. I am pointing to another issue which has been little discussed: how Jews have used antisemitism as a force for preserving the community.

The essence of the matter is exemplified by the thinking and the career of Theodor Herzl. In *The Jewish State*, the pamphlet that he published in 1896, Herzl based the argument entirely on antisemitism. This was the condition from which all who were born Jews suffered; regardless of what they tried to become, the inescapable pain inflicted on all of them by their enemies forced Jews together. Herzl spoke of the Jewish religion as, at most, a warm memory: shared faith and practice no longer bound Jews together. Herzl was even less committed to Jewish culture. Throughout his career, he was impatient with the idea that the aim of Zionism is to create a contemporary Hebraic national culture. In Herzl's view, religion and culture were side issues of importance to passionate minorities. These concerns—and many others, such as the insistence by some that the Jewish state be created according to a socialist blueprint—could be addressed in the future after the state was created. That endeavor was the only one that belonged to every Jew, for the state was the only possible cure for antisemitism, the problem which affected all Jews.

Herzl's thought was not linked to the earlier history of Zionism. He did not know, and he was not carrying forward, the work of a handful of rabbis who had argued two generations earlier that human efforts to build the Holy Land should now begin in preparation for the Messiah. He was not impressed by Moses Hess who had suggested in 1862, in *Rome and Jerusalem*, that the Jews should return to Palestine in order to refresh their religion and culture within their own polity. Herzl's acknowledged predecessors were those who had fought for the *political* emancipation of the Jews. This effort had begun in Europe when the French Revolution promised equality for all individuals, including those of Jewish origin. In the next century the emancipation of Jews, in law, had spread as far as Germany and the Austro-Hungarian Empire.

Nonetheless, discrimination had not vanished. As antisemitism rose markedly in his own time, in the last decades of the nineteenth century, Herzl became obsessed with the question of how to realize the promise of equality. The great idea of his life was that equality could not be achieved for the Jews as individuals; they must acquire a state of their own. Equality as a group was the precondition to equality as individuals. Herzl was thus the heir of Jewish political figures before him such as Adolphe Cremieu in France and Gabriel Reisser in Germany who a half-century earlier had led battles for equal citizenship for Jews. They had thought that they would defeat the antisemites by persuading governments to make personal equality for Jews the law of the land; Herzl wanted to complete their task by creating a Jewish political state.

Herzl did, however, invent one unprecedented use of antisemitism in his battle for the equality of the Jews. He suggested that antisemitism was not only a problem to the Jews, it was also disturbing the stability of Europe. Since Herzl was a rational man, he did not imagine that governments and societies had need of antisemitism because it could be used to deflect angers against the ruling powers onto scapegoats. On the contrary, Herzl was sure that even antisemites were reasonable people; they would want order in their societies. Helping Jews to become normal people in a state of their own would remove the cause of antisemitic eruptions. In Herzl's historical imagination, antisemitism thus became both the unifying factor of the Jewish community and the guarantor that the world would help Jews achieve their normalcy.

Herzl offered a new cure for antisemitism, but his suggestion was in competition with other doctrines. Revolutionary socialists followed Karl Marx's teaching that the "Jewish problem" was a result of the inequities of capitalism. Antisemitism would end only in a classless society. Most of the Jewish high bourgeois continued to insist that the cure for antisemitism was assimilation. The way to achieve equality was to remove from Jewish life any practices that might be irritatingly different from those of the majority. Therefore, after 1881, while more than two million Jewish immigrants were arriving in the United States from Eastern Europe, the established Jewish leaders worked hard to teach the newcomers American ways, to prepare them to assimilate. These leaders wanted to imagine that antisemitism in America was directed at the immigrants from Eastern Europe and not at people like themselves who had already become Americans "of the Hebrew religion." But the "German Jews" could not avoid knowing that they, too, were the targets of social and economic discrimination. They were being attacked by populist antisemites as Wall Street bankers who despoiled the poor.

The established Jewish elite had to fight for equality on two fronts: immigrant Jews had to be changed into Americans, and the endemic antisemitism of the majority society had to be answered and, ultimately, uprooted. The leaders of the established Jewish community poured their most important energies into all the aspects of the fight against antisemitism. They joined in creating a new organization, the American Jewish Committee, to protect the rights of Jews at home and abroad. From the moment of its founding, this body became the dominant expression of the ethos and interests of the German-Jewish elite.

In the United States, new organizations to fight anti-Semitism became a growth industry. Less than a decade after the creation of the American Jewish Committee, B'nai B'rith organized its own Anti-Defamation League in 1913. The American Jewish Congress made the defense of human rights into its primary purpose in the 1920s. Beginning in the 1930s, local councils to fight anti-semitism have burgeoned in every Jewish community of any substantial size. The National Jewish Community Relations Advisory Council arose in the 1940s to coordinate the efforts of all these bodies. Even the labors for Israel, which became the dominant endeavor of American Jews after 1948, were strongly motivated by anti-antisemitism. American Jews explained that they were supporting Israel as a place of refuge for other Jews who were fleeing their enemies, and as an insurance policy for themselves, if American society ever turned sour. The Palestinians, and all the other Arabs in conflict with the state of Israel, have seldom been discussed by American Jews as protagonists of Arab nationalism in conflict with Jewish nationalism. Instead, the Arab opponents of Israel have almost invariably been dubbed as antisemites, and the defense of the Jewish state has been depicted as part of the age-old battle with all the varieties of antisemitism.

If the central concerns of contemporary Jews, including the support of Israel, can be understood as aspects of the war against antisemitism, it makes sense that the community should be led by those who contribute the most money and effort to this endeavor. To keep up the morale of both the generals and the foot soldiers in this army which is arrayed against the enemies of the Jews, the community as a whole must be convinced, and reconvinced, that the threat remains serious. Such a Jewish community needs the enemy, the antisemites, at least as much as the United States needed the fear of "the evil empire," the Soviet Union, to give cohesion and elan to its foreign policy—and now misses the absence of the Cold War. As long as fighting antisemitism is at the center of the agenda, the Jewish community needs to exaggerate the power of the enemy, even to the state of paranoia.

By the light of these reflections, an explanation is possible for the revival of interest in the Holocaust only in the 1970s. That was the point when antisemitism in America had become negligible. Every major area of American life—political advancement, academic preferment, jobs in business or industry—was now open to Jews. The children who had been born after the end of the Second World War were now in college or in the first stages of their careers. They had been born after the defeat of the Nazis, and they had grown to maturity taking the existence of a Jewish state for granted. The homes in which they had been raised had, essentially, imposed few limits on their personal freedom. They were free to choose their politics (as some demonstrated in the student revolts at the end of the 1960s), their sexual mores, and their connection, or lack of it, to Jewish faith and memory.

Middle-aged parents saw what freedom had wrought and became frightened at the evaporation of the Jewishness of their children. The parents evoked the one Jewish emotion that had tied their own generation together, the fear of antisemitism. The stark memory of Auschwitz needed to be evoked to make the point that Jews were different. Young Jews needed to be told that antisemitism had not disappeared; it was only quiescent and could return to destroy them. Holocaust courses, institutes, and museums suddenly became necessary, to evoke sharp, and instant, Jewish emotions among hundreds of thousands of younger Jews who had little connection with Jewish religion or Jewish learning.

Historians of religions will no doubt see the unparalleled effort and passion which created the greatest of the Holocaust memorials in the United States on the Mall in Washington as the contemporary version of the building of a "national Jewish cathedral." It enshrines the Holocaust as the via dolorosa and crucifixion of the Jewish people. Those who come to remember are transformed in this shrine into participants in the great sacrifice. They are confirmed in their Jewishness, leaving with "never again" on their lips. It is their prayer, even as they remember that "Hear O Israel, the Lord, Thy God, the Lord is one" was the holiest of all verses for their ancestors.

This ambivalence is not limited to the United States. In France, Alain Finkielkraut, a child of survivors, wrote recently about the Jewishness of his generation in a book entitled *The Imaginary Jew*. Finkielkraut asserted that "from Judaism I drew neither religion nor a way of life but the certainty of superior sensitivity." He concluded "by calling on a generation of 'imaginary

Jews,' those who live in 'borrowed identities,' who 'harvested all the moral advantage' of their suffering ancestors, to dedicate themselves to preserving more than just the memory of pain, but the rich complexities of a profound and absorbing culture."

Perhaps the most subtle and the most important of all the uses of antisemitism by Jews in the modern era is its role in "guaranteeing" the survival of the Jewish community in the Diaspora. I have been maintaining, so far, that the striving for equality has given purpose to contemporary Jewish life. This makes sense so long as equality—of some Jews—is not completely realized. When their own equality was no longer problematic, after the 1960s, American Jews could still fight for Israel against the "Arab antisemites," and for the right of the Jews of the Soviet Union to emigrate—and their energies were fueled by the newly aroused memories of the Holocaust. But there has always been the theoretical possibility that all these battles might be won. The contemporary Diaspora community would then have to face the question of finding unifying content for its life after the Arabs make peace with Israel (as it is now possible), the Jews of the former Soviet Union are all free to go, and Israel has transformed itself (as it now seems to be doing) into a Western country with an economy that is attaining a European standard of living. At some point in the not too distant future, the Diaspora will be constrained—by good fortune—to face the question that has been implicit from the very beginning of its drive for equality: On what basis will the Jewish community survive in a completely open world?

Nahum Goldmann once answered the question by saying that the Jews, who have spent at least a century in breaking down all the discriminatory barriers against them, would have to spend the next century erecting some new barriers, out of their own free will, to safeguard the separate identity of Jews. Some twenty years ago, in the immediate memory of Martin Luther King's "I Have a Dream" speech, I dealt with the same theme in a short essay that was published in *Ha-Aretz* entitled "I Have a Nightmare." The purported contents of that "bad dream" were that the Arabs made peace, Brezhnev published a decree letting all the Jews out of the Soviet Union, and Israel struck oil in quantities to rival the reserves of Saudi Arabia. I then asked the plaintive question: "What will the American Jewish organizations do with themselves?"

In fact, Nahum Goldmann and I did not invent this concern. In the United States it had been raised more than a half-century earlier by Mordecai M. Kaplan. He had suggested that American Jews would continue their separate identity in America by redefining themselves as an ethnic minority, a people with a sub-culture of their own. Throughout his long life, Kaplan spent his energies "reconstructing" Jewish identity in the key of democracy: to be spiritually open, man-centered, and changing with the times. The hidden premise in all of his writing is an estimate of antisemitism: it would not be virulent enough in America to make life difficult for Jews, but it would continue indefinitely at sufficient strength to prevent Jews from assimilating easily into the majority. Jews would have no option but to redefine their identity in twentieth-century America within their own group, and to find their emotional sustenance within this extended family.

This assumption that even when Jews achieved as much equality as was likely, just enough antisemitism would remain to enclose them within their own domain is fundamental not only to the addiction to anti-antisemitism but also even to the theories about the survival of "positive Judaism." For example, the Haskalah, the Jewish Enlightenment in Eastern Europe in the nineteenth century, created modern literature in Hebrew. This movement has been celebrated since as one of the sources of contemporary Jewish creativity, but the writing of the Haskalah often sighed with regret that modern Jews could not easily enter Russian or Polish literature, so they are constrained to become modern men and women in their own ghetto. The evidence for this contention is in the history of Hebrew literature—and, for that matter, of writing in Yiddish—in the United States. The home of modern Hebrew letters has become the State of Israel, in which the revived language is the national tongue, but Hebrew and Yiddish writing have almost vanished in the Diaspora. The Haskalah, in Hebrew and Yiddish, is no longer a kind of refuge for modern Jews because there are now few barriers against the entry of Jews into all the expressions of culture in the languages of the majority. Jewish commitments are now in open competition with many

344

other values and identities, and the fear of antisemitism forces few to choose their Jewishness. That choice is now made by those who think that the identity into which they were born is superior or more authentic.

In the mind of American Jews, the concern about the inner content of Jewish life suddenly became popular after 1990, when the results of a large, centrally organized study of Jewish population in America were released. Two findings were most frightening: the rate of intermarriage had risen to over 50 percent, and the 4.5 million Jews who are somehow identified with the community are not many more than the 3.5 million who were found to have some inactive memory of partial Jewish ancestry. In the light of these unsettling facts, the dominant buzzword in the organized Jewish community became "continuity." But why did the leaders of the organized Jewish community have to wait for this study? The evidence of the ongoing evaporation of Jewish learning and religious practice had been widely noted for at least two generations. Nonetheless, the Jewish establishment continued to insist that efforts to deepen Jewish education and culture were the private business of those who cared; the business of the community as a whole was to fight the battles of the Jews, everywhere, for equality.

This obduracy had deep roots in the organizational structure of American Jewish life. Since Alexis de Tocqueville's description *Of Democracy in America* in the late 1830s, citizens of this land have taken pride in the voluntarism which characterizes this society. In America, any cause or opinion can easily be enshrined in an organization created by enthusiasts. Those who found, and continue, such voluntary bodies need to persuade, and keep persuading, others of the importance of their cause. Such organizations rarely admit that the situation they once addressed has changed, so that the need for their organization may have decreased. On the contrary, voluntary organizations keep competing with each other for attention and money. They insist that the evil against which they are on guard is still threatening, or that it has even become more deviously dangerous. Our hope for the good life, so the spokesmen assert, requires that we continue and increase our support for their agencies.

American Jewish organizations are part of this pattern. Each must "sell" its program as widely as possible. The organizations which have been created to oppose antisemitism must, almost inevitably, emphasize its persistence, even when it is waning. Those who write the reports, call the parlor meetings to raise big money, and send out tens of thousands of letters of appeal to the wider public do not even think that they are motivated by institutional needs. They repeat as a litany that the Jews in Germany thought that they were secure and that in the 1920s they shrugged off the first Nazis as marginal hooligans. The "defense" organizations insist in good conscience that their efforts are necessary to keep America different.

Nonetheless, the anomaly remains that the budgets keep growing, and new agencies against antisemitism keep being created, while the disease is waning. I cannot help remembering the ironic witticism of my father that when fundraising is in decline, the organizations pray for a small and, hopefully, not too murderous pogrom. More seriously, my own decades of study of modern Jewish history have convinced me that direct Jewish efforts against this plague are of marginal importance. The governing factor is economic: during depressions, such as the inflation in Germany in the 1920s or the economic disaster in the United States after 1929, the losers increase and they look for scapegoats. The basic fight against antisemitism in America today is being conducted by those who are trying to lessen the numbers of the dispossessed.

Having said this, it is important to note as well that the national Jewish defense agencies do make a difference. One cannot allow the *Protocols of the Elders of Zion* to be republished without a reply. The question is not whether the Jewish community ought to counteract antisemitism—certainly it must—but where the battle against antisemitism belongs among the community's priorities. Most important, we must understand that that battle often serves to boost Jewish morale even more than to counteract antisemitism.

Some fifty years ago, many of the American Jewish organizations joined together to commission a study by the social scientist Robert M. MacIver on how these voluntary bodies function. His report suggested that there was much duplication, and MacIver proposed that each organization limit itself to a specific task of its own. The mild proposal was much discussed, and essentially not adopted. The state of the organized American Jewish community today requires the answer to a different and more fundamental question: How can we base the Jewish community not on mostly imagined fear but on affirmation? I am not very hopeful that a leadership which has been nurtured on fighting our enemies will make this turn—but perhaps it will. Whatever the existing leaders and organizations may think, palliatives in the name of "continuity" will not do. There must be a radical new beginning to make imparting Jewish learning into the dominant communal purpose of American Jewry.

·17·
Reflections on Crown Heights: Interpretive Dilemmas and Black-Jewish Conflict

JONATHAN RIEDER

Jonathan Rieder, chairman of the Sociology
Department at Barnard College, Columbia University, is
the author of *Canarsie: The Jews and Italians of
Brooklyn Against Liberalism.* He is currently writing a
book on moral argument in American politics.

Sociologist Jonathan Rieder's aim is not to deliver another report on the August 1991 events in the Crown Heights section of Brooklyn, but to "identify larger interpretive problems in understanding antisemitism." Rieder offers a second perspective of antisemitism among American blacks, in the larger context of black-Jewish relations, to Gary Rubin's "How Should We Think About Black Antisemitism?" (chapter 7 in this volume). His analysis focuses on two areas, one methodological, the other highly practical.

As we have seen in a number of the essays in this book, the natural vigilance of the Jewish community with respect to antisemitism has translated the methods of social science used in measuring and monitoring antisemitism and other forms of racist bias. But, according to Jonathan Rieder, there are some aspects of black-Jewish relations—including antisemitism in the black community—that do not emerge from the use of the standard methodology. The other way in which we "know" antisemitism, he reminds us, is through "flamboyant rituals," occasionally virulent in nature, that move the Jewish community to higher levels of vigilance.

In practical terms—Rieder uses Crown Heights as paradigmatic—certain dramatic, indeed awful, occurrences will distract from and mask the complexities of the issue of black antisemitism. As Rieder observed in a 1995 interview, "Fashioning the events of Crown Heights into a 'pogrom' tells us little about the dynamics of the issues that caused the Crown

Heights events, and less about a crucial question: Could Crown Heights happen elsewhere?"

Rieder analyzes the elements of "class warfare" and "tribal rivalries" that inhered in the Crown Heights community, as well as a fundamental black-white conflict all too often expressed in the idiom of antisemitism but reflecting larger realties. How quickly, asks Rieder, can antiwhite feelings alchemize into anti-Korean, anti-Jewish, anti-anything expression? Further, intracommunal conflict, within communities and among members of discrete groups, needs to be examined in order to obtain a complete picture of racism, bias, and bigotry, including antisemitism. Implicit in Rieder's essay is the necessity for conducting a series of detailed ethnographic studies on the street.

J.A.C.

A ONCE-GRAND ALLIANCE: PARIAH PEOPLES
IN THE HOUSE OF BONDAGE

Blacks and Jews have been scuffling now for more than a generation. There likely is no more vivid symbol of this wrangling than the rampage of blacks against Jews that convulsed the Brooklyn neighborhood of Crown Heights for three days in 1991. One Jewish resident was full of bitter perplexity as he sought to make sense of the madness on the streets. He had always admired what he deemed the "moral courage" of African Americans, and he could not help but think back to his efforts in high school on behalf of integration, his earnest talk of racial brotherhood. The contrast with those moments in the early 1960s was striking. "What has happened to black people? Why will no black leaders condemn these black Nazis, the black Ku Klux Klan?"[1] As his lament indicates, efforts to get a fix on this tension, especially within the organized Jewish community, have often invoked as the baseline of measurement a high point of black-Jewish alliance that was pronounced in the early phases of the civil rights movement.

This narrative line, of sad devolution from a glorious past, captures many of the critical features of the changed relationship between blacks and Jews. Surely it would be a mistake, in cynical recoil from current abrasions, to minimize the genuineness of the mutual sympathy that punctuated the civil rights movement. The primacy of the Exodus narrative in both peoples' lives symbolizes the unity of experience that enabled Jews and blacks to glimpse some irreducible aspect of shared humanity across the bridge of their differences. Paying homage to the African-American identification with Israelites in the house of bondage that runs from slavery down through the civil rights movement, Martin Luther King Jr. made himself Moses in that final, haunted speech in Memphis, the night before James Earl Ray's bullet claimed him: "And He's allowed me to go up to the mountain. And I've looked over. And I've seen the promised land." Constantly, the churched part of the movement asked, in small churches and big ones, throughout the South: "Did not my Lord save Daniel in the lion's den, and the Hebrew children in the fiery furnace? And why not every man?" On the Jewish side, the imaginative reexperience of Jewish slavery was invoked to enhance the universalist import of the "as thyself" in the commandment "Thou shalt love the stranger as thyself, for ye were strangers in the land of Egypt." Thus does the memory of Egyptian bondage at once encourage empathy for all vulnerable people and a broad conception of rights. In Leo Baeck's rendering, the biblical imperative "Ye shall have one manner of law; the stranger shall be as one of your own country" aims "to protect the stranger, for the injustice done to him who can appeal only to the rights of man is an injustice done to all humanity."[2]

Against the risk of cynicism, there is the equal danger that we cling to a romance that sentimentalizes the old alliance and exaggerates current dilemmas. From the beginning, the alliance engaged some blacks and certain Jews more than others. There always were plenty of blacks who knew Jews mainly in inauspiciously unequal circumstances—as their landlords, shopkeepers, social workers, teachers, creditors—that did not make for happy relations. How many unlettered residents of the Northern ghettos or the Southern black belt knew about Abraham Cahan and Abraham Joshua Heschel? Nor did Talmudic injunctions to welcome strangers ever encompass the totality of Jewish sensibility; ethnocentric, tribal, and provincial sentiments have always been part of Jewish life too. Not all Jews were saintly "mensches." At the height of the civil rights movement, there were Jews who looked upon the affairs of "goyim" with indifference, if not distaste. There were also Jews who talked about *"shvartzes,"* and worse. To improvise only slightly on Milton Himmelfarb's old adage, Jews have incomes like Episcopalians but vote like Puerto Ricans; Jewish liberalism mainly meant that, all things being equal— "dollar for dollar and year of education for year of education"— Jews were more liberal than other groups.[3]

Meanwhile, the alliance was not a single, indivisible affair. An interorganizational network linked black and Jewish ethnic, political, labor, and religious leaders in concrete acts of litigation, social-movement participation, moral suasion, legislation, and lobbying. Within that network, the liberalism was expansive, not only ideologically but also in a more intimate fashion. It was fortified by face-to-face relationships, by the lived history of shared battles, and by institutional commitments. Even here, as Freedom Summer made so palpable, relationships of helping, when the partners were not precisely equals, invited paternalism, self-congratulation, and resentment.

The more diffuse sympathy of ordinary Jews for the civil rights movement was based on empathy for another pariah people. Dismantling a racist, antidemocratic caste system spoke to the primacy of deliverance in a poignant manner. The identities of oppressed and oppressor, victim and victimizer, possessed moral clarity; the same clarity characterized the cherished language of rights and the sacred texts of Declaration and Constitution that sustained the struggle for democratic inclusion. When the axis of racial debate shifted, the old clarities dimmed, as did the constancy of Jewish support.

The high point of mutuality was never a relationship of symbiotic merger, in which each party lacked its own separate interests, or of unconditional love. To some extent, Jewish nobility nicely coincided with Jewish self-interest. At least in one rendering, Jews support rights for others for reasons of nervous self-protection, hoping, as they say, that what goes around—in this case rights—will come around. Jesse Jackson, thinking perhaps of those amicus briefs which some Jewish organizations entered in the *Bakke* case, delivered one version of this calculus of concern: "When there wasn't much decency in society, many Jews were willing to share decency. The conflict began when we started our quest for power. Jews were willing to share decency, not power." Jackson may have been too cynical in this deflation of Jewish high-mindedness, but he captured at least a partial truth not so different from the one in another of Himmelfarb's aphorisms: Jewish liberalism was that brand of Jewish particularism that likes to call itself universalism.

With the shift from relatively painless issues of rights to trickier ones of class, of remedies for the economic and psychic injuries of the poor, and of distributing scarcity, blacks and Jews found themselves in disagreement. This dispute never turned only on avarice; in the case of quotas, it also activated rival conceptions of justice. The emergence of a strain of "Middle American" reaction among lower-middle-class Jews, fueled by complaints about quotas, welfare, scatter-site public housing, crime, and busing, added to racial abrasion.[4] The rise of black nationalism, and the pan-African identification with Palestinian people of color, further divided the two peoples. The broad rubric of "black-Jewish conflict," always overdetermined, conflates these disparate elements.

This reminder of the inescapable social conditions that underwrote liberal sympathy, and then eroded it, highlights the limits of moralism in understanding black-Jewish conflict. One cannot escape here the legacy of Jewish exceptionalism, the expectancies from within and outside the Jewish community, that hold Jews to rigorous, some would say extravagant, moral standards. This exceptionalism disables clear thinking among blacks and Jews alike. Among Jews, to consider only one of its many afflictions, moralism can make for self-righteous, hypocritical exaggerations, as in the complaint of an Orthodox Brooklyn rabbi, whose expansive "we" legitimated a capacious resentment by allowing him, and the vast majority of his fellow congregants, to free-ride on the heroic efforts and liberal universalism of primarily secular and reform Jews in the movement. "Here we were, Jews marching for civil rights, really gung ho, marching along in Selma, Alabama, but it came to the public schools and it became, 'Get out of my community, I want your job.'"

And for blacks, moralism can take the form of disappointment, and a focus on Jewish defections, even though Jews on average support affirmative action and vote for black mayoral candidates at higher rates than other white ethnic groups, and whites as a whole.

The unraveling of the alliance can be charted in at least two separate ways. First, there is a long and august tradition of social survey research, in part the result of the Jewish community's efforts to scan the environment for hints of antisemitic, populist-conservative, and antidemocratic movements that might threaten Jewish interests and survival. "Never again!" oddly enough found expression in the form of secular social science.

Yet black-Jewish tensions have burst into public consciousness in a less abstracted fashion, in flamboyant public spectacles that claim our attention and conscience. The history of black-Jewish relations is filled with such charged dramaturgies: the Ocean Hill–Brownsville school struggles of 1968, the *Bakke* litigation, the Andrew Young affair, Jesse Jackson's "Hymie-Town," Farrakhan's attack on the "gutter religion" of Judaism, and most recently Crown Heights. In these moments, low-grade, routine ethnic tensions, which are fully compatible with a state of tense but regulated competition, tend to give way to unstable pluralism and explicit vendetta.

My focus here will be on Crown Heights. Despite the many idiosyncratic elements in that situation, Crown Heights commands attention on a number of scores. Substantively, it was, if not the utterly worst moment, then arguably one of the worst moments of antisemitic violence in the United States. It disclosed the power of a street version of black nationalism which, beyond the Crown Heights case, continues to bedevil the Jewish community, most dramatically in the form of Louis Farrakhan and the Nation of Islam. Finally, like these other episodes, Crown Heights offers interpretive opportunities as well as moral disappointment.

If much can be gleaned from survey data, survey discourse is a limited, artificial genre of talk which tends to capture selective zones of opinion and is subject to interpretive errors. By contrast, these more volatile moments of conflict, although vulnerable to distortions of their own, have the benefit of a certain "naturalness." They strip away the facade of politesse and other barriers to perception and observation, laying bare that backstage of ethnic sentiment that is veiled in everyday life. They reveal historically situated actors, grappling with real-life situations in all their concreteness, and thus mobilizing what is often deeper, more heartfelt, if vulgar kinds of feeling, metaphor, and belief.

Still, we need to proceed cautiously. Whatever special opportunities are to be had in probing the meaning of such ritual spectacles, they generate other obstacles to understanding. The first involves the organized character of the Jewish community, the existence of machinery for monitoring the environment for threats. On the one hand, vigilance can become hypervigilance, producing an overreactivity to dangers.

Furthermore, the penchant for study generates symposia along the lines of "Whither Black-Jewish Relations?"; beneficial as they often are, such convocations may at times devolve into a ritualized genre which, in tacit coordination with equally stylzed African-American rejoinders, produces baroque dramas full of earnest Jewish confessions of a desire to recapture mutuality, black warnings that the time is at hand to "reevaluate" the black-Jewish relationship, Jewish demands that blacks atone and apologize and repudiate, black displays of autonomy from the white man that elicit reflexive "say-ons" and "right-ons" of appreciation, and Judeocentric cries of "Never again!" The problem here is that all this distraction makes it even more difficult to find the proper point of response to antisemitism, which lies somewhere between overreactive tetchiness and masochistic silence or nonchalant denial.

The more critical problem involves what social scientists have deemed the "availability heuristic," which refers to the ad hoc rules people use to make decisions under conditions of uncertainty, their tendency to rely on vivid events as clues to the meaning of things. Ordinary citizens, no less than social scientists, spend a good deal of their time scanning the social landscape, seeking to read the intentions and characters of other ethnic, racial, political, and class groupings. But they do so with less than perfect information, often across the distorting distance of economic and social as well as racial and ethnic difference. As a result, there is a tendency to fall back on these "available" incidents.

Unfortunately, available often means flamboyantly available, and rare to boot, all of which enhances the chance of misreading.

In a case like Crown Heights, the potential for misreading events was vast. After all, the "available" included "pogrom"-like acts of antisemitism, and the most proximate audience for those signs included many people who were primed to detect the repetition of an ancient pattern of Jewish victimization. As we shall see, however, the Crown Heights situation and context were a good deal messier than these timeless metaphors admit.

"HITLER SHOULD HAVE FINISHED THE JOB": KRISTALLNACHT IN BROOKLYN

At first glance, Crown Heights would seem to be an odd setting for a ritual explosion of ethnic violence and recrimination. Depending how you draw the boundaries, the community is a mixed neighborhood of more than one hundred thousand Caribbean blacks (the vast majority of the neighborhood, including many Jamaicans, Trinidadians, Haitians, and Guyanese), African Americans, and Jews, mainly from the Lubavitcher Hasidic sect. From one vantage point, Crown Heights can be seen as the successful realization of multicultural community.

After all, unlike affluent Jews who left the polyglot city for suburban sanctuaries, the Jews who remained live commingled with people of color. Nor did they flee south and west to onetime white urban enclaves like Canarsie and Borough Park, as did many of their Jewish neighbors. Moreover, unlike assimilated Jews, they declare their difference with gusto; in violation of the bland pieties of one version of civil religion, they wear their difference proudly on their sleeve. And so do many of their black neighbors.

Both peoples thus pose righteous questions like what is the place of communal difference and how should tribal people live it in the public life of American pluralism? And through their daily practice, they suggest at least one answer. In place of the bland indistinction of the melting pot, we find a bright palette of ethnic coloration: Jamaican dreadlocks and Jewish *payess*, West Indian Carnival and Jewish High Holy Day celebrations, calypso and klezmer.

This was the setting for what began with a tragic automobile accident, or so it appeared. A car in a motorcade of the grand rabbi—the "rebbe"—Menachem Schneerson of the Lubavitcher sect struck and killed a seven-year-old black boy, Gavin Cato, the son of Guyanese immigrants. But in racially charged Brooklyn, one person's accident is another person's racial intentionality, even conspiracy. Almost immediately a menacing crowd began to pummel and rob the Jewish driver; rumors spread that the private Hasidic ambulance had sped away without attending to the dying Cato boy. Within hours, a mob chanting "Kill the Jews" ran down Yankel Rosenbaum, a visiting Hasidic scholar from Australia, and one of its members plunged a knife into him. He died in King's County Hospital a few hours later. An antisemitic rampage shook the community for the next three days.

For many members of the Jewish community, Crown Heights was as pure a form of black antisemitism as one could find. The temptation to press the wild events into familiar narrative frames seemed natural, perhaps irresistible. Many Holocaust survivors reside among the Lubavitchers, and they especially, but not exclusively, relived a painful history. As Rabbi Shmuel Butman, one of the grand rebbe's spokesmen, told me, "We had hoped that pogroms would remain only in history books. This is not Poland in 1881! It's the United States in 1991." Yankel Rosenbaum's father, Butman noted elsewhere, "survived the Nazi concentration camps. Yankel, unfortunately, did not survive the streets of the city of New York." Former Mayor Ed Koch observed, "Not since the last pogrom in Poland in 1946 has the Western world witnessed such an event."[5]

More than a projective reading of history or some putative affliction of "Jewish paranoia" gave rise to the cries of "pogrom," "black Nazis," and "Kristallnacht." The man accused of plunging the knife into Yankel Rosenbaum held a grudge against his Jewish landlord and recently had retaliated with Star of David graffiti in the building's lobby. Black crowds gathered across from the grand rabbi's headquarters chanted, "Hitler should have finished the job." The mob, moving up President Street, systematically sought out Jewish homes, smashing windows and hurling firebombs. One resident I interviewed spotted a preteen informer among them, whose street knowledge helped identify Jewish homes where mezuzahs didn't quite do the trick. On Rosh

Hashanah, a bullet flew through the window of a synagogue. The Lubavitcher conviction that Mayor David Dinkins intentionally held back the police force reinforced this sense of "the abandonment of the Jews."

These resonant metaphors capture undeniable aspects of the conflict, especially as Jewish residents themselves felt the terror. They evoke timeless aspects of Jewish experience, above all the primal sense of physical vulnerability created by unchecked thuggery. These immemorial anxieties about safety were reinforced by the seeming inability—or, worse still, the unwillingness—of the state to protect them from "Cossack" hooligans. Finally, street-level activists with reputations for attitudes inimical to Jewish interests and sensibilities, as well as in some cases for explicit antisemitism, entered the scene and inflamed the local situation.

And yet the resonance of the metaphors and their capacity to evoke powerful collective memories carry with them the danger of clouding the complexity of what in truth was a multileveled reality. As the Korean grocers who took up automatic weaponry to protect themselves when the police could not during the Los Angeles rioting surely know, Jews have hardly been the only targets of black ghetto violence in recent years.

Closer to home, only one year earlier some of the same activists who appeared in Crown Heights were locked in an ugly, ethnocentric struggle with Korean grocers in East Flatbush, just a mile south down Flatbush Avenue. There too, Korean merchants, and the Korean community more broadly, decried the failure of an African-American mayor, and his police force, to protect them and move against the forces of street-level black power.

Moreover, Mayor Dinkins counted many Jews among his advisers and personal friends, had taken political risks to stand against black antisemitism, and was a longtime supporter of Israel. There was a less personalistic and malevolent explanation for the strange abdication that turned the community over to the rioters: an incredibly hands-off mayor, with a well-known predilection for delegating, and an even more eerily distracted police chief.

These considerations only broach the subject of the countless features of Crown Heights that do not fall neatly into the narrative frame of black-Jewish conflict. As we go on to examine some of the anomalies that radically qualify the stark imagery of *War Against the Jews*, we shall see that the swirl of events there cannot be contained in the narrow confines of black antisemitism; elements of ethnic, tribal, racial, and class conflict were all at play.

Moreover, the disturbing strain of black folk hostility to the Jews that was evident on the streets comprised a specialized dimension within the whole event, and even the meaning of that hostility was not entirely unambiguous. Although the distinctive preoccupations of vernacular black nationalism among street-level leaders have often been directed at the Jewish community, grassroots activists did not rely on a coherent antisemitic ideology. Antisemitism flowed into more general antiwhite and even anti-Asian sentiment. In discussing these complexities of the conflict, my aim is not to give a systematic accounting of the Crown Heights conflict so much as to identify certain interpretive problems in understanding antisemitism.

THE AMBIGUITY OF "BLACKNESS"

The most elemental interpretive dilemma involved classifying the nature of the conflict and coding the motives behind it. The metaphors of pogrom and Kristallnacht favor a master frame of War Against the Jews. Yet putting the rampage in a broader context of black and Jewish grievances in Crown Heights suggests other dimensions, such as black-white, class warfare, and tribal rivalry, that were operative as well. No single rubric exhausts the explanation of the multiple and shifting lines of contention.

At the most obvious level, the driver of the car that killed Gavin Cato was not just white, or even Jewish, but a Hasidic Jew from the Lubavitcher sect. Many of the Hasidim felt neglected by established Jewish organizations, which they claimed spoke to more "refined" and assimilated secular, Reform and Conservative Jews. Seen in this light, the Lubavitchers were an "embarrassment" to the pieties of civil religion.

The Cato boy, meanwhile, was not simply "black" but the son of Guyanese immigrants, while many of the notorious activists who entered the fray were African-American. The "black" part of the Crown Heights neighborhood is differentiated by class, ethnicity, nationality, and lifestyle. The spread of diversity ranges from welfare mothers to black home-owning professionals to Jamaican drug posses, with the majority falling in the category of modest working people.

Countless black residents decried the "gangsters" who temporarily gained control of the streets, drawing a moral line between the rioters' distasteful nihilism and the civility of the respectable classes. Many West Indians blamed the rioting on African Americans, and a number of Barbadians insisted to me that the West Indian culprits among them were mainly Jamaican young men; in both cases, the argument, sometimes tacit, often explicit, was that unrepresentative hoodlums threatened, through a process of collective liability, to besmirch West Indians and strip them of their moral aura.

Nor was there even agreement on the nature of the initial event which triggered the violence. All across Brooklyn, and New York City, citizens held heated debates on the legal, moral, and factual issues at hand. One subway conversation, retold to me by one of its participants, epitomized the diverse points of view. A Jamaican woman insisted that Jews had murdered a black boy and white police had refused to arrest him. A Saint Vincentian woman argued back that there was an important difference between an accident and murder, and this clearly fell under the heading of an accident. An African-American woman jumped in. Her son was killed by a car driven by a black man, and he wasn't indicted either. She wanted revenge, but understood this was not the way of the law. The Jamaican argued that this was just what whites had done to blacks in Jamaica for a long time. To some extent, this was a fight not just about facts, but about preferred stories; how to construe history, to explain affliction, to fashion identity. And in this heated zone of narrative contention, there was no unified "black" community posed against "Jews."

In the Borough of Brooklyn more broadly, African Americans and Afro-Caribbeans do not merge in one neat pan-African "black" community based on negritude. These divisions intensified during Crown Heights, as African-American activists sought to build a following along the lines of black power. In truth, African Americans and West Indians have been vying for preeminence in the borough, and power has been shifting toward the Afro-Caribbean contingent.

But neither is there some unified pan-Caribbean unity either. Underneath the facade of solidarity in the annual West Indian Day parade lies the reality of tension between the Jamaicans and southern Caribbeans from Barbados, Trinidad, and Grenada, encoded as the struggle between steel band calypso and reggae. Some West Indians, seeking to create social and moral distance from African Americans, decry "blacks," by which they intend to refer, often perjoratively, to the latter, and whom they often rebuke for shiftlessness and criminality.

The identity of the West Indians is complicated, and can include a good measure of code switching; a West Indian proud of being Trinidadian may shift from his island identity to a more West Indian one, and then again, under the impress of a generalized white racism that does not always discriminate between "kinds" of blacks, a "black" identity. "Blackness" is hardly an immutable, obvious, or essential category of human experience and perception.

These ambiguities of race and ethnicity were played out in the ethnic and ideological divisions that emerged among the various elites which sought to gain interpretive and political control of the Crown Heights incident. The entry into the fray of African-American activists like Alton Maddox, Al Sharpton, Sonny Carson, Herbert Daughtry, and C. Vernon Mason quickly disclosed the cleavages between these activists and the Afro-Caribbean leadership. From the beginning in Crown Heights there were rumbles of resentment over the African-American putsch of a West Indian community, which repeated aspects of the black boycott of a Korean grocer one year previously. In that situation, African-American activists to some extent held a Caribbean neighborhood hostage with their street demonstrations. Even the angriest Jamaican youths did not line up behind the American activists. Sonny Carson's awkward effort at the Cato boy's funeral to unfurl a Guyanese flag betrayed his own version of eating bagels and cannoli on Election Day as he sought to bridge the intrablack cleavage.

These ethnic tensions exploded in the back-and-forth discussion over issues such as whether the West Indian Day parade should have proceeded as usual after the riots, and the desirability of dialogue with the Hasidim. Sonny Carson, insisting he would fight oppression in Crown Heights "by any means necessary," repudiated the parade as an affront to the political struggle. "It was a shame before God that [2 million] people had the audacity to party ... where the [Cato] boy was killed." The Reverend Herbert Daughtry apparently criticized "grinning and skinning" at Carnival.

The Caribbean community struck back hard in the *New York Carib News*. Where did African-American activists get the nerve "to tell the Caribbean community ... how best to conduct struggles for justice"? Conjuring up derogatory images of "Black Sambo," comments about partying and grinning were taken as ethnic slights that revealed the African Americans' "disrespect" for West Indian culture, and in Brooklyn one does not "dis" ethnic heritage lightly. The paper cited one West Indian leader who replied that Caribbean people are not just "party people. . . . We do not just 'grin and skin.' . . . We are a serious people."[6] Meanwhile, Carlos Lezama, the Trinidadian-American head of the parade association, generously invited the Lubavitchers to march at the head of the parade with him. In contrast to Daughtry's inability to fathom the warm reception accorded the rabbis by the established black leadership, prominent Caribbean leaders as well as many African-American elected officials affirmed the healing of Hasidic-black dialogue.

THE AMBIGUITY OF FOLK ANTISEMITISM:
"KILL THE JEW CAUCASIAN"

There is a world of obvious difference between the abrasions of ethnic competition that unfolds in a context of managed, if tense, pluralism and the utter breakdown of pluralism that emerged in the rampaging mobs that took over the streets of Crown Heights. Once you begin to separate out the various strands of black-Jewish conflict in Crown Heights, the murderous passion of the mob that hunted down Yankel Rosenbaum comes to the fore. Especially in the context of an apparently indifferent police response, the threat to the physical security of the Jews was the most frightening aspect of the Crown Heights affair.

Neither the fear of street crime nor the dangerous classes that most often perform it were new developments for Brooklyn Jewry. But the ad hoc, spontaneous character of street crime can hardly be compared to the systematic firebombing of Jewish homes, of organized mobs screaming "Kill the Jews," of a coordinated effort among a shadowy network to intimidate, harm, and drive Jews from the neighborhood. There was persuasive evidence for the reading of the conflict as "War Against the Jews." A Jewish family who lived in the same apartment building as the Cato family found a swastika on the door with a clear warning to "leave now." One month after the car accident, a state of virtual terror prevailed near the Cato home. A black man put his face into a baby carriage and told the Jewish mother, "We're going to burn you Jews out of here if you don't get out. Leave now." One Lubavitcher leader told me how he was accosted by a man who screamed, "I'm going to get my gun and shoot one of you motherfucking Jews. I'm going to put a bullet through those glasses on your head."

In reaching for some high-minded, Olympian distance, widened further by a sociological preference for irony and complexity, then, we do not want to sanitize the ugliness of racial violence in Crown Heights, simply absorbing it in the inoffensive rubric of "ethnic competition." But we do need to circumscribe it if we are to avoid falling victim to the distorting temptations of the availability heuristic. The ferocity of the violence naturally fixated attention but by itself does not clarify the relation between the part and the whole, the hundreds of rioters in the streets and the hundreds of thousands of African American and West Indian blacks who live in Crown Heights and nearby neighborhoods like Bedford-Stuyvesant, Flatbush, Brownsville, Bushwick, East Flatbush, and Williamsburg. The representativeness of the rioters remains in question.

Indeed, it is still possible to view Crown Heights as an example of relatively successful coexistence, and even integration; on many blocks, Lubavitchers, African Americans, and Afro-Caribbeans live sprinkled among one another, and in peace. Countless dignified West Indian pluralists, who had their political and cultural quarrels with the Hasidim, did not succumb to ethnocentrism and thuggery. They were as much at odds with the rudeboys as were the Jews. Gavin Cato reportedly played with Jewish children on his block.

After the riots, many black residents went out of their way, through compensatory smiles and waves, to affirm sympathetic feelings and distance themselves from the rioters. Others were more direct in telling Jewish neighbors of their anger that hoodlums had made a fuss over an accident. A Haitian cabdriver, feeling great empathy for the plight of the Lubavitchers, detected the Jewish wariness at his approach. "As I get close, I can tell, the Jews are thinking, 'What's he going to do to me? Is he one of the guys who broke my windows?'"

If the violent thuggery was not just aberrant or sporadic, it was a specialized phenomenon within the totality of the Crown Heights affair. Crown Heights is not an impermeable enclave; Lemrick Nelson, the youth accused of stabbing Yankel Rosenbaum, lived in East Flatbush. In a heavily Caribbean community, a disproportionate number of the rioters were African-American youth, many of whom came streaming into the community from nearby housing projects as rumors of the accident and the ensuing disturbances spread. In addition, in a significant departure, West Indian youth joined their African-American brothers.

In an insightful piece in the *Village Voice*, Peter Noel captured the Jamaican presence in the violence, quoting one street orator: "We ah go bu'n [burn] dem devils, Rasta. We want justice. We nah want nonna dem marchin bizness. . . . Night time ah de right time. We ah fe dead fe justice! Dead."[7] Caribbean participation went beyond the Jamaicans, and drew as well third-generation Trinidadians, Haitians, Guyanese, and still other ethnicities.

Traditionally, the Caribbean community has abjured resentment politics and American-style black separatism, although racial succession has often been charged with intense passions; in Flatbush during the 1980s, Maurice Gumbs campaigned in calypso joints against State Senator Marty Markowitz, the incumbent in a predominantly black community, on the slogan "Massa Day Done." But among younger second- and third-generation West Indians, a more diverse pattern is emerging, with lower-status Caribbeans with less opportunity to be mobile adopting a more general "black," racialized identity while more upwardly mobile

Caribbeans hew to their island or West Indian identity and separate themselves forcefully from American blacks.

Many West Indian parents voice alarm at the way the seductions of the streets conspire with the decline of island social control to entrance their children. As Philip Kaznitz, author of *Caribbean New York,* astutely observes: "Many Caribbean parents are shocked at what their children are becoming or—as they see it—what being black has done to their children. 'You're becoming Americans,' they scold."[8]

As a result, complex permutations open up. Plenty of West Indian youth, as well as African-American ghetto kids, ape the Johnny-too-bad style of the Jamaican posses, dreadlocks and all. The cultural messages that flow through the networks linking the slums of Kingston, Jamaica, and Little Kingston, as the Jamaican section of Crown Heights is known, branch out in America to reach a wider circle of black audiences. The ethos of the Jamaican rudeboy bears a powerful equivalence to the African-American cult of the badass, or "Bad Nigger"; both embody an ethos of defiant masculinity at odds with Mayor David Dinkins's aura of decorous respectability. When Dinkins offered a crowd outside the Cato house his plea for peace, he was met with a fusillade of bottles and the cries of "Traitor" and "The mayor's not safe." These sentiments reflect an alienation that might expand the market for resentment politics among West Indians, although the predominant models remain ones of ethnic competition and pluralism, even when mixed with more than a tinge of black power and pride.

But even if we narrow the frame of "War Against the Jews" down to a distinctive element within the totality of black-Jewish relations in Crown Heights, identifying the social networks of vengeful reaction does not resolve the matter of the meanings of the racist mob. The more vital area of complexity remains the question of how to interpret its "antisemitism." The problem is that we often construe ethnic slurs against a communicative baseline not of the folk usages within the community of the speakers but of some abstracted universalist standard of genteel manners. In the process, we do not comprehend the meaning of the words for the users of the idiom.

The debate on the meaning of "Hymie-Town" (a term used by

Jesse Jackson at the time of the 1984 Democratic presidential primaries in the course of a chat with two black reporters) epitomizes such interpretive dilemmas. For some commentators, "Hymie" was a presumptively antisemitic phrase. Many of Jesse Jackson's colleagues in the campaign denied its status as a slur, and Jackson himself enfolded it under the heading of "noninsulting, colloquial language." In a more elaborate variant of this rendering, "Hymie" adhered to the rules of a specific genre of black folklore. Jackson's campaign aide Gene Wheeler, who grew up with Jackson, defined this style of ethnic naming and banter which Jackson thoroughly enjoyed:

> He has words for everybody . . . blacks, everybody. It's a tradition that people in our community call people by nicknames. . . . Hymie? It's a derivative of Mr. Hyman. . . . We had black characters we'd name Moz and Mozetta, that was any black person who was acting a certain way. . . . We'd be in a neighborhood, riding in a car and see someone and say, "Oh boy, Moz is on his way somewhere" . . . or a guy trying to jive talk us out of something, we'd say, "OK, come on Moz, give it up.". . . . We could use it in both a positive and negative way.[9]

In this counterreading, the rule Jackson broke was not the taboo on racism but that on vulgar banter, and the politesse that keeps such talk out of public hearing. This was the gist of Jackson's defense in his apology at the Democratic National Convention—perhaps he was guilty of an error of "tone" or "taste."

The phrases "goyim" or *"shvartzes"* carry a similar plurality—and thus ambiguity—of meanings. Depending on tone, circumstance, and intention, the latter may intend to demean an entire group of people, function denotatively as a way to mark blacks, impugn the less respectable members of the larger ethnic group in question, or declare the speakers' membership in a certain *"prost,"* or unrefined Yiddishkeit rhetorical community. Given black reaction to the phrase, the usage may signal insensitivity to others, but that is another way of describing belonging to a rival, less genteel moral world and the backstage linguistic norms which prevail there. Al Vorspan captured the dominion of the generic form of sotto voce "schmoozing" which governs Jewish performance of the term "*shvartze*":

> I can recall . . . a thousand conversations . . . that I regard as parallel [with Hymie]. Happens to me every day, as a matter of fact. In which someone from the Jewish community will hear me talking about race relations, or black-Jewish relations, or whatever it is I'm talking about and will say to me, not up on a platform, very off-the-record, just kind of schmoozing around, something about—"Well, you know the *shvartzes*" . . . or "you know how the *shvartzes* are."[10]

Analogously, perhaps "Hymie" was *prost* more than racist, and the invitation Jackson issued to begin the conversation in which "Hymie" was uttered, "Let's talk black talk," marked the talk as a kind of Afro-schmoozing, or "brother talk."

The larger point is that to carry on about "the Jews" or "the goyim," "the *shvartzes*" or "Hymie," may or may not have racist connotations. In New York City, as in many other tribal places, people do not see themselves simply as abstract Americans or lonely individuals; they identify with specific ethnocultural groupings, and the clustered nature of their social networks is reflected linguistically in a tendency to sort people into ethnic tribes. The nature of group difference, and group interest, is taken for granted. When Mayor Koch, on the eve of the 1988 New York Democratic presidential primary, averred that "Jews would have to be crazy to vote for Jackson," he was operating with an equally corporatist sense of Jewish identity.

These complexities of the meaning of ethnic epithets are not confined to blacks and Jews. White ethnic working-class usage of racist insults is often characterized by a similar elusiveness. While some white ethnics in Brooklyn may speak delicately, separating blacks who are "refined" from lower-class blacks, others, less genteelly, who will say without embarrassment, "niggers" or "animals" or "black shit," may mean lower-class blacks; others really mean to convey dislike of an entire race. Their neighbors may mix the idioms of class, race, and ethnicity, as when they observe that the Barbadians and other "island people" are "producing people like we are," unlike the "lower black element."

One member of a squad of Italian-American boys I once studied, who was preparing to take vengeance on "the niggers," explained to me, "We only bother with the [black] ones that are like friends with us. But then there's always them fucking arrogant ones that ... if you don't kill them, they'll kill you." Depending on the context, "niggers" can mean "all black people" or it can mean the particular blacks uppermost in the boys' mind at the time and toward whom they feel hostility.

When we peer into provincial communities from the outside, we run the risk of missing such symbolic nuances.[11] As Dell Hymes has warned of these sociolinguistic dangers, the social scientist "must first be sure of reading signs that are there, not signs imagined to be there because of ignorance of communicative conventions. . . . There arises the problem of what may be called communicative interference-misinterpretation of the import of features of communication by reading another system in terms of one's own."[12]

At first glance, it might seem as if the import of "Kill the Jews" or "Hitler should have finished the job" is about as unproblematic as it gets, especially when compared to the more ambiguous zone of meaning occupied by Hymie and *shvartze*. And yet the folk meaning of "kill the Jews" is not quite as obvious as it appears. For the more provincial blacks in Crown Heights rubbing up against the reality of difference, some of whom know Jews only as the Hasidim nearby, "Jew" at times simply indicates the local tribal opponents. Similarly, taunting the Jews with Hitler may seem perverse, and it is hardly civil or gracious.

But when deciphering ethnic barbs without knowing the thick context of meaning which gives them form, it may not be clear if this usage reflects a formally antisemitic belief system or some version of "playing the dozen," that vernacular game of insult in which tribal opponents mock, denigrate, and insult one another. The Jewish quickness to respond sometimes makes Jews complicitous partners in the rhetorical games of black nationalist orators, who exploit that reactivity as a prop in dramaturgies that proclaim their fearless character, their verbal agility at getting under the white man's skin, and their resolve not to be cowed by anyone or anything. Khalid Abdul Muhammad has adeptly developed this genre, with his expert management of college audiences and the studied outrageousness of Jew-baiting neologisms like "Columbia Jewniversity" and "Jew York City."

Finally, for many in Crown Heights "Jews" simply denotes the most immediate incarnation of white people. One agitator cursed "The Jew Caucasians." Before a mob dragged journalist Jimmy Breslin from a taxi and savagely beat him, the cry went up, "White man, white man." Breslin's black rescuer explained, "It isn't just you. They hate all white people." After the grand jury failed to indict the Jewish driver, the sound of reggae blared on President Street, "Hunt down all the white men and murder them." As Cornel West has persuasively argued, black anti-semitism is in part "a species of anti-whitism. . . . The particular interactions of Jews and black people in the hierarchies of business and education cast Jews as the public face of oppression for the black community, and thus lend evidence to this mistaken view of Jews as any other white folk."[13]

Lubavitcher Jews, whose beards, black coats and *payess* made them visible icons of difference, were prime targets of attack. Their presence was sufficient to trigger violence. In one typical case, a black mob spotted a car with two Lubavitchers and started attacking it with rocks and concrete. As shards of glass flew through the air, one of the Jews cried, "Run them over, kill them!" And later, "Those animals were going to kill us. I didn't do anything to them!"

But rampaging youths did not reserve their wrath for Jews, or even Caucasians. They looted stores owned by Iranians and Koreans, and threatened black reporters. The indiscriminate nature of violent reprisal matches a broader pattern of reaction. Across the city, and the nation, certain constituencies among lower-class African Americans have turned their rage on a variety of targets, from the Central Park jogger to Asians.

As with black suspicion of official institutions of governance and criminal justice, we are dealing here with broader patterns of underclass violence, collective vengeance, and physical modes of dispute settlement that are widely diffused in the African-American lower-class community. Salvadorian and Mexican conduct during the Los Angeles riots, as well as the murderous violence the white ethnic mob in Bensonhurst launched against Yusuf Hawkins, attest that poor black youth hardly boast a monopoly on this style of response. Conflict between Crips and Bloods makes no less clear that African-American gang members, in defense of their loyal community of homeboys, just as often apply this vision of indiscriminate payback against other African Americans.

The death of Gavin Cato thus did not provoke or reveal a formal antisemitic belief system. Rather, it mobilized sentiments of ethnocentrism, violence, and mistrust that are general features of certain strains of lower-class black life and which happened to turn against physically proximate Jews. Jews in Crown Heights became the victims of an irony of ecology; the grand rebbe's command to the Lubavitchers to remain in Crown Heights, the instruction not to follow the white stampede to Borough Park and Canarsie and Long Island, entangled his followers in the class-based passions and grievances of a highly alienated sector of black youth.

VERNACULAR BLACK NATIONALISM: "I AM ANTIWHITE!"

Some of the same ambiguities in applying the antisemitic label at the folk level emerge as well when we consider the favored rhetoric of the grassroots activists who sought to give shape to the inchoate grievances and passions of the mob. Once again, we discover the primacy of the larger enemy, the speed with which Jew dissolved into a more generalized, usually white enemy.

It is true that many of the African-American leaders who emerged during the Crown Heights incident—Sonny Carson, Alton Maddox, Al Sharpton, C. Vernon Mason, and Herb Daughtry—had a history of involvement in conflicts with sectors of the Jewish community. Mason was the author of that famous jape against Dinkins, "He wears too many yarmulkes on his head." During the 1968 school wars in Brooklyn, Carson, then head of the local chapter of CORE, gained notoriety with his florid antisemitism. Reverend Daughtry had a history of ethnically provocative statements directed against Jews. At one of the early rallies of the Black United Front in 1978, which Daughtry organized to fight Jewish domination in Crown Heights, speakers decried the

Hasidim as "terrorists" and "oppressors" and Daughtry, calling for a black citizens' patrol, warned ominously, "When the people of the long black coats meet our men, let us see what will happen." At the Cato funeral, Sharpton decried "diamond merchants."

And yet we find here not the primacy of formal antisemitism or even anti-Jewish sentiment so much as more general features of vernacular black nationalism, above all the "species of anti-whitism" to which West has alluded. In truth, Sonny Carson's penchant for theatrical displays of outrageousness sometimes carried a larger truth, as during the first mayoral contest between Dinkins and Giuliani, when he rebuffed accusations of anti-semitism with the stark rejoinder that it was whites he did not like.

In Crown Heights, Carson's statement addressed the youthful warriors who had smashed Jewish windows and heads. "White Americans, Black Uncle Toms . . . call you hoodlums. We call you the children of Malcolm X." Beneath a picture of a black youth smashing a huge wooden pole through a police car windshield ran the exhortation to "The Heroes of Crown Heights Rebellion" to remember Soweto and Palestine.

In transmuting the Boyz 'n the Hood into the Intifada, his version of "You are somebody," Carson's idiom was more black nationalist, and even pan-Africanist, than antisemitic. During the black boycott of the Korean grocers, his rhetoric had also remained derivative Malcolm X. He cited the stock phrases: "We work for the liberation of our people by any means necessary." He invoked the old Malcolm X adage about white fear of a black man with a knife in the dark. He heralded the "savagery" of black men; he wants "to unshackle their balls," to save blacks from a civilizing process that will "make faggots of them," that will refine and "educate" the blackness and outrage out of them. And he told a crowd near the grocery store, "Get ready for the Day of Outrage against racism. All the hot days are ahead. Racism lives in this country. Black power. Black power. Let's kick their ass."

The imagery of racial victimization that emerged during the Crown Heights affair further suggests the primacy of the black-white axis for the African-American activists who sought to gain interpretive and political control over the Crown Heights affair.

Thus Al Sharpton sought to enfold the Caribbeans in the larger community of black affliction, bound together by the presence of racist white—and not notably Jewish—enemies. This made a certain sense. In Howard Beach, Queens, the wilding white wolf pack did not discriminate between American blacks and their Trinidadian prey, Michael Griffith, when they chased him out onto the Belt Parkway where he was struck and killed by a speeding car.

Speaking at the Cato funeral, Sharpton used the imagery of the black family's vulnerability to transmute an accident into racist design. As if the Cato boy were brother to the Scottsboro boys, Sharpton placed little Gavin in an Africentric family formed by the line of blacks destroyed by white malevolence, including the martyrs of the outer boroughs—Yusuf Hawkins, felled by a mob of Bensonhurst badasses, and Griffith, and the four girls blown up in a Birmingham church.

As Sharpton put it, "They"—meaning the crackers—"are killing our children." Mayor Dinkins, disdainfully rebuffed only recently by some militants as "Dinkinstein," sat alone in the church, but in a show of racial solidarity, Sharpton included him in the family: "These people don't like you no better than they like us." Sonny Carson outdid everyone, loonily invoking Jeffrey Dahmer's cannibalism. "Now they're eating us."

As the variousness of the "they" makes clear, charges that Jewish doctors are injecting black babies with AIDS or Leonard Jeffries' assertion of a Jewish Hollywood conspiracy to demean blacks comprise only Jewish-inflected variants of something more general: a vivid sense of the presence of malevolent forces. This perception appears in a range of sentiments, from suspicious to frankly conspiratorial, that pervade the black ghetto. The central strain in these laments is powerlessness, of vulnerable selves beseiged by overwhelming hostile forces.

The same blurred eclecticism of the category of enemies in vernacular black nationalist discourse, and the primary sense of desperate vulnerability which it conveys, were evident in the black boycott of the Korean grocers in East Flatbush one year before. Many of the same activists, most graphically Sonny Carson, were active in that movement. Instead of threats against Jewish enemies, anti-Asian imprecation, congealed in cries against yellow "gooks," exhorations not to "buy from people who don't look like you," and the anti–Pan Asian ethnocentrism of "You Chinese, Korean motherfucker, go back to your country," predominated. Around the time of the boycott, a black teenager smashed the skull of a Vietnamese Flatbush resident with a claw hammer, and his accomplices chanted, "Koreans go home."

And yet as in Crown Heights, the precise enemy on which attention alighted was volatile and shifting, and at least in activist discourse, kept collapsing into the broader rubric of enemies. As I wrote at the time,[14] from the jump-off point of the specific merchant's disrespect for sister Jiselaine, the Haitian customer accused of shoplifting, the activists' diatribes moved in a widening spiral: gliding from the emotive image of the abused, "disrespected" Haitian woman to a diffuse sense of abused, disrespected black people; dissolving the identity of the evil merchant-perpetrator in a generalized nefarious Korean and white "they"; and eliding the demand for justice for Jiselaine and the search for black power. Out on Church Avenue, one street orator rambled:

> Make sure these Korean racists leave our community for good. . . . Our tax monies are going to protect these racists who beat up our women. . . . Wake up, black people. It's time for black people to control their own community. . . . Other ethnic groups come into black communities and exploiting people, it's happening in Harlem, it's happening in Flatbush, in Crown Heights, everywhere there are black people. . . . We are saying, no more savage racists in our community. They are sucking out the people's sweat. . . . They paint us as savages, but they caused the destruction of the entire Indian race.

ETHNIC COMPETITION: HASIDIM AGAINST WEST INDIANS AND AFRICAN AMERICANS

For obvious reasons, Jewish concern and media coverage focused on the sensational events, leaders, and statements welling up from the streets of Crown Heights. Entranced by the "available" evidence, observers could easily miss the nuances I have been describing. But if we go even further, forget for the moment about the immediate violence and look at the long-term context of black-Lubavitcher abrasions, a rather more familiar black-Hasidic rivalry over residential, political, and cultural resources comes into focus. The rampage unfolded within the context of an institutionalized state of discord which had developed over decades. The multiplicity of the grievances again pays homage to the complexity of coding the causal motives at work.

Unlike other neighborhoods where white flight left housing vacancies for ethnic turnover, the Hasidic commitment to remain placed the precise outcome of succession, and the balance of ethnic and racial power that would characterize it, in doubt. Thus, despite the economically modest situation of most Lubavitchers, there has been an expanding line of Jewish settlement, fueled by the scarcity of space and the large size of Hasidic families, reaching further into the black community. Blacks at all class levels have sometimes reacted to a sense of "invasion," and black militants resorted to the imagery of West Bank expansion and Zionist land grab to appeal to it. That some Jews have been able to make cash purchases at top-of-the-market prices added to resentment.

Moreover, for dignified Caribbeans who have a virtually Anglophilic dislike of "rudeness," a request to buy their home is chutzpah. One man fumed, "They knocked on my door! And then they had the nerve to tell me, 'Why don't you sell, I have a need, my need is greater yours.' I told him, 'I don't want to sell. This is my homestead.' And they still came back! They see nothing wrong with this aggressiveness." The tensions arising from these solicitations reached such a point that then Mayor Koch warned, "This type of persistent and unwelcome solicitation of homeowners . . . constitutes a form of harassment that can only lead to increased tensions within the community."[15]

Blacks and Jews have also engaged in cultural struggles over respect for their secular and sacred ceremonial life. At the most informal level, West Indians complain about the lack of Hasidic street deportment, the tendency of the Lubavitchers to dispense with the ritual niceties that humanize anonymous interaction in public and allow strangers to negotiate public space. "They walk down the sidewalk seven strong, and push you into the gutter," one Trinidadian fumed. At one of the powwows to enhance ethnic understanding that followed the violence, Lubavitcher spokespeople explained that Hasidic brusqueness was often the result of hurrying to and from synagogue or absorption in Talmudic reflection, and was just as often directed at other Lubavitchers.

Such earnest efforts at "brotherhood" infuriated one Jew: "And now I am supposed to go explain myself to people who don't like me because I am different. Fuck you! We're *supposed* to be different. If you want to understand me, read the Bible. I should explain my Sukkot to you so you won't kill me?"

Black residents have complained as well about the ritual roping off of streets on Jewish holidays, which impedes their free mobility. In a number of cases, black drivers found Hasidic Jews banging on the hoods of their cars because they were in violation of Sabbath proscriptions. More formally, the fight for cultural respect and ceremonial honor has unfolded in Hasidic complaints about the parade route of the West Indian Day parade, which passes in front of the main Lubavitcher yeshiva on Eastern Parkway. The parade is a carnival of steel band music and exuberant celebration. The central symbolic expression of West Indian cultural and political pride and power, the parade draws almost one million people to Eastern Parkway. But Lubavitchers code the life-affirming humanism of West Indian culture as lasciviousness, and they are uncomfortable over the often scanty clothing and sensuous dancing, which offend Orthodox taboos on immodesty.

And so it has hurt and galled the West Indians that the Hasidim, who demand so much deference to their sacred life and affirm in public their ritual concerns, seem hostile to the expression of West Indian ceremony. Following only weeks on Gavin Cato's death, the Jews feared the potential for antisemitic violence. As a result, there were calls to reroute or suspend the parade. This act of ethnic insensitivity seemed to confirm all of the West Indian perceptions of Hasidic arrogance and insularity.

Finally, blacks and the Hasidim had long been entangled in a struggle for political preeminence. The Lubavitchers, exploiting the political power amplified by their cohesiveness and bloc voting, have successfully played the game of ethnic power in a fashion that would make the most fervent proponent of black nationalism proud. Some time ago, they managed to place the predominantly black Bedford-Stuyvesant portion of the old district north of Eastern Parkway beyond the borders of the current district, thereby concentrating Jewish power. They have been energetic in pursuit of public funds. Undoubtedly, blacks have exaggerated the extent of Jewish influence, and in any case it has been declining for some time. At the time of the conflict, the mayor was an African American, as were the police commissioner and the councilwoman representing Crown Heights, and the assemblyman was a Caribbean. Still, divested of their conspiratorial edge, black complaints of Jewish power were not just projective fantasy. Mayoral, gubernatorial, and world leaders and candidates have come to pay their respects to the grand rebbe.

That the Jewish community brings distinctive resources to the mobilizing game offers scant consolation to the black community. The interaction between the cohesive power of the Jewish community and the vulnerability of the black community during the Koch and Reagan years was not a felicitous one. It prompted the general black conviction that Jews had helped themselves to an unfair portion of political resources. But this alienation materialized as well in more specific plaints, such as that police pamper Lubavitchers on Jewish holidays by letting them violate parking regulations. For years before the accident, the grand rebbe's police guard (discontinued by Mayor Koch) had drawn black resentment as the embodiment of Jewish "special treatment." That guard resulted from threats not from the black community but from the Lubavitchers' fervent rivals in the Satmar sect of Hasidim. The visible presence of a police car in front of the rebbe's house had been a graphic reminder of what many blacks experienced as political inequality and favoritism.

And so the involvement of the rebbe's motorcade in the death of the Cato boy touched a raw nerve. The nerve was inflamed even more when the rumors flew that the police, arriving on the scene to find the Hasidic driver threatened by an angry black crowd, whisked the driver away, and furthermore, that a Jewish ambulance sped away without the Cato boy. The Hasidic high command vigorously disputed this as a "blood libel." Emergency Medical Service ambulances had appeared on the scene at virtually the same moment. The Jewish ambulance departed only after being assured that the Cato boy was being cared for. Moreover, the police and a black man, aware of the crowd of young blacks beating the passengers and driver of the Jewish car amid shouts of "Kill the Jews," told the Jewish ambulance attendents, "Go over there and get that man [the Jewish driver] out of here. They're going to kill him." But to those blacks who never heard or simply did not believe the Hasidic disavowal and who did not know of the police orders, the incident loomed as an instance of Jewish heartlessness, the lack of value placed on black life. The failure of a grand jury to indict the driver for vehicular homicide or manslaughter also intensified black feelings that the criminal justice system and political authority would not treat them with fairness.

Blacks thus did not take the measure of the incident in a vacuum, with no collective memories. They deciphered the incident in the light of their local history with Jews. They also brought to the incident the symbolic and perceptual baggage of their longer history, in the nation and in New York City, of suspicion of whites and establishment institutions of governance and police. During the Koch years, black mistrust of the police and courts was exacerbated by a series of police killings of black citizens. It may have been that the six police trying to subdue the psychotic, knife-brandishing black woman, Eleanor Bumpurs, were following procedure or reasonably feared for their lives when they fired a second shotgun blast and killed her. Perhaps they would have done the same thing if she were an old Italian or Jewish or Irish woman. When police officers used a choke hold on Michael Stewart, a young black man caught spraying graffiti, and he died, maybe an accident, incompetence, or class prejudice killed him. But in all these cases, and others, many blacks could with good reason glimpse a common threat, and they concluded that racism was the culprit.[16]

Such mistrustful readings of white intention have been evident in the belief of many black youths that the Central Park jogger was raped by her white boyfriend and that police were seeking to frame the allegedly wilding, easily demonized "homeboys," just as it was self-evident to vast numbers of blacks that the white Simi Valley jurors and the police officers they refused to convict in the beating of Rodney King were acting out of racist motivations.

As a result of such circumstances of skepticism about fair treatment from whites, the ambiguous specifics of the Cato accident, especially as distorted by demogogues, could easily trigger black indignation. If you were not schooled in the nuances of New York law on vehicular manslaughter, and believed the police favored the Lubavitchers, the failure to indict and arrest the Jewish driver might confirm your conviction that Jews get special treatment. Jews, by contrast, were genuinely puzzled at this mistrust over an accident that was horribly tragic but obviously inadvertent. The driver of the car that struck Gavin Cato had recently rescued two black children from a fire. A delegation of Jewish neighbors had gone to the Cato home to express their profound sorrow. The Lubavitchers lit a *yahrzeit* candle for the little boy. And Schneerson, although somewhat cryptic in his pronouncements, affirmed pluralism in a meeting with Mayor Dinkins, who told him, "You have blessed me in the past and your prayers have helped." The rebbe wished Dinkins well in his efforts to find peace, and when Dinkins said "both sides," Schneerson insisted, "We are not two sides. We are one side. We are one people living under one administration and under one God."

Meanwhile, stung by the apparent double standard and senseless vengeance, some Lubavitchers recalled a similar incident, but with the races of driver and victim reversed. Two years previously, a black driver without license, registration, or insurance had ran over and killed a young Hasidic child. Rabbi Butman asked me, "Did the Jewish community put 150 cops in the hospital? Did Jews vandalize African-American homes?" And as another Lubavitcher recalled, "The man was shaken, so the Jews brought him coffee. They acted like mensches."

We are confronting here the moral and perceptual chasm created by two groups with quite different readings of the same events. We cannot even say that one is rational, the other conspiratorial. Such a verdict assumes that rationality can only emerge from the detached point of view of the uninvolved, neutral observer, who can suspend subjectivity. Just as the Jews read the riots in the light of their own experience with terror, blacks read the rumored actions of the Jewish ambulance, the alleged reckless driving of the Jewish driver, and the grand jury refusal to indict in the light of theirs. In a sense, then, at least part of the explanation of the Crown Heights explosion can be found in the way an oddity of fate caught the Jewish community in the pervasive alienation of a segment of the black community from the criminal justice system, a witholding of legitimacy that has powerfully shaped perception and response across the nation.

"THE JEWISH COMMUNITY IS NOT ON CRACK": THE RISE OF JEWISH MIDDLE AMERICA

Overlapping these ethnic rivalries, and intensifying the general climate of mistrust between blacks and Jews, were a series of complaints that, on the Jewish side, invoked the conduct and behavior, not so much of blacks, but of the black poor, and on the black side, invoked Jewish racism and vigilantism. As one Lubavitcher leader put it in the local unvarnished style of talking, "The Jewish community works, the Jewish community is not on crack, the Jewish community does not have single-parent families." Many in the Lubavitcher community believed black complaints about Jewish power were the product of envy and resentment, symptoms of a larger black impulse to wallow in self-pity and blame others. One rabbi's critical parry—"So who's stopping you from organizing?"—contained the moral critique of blacks for "whining" instead of following the injunction "Do for yourself." It expressed a widespread belief, not confined to whites alone, that there is a tendency in black political culture to avoid collective responsibility. As one Bajun woman put it, although angry that police did not charge the Jewish driver, "Did the Jews make those black hoodlums take crack? What does looting sneakers and gold jewelry have to do with Gavin Cato's death?" Not long after the riots, Reverend Daughtry, appearing on the black radio station WLIB, conceded that the problem was not simply "the Jews." "What is it with us? We need to take a long hard look at . . . *our* own lethargy, *our* disillusionment with the system."

No matter how indelicately put, the rabbi's barb about crack speaks directly to the most passionate of all complaints about the black poor, the prevalence of crime. In the late 1980s, stable West Indian neighborhoods like Crown Heights and Flatbush, hardly in a league with dangerous neighborhoods like Bushwick and

Brownsville, were hit hard by the crack epidemic, and they have not been immune to the violence of drive-by shootings and the Jamaican drug gangs. But Jewish fears of black crime predate the crack epidemic. Over the years, members of the Hasidic community have recurrently been the victims of crime, and the perpetrators have almost always been blacks. There had been ethnically resonant episodes of murder, most notably the 1975 killing of an elderly Jew who managed to survive Nazi concentration camps but, traveling without money in deference to Sabbath requirements, could not endure the wrath of a street mugger enraged at getting no booty. The victim's wife, who called down to the mugger from her window perch, "Leave him alone, he has no money," told a neighbor how she and her husband "had seen members of their family tortured [at Auschwitz] and had learned to have strength for things like this."[17] Crown Heights blacks interrupted the funeral procession with taunts of "Heil Hitler" and "Hitler was right."

Frustrated by the failure of official organs of punishment and adjudication to protect them, the highly organized Hasidic community had recourse to its own informal methods of dispute settlement and protection. In Williamsburg, the Satmar Hasidim fashioned block watches armed with whistles. The appearance of a suspicious Latino or black prompted vigorous tweeting, which not only summoned scores of bearded men but continued as the "suspect" made his way down the length of the block until the process began anew at the next intersection. In Crown Heights, the Lubavitchers responded in a similarly geopolitical fashion, with patrols and border guards, the Maccabees. One such guardian, a former resident of the neighborhood, a non-Lubavitcher Orthodox Jew, recalled, "We had vigilantes in Crown Heights, and we stopped the niggers there!"

Rather than trust New York courts, the Hasidic crime patrols have sometimes taken over the functions of adjudication and punishment as well as the policing. Local blacks have at times exulted when the Jews beat a suspected mugger or car thief, and over the years there have been occasional efforts at joint black-Jewish patrols. But the Lubavitchers' vigorous questioning of blacks they deem out of place has rankled many blacks as racist presumption. Informal methods are often based on street hunches, probabilistic notions of what people "are really up to," recipe knowledge of bad people and good ones.

The problem with such folk estimates is they are rather crude and follow a risk-averse logic that presumes it is better to make the mistake of suspecting an innocent person than of missing a guilty person. This pragmatic logic, which reverses the ethos of innocent until proven guilty, can make for flagrant mistakes, and there have been notorious cases in which Jews ended up manhandling respectable black people.

Black anger was intense in 1978 when a large group of Lubavitchers, following an unrelated police killing of a black businessman, beat a black youth to a pulp—he nearly died—after he allegedly grabbed a man's yarmulke. The trial strategy of the Hasidim did not suggest Jews were a justice-loving people, who put race-neutral universal determination of guilt and innocence above their own sense of racial solidarity. They filled the spectator section with many other Jews with black hats and beards, so the witnesses could not "tell them apart." It was that incident, and the tensions that produced it, which spurred the formation of the United Black Front. The reaction to the death of young Cato did not take place in a vacuum; a long history of mutual abrasion set the context.

It is important to note that Lubavitcher reaction to the black lower classes was not distinctively Jewish. More precisely, it offered a local version of a more general dynamic. The complaints about underclass crime, family structure, and drug use, while couched in ethnic and racial terms, were essentially class-based laments, not limited to whites, which have been prominent features of white ethnic lower-middle-class and working-class urban neighborhoods since the 1960s. As early as the 1966 referendum on a civilian review board, the issue of law and order was cleaving the Jewish community into its liberal, educated cosmopolitan and a lower-middle-class provincial segments.

This schism between Jews in outer-borough neighborhoods and "limousine liberal" Manhattan Jews was balanced by the convergence of lower-middle-class Jews and lower-middle-class Catholics in attitudes and elections. The central spur to that realignment, and the defections from liberalism that accompanied it, was the cluster of race and class issues like crime and welfare.

From the mid-1960s on in Brooklyn, Jews who felt threatened by black street crime were more likely to reject the civilian review board and support the weakening of protections of due process for criminals. Beyond crime, on issues as diverse as busing, scatter-site public housing, the death penalty, and black nationalism, Jewish neighborhoods in Brooklyn and Queens increasingly turned against liberalism, and more Orthodox and observant Jews were in the forefront of that conservative surge.[18]

The more general features of Jewish "Middle America" remind us of the need to control for variance in assessing black-Jewish relations. To step out of the immediacy of Crown Heights for a moment, it has always been true that unequal relations between clients and patrons, customers and merchants, the dominated and the dependent, generate resentment. When each side of the divide is also unified by race or ethnicity, these interest-based clashes are often expressed in the idiom of ethnicity or race. And so the class and status conflicts created by the dependence of black clients and customers on Jewish landlords, retail merchants, social workers, and teachers inevitably produced a certain amount of black antisemitism. The antimercantilism of Harlem "buy black" campaigns of the 1940s, which often targeted Jewish store owners, reflected the social tensions generated by merchant-customer relations. One of Jesse Jackson's close advisers, who grew up with him in North Carolina, recalled the edge of ambivalence in the black community's relationship with "Hymie" the store owner: "Mr. Hyman was not necessarily a great guy with us. It was a bittersweet relationship. I mean, he was kind enough to give us credit, but he was not such a good guy that he would treat us fairly in the repayment of the credit."[19]

These sentiments, then, flow from an ethnically intensified variant of a more general sociological category. The more recent focus on anti-Korean boycotts in black neighborhoods across the country underscores the structural sources of ethnic competition. The ethnic framing is a consequence, not a cause, of the social conditions of unequal encounter. As Koreans have filled once-Jewish retail niches, antimercantilism now takes an anti-Asian form. On Flatbush Avenue during the boycott of the Korean grocers, some residents nostalgically recalled the Jewish merchants who, compared to what they see as "cold" and "arrogant" and "disrespectful" Koreans, loom in retrospect as warm, credit-dispensing mensches. In sum, much of what appears to be "black" antisemitism and "Jewish" antiblack sentiment has elements of racial, ethnic, class, and interest group elements. We need a sufficiently complex vocabulary to match the analytical complexity of the phenomena we are addressing.

In countless ways, the conflict in Crown Heights is full of idiosyncratic and unrepeatable elements. At the same time, the complexities of identity, mobilization, and alliance we have been exploring reflect a broader rearrangement of the lines of communal conflict in American life. As the history of Protestant-Catholic and immigrant-native rivalries indicates, the central lines of demarcation in America have varied widely. During the civil rights movement and the backlash that followed, black and white were vivid, articulated demarcations of cleavage. But class divisions within the African-American community, and new immigrant waves of Asian, Latino, West Indian, and other nationalities, have blurred the clarity of black-white as an organizing principle in American life.

There has emerged a looser, more volatile and shifting pattern of conflict. During the Los Angeles riots, the initial fault line encoded in black anger over white racism quickly expanded to black-Korean conflict, and the class anger of Chicano youth against the central institutions of society was evident as well. In other places, black-Latino rivalry has been critical. In Miami, Cubans, African Americans, and Anglos vie for hegemony. The Proposition 187 referendum to some extent polarized blacks and Mexicans, but also legal Mexican immigrants and their undocumented brothers and sisters. In the Brooklyn neighborhood of Williamsburg, Hasidic Jews from the Satmar sect—who have sometimes engaged in violent struggle with the Lubavitcher branch of Hasidim—had been locked for a decade in struggle with a primarily Hispanic community.

Whether these rivalries erupt into full-scale assaults on democratic pluralism, as in Crown Heights, or remain compatible with it, no matter how tensely, is not ordained. Nor is the degree to which Jews and blacks will become swept up in such conflicts. There is a margin of slack, and to some extent the fate of black-

Jewish relations will depend on the vagaries of chance and the two peoples' efforts at healing and harmony. Beyond sheer accident and intention, however, there is, as we have seen, a realm of more causally powerful forces shaping encounters between blacks and Jews. These forces are often only tangentially related to the events that trigger episodes like Crown Heights or to the "Jewishness" and "blackness" of the participants. As a result, the endurance of antisemitic brands of resentment politics will turn on the ability of the black community and the larger society to reduce the level of suffering in black life and the desperate alienation it breeds.

NOTES

1. This quote, and others to follow, comes from research I carried out in Crown Heights immediately after the riots. Many of these quotes, as well as some paragraphs, first appeared in my piece "Crown of Thorns" in *The New Republic*, October 14, 1991.

2. Leo Baeck, *The Essence of Judaism* (New York: Schocken Books, 1961), pp. 197–98.

3. Milton Himmelfarb, "Jewish Class Conflict," in Murray Friedman, ed., *Overcoming Middle-Class Rage* (Philadelphia: Westminister Press, 1970).

4. Jonathan Rieder, *Canarsie: The Jews and Italians of Brooklyn against Liberalism* (Cambridge, Mass.: Harvard University Press, 1985).

5. Reprinted in *The Jewish Press*, vol. 41, no. 36, September 6–12, 1991.

6. *New York Carib News*, September 17, 1991, p. 3.

7. Peter Noel, "Crown Heights Burning," *Village Voice*, September 3, 1991, p. 37.

8. Philip Kaznitz, quoted in Rieder, "Crown of Thorns," p. 28.

9. Quoted in Bob Faw and Nancy Skelton, *Thunder in America: The Improbable Presidential Campaign of Jesse Jackson* (Austin, Texas: Texas Monthly Press, 1986), p. 57.

10. Ibid., p. 53.

11. Jonathan Rieder, "Inside Howard Beach," *The New Republic*, February 9, 1987. See also Rieder, *Canarsie*.

12. Dell Hymes, "Linguistic Aspects of Comparative Political Research," in R.T. Holt and J.E. Turner, eds., *The Methodology of Comparative Research* (New York: The Free Press, 1970).

13. Cornel West, *Race Matters* (New York: Vintage Books, 1994), p. 111.

14. Jonathan Rieder, "Trouble in Store," *The New Republic*, July 2, 1990.

15. Quoted in Jerome Mintz, *Hasidic People: A Place in the New World* (Cambridge, Mass.: Harvard University Press, 1991), p. 329.

16. Rieder, "Inside Howard Beach," p. 17.

17. Mintz, *Hasidic People*, p. 143.

18. Rieder, *Canarsie*.

19. Quoted in Faw and Skelton, *Thunder in America*, p. 57.

·18·

Antisemitism and the Law: Constitutional Issues and Antisemitism

MARC D. STERN

Marc D. Stern is codirector of the Commission on Law
and Social Action of the American Jewish Congress.

"America is different!" Nowhere does this verity become more apparent than in an examination of the contours of the legal system of the United States, particularly with respect to the American Constitution, especially the Bill of Rights, most centrally the First Amendment. Marc D. Stern develops an analysis of a number of areas of constitutional protections that together ensure the security of American Jews (even as, in the American system, there can be no law or judicial procedure that can "outlaw" antisemitism). Stern telescopes the history and impact on Jewish security of antidiscrimination provisions, civil rights laws, "hate crimes" legislation, and, of course, church-state separation.

The range of legal measures analyzed by Stern have been for the most part enthusiastically endorsed by the American Jewish—and other—communities. Stern's contribution in his essay, in questioning many of these measures in the context of American constitutional pluralism, is to provide a somewhat skeptical second look at the legal arena when it comes to legislating and adjudicating matters related to bias and bigotry.

J.A.C.

An article written about almost any other country with a two-hundred-year history of Jewish residence addressing the question of antisemitism and the law would first have to address the growth and decline of explicitly anti-Jewish legislation. One would address bans on citizenship and voting, especially onerous

Jewish taxes, government-instigated pogroms, exclusions from educational institutions, and the like. Almost none of this has existed to any significant degree in the United States, at either the federal or state level. With a few notable exceptions, American law has not institutionalized antisemitism in any way that has had an appreciable impact on Jews. In recent years, it has adopted a broad panoply of laws prohibiting official or private persons or institutions from implementing antisemitic discrimination.

Official antisemitism has not taken the form of legislation in the United States for at least one hundred and fifty years. When it did exist, it took the relatively mild form of exclusion from office holding in some few states. These restrictions were more pro-Christian than antisemitic and did not deny all other citizenship rights and benefits to Jews. They surely did not endanger the physical security of Jews.

There were, of course, antisemites in public office here or there, and some of these on occasion took advantage of their official capacities to implement their hatred of Jews: an example is General Ulysses S. Grant's infamous and short-lived General Orders Number 11 barring Jews from the Department of Tennessee. These have been purely local phenomena, personal to the official, and typically of fleeting significance. No significant political party—not even the Know-Nothings of the mid-nineteenth century—ever ran candidates on a platform of antisemitism. There is one quasi-exception, which in retrospect amounted to little, but at the time was regarded as a clear and present danger to American Jewry.

The efforts by the National Reform Association (NRA) and its immediate predecessors during the Civil War and afterward to amend the Constitution to include a recognition of America as a Christian nation was seen as an effort to relegate Jews to second-class status. In addition to seeking official recognition of Christianity, the movement sought to implement the teaching of Protestantism by urging Prohibition, ensuring that Protestantism was part of American public education, and preserving and strengthening Sunday blue laws. Those affiliated with the NRA frequently lapsed into theological antisemitic utterances of the worst kind.[1] The NRA failed to secure enactment of its Christian

America amendment, in large part because Congress recognized that a Christian nation amendment was inconsistent with the Founding Fathers' deliberate decision to create a religiously neutral federal government.

At least until the rise of secular, racist theories of antisemitism in Europe at the end of the last century, antisemitism has been intimately related to Christian (and to a somewhat lesser extent, Islamic) theories of religious superiority which were implemented by states which saw themselves as charged with defending the one true faith. Necessarily, those who did not share that faith were relegated to second-class citizenship. Sometimes that status was relatively benign; more often it was malignant, leading to economic, physical, and political oppression, powerlessness and expulsion. What is important is that these were not mere private religious prejudices, but constituted the divinely sanctioned official order. This was distinctly not an American pattern, but an almost universal one elsewhere. Indeed, one of the first forays of American Jews into foreign affairs was aimed at ameliorating that second-class status in Switzerland in the mid–nineteenth century or, more precisely, preventing the United States from accepting that status as it might affect Jewish Americans visiting Switzerland. The American dissent from this traditional pattern of social organization is embodied directly in the Constitution.

The federal government itself was barred from imposing any religious test for public office by the very text of the Constitution. That standard served as the ideal to which the states accommodated themselves (if they had not already attained it), although it took some longer than others to realize it.[2] The Founders went further than merely barring religious tests. At the insistence of the states (albeit for wildly different reasons) they inserted a provision prohibiting the federal government from establishing an official religion. Most or all states had similar provisions. The importance of the separation of church and state as a barrier to official antisemitism cannot be overstated.

In the United States, the congeries of ideas we now know as the separation of church and state, together with the federal ban on religious tests for public office, prevented theological antisemitism from ever taking official hold and, in turn, from lending sanction and support to private forms of discrimination. Resulting in varying part from the confluence of the Enlightenment, religious skepticism, political idealism, a religiously diverse and shifting population, frontier tolerance for difference, and indifference toward religion, Americans gravitated toward legal barriers against establishments of religion, the most famous of which is the First Amendment's guarantee against "laws respecting an establishment of religion." But these barriers did not remain merely legal. They became part of the national ethos, available to be called on by Jews in their defense as the need arose, as indeed they were used successfully to thwart the efforts to Christianize America led by the National Reform Association.

To be sure, the issues that arise today in connection with that guarantee are typically only secondary or tertiary (and usually involve questions of all religion versus none, not Christianity versus any other faith) in comparison with the question of whether some church is identified as the "official" church of the state, with the state as guardian and protector of its interests. Today as well it is necessary to consider the argument that the government is not merely separating itself from religion but suppressing it under the rubric of nonestablishment.[3] In the nineteenth century, however, after the bans on non-Christians holding office fell, the issues were far more important and direct, with the issue being whether the government had some special duty to foster Christianity, through Bible reading in the schools or the insistence or universal enforcement of the Christian Sabbath. The most important of these protective laws for most of American history were the Sunday "blue laws." Again, these were passed not to hurt Jews—they were often enacted before there were significant numbers of American Jews in the jurisdiction—but to preserve the sanctity of the Christian Sabbath, and therefore Christian morality, which was thought to be essential to the well-being of the community. No matter what their intentions, these statutes had a harmful impact on Jewish merchants who wished to observe the Jewish Sabbath and remain economically viable, but could not do so in a five-day week.

American Jews were divided at first whether to oppose these laws, some being willing to accept them as a price of living in a Christian country. Those who did struggle against the laws occasionally met with a virulently antisemitic response. That is, American Jews were told that this was a Christian country and that they should not complain about the disabilities that came with that status. It was not until the mid-twentieth century that these laws were repealed, and then more by the demands of commerce than by Jewish opposition. Ironically, by then most American Jews had long since stopped observing the Sabbath.

The Jewish insistence on prohibiting those practices which might grow into an establishment of religion, or which suggested that the government had religious favorites, has contributed directly to forestalling the growth of officially sanctioned theological antisemitism. As the Supreme Court has noted, late in the twentieth century (in a case not involving Jews) the most fundamental assumption of the Establishment Clause is that all faiths are equal in the eyes of government.[4] The extent of the change this represents in the cultural environment can be gauged by comparing it with Justice Story's nineteenth-century treatise on constitutional law:

> Probably at the time of the adoption of the constitution, and of the amendment to it, now under consideration, the general, if not the universal, sentiment in America was, that Christianity ought to receive encouragement from the state, so far as it is not incompatible with the private rights of conscience, and the freedom of religious worship. An attempt to level all religions, and to make it a matter of state policy to hold all in utter indifference, would have created universal disapprobation, if not universal indignation. . . .
>
> But the duty of supporting religion, and especially the Christian religion, is very different from the right to force the consciences of other men, or to punish them for worshipping God in the manner, which, they believe, their accountability to him requires. . . .
>
> The real object of the amendment was, not to countenance, much less to advance Mahometanism or Judaism, or infidelity, by prostrating Christianity; but to exclude all rivalry among Christian sects, and to prevent any national ecclesiastical establishment, which should give to an

hierarchy the exclusive patronage of the national government. . . .

This is not to say that every jot and tittle of Establishment Clause decisionmaking is essential to forestalling the growth of official or private antisemitism. Moreover, it is not the case that the separation principle was universally accepted and acknowledged without difficulty merely because the Jewish community endorsed it, or even that the community itself is or has been in agreement on all points. There are issues, such as aid to parochial schools and the display of publicly sponsored religious symbols, over which the Jewish community itself is today seriously divided. Still, there have been many fights over the Establishment Clause which have divided Jews and Christians. While these disputes are often heated, the Jewish insistence on a relatively high level of separation has not resulted in any sustained antisemitic reaction.[5]

Since the large influx of Eastern European Jews at the end of the nineteenth and beginning of the twentieth century, then, Jews have never found their legal status as citizens threatened. They did not need to expend substantial energies and political capital to put an end to discriminatory laws affecting their physical well-being or their opportunities for economic or social advancement. The major, and probably the only significant exception to this generally rosy picture—and it was an important exception—was the enactment in 1922 of restrictive immigration laws which were designed to choke off the flow of Eastern European and Italian immigrants. The motivation for this law was largely to preserve the "purity" of the racial stock of Anglo-Saxon America from dilution by inferior elements from Southern and Eastern Europe (Italians, Jews, and Poles), and hence had distinct roots in racial theories of antisemitism.

Jews vigorously opposed the enactment of this discriminatory law, and constantly sought its repeal when that was politically feasible, as it often was not. During the Depression, for example, it was unthinkable for the still largely immigrant Jewish population to seek to open the country up to new waves of immigration and cheap labor competing for scarce jobs.

The enactment of this discriminatory immigration law closed the doors to further large-scale immigration from Poland and parts of what was the Soviet Union just prior to the rise of the Nazis to power, and at a time of substantial economic hardship for Eastern European Jewry. Passage of the so-called national origins immigration law—which remained on the books until 1965—undoubtedly kept the American Jewish community smaller than it might otherwise have been, in addition to condemning to death Jews who had no place to flee Hitler's soon-to-be Holocaust. Still, one would be hard-pressed to identify any domestic antisemitic consequences of this legislation beyond these obvious ones. The position of Jews already in this country was not materially affected by its enactment or enforcement.

LAWS AGAINST ANTISEMITISM

The Scope of Private Antisemitism

That combatting official antisemitism has not been (and is not) a significant problem for American Jewry does not mean that antisemitism and anti-Jewish discrimination have not existed in palpable and important ways. Surely, they have. Jews felt the impact of that discrimination in many ways, some visible, some not. In many communities, it was unheard of to sell a house to a Jew, a practice often reinforced by the use of restrictive covenants entered into by neighbors prohibiting each of them and anyone who purchased property from them from selling that property to Jews or Negroes.

Employment discrimination was rampant against Jews in particular industries—for example banking, insurance, and law—or segments of industries, particularly at the level of upper management ("executive suite discrimination"). In this century, in the wake of mass Jewish immigration many of the most prominent private colleges imposed quotas on the number of Jews admitted in order to prevent the "Judaizing" of these institutions. (That practice is largely responsible for the modern Jewish ambivalence or opposition to various forms of affirmative action.) Discrimination in places of public accommodation (the proverbial hotel with the "no dogs or Jews" sign) was rampant. By anecdotal reports, anti-Jewish discrimination remains most common at upscale country clubs, no doubt the longest lingering form of formal anti-Jewish discrimination.

The reader familiar with the black civil rights movement beginning in the 1930s and gathering momentum in the post–World War II era will notice the substantial overlap between this Jewish civil rights agenda and that of the civil rights movement. That overlap explains in large part the closeness with which Jews and blacks would cooperate in pursuing civil rights legislation and litigation in the two decades following World War II. But there were significant differences between the two groups. Most important of these was the cold fact that the black civil rights movement had to combat de jure discrimination (discrimination by force of law) in addition to private bigotry, while the Jewish community had (as a general matter) to combat only private discrimination to further its own interests.[6] Of course, where official antisemitism has surfaced, the Jewish community continues to react strongly and vigorously, typically with great success.

Second, in important ways the black civil rights agenda was broader than the Jewish one. Jews did not have to fight for the right to vote and exercise political power as did blacks. And whatever the case with antisemitism in regard to local units of the criminal justice system or individual police officers or prosecutors, Jews did not face systemic hostility in the criminal justice system the way blacks did, nor did they fear the systematic invocation of the criminal sanction as an obstacle to efforts by Jews to achieve equality as blacks surely did.

The difference between private and official discrimination may be of scant comfort to the victim, although in a democratic society official discrimination carries far greater stigma than private discrimination. But for lawyers, historians, and sociologists the differences are crucial. For lawyers, official discrimination is subject to scrutiny under various constitutional provisions including the Establishment Free Exercise and Equal Protection clauses; private discrimination, if not affirmatively ratified by government, is not unconstitutional because, with the exception of slavery, the Constitution does not address the activity of private actors. On the other hand, official discrimination is generally (but not always) more visible and hence more easily detected and regulated than the discrete actions of hundreds of thousands of private individuals.

Antidiscrimination Laws

In contrast to other countries which have specific laws against various forms of antisemitism, neither the federal government nor the states have specific laws explicitly prohibiting anti-semitism in any of its various manifestations. Some forms of antisemitism are easily redressed under general principles. Assaults on Jews because they are Jews may be redressed through a common-law action for assault, whether the attackers were public officials or private hooligans.[7] For laws against antisemitism one must turn to general laws against discrimination, particularly those provisions banning religious discrimination.

The very first federal civil rights laws passed in the wake of the Civil War were designed to protect the newly freed slaves. These laws did not explicitly prohibit religious discrimination by name, much less discrimination against Jews, but provided generally that all persons should henceforth enjoy the same rights under law as "white persons." A counterpart statute gave all citizens the same right to hold property as "white persons" enjoyed. When the statute was rescued during the 1960s from nearly a century of neglect as a potent weapon against private racial discrimination, it was not thought to protect Jews or other religious groups. The statute was cast in racial terms, and if there was anything that American Jews were certain about after European scientific theories of antisemites were put into practice by the Nazis, it was that Jews did not constitute an identifiable race.

In 1979, a synagogue in a Maryland suburb of Washington, D.C., was vandalized by teenagers who painted swastikas and other antisemitic graffiti on the building. The perpetrators were arrested and convicted of various crimes. The synagogue, not content with the state's successful pursuit of criminal sanctions, and not willing to rest solely on traditional tort law theories such as trespass which would have allowed for a full recovery of damages against the impecunious defendants, brought an action for damages in federal court alleging that the vandals' criminal action had denied it the same right to hold property as "white persons" enjoyed. The lower federal courts dismissed this claim on the ground that Jews were not a race.

The Supreme Court reversed.[8] While it agreed that the act was cast in racial terms, it found that the concept of race had

393

undergone a change of meaning since the statute had been written, and that the original meaning controlled. The Court relied extensively on the original legislative debate (brought to its attention by the NAACP Legal Defense and Education Fund) in which it is clear that the nineteenth-century Congress understood by the concept of race, not only what we would call race, but ethnicity:

> Congress intended to protect from discrimination identifiable classes of persons who are subjected to intentional discrimination solely because of their ancestry or ethnic characteristics. Such discrimination is racial discrimination that Congress intended in [the Civil Rights Act] to forbid, whether or not it would be classified as racial in terms of modern scientific theory.[9]

The Court thus added an additional level of legal protection for Jews, although it did so by emphasizing the identity of Jews as an ethnic group, not a religious one. Perhaps by the end of the twentieth century, that description of American Jews was, in any event, more apt. Jews have invoked *Shaare T'fillah* in only a handful of subsequent cases.

Public Accommodation and Employment

Laws against private discrimination first began to be enacted in the early part of the twentieth century. These early laws generally prohibited discrimination in places of public accommodation. From this remove, it is difficult to discern what impact these laws had on the real world. There are surely not many decided cases under these laws before the middle of the twentieth century. One of the weaknesses of these earlier acts is that they did not have an enforcement mechanism other than the unlikely remedy of a criminal prosecution or the cumbersome and expensive route of private lawsuits, although at least some public officials devised ways to enforce them.[10] It would appear that the laws at least forced some illicit discrimination underground or into less blatant forms in the states with such laws. But by the time a federal public accommodation law was passed in 1964, banning, inter alia, religious discrimination, such discrimination against Jews was no longer a serious social problem.

The demand for labor during World War II, and pressure from civil rights groups taking advantage of the pressing needs of the war effort, led to a major federal initiative to end discrimination in employment, the Fair Employment Practices Committee (FEPC). The FEPC theoretically had power over fair employment in all war-related industries, but in reality made little dent in the actual practice of employment discrimination. It did, however, establish the principle that employment discrimination was wrong. Perhaps more important, its creation in 1941 established the precedent that the federal government (and the states) had an interest and legitimate role in suppressing employment discrimination. The modern reader may not fully appreciate what a revolutionary step it was in the 1940s for the federal government to inject itself into an employer's decision about whom to hire, but it was such at the time.

After the war, states and municipalities, primarily in the North, began to enact fair employment laws, often with a newly created executive agency charged with enforcement. Whether because of these laws or because of changes in attitude which allowed the laws to be passed, barriers to Jewish employment began to fall, and fall rapidly. Of course not all barriers fell at once. Executive suite discrimination lingered longest. These changes were not the result of a wave of lawsuits; to judge from the reported decisions, large numbers of cases were not brought. Whether due to a simple desire to comply with the law, a change in social attitudes, the fear of successful suits, or the assimilation of Jews to the point where it was harder to identify them, is not clear, but whatever the cause, the result was an opening of opportunity for Jews. By the time the federal law banning employment discrimination based on sex, race, national origin, or ethnicity was passed in 1964, there was relatively little use made of the federal law in attacking employment discrimination against Jews. In the almost thirty years of the law's existence only a handful of meritorious lawsuits have been brought under this rubric by Jews, some of which involved antisemitic hazing on the job. One such case involved compliance by American employers with the Arab boycott of Israel, or at least a desire to avoid giving offense to Arab clients.[11]

Another issue that was addressed relatively late, and then

really only after the 1964 act was enacted, was whether a ban on religious discrimination banned not only outright refusals to hire Jews, but also a failure to accommodate religious practice by, for example, allowing employees to have their Sabbath off. The courts initially hesitated over this issue, dividing over whether such discrimination was banned by the 1964 Civil Rights Act. Congress ultimately resolved the issue by requiring accommodation of religious practices provided that accommodation did not impose unreasonable burdens on the employer or other employees.

Although the federal provision has twice been read narrowly by the Supreme Court,[12] its passage as well as that of somewhat broader state statutes in many of the states has greatly facilitated the entry of observant Jews into all sectors of the economy. Whether, however, this statute can be said in any meaningful way to address antisemitism in a real sense is doubtful at best. The Congress, incidentally, will shortly be asked to strengthen these provisions.

Housing Discrimination

It was not until 1968 that Congress banned discrimination in housing. Some states had done so earlier. However, the major blow against housing discrimination against Jews came in a lawsuit resolved in the late 1940s. There, a white home owner sued to enforce a restrictive covenant barring the sale of adjoining houses to blacks, who in fact had managed to purchase a house notwithstanding such an agreement. The Supreme Court held that judicial enforcement of a racially restrictive covenant amounted to state support of racial discrimination, impermissible under the Equal Protection Clause of the Fourteenth Amendment.[13]

The same reasoning of course applied to contractual provisions banning sales to Jews. Although these anti-Jewish clauses did not disappear immediately, lingering for decades in deeds, they lost substantial force with the decision. Jewish groups were quick to urge the invalidating of these agreements when they were discovered. In any event, the leading treatise on housing discrimination does not report even a single case of anti-Jewish discrimination redressed in the context of actual sales of houses under the 1968 federal fair housing law. Given the documented geographical dispersion of the Jewish community, this can only mean that antisemitism or anti-Jewish discrimination is not a major factor in the housing market. As far as it appears, it is not at all a factor in the financing of home purchases, which is not the case for other minority groups.

There are, however, a handful of cases in which zoning laws have been challenged under the Fair Housing Act, where their purpose or effect was to exclude Orthodox Jews from a community as by making it impossible to erect synagogues within walking distance of residences.[14] Similarly, the Anti-Defamation League successfully challenged a realtor's use of an evangelical Christian symbol (a fish) on its advertisements, on the theory that the symbol would likely have the effect of excluding Jews from using the firm's services.[15] Although this latter victory is commonly thought of as a victory against antisemitism, it is doubtful if it is that in any meaningful sense. The purpose of the symbolic display was primarily to attract a particular segment of the population on the basis of compatibility, more than a desire to exclude or repel any other population segment.

WHAT CIVIL RIGHTS LAWS HAVE ACCOMPLISHED

All in all, the federal government and the states have enacted an impressive interlocking network of antidiscrimination laws covering many, if not almost all, human endeavors. Ironically, under this complex web of statutes Jewish organizations themselves now have to justify policies which limit membership or participation in their own activities to Jews.

A review of the reported cases, however, reveals only a handful of cases in which Jews have invoked these statutes, and an even smaller number in which they have done so successfully. A somewhat greater number of cases are filed and resolved short of a formal decision, often by a small financial settlement. The relative social and economic success of Jews, much of which predated the enactment of these statutes, cannot be laid primarily to their passage. Moreover, these same laws prohibited racial and sexual discrimination in employment, which (particularly the former) have not gone away anywhere nearly as totally as anti-Jewish discrimination has. For those seeking to explain the phenomenon of Jewish success in America, one has to look elsewhere.

Civil right laws, then, are useful in aberrant cases where antisemitism takes tangible form. More important, they help in shaping public reluctance to act on whatever stereotypes and biases exist in the society. But they are not more than that for Jews.

PUNISHING ANTISEMITIC TEACHING, PREACHING, AND INCITEMENT

Antisemitism has not disappeared in this country. Indeed, antisemitic ideas and publications are unfortunately not a rarity. Sometimes these surface in "respectable" elements of society, when a stiff complaint is usually sufficient to obtain an apology and retraction. But there are publications and organizations on the right and left margins of society which are dedicated to the spread of antisemitic ideas, and whose publications and utterances are aimed at segments of society where they may be heard by willing listeners. In contrast to most of Western Europe and Canada, American law has repudiated any punishment of speech under the rubric of freedom of speech. It is true that the Supreme Court upheld the constitutionality of a law making incendiary racist speech criminal. The Court said in *Beauharnais* v. *Illinois*:[16]

> In the face of this history and its frequent obligato of extreme racial and religious propaganda, we would deny experience to say that the Illinois legislature was without reason in seeking ways to curb false or malicious defamation of racial and religious groups, made in public places and by means calculated to have a powerful emotional impact on those to whom it was presented. There are limits to the exercise of these liberties [of speech and of the press]. The danger in these times from the coercive activities of those who in the delusion of racial or religious conceit would incite violence and breaches of the peace in order to deprive others of their equal right to the exercise of their liberties, is emphasized by events familiar to all.

This decision, however, is widely and probably correctly treated as a lifeless relic. Several courts of appeal and federal district courts have so treated it, flatly pronouncing it dead and refusing to follow it.[17] Thus, for example, every district court to consider state[18] university campus speech codes which penalize racial or ethnic epithets (including antisemitic ones) has invalidated them as a denial of student free speech.[19] Still, it would be premature to finally dismiss the possibility of the reinvigoration of group libel laws in some form, since these now enjoy powerful support from certain academics and activists in both minority and feminist circles.

The supporters of punishing speech taking the form of the racist or sexist epithets argue that such usage serves to oppress minorities and women and deny them equal opportunities to succeed. While one can easily imagine extreme cases where the cumulative effect of verbal assaults is to deny someone access to some activity, this argument encourages the thin-skinned to revel in their sensitivity and to nurture a sense of victimization far beyond any legitimate grievance at the occasional and hurtful remark.

There have been some efforts in special contexts to penalize racist speech or antisemitic speech. Several challenges have been made to the renewal of licenses of broadcasters who systematically broadcast antisemitic or racist programs. Although recently repealed, for many decades federal law imposed an obligation on broadcasters to provide a platform of opposing views under the now repealed fairness or personal-attack rules. These obligations were correctly viewed as inadequate responses to the problem. How does one respond to the charge that all Jews cheat at business without, by the very act of responding, lending credibility to the charge? These challenges to licenses were the result, but they were uniformly unsuccessful given the constitutional guarantee of free speech. Indeed, for this reason the challenges did not even enjoy full support from the Jewish community, some of which viewed these challenges as infringements on civil liberties.

From time to time, the courts are confronted with the question of requests for marches by overtly antisemitic or racist groups. The most famous of these is the Nazi march through Skokie, Illinois, a town with an unusually large number of Holocaust survivors.[20] Such questions have posed anguishing problems for the Jewish community. It is now clear that American courts will not permit government to ban marches because of the despised and despicable message they seek to promote. Even if not much of the Jewish community were itself fervently committed to the defense of these civil liberties principles, as a practical matter Jews cannot achieve much by pursuing legal recourse against rallies by the likes of the neo-Nazis or Minister Farrakhan because the courts have held that these events enjoy constitutional protection.

But it is also the case that the temper of much of the community—particularly that of Holocaust survivors and their children—is such that the affront of quietly accepting mass organized antisemitism through their communities cannot be tolerated. Where this mood carries the day, the inevitable result is to convert racists of various stripes into martyrs to the censorious, conferring on them far more notoriety and publicity than they would otherwise enjoy.

Finally, occasional efforts are made to deny tax-exempt status to racist groups. First Amendment principles would seem to preclude the denial of government benefits, such as tax exemption, to a group because of its point of view. However, the precedents here are in some disarray,[21] and occasionally an extremist view is denied tax exemption on what appears to be the basis of its viewpoint.[22]

HATE CRIMES

No one has ever seriously contended that actual physical assaults or murders motivated by a desire to express revulsion or disdain for a group, or to condemn it, are protected expression. Similarly, it cannot be and has not been argued that painting antisemitic graffiti on the wall of a synagogue or equally offensive graffiti on a church is constitutionally protected expression. Moreover, it is surely true of the most serious offenses that the potential penalties are sufficiently stiff to constitute serious punishment, leave no doubt about society's attitude toward the crime, and, to the extent that the potential strength of the penalty is sufficient to deter similar crimes, offer deterrence.

In the wake of a series of reports purporting to show a startling increase in antisemitic violence, there were complaints that existing laws were not severe enough to deter what came to be known as hate crimes. These calls led to the enactment of what have become known as sentence-enhancement laws in almost every state and the federal government. Although the Jewish community as a matter of fact is not the target of most of such crimes, it took the lead in drafting and pushing for the enactment of these laws, most of which are modeled on a draft prepared by the Anti-Defamation League. These statutes provide, in a variety of formulations, that where an existing crime is committed with a racist motive, the sentence may be "enhanced" or raised by so many years of imprisonment. At the same time as these laws were enacted, Congress, following the lead of the states, required police departments to collect data on hate crimes.

Before turning to the legal legitimacy of these statutes, it is worth exploring the justification for the enactment of these statutes. First was the purported upswing in antisemitic crimes. But the fact is that no one knows whether there in fact has been an upswing. "Formal" reporting of hate crimes of any sort is a relatively new phenomenon, and official reporting of hate crimes is even more recent. No one knows, then, if these crimes are more common today than, say, twenty or forty years ago. The general decline in antisemitic attitudes among the general population, which is well documented, makes this an unlikely, although not impossible, scenario. Moreover, as the police and others become more accustomed to the obligation to report cases which might have gone unnoted ten years ago, or not been thought of as bias crimes, they are now so reported.[23] There may well even be over-reporting as a result of a tendency to include doubtful cases.

Second, the enhanced-sentencing laws are often defended on the ground that increased sentences are necessary to deter other violators. But there is precious little evidence that increased sentencing has had a substantial impact on crime rates. Stiff penalties for drug violations have not done much to reduce the drug problem, but they have swelled prison populations. A more likely justification for these laws is that they serve as an additional reminder that society regards racist acts with special horror, if that were not already sufficiently known.

Finally, it is useful to unpack these statistics, so that not all "antisemitic" incidents are lumped together as a justification for laws against hate crimes. Almost all of the reported crimes tend to be garden-variety vandalism,[24] either graffiti or cemetery-related offenses, almost always committed by teenagers on drunken binges. Although one would never know it from reading the Jewish media, other churches find themselves victimized by this conduct as well. It is unclear what purpose more draconian sentences serve in preventing recurrences of this kind of behavior by adolescents who are notoriously impervious to sanctions dependent on thinking of the consequences of one's behavior.

Whether or not necessary or desirable, enhanced-sentencing laws are politically irresistible and here to stay. They carry with them several potential constitutional problems. First, to the extent that they wrap around existing offenses, they bear any infirmities of the underlying offenses, a particular problem in the case of the offense of harassment, which is often vaguely defined, to the point of unconstitutionality.

Second, and most relevant, because they focus on motivation, these statutes call into question a person's thoughts, ideas, and associations. Prosecutors will have to prove, usually beyond a reasonable doubt, that racial or religious hatred motivated an act—and to do so they will be tempted to introduce evidence of the books a person has read, persons he or she has associated with, and things they have said. More fundamentally, some have charged that the very fact that a stiffer sentence can be imposed for acting from the wrong motivation or ideas constitutes a constitutionally impermissible form of punishment for holding the wrong ideas.

The courts have begun to grapple with these issues. The outlines of the judicial response are now evident, although there is much yet to be clarified. Basically, the courts will uphold enhancement laws, at least under the federal Constitution, if they are carefully and precisely written. Some state courts, however, have been surprisingly suspicious of these statutes.

The first case to discuss enhancement laws involved a St. Paul, Minnesota, ordinance which was a model of poor legislative draftsmanship. It provided:

Whoever places on public or private property a symbol, object, appellation, characterization or graffiti, including, but not limited to, a burning cross or Nazi swastika, which one knows or has reasonable grounds to know arouses anger, alarm or resentment in others on the basis of race, color, creed, religion or gender commits disorderly conduct and shall be guilty of a misdemeanor.

In a bold effort at statutory cosmetic surgery, the Minnesota Supreme Court in *RAV* v. *St. Paul* held that the ordinance punished only fighting words, that is, words which "itself inflicts injury or tends to incite immediate violence."

The United States Supreme Court was not persuaded, although the Court was badly divided on rationale.[25] A majority held that although as construed the statute reached only fighting words (words aimed at a particular individual and likely to produce a violent reaction), it was selective in which fighting words it prohibited. Fighting words aimed at obese people, for example, were outside the statute, but not those aimed at Jews. Even though fighting words are unprotected by the Constitution, Justice Antonin Scalia wrote they may not be selectively punished—that is, one may not punish fighting words aimed at Republicans but not those aimed at Democrats.

Four concurring justices thought that the state could freely punish only some subset of fighting words, although it is not clear how they respond to Justice Scalia's point about Republicans and Democrats. They nevertheless thought the statute unconstitutional because it was too loosely drafted and reached conduct which only caused "hurt feelings, offense or resentment," feelings which are insufficient to justify invocation of the "fighting words" doctrine.

The scope of the majority opinion in *RAV* gave rise to fears that all sentence-enhancement statutes would be held unconstitutional under a similar rationale. Those fears grew when some (but not all) state courts, deciding to pass on such statutes after *RAV*, held that *RAV* compelled their invalidation.

The Supreme Court quickly took one of those cases, *Wisconsin* v. *Mitchell*,[26] to decide whether *RAV* compelled invalidation of all hate-crimes enhancement statutes. In an opinion widely criticized for fuzzy thinking, the chief justice held that it did not. Although the opinion is not perfectly clear on this point, the Court apparently distinguished between statutes drafted in terms of speech, which would be unconstitutional, and those based on action, which would not be. If it were otherwise, the chief justice observed, all civil rights statutes would be of questionable constitutionality.

The Court also dealt with the problem of pure speech as evidence of an element of a crime (to wit, a racial animus). Pointing to prior decisions in death penalty[27] and treason[28] cases, the Court held that such evidence was admissible, if the evidence was relevant and credible and introduced for some purpose beyond showing that the defendant was a bad person. The Court's discussion of this point was sketchy and dismissive. Even but a moment's thought should have persuaded the Court to proceed more carefully.

The decision in *Mitchell* upholding the constitutionality of Wisconsin's hate-crimes sentence-enhancement statute has proven decisive. As far as I am aware, no state appellate court has held such a statute unconstitutional under a state constitution since *Mitchell* was decided. This is somewhat surprising. Prior to *Mitchell*, several state courts found substantial problems with such statutes, albeit under the federal Constitution.

Of course, *Mitchell* did not resolve all outstanding issues. Older statutes in the mold of *RAV* continue to be invalidated. The federal courts have struggled with the constitutionality both as written and as applied to specific incidents of a federal criminal statute prohibiting the intimidation of persons exercising their rights under the federal fair housing law.

Courts have predictably struggled with the admissibility of evidence that a person charged with a hate crime belonged to a hate group when that fact is introduced to prove that the defendant acted with a racist motive. The concern, of course, is whether the introduction of such evidence chills the First Amendment right of political association.

And finally, it seems fair to ask whether sentences imposed in these cases are too draconian (thirteen years in one cross-burning case) and whether judges at all levels will be courageous enough to challenge government overreaching in these cases. So far the evidence is that they are reluctant to do so.

An effort by the U.S. Equal Employment Opportunity Commission to promulgate regulations on religious harassment in the workplace was withdrawn in the face of intense pressure from the religious right, which charged that the guideline would suppress legitimate religious expression. While there was some basis for that complaint, the regulations could have been cured relatively easily. In any event, religious harassment remains illegal, although employers are now without official guidance on the subject and are likely to remain so for some time.

Antisemitism in America is not now a major threat to American Jewry. An impressive body of legislation and judicial decision, to say nothing of public attitudes, stands as defense against outbreaks of antisemitism. Barring an apocalyptic change in the social climate, not now over the horizon, these laws ought to reassure American Jewry that its physical, social, and economic security is not in any danger, at least not from forces that single out Jews. If one can be sure of anything, however, it is that the Jewish community will not be so persuaded.

NOTES

1. See N. W. Cohen, *Jews in Christian America: The Pursuit of Religious Equality* (1992), pp. 69–74.

2. See Borden, *Jews, Turks and Infidels* (1984).

3. See for example *Lamb's Chapel* v. *Center Moriches School District*, 113 S.Ct. 2141 (1993); *Witters* v. *Washington*, 474 U.S. 481 (1984); *Widmar* v. *Vincent*, 454 U.S. 263 (1981).

4. *Larson* v. *Valente*, 456 U.S. 228 (1982); see also *Church of the Lukumi Babalu Ave* v. *City of Hialeah*, 113 S.Ct. 22176 (1993).

5. Perhaps the most infamous exception was the editorial in the Catholic periodical *America* after the decision of the Supreme Court in the first school prayer case, *Engel* v. *Vitale* (1962), in which the Court held that schools could not begin the day with an officially composed prayer. The editorial warned American Jews that they were risking an antisemitic backlash by seeking to separate church and state.

6. Early in the struggle to end various forms of private anti-Jewish discrimination, Jews sought to link private activity with government so as to subject it to constitutional limitations. Thus, in the mid-1940s the American Jewish Congress sued New York City seeking to have it deny tax exemptions to discriminating universities and (unsuccessfully) challenged tax abatements given a large private housing development which excluded Jews.

7. For an early example, see *Munick* v. *City of Durham*, 181 N.C. 188, 106 S.E. 665 (1921), a North Carolina case in which an elderly Jewish merchant was assaulted by officials of the municipal water company because he paid his water bill in coin. The North Carolina Supreme Court brushed aside a variety of technical defenses, indignantly insisting that North Carolina was not Russia, where official pogroms were an acceptable mode of official response to the real or perceived faults of Jews. This, of course, was the same North Carolina where de jure discrimination against blacks, and even lynchings, were routine crimes that went unpunished.

8. *Shaare T'fillah Congregation* v. *Cobb*, 481 U.S. 615 (1981).

9. 481 U.S. at 617 (citations omitted).

10. *Camp-of-the-Pines* v. *New York Times*, 184 Misc. 389, 53 N.Y.S.2d 475 (Albany Co. 1945). The newspaper had refused to publish an advertisement for a camp boasting that Jews were excluded, after the district attorney had warned papers against publishing such advertisements.

11. *Abrams* v. *Baylor College of Medicine*, 581 F.Supp. 1570 (S.D. Tex. 1984), aff'd, 805 F.2d 528; compare *AJ Congress* v. *Carter* (ARAMCO), 9 N.Y.2d 223, 213 N.Y.Supp.2d 60 (1961).

12. In *Ansonia Board of Education* v. *Philbrook*, 479 U.S. 60 (1985) and *TWA* v. *Hardison*, 432 U.S. 63 (1977).

13. *Shelley* v. *Kramer*, 334 U.S. 1 (1948).

14. *LeBlanc-Sternberg* v. *Fletcher*, 781 F.Supp.261 (SD NY 1990), *appeal pending* (2d Cir. 1995).

15. *Lotz Realty* v. *HUD*, 717 F.2d 929 (4th Cir. 1983).

16. 343 U.S. 250, 261 (1952).

17. *Smith* v. *Collins*, 578 F.2d 1197, 1204 (7th Cir. 1978); *Dworkin* v. *Hustler Magazine, Inc.*, 867 F.2d 1188 (9th Cir. 1989). There was a cryptic reference to *Beauharnais* in the *RAV* decision discussed below.

18. As noted, the Constitution applies only to government regulation of speech. Private campuses are theoretically free to censor if they choose to do so. Some private schools have maintained such codes, but most private universities have chosen to abide by Constitutional standards.

19. *Doe* v. *U. Of Michigan*, 721 F.Supp. 852 (E.D. Mich. 1989); *UMW Post, Inc.* v. *Bd. of Regents*, 774 F.Supp. 1163 (E.D. Wis. 1991).

20. *Collins* v. *Smith*, 578 F.2d 1197 (7th Cir. 1978).

21. Compare *FCC* v. *League of Women Voters*, 468 U.S. 364 (1984) (holding government could not refuse to subsidize public television stations which endorse candidates) with *Regan* v. *Taxation Without Representation*, 461 U.S. 540 (1983) (government may decide what speech to subsidize). Also compare *Rust* v. *Sullivan*, 111 S.Ct. 1759 (1991) (upholding refusal to fund clinics counseling abortion).

22. *National Alliance* v. *U.S.*, 710 F.2d 868 (D.C. Cir. 1983).

23. The very question of whether a particular incident is or is not classified as a bias crime is not always simple. In New York, there have been several incidents where the very act of classifying a crime as either a hate crime or an ordinary crime has led to charges of antisemitism or, conversely, of favoritism toward Jews.

24. The 1992 ADL *Audit of Anti-Semitic Incidents* reported a total of 1,730 antisemitic incidents. Eight hundred and fifty-six (nearly half) were classified as vandalism, and 874 as "harassments, threats and assaults." Of the 856 acts of vandalism, 7 were classified as "serious crimes." The proportions are telling.

25. 112 S.Ct. 2538 (1992).

26. 113 S.Ct. 2194 (1993).

27. *Barclay* v. *Florida*, 463 U.S. 939 (1983); *Dawson* v. *Delaware*, 112 S.Ct. 1093 (1992).

28. *Haupt* v. *U.S.*, 330 U.S. 631 (1947).

·19·

Contemporary Antisemitism: The International Context

ANTONY LERMAN

Antony Lerman is executive director of the Institute of Jewish Affairs (IJA), London. He is joint editor of *Patterns of Prejudice*, the international journal on racism and antisemitism, and coeditor of the yearly *Antisemitism World Report*, produced by the IJA.

The complexity and the nuanced nature of antisemitism are brought forth in Antony Lerman's chapter on international antisemitism. Antony Lerman's implicit question: Can we in fact talk about antisemitism "around the world"? In his overview of the international picture, Lerman argues that the issue of international antisemitism is far from straightforward, that there needs to be a question mark with respect to a monolithic approach to "world antisemitism." Lerman asserts that sweeping generalizations concerning the seriousness of international antisemitism are inappropriate and that international antisemitism must be broken down into its constituent parts. Nuanced judgments with respect to assessments of the cluster of issues surrounding each national situation are called for.

J.A.C.

Generalizations about the worldwide state of antisemitism are easy to proffer and are continually being made. Nothing wrong with that, of course, if preoccupation with the subject reflects eternal vigilance. But global assessments of antisemitism are often diametrically opposed. Some say it is getting damagingly worse. Others say it is in decline.

Compare two recent judgments. Historian Robert Wistrich:

"The virus of anti-Semitism is embedded, as it were, in the heart and the very bloodstream of European society and culture, ready to be activated at the first major crisis—whether it be war, revolution, the fall of empire, economic depression, or the unleashing of ethnic conflict. With the end of the Communist era, many of these conditions are now in place—a not very encouraging prospect."[1] Historian Michael Marrus: "I see no coherent, world-wide antisemitic sensibility, appearing in different guises in different situations but operating everywhere with a single aspiration—hatred of Jews simply because they are Jews. My sense is of an antisemitism of waning strength and significance".[2] These are by no means the most extreme examples of opposing views.

Why is there such divergence and how can the international context of antisemitism be reliably described when there are such differences of opinion? If this were only an academic exercise the question would hardly be important. But at its most extreme, antisemitism kills. Therefore descriptions of antisemitism and judgments about its seriousness very often have implications for action. Faulty judgments can have consequences. The reasons for such varied views need to be explained and the explanation should add to our understanding of the state of contemporary antisemitism.

That there are such variations must be puzzling to many who are concerned about antisemitism but take no part in any monitoring or research activity. After all, there is no such variation in assessments of the general state of human rights, in which category antisemitism is rightly placed. There is very broad agreement between human rights monitoring bodies about the state of human rights throughout the world. Some governments naturally reject human rights reports which are critical of their behavior, but expert opinion is, on the whole, of one mind. With antisemitism, governments are also reluctant to admit that problems exist, while experts—whatever that means in this context—do not agree.

There are some very clear reasons for the disagreement. An understanding of those reasons should make it easier to decide which analyses and assessments of antisemitism carry more weight. There are two sets of problems: difficulties arising out of the nature of the subject itself, and complications arising out of external pressures on the study of antisemitism. I will consider these before discussing trends in antisemitism.

THE NATURE OF THE SUBJECT

Antisemitism is, among other things, a form of human rights abuse. However, it is difficult to monitor and measure because it very often manifests itself in verbal or written forms, as propraganda, hidden insult, hard-to-identify discrimination, and ideology, and not in imprisonment, torture, murder, or denial of civil rights. Two kinds of problems loom large: first, whether certain forms of social phenomena do or do not constitute antisemitism; second, whether the methodology employed in analyzing anti-semitism is adequate or appropriate to the task.

What Is Antisemitism?

Several forms, expressions, and manifestations of antisemitism are easy to recognize, but there are gray areas. One of the most contentious has been anti-Zionism: when should it be considered antisemitic?[3] Logic would suggest that antisemitism and anti-Zionism are not synonymous, but many writers on antisemitism regard them as indistinguishable, or at least distinguishable only on very rare occasions. When people monitoring antisemitism are asked to report on manifestations, many automatically include any severe criticism of Israel. At its most extreme this approach has led to the conclusion that there is a genuinely new anti-semitism: the denial of the Jewish collective right to self-determination, which has superseded the denial of the individual right of the Jew to equality in liberal societies.

Another gray area is media representations of Jews. There is often an outcry whenever a Jew is portrayed negatively in the media, and accusations of antisemitism are leveled, or at least implied, in representations made to editors and producers. But the implications of seeing *all* critical representations of Jews as anti-semitic are absurd.

Methodological Pitfalls

The methodological problems are even more difficult.[4] Take the level of antisemitic incidents, often used as a guide to the state of antisemitism. Great store is set by percentage changes in the number of incidents each year, but the basis of analysis and measurement of incidents are rarely revealed or discussed. What, for example, is an antisemitic incident? Who reports them and is any corroborating evidence required before an incident is recorded as being antisemitic? What proportion of total racist incidents do antisemitic incidents occupy? Is any correlation made between the number of antisemitic incidents and the total number of Jews in the areas under consideration? These questions are not new but they are rarely taken into account when data on incidents are presented.[5] Similar sorts of questions can be asked of other categories and kinds of data.

These problems are often ignored although attempts are sometimes made to circumvent them by the employment of apparently rigorous scientific and academic approaches. Much of this kind of writing on antisemitism is unconvincing and contrived. Although some aspects of the study of antisemitism lend themselves to a rigorous scientific approach (for example, opinion polling), most do not.

Examining the Data

The quantity of data available to researchers is vast. Manifestations of antisemitism can appear in mainstream newspapers, on radio and television, in local media, at political meetings, in school classrooms and textbooks, as well as in the great quantity of material produced by organizations, movements, and parties which espouse antisemitism either overtly or covertly. Add also the activities and publications of religious groups, international political gatherings, popular literature, the specialist press, debates in parliaments—and it becomes clear that there is no shortage of raw material. Of course, scanning large quantities of human activity of this kind can produce nothing in the way of antisemitic expression or it can produce a great deal. The problem is how to differentiate between significant and insignificant data; what weight to give both what does appear and what does not appear.

Someone studying the many publications of the far right in Russia, for example, will find numerous antisemitic articles; someone looking for antisemitism in establishment circles in Britain will find few overt examples. But would one conclude from such information that the situation in Russia is dire and the situation in Britain gives no cause for concern? Not necessarily. To make such a judgment about Russia we would need to know the circulation figures of the publications, something about the readership and its receptivity to antisemitic ideas, the place of antisemitic attacks in the context of attacks on other minority groups in Russian society, the current political context, and so on. Establishment silence on Jews in Britain may mask underlying antipathies which do not show up in the usual ways of measuring these things. But then again, to assume that antisemitic attitudes are widespread in the British establishment, just because they once were, would be sloppy reporting. And even if the existence of such attitudes could be verified, one would still need to question the significance of such attitudes.

The data must be treated with a certain degree of subtlety, yet this does not always happen. In its absence, simplistic conclusions are drawn which can be misleading.

The Problem of Anecdotal Evidence

The study and assessment of contemporary antisemitism seems to be particularly vulnerable to the use of purely anecdotal evidence. A Jew may be killed, attacked, falsely imprisoned—and antisemitic motives imputed without any evidence. Incidents of antisemitic expression may be reported but without any corroborative information. Numerous exchanges occur of the kind where one person will tell a friend of an instance of antisemitism in their place of work: X said something to Y, either explicitly unpleasant about Jews or by implication. There is no way of checking such incidents and yet they easily become part of the currency of antisemitic data and feed into conclusions and assessments. Thus an agglomeration of single anecdotal incidents can easily form the basis of "expert" assessment.

In general, there are great difficulties associated with moving from a description of what there is, to an assessment of its significance, to a conclusion about the threat posed to Jews and to society as a whole. So much writing on contemporary antisemitism seems wrongly to assume that it is enough to describe what exists—that significance and assessment are encapsulated in description.

EXTERNAL NONSCIENTIFIC PRESSURES

I would argue that the Holocaust acts as the greatest nonacademic pressure on the study of contemporary antisemitism.[6] Everyone writing about antisemitism post-1945 writes in the shadow of the Holocaust, and under the veil of genocidal antisemitism developed and implemented by the Nazis. How this form of antisemitism emerged and how it turned from words into deeds are questions which academics have had to confront. Their answers have become part of the canon of knowledge about antisemitism in the twentieth century and about the strength and persistence of antisemitic stereotypes. But it is easy to forget that there were other forms of antisemitism before the Holocaust which fell short of genocide, and that those manifestations of antisemitism continue to exist post-Holocaust. The Holocaust did not supplant them. Nor is there anything to suggest that they automatically lead to genocide against Jews.

And yet the assessment of antisemitism today is so very often colored by the unstated yet clearly discernible assumption that all antisemitism tends to genocide and by the question of whether the state of antisemitism in a certain place will lead to another Holocaust. That the Holocaust should exert such pressure on the study of current antisemitism is by no means surprising, but its effect is to distort our understanding in various ways. First, researchers tend to lay undue emphasis on contemporary reflections of the kinds of antisemitic movements, organizations, and parties which existed in the 1920s and '30s, no matter how small

413

or insignificant they may be. Second, the hunt for genocidal anti-semitism obscures other forms of antisemitism which may be causing more harm than rhetorical threats made in small-circulation magazines to destroy Jewish communities. Third, while the Holocaust also exerts tremendous moral and emotional pressure on all those involved in either studying or combating anti-semitism, the study of contemporary antisemitism, like the study of any social movement, requires a certain emotional detachment, and there is no doubt that the Holocaust inhibits that distancing.

The impact of the Holocaust on the study of antisemitism is also bound up with other enormously significant pressures—political, ideological, and financial.

Ideological, Political, and Financial Pressures

Antisemitism is a political football, used by the left to prove fascist inclinations of rightist governments; used by the right to discredit the left; used by pro-Israel groups to discredit the Palestinians; used by Jewish organizations in their struggle for dominance in the Jewish world. Steering an objective path between these and other political game plans is not easy.

The influence of ideology can be found among Jewish, Israeli, and Zionist groups and institutions involved in monitoring and combatting antisemitism. Antisemitism was a powerful force behind the creation of the Zionist movement. The belief that Jewish life in the Diaspora is doomed is due in part to the fact that antisemitism remains an intractable tenet of modern Zionism. And since, to all intents and purposes, modern Zionism is an arm of the State of Israel, such a view must weigh heavily in Zionist or Israeli-based institutions studying contemporary antisemitism. At its crudest level, this view results in the exaggeration of the current dangers of antisemitism in order to encourage more Jews to live in Israel. Of course, the intrusion of an ideological imperative in antisemitism studies is not always so blatant,[7] and the assumption must be that Israeli academic institutions studying current antisemitism are not unduly affected by such an imperative. Lately, however, there are signs that the ideological element in antisemitism studies has become far more significant.

Institutions studying current antisemitism need money in order to survive, so there is nothing unusual in appealing for funds. But funds are not necessarily given on the basis of who is doing the best work. Often what counts is who shouts loudest— through access to the media, for example—and who possesses surface credibility—a well-known name, either person or institution. In effect the allocation of funds is distorted by the fact that in the Jewish world, antisemitism, properly packaged, is a hot commodity, as the success of the U.S.-based Anti-Defamation League and the Simon Wiesenthal Center testify. And what tends to happen is that even organizations with only peripheral involvement in studying or combatting antisemitism play up that part of their work in order to attract funds. And invariably, the Holocaust is invoked in some way in these fundraising efforts.

Given the pressures on the study of contemporary antisemitism, it is not surprising that contradictory assessments of antisemitism worldwide are produced by individuals and institutions who all claim to be experts on the subject.

A Phase of Heightened Concern and Activity

I do not doubt that there have always been pressures on the study of contemporary antisemitism and that these pressures are more acutely felt during periods of perceived resurgence. Greater efforts will be made to raise funds for work on antisemitism and more funds are likely to become available during times of highly publicized antisemitic and anti-Jewish outrages. We are passing through one of these phases as I write. This is probably a cyclical phenomenon. But a combination of general social and political factors on the one hand, and a new internal Jewish dynamic following the collapse of Communism and developments in the Middle East peace process on the other, indicate that these pressures are especially acute during this current phase.

This is evident from the constellation of organizations and institutes, some new, some old but now more prominent than before, operating in this area and making statements about antisemitism. Some organizations which were devoted to such problems as the struggle for Soviet Jewry and the defense of Israel, but now without a role, have seized on antisemitism as a means of providing themselves with a new raison d'être. In the Jewish world, in the United States the Anti-Defamation League and the Wiesenthal Center, both active in other countries, dominate and are unique in that almost their entire budgets—something in excess of $60 million per year—are devoted to antisemitism and bigotry. Both organizations have come to occupy increasingly significant positions as a result of the way they have responded to the current resurgence of antisemitism.

In Israel, the government's Antisemitism Monitoring Forum has been especially active in developing an international role in this area. It was the driving force behind the establishment of the new Project for the Study of Antisemitism at Tel Aviv University and has been developing ties with a Jewish community–based network of people monitoring and researching antisemitism. For both the Israeli-based initiative and the two U.S. organizations, research and action are inextricably linked.

From the point of view of research, the Institute of Jewish Affairs' annual *Antisemitism World Report*, launched in 1992, has become the most authoritative international documentation of antisemitism worldwide and the first of its kind. A series of opinion polls conducted during the last few years by the American Jewish Committee in various countries, covering not only antisemitism but also knowledge about the Holocaust, have added greatly to the stock of more reliable information about antisemitic views. The Sassoon International Center for the Study of Antisemitism at the Hebrew University has begun to publish a useful series of papers on contemporary antisemitism.

The problem of antisemitism has also been taken up more seriously by interfaith organizations, other bodies monitoring racism, international bodies like the Council of Europe and the U.N. Human Rights Commission, and numerous other organizations.

The above is only a brief and partial review, but I do not think there is any doubt that there appears to be a greater general willingness to speak out against antisemitism and a more robust and uncompromising approach to combatting antisemitism being taken by Jewish organizations. Something, it seems, has changed in the last five years. The problem is to determine whether that change is purely a result of the resurgence of antisemitism or whether other forces have helped produce it.

The discussion that follows deals with antisemitism outside of the United States.

THE MAIN TRENDS

The Collapse of Communism

There is little doubt that the collapse of Communism was a critical moment in the development of antisemitism outside of the United States. Certain specific changes in the antisemitic climate occurred with the end of Communist hegemony in Soviet Russia and Central and Eastern Europe, and those changes were further influenced by decisive developments in the Middle East peace process. It is also possible to see this period as a time when certain existing processes relating to antisemitism reached significant new levels.[8]

Before 1989, the most damaging forms of antisemitism, both for Jewish communities and for the societies in which they lived, thrived in the Communist states. Despite the Communist claim that antisemitism simply could not exist in socialist societies, antisemitism had become a political weapon in the hands of the Communist authorities, both at the level of national governments and at that of official organizations and administrators. Its most public expression was the Communists' anti-Zionist campaign, which was in great part a thinly disguised form of antisemitism. But it also expressed itself in endemic discrimination against Jews in employment and higher education, and in the suppression of all but the most controlled and supine forms of Jewish self-expression. Although this antisemitism did not involve mass violence against Jews, it resulted in the destruction of Jewish communities and severely disrupted the transmission of Judaism and the Jewish heritage from generation to generation.

As Communism collapsed, this whole antisemitic and anti-Zionist edifice crumbled. Within a remarkably short space of time, state-sponsored anti-Zionism and all the structures associated with it simply came to an end, officially sanctioned dis-

417

crimination against Jews withered, and Jewish communities were able to practice their religion and culture freely, establish ties with Jewish organizations abroad, and have open contact with Israel. The opening or restoration of diplomatic ties between the former Communist states and Israel was a further example of the rapid demise of state-sponsored antisemitism.

These remarkable changes had a profound effect on the global level of antisemitism, since the influence of Communist-inspired antisemitism was widespread. Not only did it affect many hundreds of thousands of Jews living under Communism, it had a marked influence in international organizations and Third World forums, it boosted and worked together with the Arab and Palestinian anti-Zionist campaign—which in part was antisemitic and in various countries had an antisemitic effect—and it fed into the ideological and political offensive waged by many Communist and pro-Communist groups and parties in the West. As Communism collapsed, its antisemitic influence outside of the Eastern bloc rapidly waned and a whole area of antisemitic activity ceased to have any serious significance.

As the first walls of Communism were torn down and it soon became apparent that others would inexorably follow, there was an initial burst of naive optimism that democracy would rapidly take hold and antisemitism would play no significant part in the development of the post-Communist world. Almost as quickly as Communism collapsed, however, the grassroots antisemitism that existed in Communist societies, and had been either suppressed or sometimes harnessed to state ends, bubbled to the surface. Freedom from Communism also meant freedom to be openly antisemitic, to establish antisemitic organizations, to create political parties with antisemitism as part of their political ideologies, to publish antisemitic newspapers, magazines, and pamphlets, and to republish traditional antisemitic tracts like *The Protocols of the Elders of Zion* and *Mein Kampf*. Had this outpouring of antisemitism been confined to publications and fringe political propaganda, it might not have created such a stir, but it soon became clear that antisemitism was being used by mainstream politicians and political parties to appeal to their electorates in a cynical struggle for power. It was one thing for a reviled system like Communism to make use of antisemitism politically, but quite another for free citizens in post-Communist societies, the future leaders of governments, to use political antisemitism, one of the most dangerous forms of Jew-hatred.

Jewish organizations and bodies concerned with human rights in Eastern Europe quickly focused their attention on post-Communist antisemitism, and there was a flurry of activity and pronouncements designed to persuade Eastern and Central European leaders to condemn antisemitism and to eschew its use in the emerging democratic politics. Many leaders were slow to respond in a satisfactory manner, giving assurances to Western audiences but being far more equivocal when addressing their own constituencies. This expressed itself particularly clearly in the way such leaders lent their support to movements which aimed at rehabilitating pre-Communist leaders who were either allies and supporters of the Nazis and fascists or purveyors of homegrown versions of Nazism and fascism.

Despite the attention drawn to antisemitism in post-Communist Europe, and the condemnation of it in the West by government leaders and international bodies, it continues to manifest itself strongly, particularly in Russia and Romania, albeit in varying forms. But the more dire predictions of its impact have so far proved unfounded. On the contrary, there has been a marked lessening of the significance of antisemitism in the political process in general. With countries like Poland, Hungary, and the Czech Republic showing strong signs of growing democratic maturity, there must be reason to hope that antisemitism will become steadily more marginalized.

As deeply disturbing as the upsurge of grassroots antisemitism in Eastern and Central Europe has been, how does it compare with the state-sponsored antisemitism of the Communist years? This is a most important question since there is clearly a sense in which the attention devoted to post-Communist antisemitism seems to imply that it is somehow worse than Communist antisemitism and could lead to more serious consequences. I pose this question here but will return to it after considering other elements of antisemitism which are integral to an understanding of its international context.

The Progress of the "Respectable" Far Right

The upsurge of antisemitism in the former Communist countries is one important determinant in the generally held view that there has been a resurgence of antisemitism worldwide since the end of the 1980s. Another important determinant is the increasing prominence of far right parties in Western Europe which present a respectable image to the public, participate in the electoral process (aiming to gain power through legitimate means), advocate policies of racial exclusion, and express a mostly covert antisemitism.[9]

The parties concerned—the Front National in France, the Republikaner in Germany, the Freiheitliche Partei Österreichs in Austria, the Vlaams Blok in Belgium, the Movimento Soziale Italiano in Italy (now subsumed in the National Alliance), for example—have established significant bases of support for themselves among their countries' electorates and in some cases have made significant inroads into mainstream politics. Their growing, yet inconsistent, success predates the collapse of Communism and must to a great degree be put down to the existence of a set of conditions conducive to the growth of racist movements.

First, there has been a weakening of traditional mass ideologies. Many Europeans have become disillusioned with mainstream political parties and have seen the decline of other institutions, like trade unions, which have traditionally defended their interests. These institutions served both as a bulwark against extremism and as a means of integrating into the mainstream individuals predisposed to far-right ideas. But it is not only the far right which is benefiting from this state of affairs; other nontraditional groups like the "green" parties, regional independence movements, single-issue pressure groups, and anti-politics parties have also received increased support.

The past few years have also seen the end in many European countries of expectations of consistent economic growth. Indeed, many European countries are experiencing serious economic difficulties of a structural nature. More than 20 million people in the European Union are now unemployed, and the recession that has affected so many of them is shifting only slowly. Significant numbers of people were not receptive to extremist messages earlier, as long as political consensus could be built around expectations of increasing affluence, better welfare provision, and peaceful redistribution of wealth through the tax system.

In addition, the numbers of migrants, asylum seekers, and immigrants seeking to enter Western Europe, and the prominence given to these developments in the media, has proved to be fertile ground for the far right. Where it is easier to keep people out, as with Britain, the pressure from newcomers on society in general is limited, but even in Britain, anyone who raises the immigration issue is guaranteed strong emotional responses. In other Western European countries, where borders are permeable, it is far harder to prevent the flow of migrants, and as the situation in Germany has shown, considerable social tensions and pressures resulting from the need to absorb large numbers of foreigners exist. It may well be that the long-term contribution of immigrants to the economy outweighs the short-term impact on social services, but this is not an argument which political leaders generally espouse with much conviction, and it carries little weight with people who see immigration as producing other negative consequences. For example, immigrants are perceived to be diluting the national character of what are viewed as ethnically homogenous societies, so that people feel like strangers in their own homes.

The far right has successfully capitalized on dilemmas faced by governments in dealing with questions of asylum seekers and immigrants, and on the popular fears that arise when newcomers are perceived to impinge on national identity.

What is more, not everyone has viewed the quest for European integration as an opportunity to create a new political consensus and stability. Some have seen it as a threat to national sovereignty and, therefore, national identity. In some countries, the desire for integration has translated into more votes for democratic forces which have voiced some of these fears, or in support for anti-Maastricht referendums. In others, racist movements and parties have capitalized on opposition to European integration. Thus among the issues that dominate the "new" Europe, that of borders offers another opportunity for the extreme right to attract support.

Following these factors is the eruption of nationalism throughout Europe as a whole. Much of this nationalism does not stem from liberal impulses. It may be based on race and ethnicity, rather than on shared history and culture. It can be exclusivist and intolerant.

The collapse of the USSR and the end of the Cold War have further transformed international relations, dissolving the sense of certainty that the bipolar world provided. In particular, the reunification of Germany has transformed the political and economic balance in postwar Europe. Many of the dominant political forces that drew strength from their opposition to Communism have now disintegrated, leaving large numbers of people unsure of the political direction to take. The Cold War shaped a certain kind of national identity which has now been undermined, leaving many searching for new certainties and allowing racist movements to capitalize on the situation.

Finally, Nazism and fascism became taboo ideologies at the end of the Second World War. In many countries, expression of either doctrine was prohibited and political organizations were proscribed. The passage of time and the coming of generations which did not experience the war or its difficult aftermath has led to a blurring of the true picture of fascism. Nostalgia for a time when "the trains ran on time" and "there was law and order and discipline" has become an attractive option. And this is especially so in relation to the social and economic problems which so many people face.

The full force of these conditions is evident in Italy, where the neofascist party, the MSI, is now part of the ruling coalition led by Silvio Berlusconi and his Forza Italia. The MSI pronounces itself "postfascist" and its leaders have made attempts to distance themselves from the worst excesses of the fascist past. But they have found it hard to hide their admiration for Mussolini, and at street level MSI supporters show clear signs of an unrepentant neofascism. There is no suggestion that the MSI will begin to espouse antisemitism, but it is already influencing the government to cut or abandon funding for the activities of certain minority organizations.

Although many are naturally alarmed at the rise of political parties in Europe which clearly take some inspiration from traditions which led to the mass murder of the Jews of Europe, antisemitism's precise role and significance in the electorally respectable far right is easy to exaggerate. A much clearer role can be discerned in the many more extreme parties, groups, and movements on the far right which are more interested in direct action than democracy and which concentrate most of their attention on the publication and distribution of racist propaganda. The more extreme the party or group, the more overt its antisemitism. But the far right currently displays greater concern with visible minorities such as blacks, Asians, Turks, Muslims, and Gypsies than with Jews. These groups bear the brunt of increased racist activity, violent and nonviolent, organized and spontaneous. Reported antisemitic incidents have also increased although they represent only a small fraction of overall racist incidents.

The significance of the far right for current antisemitism lies in three elements. First, there is the disguised or semidisguised antisemitic innuendo employed occasionally by the leaders of far-right parties. Statements are made which do not necessarily refer to Jews directly but which clearly signify approval of antisemitic sentiments and are so understood by sections of the electorate to which those leaders are appealing. Second, the overt antisemitism eschewed at the national political level often emerges in the raw at the local level, especially through local party newsletters and other forms of political material. Third, the respectability that the far right has achieved tends to widen the space in which antisemitic ideas, and other forms of racism, can gain legitimacy.

HOLOCAUST DENIAL AND OTHER FORMS OF INTERNATIONAL ANTISEMITISM

While the thrust of far-right politics directed at immigrants, asylum seekers, and visible minorities appears to be concerned with the preservation of "national" culture and "national" identity, there is one form of antisemitism that is common across the entire far-right spectrum, though varying in intensity: denial of the Holocaust.[10] Whereas most antisemitism is country specific in its expression and means of operation, denial of the Holocaust is a truly international form of antisemitism, with certain basic texts and propagandists appearing in many countries. And the fact that

Holocaust denial is a common denominator among far-right organizations, and is also used by Islamic fundamentalists and some extreme left-wing organizations, is evidence that open antisemitism has been largely unacceptable in the postwar period. Denying the Holocaust provides a pseudoacademic framework in which to attack Jews and to do so in a highly unpleasant and insidious fashion. Because it is couched in terms of historical revisionism, antisemites believe they can sidestep charges of antisemitism.

Holocaust denial is the most prominent example of an organized antisemitism which extends across national boundaries. But there are others. Far-right and extreme far-right organizations have increasingly developed international contacts in recent years, drawing on each other for funds, ideas, and material. Publishers of antisemitic books and pamphlets distribute their publications worldwide. In countries where the magazines of neofascist groups are banned, printers in Spain, the United States, and elsewhere are used. Antisemitic material is available on computerized databases, through computer bulletin boards, on computer discs, and on racist telephone networks—all accessible from practically any part of the world.

Islamic fundamentalist antisemitism is also an international phenomenon. It largely manifests itself as part of Islamic opposition to the existence of the State of Israel. Not by any means new, but certainly more significant in recent years, fundamentalist antisemitism is evident within Islamic states, like Egypt and Iran, which either allow its expression or officially encourage it; it operates through fundamentalist organizations which have international networks like Hizbollah and Hamas; and it emerges through local Islamic organizations in Western countries with growing Muslim populations. The international groups have proved themselves capable of murderous bombing incidents directed at Israeli and Jewish targets, like those in Argentina and Britain in June and July 1994. Not that they have claimed responsibility, and even if they had, they would no doubt insist they were demonstrating opposition to the agreement between Israel and the Palestine Liberation Organization (PLO), and to the Zionist state. But whatever the motive—and there can be no guarantee that the motive is an antisemitic one, as that term is commonly understood—an attack on Jewish targets is bound to be perceived as antisemitic and may well have an antisemitic affect. The bombing in Argentina, in which more than a hundred people died, was devastating for the Jewish community. Elsewhere, however, Islamic fundamentalist antisemitism has been largely rhetorical in character, and in Western countries, directed at Jewish students on university campuses.

COUNTERVAILING FORCES

As this brief review indicates, there have been new and troubling developments in antisemitism in the last decade, and particularly since 1989: the preconditions in Western Europe, the emergence of grassroots and political antisemitism in Eastern Europe after the collapse of Communism, the electoral advance of the far right in certain Western European countries, the growth of the Holocaust denial movement, increasing international contacts between antisemites, and the growth of Islamic fundamentalist antisemitism. But just as the post-Communist antisemitism of Eastern and Central Europe must be set against the context of the situation before 1989, so too must the other aspects of antisemitism today be considered in the light of other circumstances and countervailing forces.

Changes in the Middle East

Possibly most significant in the long term, and closely related to the developments in Eastern and Central Europe, are the moves toward peace in the Middle East. Antisemitism in that region is a complex issue, derived as it is from a variety of sources and its expression still largely controlled by the authorities.[11] But there is no doubt that antisemitic tracts circulate in the Middle East in large numbers, antisemitic images are ubiquitous in Arab media, and where Jewish minorities exist they have been subject to restrictions and have had to tread very carefully. When Communism collapsed, the Arab states and the PLO lost their main partners in their anti-Zionist campaign. Countries which had trained and harbored PLO terrorists ceased to offer them hospitality and opened diplomatic relations with Israel. Israel, already less isolated in international forums as a result of growing Third World disillusionment with Arab oil producers, radically improved its international position. The Arab states were unable to ignore the change in the international climate, especially after the Gulf War, and entered the Madrid process brokered by the Bush administration.

A number of developments began then which resulted in the lessening of antisemitic pressures in the Middle East. Shortly after the Madrid conference, Syria relaxed its restrictions on Jews leaving the country and in effect opened the way for the emigration of Syrian Jewry. In Egypt, and in other Arab countries, there has been a marked lessening in antisemitic expression. This process was given a further boost following the signing of the Israel-PLO accord in October 1993 and subsequent meetings between Israeli leaders and Arab leaders such as Morocoo's King Hassan and Jordan's King Hussein. Crown Prince Hassan of Jordan agreed to become a member of the Inter-Parliamentary Council Against Antisemitism, a body set up by Greville Janner, a British Jewish member of Parliament.

If it continues, this trend is of great significance for the future diminishing of antisemitism. While the Arabs have justified their campaign against Israel on purely political and historical grounds, there is no doubt that antisemitism has played its part. This anti-Zionist antisemitism has been echoed outside of the Middle East and has helped sustain a certain level of antisemitic expression. But further progress in the peace process is bound to lead to a further lessening of antisemitic pressures in the Middle East generally (excluding Iran, whose anti-Jewish hostility remains at a high level), as well as among those outside of the region whose antisemitism has drawn succor and inspiration from Arab antisemitism.

Opinion Polls

Antisemitic sentiment as measured by opinion polls provides a further indication of worldwide trends.[12] Of course polls have not been conducted in all countries and not all polls are reliable. But since the collapse of Communism, one can construct a much broader picture of antisemitic sentiment than before. In most Western countries where reliable polling has been conducted, the evidence suggests a long-term decline to a specific bedrock level of antisemitic prejudice. Polling in Eastern Europe has revealed high levels of antisemitic sentiment in some countries—Poland and Slovakia, for example—but these results hardly came as a surprise. Even where antisemitic sentiment is high in Eastern Europe, other minority groups often attract greater enmity, with Gypsies being regarded as the most reviled group of all. Follow-up surveys will provide a more informed picture of the effect of democratization and economic liberalization on former Communist societies.

Changes can certainly be expected, although not necessarily for the better. Surveys indicated lower levels of antisemitic sentiment in eastern Germany than in western Germany in the immediate aftermath of reunification. But after a year or so recorded levels increased in eastern Germany to match western Germany. In Russia, recent polls indicate that antisemitic views are now held more evenly among different age groups and social strata than before, but even there, where the antisemitic movement is extensive, levels of antisemitic sentiment are not as high as in some of the other countries of Central and Eastern Europe.

Declining levels of antisemitic sentiment are usually associated with improved levels of education, higher standards of living, and the passing of older generations. These are medium- to long-term developments and can only be achieved within the framework of social, economic, and educational policies pursued by governments. Efforts to do something about the problem of anti-semitism in the here-and-now may not have an immediate impact on levels of sentiment, but they are designed to prevent occurrences of antisemitism and to punish those who perpetrate antisemitic acts.

Legal Developments

Among the most sustained efforts to combat antisemitism have been those in the legal field and in the field of international human rights instruments. The last decade has witnessed a considerable increase in the adoption of legal measures which can be used to prosecute antisemites.[13] For example, increasing numbers of countries now have laws against incitement to racial hatred, and with the collapse of Communism, many former Communist countries have adopted such legislation. By no means all countries include antisemitism by name in the laws passed, but the wording used is invariably broad enough to cover antisemitism. Some countries now also have specific laws outlawing denial of the Holocaust and more are considering adopting such laws.

On the international level, considerable efforts have been made to ensure the inclusion of antisemitism in the concluding documents of the CSCE process meetings. (The Conference on Security and Cooperation in Europe is the framework created, following the signing the Helsinki Accords in 1975, to enable discussion of security and human rights issues between Western and Eastern Europe during the Cold War.) And at the United Nations, the culmination of a long campaign came when the Human Rights Commission made an explicit formal condemnation of antisemitism in March 1994, the first ever such resolution by a UN body.

Use of legislation to prosecute antisemites has been patchy, but it would be wrong to evaluate the impact of legislation on antisemitism only in this narrow way. The existence of such legislation indicates that there is a greater readiness to make a public stand on incitement to race hatred; it shows the degree of consensus on this issue, and it may have a longer-term educational effect. Politicians in many countries find it advantageous to be seen to be associating themselves with such measures. The thrust is definitely toward more and better legislation of this kind.

Legislation passed in Canada, Australia, and the United Kingdom to allow the prosecution of suspected Nazi war criminals who committed their crimes in other countries must also be seen as part of the legislative effort to combat antisemitism. This was certainly in the minds of many who pressed for the introduction of these laws, although the motivation to combat antisemitism was generally couched in terms of the argument that prosecuting these suspected criminals would have an educational effect, helping to ensure that such things never happen again.

But the legislative and international human rights effort is only one of the countervailing forces against antisemitism. Other initiatives include dialogue with the churches (still to be fully developed in many former Communist states); the willingness of many prominent political leaders to condemn antisemitism; measures available in some countries to ban antisemitic groups; the educational effort, both formal and informal, on racism and specifically on the Holocaust; the greater public awareness of the Holocaust as a result of increasing numbers of documentaries, feature films, and books; the monitoring of antisemitic incidents by the authorities in some countries; and public demonstrations when major incidents occur. The taboo on public expressions of antisemitism may well be weakening, but it remains something which societies are officially unwilling to tolerate.

As noted earlier, many national and international Jewish organizations have geared themselves up to deal with the problem of antisemitism. On the international level, the Israeli government, the World Jewish Congress, the Simon Wiesenthal Center, the Anti-Defamation League, the American Jewish Committee, the International Association of Jewish Lawyers and Jurists, organizations of Holocaust survivors, and others speak out, conduct prejudice reduction programs, and make representations to governments. Numerous conferences and seminars on antisemitism have been held in recent years, and many of those gatherings have been organized in conjunction with non-Jewish bodies. Students have been increasingly active in working to combat antisemitism. In individual countries, defense activity of this sort has become increasingly sophisticated.

Historians have shown that monitoring, marching, and making laws and representations are nothing new and may not be enough to stem an upsurge of antisemitism, should one occur.[14] But there is certainly something different about the current wave of activity.

THE INFLUENCE OF THE HOLOCAUST

The link that is made between this activity and the Holocaust is often very explicit. The message of "Never again!" is always implied and very often stated openly in various ways. The establishment of two multimillion-dollar Holocaust museums in the United States, the stress on Holocaust studies in universities, colleges, and schools, the wish to educate against prejudice through educating about the Holocaust, the huge growth in scholarly studies about the Holocaust, the increasing number of Holocaust memorials, the great interest of documentary and feature filmmakers in the Holocaust, and the effort to obtain restitution and compensation for Jewish property expropriated by the Nazis in Eastern Europe during the Holocaust—all these developments and more indicate clearly the degree to which action on antisemitism is inspired by increasing awareness of the Holocaust.

The assertive willingness of Jewish organizations to speak out on perceived antisemitism, and to organize campaigns against countries, organizations, and individuals who espouse or condone antisemitism, has an edge to it which was not present five or ten years ago. I believe that this activity is increasingly fueled by a desire to right the wrongs of the Holocaust, not to let those involved get away with it, to settle accounts before it is too late.

In my view this is a very significant development both for Jewish life and for antisemitism. On the one hand, it makes for increased vigilance by suggesting that, no matter what the true state of antisemitism worldwide, Jews have become more sensitized to antisemitism in the post-Holocaust period. On the other hand, it can lead to an exaggeration of the degree of antisemitism worldwide and the threat it poses to Jewish communities and society in general.

Both the level of antisemitism worldwide and the Jewish capacity or willingness to fight it are heavily influenced by the normalization of the Jew, by a diminishing of his or her visible otherness. This is not a simple development because it consists of seemingly contradictory processes. Integration and assimilation contribute to normalization. Most Jews look no different from their fellow citizens. The existence of Israel has contributed to normalization because Jews are seen to be involved in the whole range of human activity.

Jewish self-assertion—more prevalent among the young, among the North African Jews now part of the French Jewish community, and among Hasidic groups—also contributes to normalization because difference is more the norm in many societies. As far as dress is concerned, it is increasingly the case that all styles are acceptable.

But normalization also means that Jews are more likely to be subject to criticism as a group, less likely to benefit from a sense of being untouchable because of the Holocaust. And it also means that Jews are more likely to speak out when they perceive they are under attack, since they care less about how others see them. The willingness to speak out more on antisemitism often generates more antisemitism. Those who do so, however, feel it is a price worth paying.

INTEREST AND IGNORANCE

Jews find themselves at times the object of both intense scrutiny and ignorance. There are millions growing up with no knowledge of Jews whatsoever. Even in societies where there are relatively sizable Jewish communities, it is common to encounter people who have never met a Jew. But the scrutiny and the ignorance are double-edged, and deciding which edge is the significant one is a matter of interpretation. The Middle East conflict, interest in the Holocaust, antisemitism, the recovery and reclaiming of the past in Eastern Europe—these and other factors ensure that attention is focused on Jews. In some countries this interest is mostly seen as a product of a genuine desire to inquire and to know; in other countries, it can be an excessive, intrusive interest playing on unstated fears of Jewish influence. The airtime and column inches devoted to the Israeli-Arab conflict are often put down to questionable attitudes to Jews, to the application of double standards whereby Israel is expected to adhere to norms which are not demanded of other states. But this view has become out of date, given developments in the peace process.

Since education is regarded as a principal means of reducing prejudice, ignorance about Jews is likely to be seen as a source of antisemitism. But I doubt whether such a perception is universally applicable in 1994. In the past, ignorance often went hand in hand with obscurantism, the automatic acceptance of the Christian claim that Jews killed Christ and other antisemitic stereotypes.

In Western societies today, lack of knowledge of Jews no longer leads invariably to negative views of Jews; a degree of benign ignorance prevails. The encouragement of a liberal and tolerant society, however incomplete, means that when confronted with Jews, people do not automatically adopt negative attitudes, even if they have been on the receiving end of antisemitic stereotypes in the past. Some would argue that the liberal consensus is itself a form of antisemitism, since it is ready to the accept the Jew as an individual if he no longer wishes to assert his identity, but not the collective Jew who insists on remaining rooted in a community determined to maintain its difference. This is a contentious view, but it indicates again the double-edged nature of interest and ignorance.

HIDDEN AND LATENT ANTISEMITISM

The argument about the liberal consensus takes us into the realms of hidden and latent antisemitism. I referred to the question of hidden antisemitism above in relation to the electorally respectable far right and Holocaust denial. The phenomenon certainly exists, but it is very difficult to judge whether more people are demonstrating their hidden antisemitism by making antisemitic statements which are thinly disguised or whether there truly is more hidden antisemitism. If the former is the case, it does not seem to be very effective for the hidden antisemites, since so much attention has been drawn to those who indulge in it. If the latter applies, it suggests that the taboo against expression of antisemitism remains strong.

Latent antisemitism is even more difficult to assess, and yet when assessments of antisemitism are made, support for the idea of widespread latent antisemitism is often implicitly or explicitly given. But even though there is certainly some latent antisemitism, there is no direct evidence to suggest that it has become especially significant in recent years. In many ways, given the preconditions in Europe described above, one might expect high levels of latent antisemitism. In fact, the resurgence in antisemitism comes largely from sources which either do not hide their antisemitism, or if they do so, they thinly disguise their hate for Jews.

ANTISEMITISM OUTSIDE OF EUROPE AND THE MIDDLE EAST

This essay has focused mostly on Europe—given the importance of antisemitism in Europe and the importance it exerts elsewhere—and to some extent on the Middle East. Antisemitism also exists in Latin America, South Africa, Australasia, and to a much lesser degree in Asia. But there is little to suggest that any other significant trends have emerged in these places which change the world context.

The one possible exception is the bombing of the central offices of the Argentine Jewish community in June 1994, which resulted in the death of more than one hundred people. Most observers would have argued that antisemitism in Latin America was not a growing threat; indeed, developments in the last year or two indicate a general improvement. The bomb—whoever planted it, and there are suggestions that local neo-Nazis might have been involved even if only "contracted" to carry out the bombing by Islamic fundamentalist elements—showed that Latin America constitutes a soft underbelly for this kind of outrage. The bomb's impact may be antisemitic in nature, frightening Jews who will feel unwilling to demonstrate their identity and giving encouragement to local antisemitic groups, but it is too early to predict the consequences.

The state of antisemitism worldwide presents a complex picture and allows for no facile conclusions. That the social, political, and economic preconditions now exist for an increase in antisemitism in some parts of the world, to a degree not apparent since the passing of the immediate postwar period, is clear, but they are at most necessary and not sufficient conditions. An increase in violent ethnic conflicts, the growth of racist incidents, the increasing popularity of exclusivist extreme nationalism—all these have occurred and antisemitism has been a part of all these developments. But on the whole, Jews have been peripheral, both as propaganda victims or as victims of violence. The main targets in these conflicts are not Jews. What is surprising, therefore, is that there has not been more antisemitism.

Similar conclusions could be drawn about the evident relaxation of taboos on Nazism and fascism and the passing of time since the Holocaust and the Second World War. As the advance of the far right and the coming to power of the MSI in Italy have shown, the connection between these parties and the parties which led Europe to the death and destruction of the Second World War is not a sufficient deterrent for many of today's voters.

But again, there is absolutely no evidence of a mass return to fascism and Nazism, even in those countries suffering most from economic dislocation, political instability, and social collapse. For all the justified concern about neo-Nazism in Germany, the last thing most Germans want—east and west—is a rebirth of totalitarianism. Some would argue that it is the concern with dilution of national identity which signals creeping fascism, but here we enter the world of political opinion and sloganizing; however legitimate it may be to question such fears about national identity, to paint it as the return of Nazism is groundless.

As regards the growing number of years since the occurrence of the Holocaust, there is very little evidence that time itself is actually encouraging more people to be antisemitic. It may be the case, however, that more extreme antisemites are more ready to express their antisemitism, which would help explain increases in antisemitic incidents.

While the notion of a new antisemitism does not stand up to scrutiny, many of the indicators discussed above do point to a qualified resurgence in antisemitism. There appears to have been an increase in antisemitic incidents and dissemination of antisemitic material in some countries, with antisemites more ready to act out their hatred in violent forms. But it is hard to estimate the reliability of such a conclusion because of inadequate data going back over time. While the far right has made progress in Western Europe, it is difficult to assess the role antisemitism has played in the process. Grassroots and political antisemitism in Eastern Europe blossomed after the collapse of Communism. But compared to the antisemitism which was used by the Communist authorities, this antisemitism is far less damaging in its effect on Jewish communities. Holocaust denial thrives, but despicable and vile though it is, there is no evidence that it has infected mainstream opinion. Islamic fundamentalist antisemitism is probably the most worrying as far as Jewish security is concerned, but as yet it remains more of a potential than an actual danger.

And if we set these elements of qualified resurgence against factors indicating a lessening of antisemitism, the international context of antisemitism becomes clearer. Over recent years, antisemitic sentiment has declined in some countries and stabilized in others. Evidence of discrimination against Jews in employment, in social situations, in politics, and so on, is minimal. In most countries, antisemitic incidents are but a fraction of overall racist incidents. Other groups bear the brunt of racist activity. There are no mainstream parties with antisemitic policies as part of their platforms. Christian antisemitism prevails and churches in Eastern Europe have a long way to go to catch up with interfaith dialogue in the West, but the churches are in the forefront of combating antisemitism and have made great, albeit imperfect, strides in setting their own houses in order. Finally, there is a serious and growing body of legislation and international human rights instruments which allow for the prosecution of antisemitism.

The objective conditions do not give cause for great alarm, but they must be set in the context of a lower threshold of tolerance of antisemitism among Jewish organizations, heightened Jewish concern, and greater readiness to speak out and demand action. This more militant Jewish view is in part a manifestation of what Tom Smith describes: "that Jews, for understandable reasons, overestimate the extent of anti-Semitism, its direction of change, and its potential for the future."[15]

But it is also part of a historic shift which has made the exaggeration of antisemitism even more acute. Jewish fear that the Holocaust will be forgotten—no matter what the evidence—has led to both the demand for a settling of accounts before it is too late and a desire to remind the world of the dangers of antisemitism. Understandable, and in part worthy, though these processes may be, they are fraught with dangers. But they too are part of the international context of antisemitism.

NOTES

1. Robert S. Wistrich, "Antisemitism in Europe Since the Holocaust," in *Working Papers on Contemporary Anti-Semitism* (American Jewish Com-

mittee, 1993, appeared originally in the 1993 *American Jewish Year Book*), p. 21.

2. Michael Marrus, "Antisemitism and Xenophobia in Historical Perspective," in *Patterns of Prejudice* 28:2 (1994), 81.

3. The most comprehensive exploration of this issue is Robert Wistrich, ed., *Anti-Zionism and Antisemitism in the Contemporary World* (London, 1990).

4. For a comprehensive attempt to deal with these problems, see the Methodology section in "Introduction," *Antisemitism World Report 1994* (London: Institute of Jewish Affairs, 1994), pp. xxiv–vi.

5. For a critical approach to the Anti-Defamation League audit of incidents in the United States, see Tom W. Smith, "Anti-Semitism in Contemporary America," in *Working Papers on Contemporary Anti-Semitism* (New York, American Jewish Committee, 1994), pp. 13–16.

6. See also Antony Lerman, "Antisemitism in the 1990s: A Symposium," in *Patterns of Prejudice* 25:2 (winter 1991), 3–78.

7. See, for example, the Introduction by Dr. Elyakim Rubinstein, chairman of the Anti-Semitism Monitoring Forum of the Israeli government, in *Anti-Semitism Worldwide 1993*, produced by the Project for the Study of Anti-Semitism, Tel Aviv University, in cooperation with the Anti-Defamation League, pp. v–vii.

8. These developments are covered in Charles Hoffman, *Gray Dawn: The Jews of Eastern Europe in the Post-Communist Era* (New York: HarperCollins, 1992); Paul Hockenos, *Free to Hate* (London/New York: Routledge, 1993); *Anti-Semitism in Post-Totalitarian Europe* (Prague: Franz Kafka Publishers, 1993); *Patterns of Prejudice*, vol. 27, nos. 1 and 2.

9. For background and an assessment of the far right see Peter H. Merkl and Leonard Weinberg, eds., *Encounters with the Contemporary Radical Right* (Oxford: Westview, 1993); and *Political Extremism and the Threat to Democracy in Europe: A Survey and Assessment of Parties, Movements and Groups* (London: Institute of Jewish Affairs, 1994, for Centre Européen de Recherche et d'Action sur le Racisme et l'Antisémitisme).

10. Deborah Lipstadt, *Denying the Holocaust: The Growing Assault on Truth and Memory* (New York: Free Press, 1993) is the best account of Holocaust denial published so far.

11. A useful summary of the nature of Arab antisemitism can be found in *Antisemitism World Report 1994*, pp. 160–61.

12. A summary of some of the polls can be found in Arthur Hertzberg, "Is Anti-Semitism Dying Out?" *New York Review of Books*, June 24, 1993. Herzberg's article is one of the most important recent contributions to the debate about contemporary antisemitism.

13. See the various articles and papers by Stephen J. Roth, and most recently "The Legal Fight Against Antisemitism: Survey of Developments in 1992," *Israel Yearbook on Human Rights*, vol. 23 (1993).

14. See for example Simon Epstein, "Cyclical Patterns of Antisemitism: The Dynamics of Anti-Jewish Violence in Western Countries Since the 1950s," in *Analysis of Current Trends in Antisemitism*, no. 2 (Sassoon International Center for the Study of Antisemitism, 1993).

15. Smith, "Anti-Semitism in America," p. 18.

PART FIVE

ANTISEMITISM IN CONTEMPORARY POPULAR CULTURE

·20·

Antisemitism: Our Constant Companion?

ANNE ROIPHE

Anne Roiphe, a novelist and journalist, is the author of
*Lovingkindness, The Pursuit of Happiness, A
Generation Without Memory,* and *A Season for
Healing.* She is a columnist for the *New York Observer.*

Anne Roiphe challenges the reader with a number of questions in her
provocative essay with which this volume closes, and she reflects upon a
number of controversial issues. The response in America to the Holocaust, the Jewish communal stance on core constitutional questions such
as the separation of church and state, approaches toward intergroup and
interreligious relationships, stereotypes and prejudices—all inform Roiphe's
observations on antisemitism and lead her to her conclusions that tolerance is not the same as acceptance; that antisemitism may very well be
our constant companion in America; that, with all of their successes, Jews
in America may yet be not entirely secure. (Compare in this regard chapter 4, "Can Antisemitism Disappear?" in which Earl Raab argues for the
terminability of antisemitism, and my introductory chapter to this volume.)
Roiphe's "bottom line" question, in essence a challenge to the thesis of
this volume: Is not the security of Jews in this country still at risk?

Many Jews will identify with the feelings and emotions expressed by
Roiphe. Her down-to-earth essay in fact illumines for the reader the "perception gap" (also discussed in my Introduction): the data indicate an antisemitism on the decline, yet most Jews perceive antisemitism as a serious problem, perhaps on the rise. As Roiphe addresses this phenomenon,
her reflections enhance our understanding of it.

Roiphe's essay, however, may be read as going beyond identifying a
long history of anti-Jewish persecution. Even as she asserts "we are not

the sum of our persecutions," Roiphe's message, at least to this reader, is that persecution is so ingrained in the Jews' collective psyche that being persecuted and being Jewish are synonymous.

The feeling that the history of the Jews is coterminous with the history of antisemitism—"the lachrymose theory of Jewish history," to invoke the usage of historians Cecil Roth and Salo Baron—is in my view a misrepresentation of that history. While antisemitism has surely been an important factor in Jewish history, it does not *define* Jewish history; it is not its central dynamic.

Roiphe is right on the mark, however, in her prescription for antisemitism; she calls upon Jews to support programs that will enhance social and economic justice. She offers two reasons: first, such activity is a positive and powerful affirmation of Jewish identity—particularly, I might add, in a time during which Jewish identity and continuity are considered to be at risk—and second, as is discussed elsewhere in this volume, prejudice is reduced not by changing the individual, but by changing the conditions of society.

An observation on Anne Roiphe's pointed views on the separation of church and state: Roiphe posits that a Jewish community "bold enough, fearless enough . . . could live more easily with their [Christian] symbols and put ours in public." In other words, we should be able to live with a lower "wall of separation"—to use Jefferson's phrase—between church and state. Roiphe seems to suggest that the American Jewish commitment to an impenetrable wall of separation stems from a fear that a breach in the wall would emphasize the distinctiveness of Jews and, presumably, leave them exposed and unprotected. But Jews ought not have that fear, Roiphe argues. Jews ought not be reluctant to display their symbols, even in the public square itself.

It seems to me that Roiphe's analysis of church-state separation stands the issue on its head; it is better suited to those societies that are not based on the principles of democratic pluralism. The separation of church and state is the central constitutional mechanism in the protection of individuals, groups, and minorities, balancing off the interests of majorities and the state. The American Jewish commitment to church-state separation is premised upon the very fact of the Jewish community's distinctiveness. Lowering the "wall of separation" does not enhance or emphasize a group's distinctiveness; quite the contrary, it compromises, and may ultimately destroy, that distinctiveness. The wisdom (or lack thereof) of having a Hanukkah menorah on the steps of City Hall has nothing to do with fearlessness and chutzpah.

This is not an unimportant point. An analysis of constitutional protections—particularly church-state separation—is crucial to our understanding of Jewish security. American associationalism, American voluntarism, American exceptionalism, above all American pluralism, are informed, protected, and guaranteed by the "religion clauses" of the First Amendment that define the separation of church and state, provide for religious liberty, and ultimately guarantee the security and status of individuals and groups in this society.

J.A.C.

How can a Jew not be bitter, how can a Jew not be bent by the weight of the stories we know, stories that have come to us through the generations, so many stories of communal disaster, of individual pain, of lies and exclusions, of expulsions and blood libels, of Cossacks riding down on our villages, inquisitors and their instruments of torture, of cold shoulders and cold murder, of blame placed on our children's heads for plagues, for drought, for flood, despised for our enforced poverty and envied and loathed for our assumed wealth? We have merged them, the tales of our oppression, stylized them, remembered them, echoed them in our hearts, in our liturgy, in our responses to newspaper headlines, the glance of neighbors, the whispers of those in power. We startle easily, we try not to panic and then fear we have become alarmed too late. We have learned to laugh at ourselves while keeping a sharp eye out for a change in the weather, for the approaching storm, for heartbreak dead ahead.

How can a Jew not be angry at the injustice, the cruelty, the brutish savage behavior of the antisemitic thugs who beat us up in the streets of Cracow, Charleston, or New York, who wrote fine-sounding articles about our venality in the literary presses of Vienna, Bruges, or Kansas City; or who are today cheering Kahlid Abdul Muhammad at universities around the United States? We know where it led, and while once it couldn't be imagined, now it can. Even with a state of our own, land of our own, can we ever be a normal people, trusting, friendly, neither defensive nor offensive, proud but not belligerent, easy in our sleep, with memories like the ones we have? Are we Jewish Americans or American Jews, and just because America has allowed us to flourish in this century will it do so in the next?

We scold ourselves when we threaten to drown in the rising waters of our lachrymose history and remind ourselves that we are not the sum of our persecutions, we are not bound together merely by our enemies. We remind ourselves of our splendid books holy and secular, our law, our commentaries, our fables. We remind ourselves of our skills in the world of finance, medicine, law. We speak of our ethics, our traditions, our holidays, our families, and we know we are not what they say of us, we are not their scapegoat, we are people of our own imagining.

Nevertheless we carry with us, each Jew, not simply the escape from Egypt with the pharaoh's army at our backs but the swords of the Syrians and the ropes of the Romans, and last and most terrible, the barbs of the Gentiles, the stereotypes about money, greed, exclusiveness. Even here in America stepping up and down in the aerobics classes of our local Jewish community centers we remember the trains of the Christians, those nation builders who called us "Christ killers" as they killed us and who used our presence between the social cracks to grease the wheels of commerce while despising our stubborn hard-won survival, robbing us of our successes, our dignity, our lives. In America we faced the fact that our beloved Roosevelt did not come to the rescue. We know that the immigration laws were there to keep us out, that those laws resulted in the deaths of many who might have been saved. We remember when the American president, the American generals, the Princeton, Harvard, Yale men of the Cabinet, could not spare even a few bombs to blast the tracks that ran to Auschwitz.

We remember when they thought our heads were smaller, our brains were less. When hotels and universities, medical schools, golf clubs and law firms, apartment houses and neighborhoods, were openly restricted. How can we possibly be calm, fair, forgiving? Our story is not for the faint of spirit. We remember our parents saying, "Sh, sh, don't call attention." We remember our parents saying, "Don't talk with your hands, don't let your hair curl, off to the plastic surgeon with you, watch out, sh, sh."

Those were the days when identity politics were not invoked to increase pride or the membership in communal organizations but to influence the odds of survival.

Antisemitism may represent the moral failure of the majority, but it also, especially after the Holocaust, confounds our relationship with our God. If we are covenanted, what kind of a covenant is this? Are we the only people on earth to continue a relationship with a deity that has failed to protect us, again and again? We make excuses, we blame ourselves for our impurities, but as the centuries pass it becomes increasingly hard not to point a finger at God. "Where were you when the crematoria were working through the night, sending ash up to the stars?" We wonder about the God of our fathers who even in the beginning was willing to taunt us with the lives of our children and threatened to take Isaac. What kind of a God sacrifices or pretends to sacrifice or allows the sacrifice of His own children?

Most of us do not accept antisemitism as the tool of a punishing and vengeful God. Those Jews who tell themselves that the Holocaust occurred because some Jews broke the Sabbath or defied kashrut or mocked the law contort, turn inside out reality to hold on to their faith. They blame other groups of Jews rather than suffer the anguish of their uncertain arrangements with the indifferent firmaments. Rabbi Hillel, Rabbi Akiba, would never have let this stand. They sought ways of gentleness, forgiveness, humanity, working within the outlines of the law to allow Jews to stretch in the sunlight of life.

The long story of Jewish punishment has so outweighed any possible Jewish crime against God or man that we can't but feel that a religion that blames the victims for their story will be abandoned in the dust of time. In a pragmatic, nonspiritual age such as ours, the Jewish experience in America has made some of us godless, some of us questioners, and has shaken some of our faith, loosening ties with the tradition, stripping, weakening our recognition of ourselves as a nation with a purpose, with a destiny, with a direction.

In America our Reform, Conservative, Orthodox congregations became Holocaust-fixed and Israel-animated. The trees we planted, the blue boxes we filled with coins, the Israel we cheered at peace and war—this was our answer to the antisemites. We are still here. We have an army that all the world admires or fears. Next time we won't need your passports, your pity, we won't suffer your indifference. For the most part the congregation was involved with History, not with God; with nation building rather than piety; with fitting into America, not with making waves. The theological problems will need more discussion, more public debate, more inventive and tolerant solutions.

What is God to the Jews and what are the Jews to God is a subject that the next century can follow creatively, imaginatively. And why not? We have room in the Jewish nation for all kinds of solutions, all kinds of answers to theological doubt and belief. In the current climate, where antisemitism is not at the moment knocking down our doors, we can use the breathing time to create: Jewish philosophy, Jewish art, Jewish literature.

Our anger goes out from us in all directions, to the Gentiles, to the political authorities, to the Vatican and the quota-makers in other countries, to the excluding aristocracies and the brutal peasantry and the wishy-washy intellectuals. Our anger turns on ourselves, grinding away in our bellies, affecting our judgments, distorting our politics, blinding us to our true friends, and isolating us when we need not be isolated. It is hard for a Jew not to feel that the plot of the world, its most central story, is about his or her destruction, exclusion, failed attempts to find a safe spot. We are a small group, hardly a fraction of a percent of the global population, but our mark is often there wherever grief comes raining down.

The author Jerzy Kosinski wrote in *The Painted Bird*, "A person (concludes the boy) should take revenge for every wrong and humiliation. There were far too many injustices in the world to have them all weighed and judged. A man should consider every wrong he had suffered and decide on the appropriate revenge."

The problem is that we cannot exact punishment, we will not catch the most prominent Nazis, and we can never achieve revenge against all those who were indifferent, those collaborators, those mild antisemites glad to see their towns cleansed. Our need for revenge hangs over us and we need to take care that it not express itself on the heads of historic innocents, passersby. We are both threatened by Holocaust "revisionism" and left unsatisfied in our natural desire to harm those who have harmed us.

In addition we find ourselves today in an America aware of a new antisemitism that ripples and plays across the black community, mocking us, taunting us, saddening us. Some Jews in their fury have turned against the blacks, giving up their natural and moral identification with the victims of racism and identifying themselves instead with the wealthiest, strongest portion of America.

Why not? It's an old story. The peasants most loved by the socialists of Russia and Poland were the first to turn on the Jews. The Communists as soon as they had power began their Jewish purges. The leftists in America turned on the Israelis, the blacks took the Palestinian cause to heart, and as always when Jews go searching for allies we find our most hopeful loves unrequited.

In America the traditions of liberty have served many white people well, and public order has been maintained despite fighting at the edges of ethnic neighborhoods, rudeness in the boardrooms, among the club members, in the banks. The center-stage drama in America has been that of the whites against the blacks. This is the morality play that seems to have sucked the floating hatred into its vortex, and we Jews have for the most part, up to now, been able to avoid the tornado.

In America, the disaffected, the Ku Klux Klan, the skinheads, the teenage vandals, the white majority making antisemitic jokes in the locker rooms, may not have any special affection for Jews, but we are the secondary enemy, not the primary. In the dust stirred up by the black-white conflict we have been able to go about our lives, using the schools, the banks, our own communal structures to build a society so comfortable that the major threat comes from within as our children mingle and merge and leave us behind.

In America there are so many kinds of snobbisms, prejudices, dislikes, that antisemitism almost has to wait its turn to catch attention. The Catholics and the Protestants, the fundamentalists and the Episcopalians, the Irish and the Italians, the ones who have been here longest versus the latest newcomers, the West versus the East, the city people against the rural, the lawyers versus everyone. The blacks can hate the Koreans and the Koreans can loathe the Dominicans and the Puerto Ricans point out that the Dominicans are lazy, the fundamentalists hate the gays and the pro-lifers go toe to toe against the pro-choicers, and everyone hates New Yorkers, which is a polite way of being antisemitic and antiblack and -Hispanic too—and so the merry-go-round turns. Jews seem relatively safe behind the reality of omnipresent social dislike which provides the voice-over for those wonderful dreams of the Founding Fathers of brotherhood and opportunity for all.

What a success story it has been. The Jewish immigrant parents had extravagant hopes for their children and those hopes have been more than fulfilled. "Greenhorns," aliens, sweatshop workers have been transformed into doctors and lawyers, journalists and businesspeople. In disproportionate numbers we speak in public, we talk, we make movies, we write articles, we add our two cents to the political scene, to the theater, to the biologist's laboratory, to the classroom. Some say antisemitism has been beaten, vanquished in America. Others say wait, it pauses, it sleeps, it will come slouching toward us again. It certainly isn't a strong enough beast at the moment to force our children to marry each other, to drive the community into a renewed sense of urgency.

And yet most of us believe that we are not safe, we do not sleep well at night, we startle at the slightest sound. We know that we are not loved and the laws that protect us, make us equal, give us our opportunities, are man-made and man-made can be man unmade.

Jewish communal life depends financially to some extent on our fear of antisemitism. The reports are issued, the pleas for funds follow. It appears that we wouldn't give if our very lives and our children's lives were not on the line. Are they? The antisemites of America, loony Aryan-rights groups, Nation of Islam followers, and the fellow who sells you your car and then tells an antisemitic joke behind your back, today they are either powerless or bound by the laws of the land to let you go your own way. But tomorrow?

The half-Jew Jean Amery, a literary critic and a survivor of Auschwitz, reported seeing a crèche in Austria at Christmastime, 1938. Beneath the cradle was a sign which said, "Let the hungry be fed and the poor be welcome and the Jews shall die like dogs." In America when we wake up and see a swastika on a temple door or hear a religious leader speak of Judaism as a "gutter religion," we are not so much frightened as furious. How dare they again? How is it possible?

Because of the Holocaust all antisemitism, from the mildest to the most brutal, alarms. Most of us no longer shrug our shoulders and expect the worst to pass. We know that the Farrakhans of the world speak not just to African Americans but that the brushfire they have started could, just possibly, ignite the country, heating up the ethnic poor, the fundamentalist South, the Christian coalitions, and after ensuring that homosexuals are deprived of equal rights they might attack Jewish businesses, boycott Jewish professionals, make it hard for firms to hire Jews once again.

Given our financial success, our professional organizations, the Bill of Rights, the Constitution, the safeguards of our legal system, this scenario seems paranoid, but paranoia is sanity in this benighted century.

Our anger, particularly our Holocaust rage, affects each one of us in a primary and personal way. What are we to do with it, this roiling of feelings that we all nurse, this resentment, grudge, and fear that we have reasonably acquired in response to the facts of our history? Jean-Paul Sartre says in his book *Anti-Semite and Jew*, "Since the Jew is dependent upon opinion for his profession, his rights and his life, his situation is unstable and he carefully watches the progress of antisemitism. He tries to foresee crises and gauge trends in the same way that the peasant keeps watch on the weather and predicts storms."

Of course recent polls done by Jewish organizations which unduly alarmed us appear now to be as accurate as the old cuckoo clock in divining the future. We are a traumatized people and we are right to be cautious, to send our census takers out into the hinterlands and test the pulse of the people among whom we live—do they hate us today as much as they did yesterday, do they doubt the Holocaust, do they think we own the media? The polls may be off, the questions can provoke more or less troubling answers, but our need to know, to test the waters, is as reasonable as an aviator checking his parachute before takeoff; nothing is to be taken for granted.

On the other hand our caution, our anger, can make us insensitive to other realities, we can be caught looking in the wrong direction, our commitment to justice and repairing the world can be diluted, and in protecting ourselves we can forget who we are. If the past holds us too tightly in its grip we can be smothered.

It's hard to fight against antisemitism. It is not an enemy that always stands up and confronts you. It is whispered behind your back and its damage is often just behind the legal, just under the surface of the culture, and is more in the mind than in the open.

The Jewish community has decided that its well-being depends on the separation of church and state and presses everywhere to keep religious symbols such as Christmas trees and crèches out of public squares and off of public property. Of course we do live in a Christian culture and we are a small minority. While the arguments for maintaining the neutral condition of the town hall and the school are compelling, I am also certain that if Jewish life in America becomes bold enough, fearless enough, less angered by the Christian symbols which could in time lose their association with persecution and terror, we could live more easily with their symbols and put ours in public, along with theirs, wherever we might have a community.

It may be that one day the religious and ethnic differences in America can be celebrated, inclusively, respected by all, instead of hushed and removed from the public arena. In this sense the Lubavitch menorah by the horses and carriages on New York's Central Park South is a good representation of the glorious if difficult cacophony of American life. It seems absurd to think that our fight against antisemitism must include objections to every Rudolph the Red-Nosed Reindeer that appears on the courthouse square.

This is a complicated issue. But I think that some of the policies of the organized Jewish community need revisiting in light of the changes in America. In the days when Jews were trying to be inconspicuous it made sense to wish for a blank public area. Does it still? Will our less Holocaust-traumatized children and grandchildren be more comfortable with the signs of the Christian religion and less alarmed by the majority culture going about its business?

The truth is that today we are doing famously well by all measurable standards. By the 1980s and early 90s Jews had been appointed to the presidencies of some of the most prominent schools in America—Bard, Barnard, Columbia, Dartmouth, M.I.T., Harvard, and Princeton (which of all places opened a kosher kitchen for students in 1971). There are more Jewish executives at the top levels then ever before. Leonard Dinnerstein in his historical work *Anti-Semitism in America* says that "by emphasizing the hostility of some Americans toward Jews, one attributes too much power and or influence to fringe people and overlooks the whole new network of positive and diversified interactions between Jews and Gentiles, black and white. Much less prejudice exists in our own time than in any other period in the history of the nation."

The fears expressed by some in the Jewish community that the Wall Street junk-bond cases would create a groundswell of antisemitism did not prove true. The Pollard case passed by with its inherent antisemitism and certain injustice, but unlike the Dreyfus catastrophe did not awaken mobs to threaten the Jews of Bloomington and Shaker Heights. The radical left and the radical right stirred up antisemitism throughout the 1980s without starting a trend, without creating large numbers of converts. Black antisemitism may be spreading, but aside from sending chills down our communal spine it seems to affect neither the problems of the black nor the well-being of the Jew.

The American Jewish Committee reported in 1988, "There is no widespread discrimination against Jews in the executive suite." In the late 1980s Jews, who constituted less than 3 percent of the nation's population, accounted for 13 percent of executives under the age of forty. In 1992 an Anti-Defamation League study reached the conclusion that 17 percent of white Americans and 37 percent of black Americans are hard-core antisemites.

This is either alarming or reassuring in the old doughnut-and-hole dilemma. What seems clear is that our worst fears have not yet come to pass. What seems equally clear is that we can't let our guard down yet, and while we shouldn't react to every swastika on a synagogue wall with panic, we can't assume that the tide of history will ever after go our way. Tides change.

In searching for the causes of antisemitism, hope rises that whatever insights are found will apply not just to our condition but to the whole of humanity—poor, benighted, blighted, untrustworthy, almost guaranteed to be vicious humanity.

Hannah Arendt in her book *The Origins of Totalitarianism* talks about the myth that antisemitism is normal, that the outbursts of rage against the Jews that occurred all through the history of Western Europe need no explanation because they are as natural to life as the wheat that grows in the fields and the cemeteries whose stones rise on the hills. This understandable but woolly-headed view subverts careful examination and can lead to a shrug of resignation, a mystical acceptance of calamity that may help to blunt our rage but opens no new doors of understanding. If we believe that a demonic force, loose in the world, has chosen for its victim the Jewish people, we allow for the possibility that antisemitism is part of a divine order, has a purpose in the celestial scheme of things. It turns Jews into actors in a play that is destined to repeat, the script never varying night after night.

When we hear that the Romanians in a country without Jews are increasingly antisemitic, when we hear that the Poles and the Hungarians are mounting antisemitic attacks against their elderly, fading Jewish populations, that blacks in America have forgiven the Arab slave traders and now blame us for their transport, we can become convinced that Jews will be a target of abuse even when all that remains is our shadow against the historical wall, a fossil buried deep in the layers of rock. It's hard to resist this view; it seems to fit our experience both historical and contemporary, but it is a dangerous and fatalistic position and allows many of our children to ask, Why are you doing this to me, binding me on the altar so that I too can be harmed? It seems better to examine the more difficult question: What could antisemitism be about?

Hannah Arendt reports the joke in which the first man says to the second, "The Jews and the bicyclists caused World War I." "Why the bicyclists?" asks the second. We can begin to answer why the Jews, but each answer is just a small piece of the puzzle, and as we begin to understand the social and political forces that lie behind the continuing antisemitism of the Christian world we remain confounded by the unreason of it, the absurdity of it, the illogic compounded by meanness, the recurrent flood of hatred that seems larger than any explanations, stronger and more malevolent than our reasons would explain. We are left, after the best of analytic thought, staring evil in the eye. We blink.

Nevertheless we can list the apparent causes of antisemitism easily enough. There is the "Christ killer" accusation. Here we have, aside from the historical inaccuracy of the charge, the peculiar blurring of lines of individual and group, past and present, which is essential to all prejudices, which is the intellectual problem of all human beings: Who am I, what part of myself belongs to me alone and what part to the group, the nation, the religion of which I am a part?

Can a person be held responsible for errors of his or her ancestors, for others of the group? How many generations does it take to expiate a crime and how can I be responsible for the future, present, and past all at once? This charge, this source of antisemitism, represents a kind of primitive thinking, as if people were not moral beings with potential for choosing good or evil but rather vessels in which the whole is represented literally by the specific.

Of course our own Book of Genesis makes this charge against mankind when Adam and Eve are thrown out of the Garden of Eden and condemned to daily toil and painful childbirth and death because the first couple succumbed to a temptation planted by God. The covenant itself between the people of Israel and God is one that binds future generations and commits future generations to the law; circumcision is hardly an infant's free choice. So we do live our lives in part in historical group time, and group guilt is a reality that we understand perfectly well.

The greatest original sin of Americans was surely slavery, and the ways in which this sin has come back to haunt the American dream seem not unjust, not unreasonable, even though no American alive ever owned a slave or directly benefited from slave labor. The second original sin of Americans was against the native inhabitants. We seem to have gotten away with this injustice, aside from pangs of conscience that have emerged in portrayals in our recent movies. So we struggle with the fact that the most upper-crust, Episcopalian American was not really responsible for slavery and we wouldn't think of excluding him or his children from our presence, and yet they were guilty, as a group, as a type: their forebears did it. The yes they did and no they didn't of this problem is determined positively in the minds of antisemites without regard to individuals, reality, historical place.

The fact is that all people think in stories, simplify and codify into good and evil, reducing other people's selves to the type, tribe of origin, and mythologizing without regard to particular face, particular taste. Freedom of choice, respect for the individual, is a late historical invention and we all sometimes slip back into the fairy tales of our childhood when all the witches were bad and all the fairies were good and above all we ourselves were the innocents who wandered into the dangerous woods.

With the Vatican repudiating its antisemitic positions, and with the increased obvious blood guilt of every other ethnic group—the Somalis, the Rwandans, the Iraqis, the Haitians—the focus on the death of Christ is blurred. In Protestant America this taunt of Christ killer was never so central, since love of the actual body of Christ is less central to the Protestant vision. It is more our religious difference that marks us off. In many parts of America questions of damnation and salvation are probably more isolating for Jews than accusations about the Crucifixion.

Then there is the peculiar role Jews have played as lenders, financiers, middlemen, marketmen, merchants taking the money from those who till the land, whose traditions are rooted in place, who have always lived on the lands that we travel through. Money and antisemitism are like flower and bee, intimate. The Jew sees this attack as particularly unfair because our expertise in financial matters came about as a matter of necessity, our having been denied ownership of land and forced to the margins of the economy.

The Gentile of course has another view. Remember in Claude Lanzman's *Shoah* the peasant woman talking about the departed Jews of the village and their secret hoards of gold; she believes it still. The Jews of that village had nothing of value hidden in their closets.

But the myth, the power of that myth of Jewish accumulation, never seems to entirely fade. Our success, our adaptability to the market, made us the target of envy, fear, and rage of those who failed where we succeeded, those who were rooted to place, village, town, and could not imagine the larger world and did not weave the financial webs that we did. In America the Jewish success in schools and colleges opened up for us the professional class with its automatic financial rewards. Again we become by our success the objects of others' frustrations.

The financial success of Jews in America particularly mocks blacks and poor ethnics. Our rapid rise says to other groups, Why didn't you, why couldn't you? Although there are many reasonable answers to that question, it rankles anyway and provokes a particularly bitter kind of antisemitism. Our school smarts, the high numbers of Jewish doctors and lawyers, provokes admiration and envy. It provokes the question What's wrong with me? It is far easier to hate the accomplished Jew than to feel inferior.

On the other hand we have also been despised for being poor and ignorant, having the manners, smells, aggressiveness of the marginal. So it does not seem our bank accounts determine the degree of hate that storms over us.

Money is of course connected to well-being, security, but also to pride. And Jewish wealth and Gentile poverty makes the Gentile rage. (Is it no accident that confiscation of Jewish goods ended finally in the piles of gold teeth?) The labeling of Jews as greedy and materialist allows the Gentile public to displace, project, and avoid its own greediness and desire for earthly goods. It also conveniently explains the economic failure of many who can blame their own poverty on the existence of the Jews instead of on lack of wit, foresight, or earned education.

This twinning of anti-Jewish feeling and money is most clearly seen in the prevalent Jewish American Princess joke. As after the news of the Holocaust reached these shores it became unfashionable to be openly antisemitic, the jokes about the greed of Jewish women began to spread and they contained the message of Jewish materialism. But by directing antisemitic whisperings against females, bigotry was slipped past the general public, and Jewish males became vehicles for antisemitic propaganda as they happily repeated slurs aimed against their wives and sisters.

It is well known that money and excrement are connected in slang language, and in our unconscious, as Freud has shown. When we add Jews to the equation we have a way to despise Jews through their connection to money, and we have a way to equate Jews with the waste products of society, of our body, to wish to flush them away. It's a nasty turn of thought.

Then there is the social antisemitism which assumes that Jews are loud, bad-mannered, deceitful in their business dealings, and uncouth as well. Early on this was a class issue in America as the immigrants flowed off the boats and their manners were different from those of the upper classes in America. Class in America is today such a taboo subject that we can barely see that the Jew is always of a lower class even when he becomes a Warburg or a Loeb. Jews absorbed the class dislike from above and below. That of course is still apparent.

But the politeness issue is a terrible cover for the savagery of society. Freud describes the fateful incident in which he is walking with his father and a Gentile knocks his father's hat into the gutter and his father humbly retrieves it. The bad manners here are on the part of the non-Jew. The social accusations against Jews are covers for the brutality of Christian society which if it is polite at all, is not polite to Jews.

Of course there are many ways in which Jews set themselves apart from the whole. There are the languages that we speak, the Hebrew that is alien to the natives, the other European languages that marked us as internationalists, patriots of other countries, and the dialect of our own, the almost understandable Yiddish, the Sabbath that we celebrate, the foods that some of us will not eat, the look of our faces, the color of our hair, the differences that separate us from them, the ones that were the result of their rules and the ones that are the result of our rules. In America we have for the most part become just like everyone else, baseball fans, barbecuing on our patios, paying mortgages and college tuitions, playing tennis, going skiing, watching TV.

Nevertheless we remain separate from their populism, the folkness of the folk, who gain their strength from the common myths, the old stories, the religion they share, their steeples pointing up to the sky, standing high on the hill where their people have always gone with the newborns, with the dead, in times of celebration and times of woe: a place that we do not share, a place that we turn our backs on as if we were the silhouette, the inverse of the real world, the shadow of the good, the sign, like a sudden chill, of the bad passing through.

Antisemitism was expressed in pogrom, in exclusion, in cruelty toward us, because we had no communal army to stop it, no force strong enough to protect our children when the bullies came marching into our streets, because we weren't a nation but at the mercy of the host nation, whose police, whose soldiers were encouraged to despise us. Antisemitism spread because we were the other, the alien, the ones who were not attached, were not alike, were from abroad, who didn't belong to the land, whose fathers Abraham, Isaac, and Jacob were not buried in the small cemetery just beyond the apple orchard but were far away in a homeland we longed for, spoke of, but didn't live in: a homeland that was the stuff of legend and fancy.

We were cosmopolitan, urban, traders of goods, quick of wit, unlike the folk, the folk who knew themselves to be good because they had always been the folk, whose inheritance was their entitlement to the place, whose priests tolled the bells of the church and the peals rang out over the fields just as they always had, whereas for us there was no "just as it always had been," there were no bells whose sounds were as close to us as our breathing. Our otherness defined their sameness. Their sameness was the river in which the stones of our otherness fell.

The cosmopolitanism that has helped us create financial empires and has created in our people, those at the edge of assimilation, a kind of exciting tension that has fed our art, our literature, brought to the world the insights of a Kafka, of a Marx, or a Freud, has erupted into universalism, science, culture that is based in criticism rather than applause—this cosmopolitanism has made us the object of their fury, the fury of the folk who do not want to think in terms of mankind, but root themselves in the furrows of their ancestors, who think in terms of unchanging horizons, the same sunset, year after year, the music of pride, the poetry of self-satisfaction, the polarization of good and evil.

This folk will always be antisemitic because we will always stand for the broader perspective, the ironic smile, the underground thought. Jews living in the modern world know about the dark side of human nature. The folk don't want to believe it. They think themselves good. We barely believe in goodness.

When the folk think of home they feel themselves like a strong oak tree soaking in the sunshine, rooting in the dark earth. When Jews of the Diaspora think of home we think of closets to hide in, places to leave, passports to be kept ready, we think of mothers and fathers, brothers and sisters, but we don't think of rocks and running brooks.

We think of home as a state of mind, easily portable. They think of home as a place you recognize as yours. We think of home as a place we may one day arrive. This difference is profound. It makes us appear to be the enemy of their home. It makes them the enemy of our arrival.

Whenever populism has risen in America, antisemitism has followed. From Father Coughlin to David Duke the antisemite is one who wants the old, the nostalgic, the good people, the pure race, the simple truth, the flag-waving, no subversive questions allowed. Populism has no room for irony. Irony is the Jewish lifeboat.

So those are the obvious excuses for antisemitism, the reasons given and the ways they are manipulated. But then there is the matter of the nursery and the playground. In the musical *South Pacific* Oscar Hammerstein writes in a lyric of uncommon sweetness, "You've got to be taught, to learn to hate." The Jewish Rodgers and Hammerstein felt not quite comfortable about discussing antisemitism, so impolite a subject it was then—not to mention uncommercial—that they made the object of prejudice South Pacific islanders and set their wartime tale as far away from Jews as the geography of the globe would allow.

Also the lyric is wrong. Anyone who has cared for a seven- or eight-month-old baby in their arms knows that if a stranger's face looms into view, the baby will let out a wail of terror and begin a sobbing that subsides only when the offending face is withdrawn from view. Pediatricians the world over recognize this as perfectly normal separation anxiety. In fact they worry about infants in whom this does not appear. This anxiety is a signal that development has gone well up to this point. The baby has consolidated in his mind the image of his mother caretaker and has grasped the idea that he is a separate being, that without his parent he cannot survive, that he does not control the world and that the outside will do as it pleases without necessarily regarding his enormous, sometimes urgent, needs. The birth of our minds, the beginning of ourselves contains the first knowledge of our death, our separateness, and this not only makes the baby angry, but makes him fearful as well. When the strange face appears, the illusion of permanent unity is dashed and who knows what ill this stranger, this nonmother, may bear toward the helpless infant.

It is irrational of course, Aunt Millie means no harm, Uncle Joe is just trying to get a smile from a new nephew, but to the baby there is no difference between the faces of doting relatives and the tiger who would eat him or the car that would run him over. Strange to an infant is dangerous, it signals disaster.

Soon, within weeks usually, this sharp stranger reaction dies down and the baby learns that human faces are not the harbingers of doom and is increasingly able to comprehend that mother disappears from view but will reappear in time, before catastrophe strikes.

But it seems as if the fear of the stranger, the anger that the stranger provokes, remains with us a lifetime through. It can be triggered by an odd accent, by a different color of skin, by the otherness of the face or the hair. The grown-up doesn't wail when the Jew passes by, but perhaps a touch of fear rises, a sense of alarm—not mother, not self—causes a tightening of muscles, a spasm of hate, and a turning away of the head follows.

Antisemitic literature is rife with descriptions of disgust. Jews are said to smell bad, their clothes offend, their breath is bad, they are said to be repulsive and to kill and eat little Christian babies. The Jew then is in society what the stranger is to the nursery: the feared one, the person who rips apart the dream of permanent safety, of mother's arms eternally enclosing and protecting. Why, one wonders, should such an infantile thought persist in the adult and become transformed into the rules of the country club that doesn't permit Jews or the university that holds quotas or the Nuremberg laws that forbade intermarriage? Why do the Hutus consider the Tutsis the stranger and vice versa? Why do the Serbs and the Croats and the Muslims use the most minor of differences to draw bloody lines across their maps?

It must be that the human mind matures but holds on to its oldest of traumas, its most primitive of fears; its first thoughts lie just beneath its second and third and shape them, direct them, attach to the most complicated. Prejudice is then an echo of a child's scream, Where is my mother and who are you? The infant's terror is real enough and the offending stranger hurries to withdraw. The baby may close its eyes to avoid the horrid sight. The mother will speak soothingly but the anger remains, anger at having been so frightened. Perhaps this is the anger we see when Germans compared Jews to vermin, to cancer, to polluting bacteria.

This stranger-reaction in the infant shows that a good attachment to the mother has been made and the child is connected to its homeland, its motherland, its place. Without that attachment learning stops, serious mental incapacities develop, speech is retarded or denied, psychosis is threatened. Infants who have not made that primary attachment are prone to die of passing minor illnesses. Psychoanalyst Rene Spitz illustrated that infants given impersonal care in orphanages die at extraordinary rates of simple infections.

The way in which we become human is through the ferocity, the brilliance, of our first attachments. The stories of children brought up by wolves only prove the point. Without a human hand cradling the infant, without the specific of human affection, touch, eye contact, voice, the child cannot become a person. So our viability as human beings, capacity to love, abstract thought, speech, are born with our fear of strangers, with our rage at others. What makes us human makes us kill humans, an irony we have little possibility of avoiding or altering.

The universality of babyhood cannot be questioned, and if we all experience the same helplessness as infants and our angers last with us as we grow, then Jews too must be capable of prejudice. And we know that is true. In the early days of rabbinic culture there was the ghastly argument recorded for all time about whether or not it was permitted to save a non-Jewish life on the Sabbath. It was permitted to dig in a pile of rubble to save a Jew even on the Sabbath, but could you grab a shovel if the voice that called for help wasn't Jewish?

Eventually the rabbis decided clearly that you should, that you must save even a non-Jew. But the debates continued about responsibility—legal, financial, moral—to the non-Jew. Clearly there was some question when we were the ones with a homeland about the full humanity, under the law, of the stranger. There were rules about not hiring Gentiles to take care of your children, or tend your cattle. There was grave suspicion about the moral intentions of a non-Jew and a fear that he or she might kill the children.

Our biblical interest in keeping the Jewish line and the priestly line pure, free of those of unknown lineage, is clear. Our fear of intermarriage was both a fear of assimilation and of pollution of the people. We too had myths of purity. Later in watered-down versions of antisemitism we picked up antisemitic attitudes, and the German Jews in America excluded from their hospitals and their clubs the newly arrived Russian Jews. In Israel the Ashkenazim were hardly gracious to the Sephardic newcomers. This is not to equate Jewish norms of two thousand years ago with the vile hatreds of our own century or the habits of snobbism or exclusion of parts of the Jewish community with the extremes of murderous antisemitism, but to suggest that the capacity for fear of the stranger is in us as well as in our neighbors.

The scale and terror of the Holocaust makes it clear that Jews are an innocent and wronged people, murdered and abandoned to their fate. This makes Christians, even Christians who were not in Europe at the time, a guilty people. Their moral code failed. Their society with its great cathedrals and orchestras and legal system did not stop the killing machines. They know it. They try to forget it.

In America we hear the rumbles of Christian, Gentile irritation with the implied guilt that rises as there is talk of the genocide directed against the Jews. Many Americans feel that Jews are too focused on the Holocaust, they don't want to hear anything more about it. They feel subtly accused. This itself becomes a contributing cause of antisemitism in America.

The recent scenes of Israeli soldiers in occupied territories came as a relief to many Christians. It weakened the Jewish moral position. "If Jews are not really victims, then we Christians are not guilty."

This sensitivity to guilt is why a movie like *Schindler's List* can convey the Holocaust better than a film told from a Jewish point of view. If the audience is able to identify with a rescuer they can better tolerate the truth.

"Zionism is racism" is a vile slogan intended to weaken the Jewish moral position. If Jews are like Nazis then they don't deserve the land that they were allotted in the rush of concern after the war.

For blacks the emphasis on the Holocaust can be especially frustrating because their own moral claim is put up against ours. Not by us, not in reality, but in some terrible victim sweepstakes in which Jews have appeared to be the winner. If a group has been wronged it gathers a kind of moral armor, a kind of entitlement to reparations, that some blacks feel was stolen from them by Jewish insistence on Holocaust issues.

Of course this is absurd, there is enough guilt to go around, and slavery was a moral and human tragedy on its own without comparison to any other event in history. But just as poor peoples—Hispanics, Jews, and blacks—tend to quarrel about the available housing in bad neighborhoods, so do they squabble about the misery count, so do they fight for the moral high ground.

Black antisemitism is now a fact of life in America, but how we respond will tell us who we are, and what will become of us. We do not have to follow the conservative Jews among us who ask us to turn our backs on little children who need school lunch programs. We do not have to abandon any of our traditional Jewish commandments to care for the stranger, to care for the poor, to protect the sick, to make the world a better place. We can continue to insist on our alliance with those in the black community, where are many who shudder at the bigotry of Farrakhan and Jeffries and their young supporters.

If the American Jewish community turns its back on the poor or the troubled and pretends that the inner city is none of our business, that it is the home of our enemies, then we will erode the ethical meaning of Jewish existence in the Diaspora. We will become a people like any other people, self-serving, dull, satisfied with consuming, and prey to the anger of those who stare in the window as we lead our lives. The one thing that black antisemitism must not do is to change us, turn us into people who hate. Of course we shouldn't ignore the vile language and we shouldn't pretend it isn't happening. But our outrage needs to be tempered by the political reality. It needs to be tempered by our understanding of and sympathy for the black dilemma.

Of course there is denial of the Holocaust, so-called Holocaust revisionism, afoot in the United States. This "revisionism" is a disguised expression of Jew-hate. On the other hand we can understand that the Christian need to forget, deny, or distort stems from their inability to face what their culture and religion have done. When we create more guilt, engage in a match of virtue and moral superiority, we do not clear the air. Christian guilt and Jewish anger are very complicated and do not necessarily match simple antisemitic patterns.

But also, along with deniers and their followers there are the crowds pouring into the United States Holocaust Memorial Museum in Washington, silent, respectful, largely not Jewish: they are not likely to encourage antisemitism in their children. The visitors at the museum, now Washington's most popular tourist attraction, will more probably understand the need to imagine the other, the stranger, as not so much a stranger but as a child with a size 3 shoe, or a boy with homework to do, or a man who loves the Phillies, or a woman whose dream is to be an astronaut.

We are so apt to bristle, so prone to protest that some Jews objected to the Holocaust Museum as if it cheapened, or commercialized, or watered down the history of the Jews. It doesn't. It allows us to use ourselves to illustrate the danger of stranger-fear, where it leads, what it means. The Holocaust Museum becomes a great weight pulling us away from generalizations about people, away from accusations of group guilt, away from tribal self-congratulation that feeds on mortifying others. If we had as powerful a museum about slavery, it too would serve the same purpose.

In recent years, however, since the opening of the gates of Auschwitz, political events across the earth have made it clear that antisemitism is only one of the terrible prejudices, majority against minority, tribe against tribe, that despoil the human endeavor. As we read about Rwanda and learn of the Hutus entering the orphanage at Kigali and chopping off the arms and legs of children, slashing at the heads of three-year-olds with machetes, we all recognize the beast that is man. Cambodia's death toll, Stalin's Gulag, the militias in El Salvador lining up the priests and their housekeepers and shooting them in the field, the terrible visions of brutal apartheid that crossed our television screens, the Muslims in Lebanon calling for the death of the Christians, the

Hindus attacking the Sikhs of Kashmir, the Armenians and the Azeris, the armies of Saddam against the fleeing Kurds, the Croats and the Serbs raping, sniping, executing—all remind us that we live in a madhouse in which the Jewish story, so important to us, is no more than a single blood-soaked thread of the endless plot. We despair not just for the Jews but for the entire human enterprise.

America is part of this earth, and as we go city to city across the country we see many different groups segregated in their own neighborhoods, isolated in public schools, religions split by school or geography. We see the many colors of mankind of course, but we know that the tendency to group, to prefer one's own, to make slurs on the other, is as widespread as the television which pretends we don't, makes nice where we make nasty. It's hard of course to imagine America torn like the former Yugoslavia. We built into our nation a kind of acceptance, tolerance of difference, at least at a formal legal level.

But I don't really trust it. It's not the same as real acceptance. I remember as a child at a Jewish camp in Maine being told to be quiet in the ice-cream parlor of the local small town so no one would think badly of the Jews. I remember looking into the Yankee faces of the other customers and wondering if their children whispered when they walked in the streets. Quotas and restricted neighborhoods were everywhere. My grandfather started a shirt business. The stores of the Gentiles would not buy his shirts. The Gentile shirt companies would not hire Jewish salesmen. Lionel Trilling nearly didn't get his professorship, and being Jewish in America was like entering a marathon race with a clubfoot. It makes us angry to remember. It makes us angry to hear the echoes now.

How long can a society keep the lid on its worst instincts and how long can the objects of scorn hold themselves in until they turn on someone else? When in the 1970s I heard talk of "gooks" and saw the pictures of My Lai I knew that Americans were no better than anyone else. Americans could do it too under the right political-economic circumstances. Which brings me back to the question of whether we are American Jews or Jewish Americans. The dual loyalty question is one that antisemites use to isolate us politically in America. We're not supposed to discuss it.

But the truth is that most of us, after the Holocaust, will not make the mistake that good German Jews made, owners of war medals and higher degrees. We are American only as long as America reins in its antisemites. We are Jews forever under all circumstances. But our Holocaust terror has led us to exaggerate the power and the spread of antisemitism in this country.

Of course these polls that tell us that almost everyone doubts the reality of the Holocaust and almost everyone thinks we control the media are not really to be depended on. The way in which the questions are asked, the prejudgments of the pollsters, the way people lie, tell you what they think you want to hear, and so on, make us uneasy. Social scientists are always to be taken with a grain of salt and a large dose of skepticism.

The Jewish community often uses fear of antisemitism to hold us together when energies might better be spent teaching, writing new midrash, sharing our comforts to those in the community and out to those who need us, building libraries instead of spreading anxiety.

The former British chief rabbi Sir Immanuel Jacobovits said, "Would it not be a catastrophic perversion of the Jewish spirit if brooding over the Holocaust were to become a substantial element in the Jewish purpose and if the anxiety to prevent another Holocaust were to be relied upon as essential incentive for Jewish activity?" He called for a shift from the survival of the Jews to the survival of Judaism. "For without Judaism, Jewish survival is both questionable and meaningless."

Our religion serves as a history book. It also serves as a communal support, a spiritual deepener, an ethical column in an world that can otherwise be stripped of value, meaning, sanctity. The God of the Holocaust has to be acknowledged and each person's difficulty with belief understood and welcomed. The secular Jew needs the pious Jew to express his ties to his people and the past and the pious Jew needs the secular Jew to express his doubts, his angers, his human universality. We are together in this, doubters and believers, not because of antisemitism but because without Judaism, without Jewish life, we dry up. Individually, without each other, we will be frightened and alone in the dark.

My Hungarian-born father was an assimilated, agnostic, unaffiliated Jewish man, married to his second wife who had been raised as a Catholic. He went to Italy on a vacation. There he spent his days visiting the Jewish cemetery in each town. "What were you doing?" I asked. He shrugged. What he was doing was reminding himself that he belonged somewhere. It was a sad sign of his fragile connection, like the wisp of smoke that escapes the Hanukkah candle as it expires.

If American Jewry can imagine itself as more than just an opposition to antisemitism but as a flourishing, nourishing, exciting tradition with a contribution to make to the future, which buttresses, bulwarks, decorates, furnishes the Jewish mind, then we won't have cemetery Jews anymore, and antisemitism, if it comes, will find us formidable in our life's joy, in the quality of our Jewish connections. It won't blow us away because we will be so rooted, so firmly here. If that is to happen we will have to defend ourselves by our Jewish education, enriching, deepening our Jewish knowledge, not of our tragedies but of our accomplishments.

It is highly possible that we have not evolved as much as we should, that we need to mutate into less tribal people if we as a species are going to survive. One can't will this mutation or demand of evolution a speedier rate, but we can observe our darker selves, check our own cruelty when possible, know that to love your tribe is not always a good thing, especially if you need to harm someone else in order to mark out your borders. We can watch in ourselves for signs of moral weakness, selfishness, coldness, freezing of the heart or imagination when it comes to the needs of others.

It is perfectly reasonable for Israel to be a state like any other, prone to flex muscle, step on the weak neighbor, fight for survival with all the available tools, but it is not so reasonable for Jews in the Diaspora to forget what we are about, some purpose that is more than just survival and must have to do with, if not great flaming torches for the nations, than perhaps a small glow, a small candle that never goes out.

Index

WITHDRAWN

DATE DUE			
FEB 2 5 07			